THE
CROWN OF HINDUISM

THE CROWN OF HINDUISM

J. N. FARQUHAR

GYAN

Published by

GYAN

Gyan Publishing House
5, Ansari Road
Daryaganj, New Delhi-110002
Phone: 011-47034999, 9811692060
E-mail: books@gyanbooks.com

Distribution Network
gyanbooks.com
India, USA, Canada, UK, Australia

ISBN: 978-93-6780-524-4 (HB)

First Published, 1913

2nd Impression 2024

Printed at: Gyan Press, Delhi.

THE CROWN OF HINDUISM
Author: J. N. FARQUHAR

THE CROWN OF HINDUISM

BY

J. N. FARQUHAR, M.A.

LITERARY SECRETARY, NATIONAL COUNCIL OF YOUNG MEN'S CHRISTIAN ASSOCIATIONS, INDIA AND CEYLON

HUMPHREY MILFORD
OXFORD UNIVERSITY PRESS
LONDON EDINBURGH GLASGOW NEW YORK
TORONTO MELBOURNE AND BOMBAY
1913

PREFACE

THIS book is an attempt to discover and state as clearly as possible what relation subsists between Hinduism and Christianity. It is not meant to be an exhaustive account of Hinduism, though it deals with most of its prominent features. There are other aspects of the religion which might have been included. Among these the chief is sacrifice and the priest, a subject not less interesting and fruitful than those dealt with in the volume. The reason for its omission is this, that there are large parts of the subject which have not been investigated by scholars, and it was impossible for me to undertake that serious piece of exploration myself. Yet, despite this and other omissions, the book probably contains sufficient material to enable readers to decide whether its main thesis is justifiable.

The book was begun in the hope that all that had to be said could be built on foundations already laid by the great scholars; but that proved impossible, and it became necessary for me to undertake several pieces of original investigation myself. It was not my wish to do so; but it was inevitable. The truth is that a large number of scholarly studies of very high quality have been conducted within the realm of Hinduism during the last century, but comparatively few of them have viewed Hinduism as a practical religion; and it has been necessary, for the sake of the subject, to regard the religion from that point of view throughout this volume.

The foot-notes indicate with some degree of accuracy my indebtedness to books, but there is no way in which I can show how much I owe to scores of friends, Hindu, Brāhma, and Christian, in every part of India, who have given me unlimited help both in conversation and by correspondence. To all such friends I wish to express here my most sincere gratitude. I owe very special thanks to the Rev. C. F. Andrews of Delhi, who read the whole work in manuscript with extreme care and made many suggestions of great value. I am also indebted to the Rev. D. Emlyn Evans of Mirzapore, who has done me the great kindness of reading the proofs.

OXFORD,
July, 1913.

CONTENTS

INTRODUCTION

CHAPTER I

THE INDO-ARYAN FAITH

CHAPTER II

THE HINDU FAMILY

CHAPTER III

The Eternal Moral Order

CHAPTER IV

The Divine Social Order

CHAPTER V

The Essentials of Hinduism

CHAPTER VI

The Summit of Indian Thought

CHAPTER VII

THE YELLOW ROBE

CHAPTER VIII

THE WORK OF MEN'S HANDS

CHAPTER IX

THE GREAT SECTS

CHAPTER X

God with Us

CHAPTER XI

The Religious Organism

ABBREVIATIONS USED IN THE NOTES

A.	*Āraṇyaka.*
Andrews	Andrews, *The Renaissance in India.*
Āpastamba	*Āpastamba Dharmasūtra.*
Āśvalāyana	*Āśvalāyana Gṛihyasūtra.*
B.	Brāhmaṇa.
Baudhāyana	*Baudhāyana Dharmasūtra.*
Brāhmaṇism and Hinduism	Monier-Williams, *Brāhmaṇism and Hinduism.*
Deussen	Deussen, *The Philosophy of the Upanishads.*
Divine Wisdom	Govindāchārya, *Divine Wisdom of the Drāvida Saints.*
E. R. E.	*Encyclopaedia of Religion and Ethics.*
Gautama	*Gautama Dharmasūtra.*
Glover	Glover, *The Conflict of Religions in the Early Roman Empire.*
Great Epic	Hopkins, *The Great Epic of India.*
Griffith	Griffith, *The Rāmāyaṇa of Vālmīki in English Verse.*
Growse	Growse, *The Rāmāyaṇa of Tulsī Dās.*
Heart of India	Barnett, *The Heart of India.*
Holy Lives	Govindāchārya, *The Holy Lives of the Āzhvārs.*
Iyengar's *Outlines*	Śrīnivāsa Iyengar, *Outlines of Indian Philosophy.*
I. R. M.	*International Review of Missions.*
I. S. R.	*Indian Social Reformer.*
J. R. A. S.	*Journal of the Royal Asiatic Society.*
Kaegi	*The Ṛigveda* by Adolf Kaegi.
Macdonell	Macdonell, *Sanskrit Literature.*
Madhva	Padmanabha Char, *The Life and Teaching of Sri Madhvacharyar.*
Manu	*Mānava Dharmaśāstra.* Bühler, *S. B. E.*, xxv.
Modern Jainism	Mrs. Sinclair Stevenson, *Notes on Modern Jainism.*

Oman	Oman, *The Mystics, Ascetics, and Saints of India.*
Pāraskara	*Pāraskara Gṛihyasūtra.*
Phillips	Phillips, *The Outcastes' Hope.*
Pope	Pope, *The Tiruvāçagam.*
Rāmakṛishṇa	Max Müller, *Rāmakṛishṇa, His Life and Sayings.*
Rāmānuja	Govindāchārya, *Life of Rāmānuja.*
Ranade	Ranade, *Rise of the Maratha Power.*
Ranade, *Essays*	Ranade, *Religious and Social Reform, A Collection of Essays and Speeches.*
Religious Sects	Murdoch, *The Religious Sects of the Hindus.*
Śaiva Siddhānta	Nallasvāmī Piḷḷai, *Studies in Śaiva Siddhānta.*
S. B. E.	*Sacred Books of the East.*
Śiva Bhakti	Murdoch, *Śiva Bhakti.*
Six Systems	Max Müller, *Six Systems of Hindu Philosophy.*
Śrī Śaṅkarāchārya	*Śrī Śaṅkarāchārya, His Life and Times,* by Krishnasamy Aiyar and Sitanath Tattvabhushan.
Suzuki	Suzuki, *Aśvaghosha's Awakening of Faith in the Mahāyāna.*
T.	Tantra.
Trevelyan	Trevelyan, *Hindu Family Law.*
U.	Upanishad.
Vasishṭha	*Dharmasūtra of Vasishṭha.*
Vivekānanda	*Speeches and Writings of Swāmī Vivekānanda.*
Warren	Warren, *Buddhism in Translations.*
Westcott	Westcott, *Kabir and the Kabir Panth.*

INTRODUCTION

I. We have entered upon a new era. All parts of the world have at last been brought into communication with one another. We read news of every land at our breakfast tables. The nations have become one city: we buy each other's goods; we read each other's books; we think each other's thoughts. The unity of the human race has become effective for the first time in human history. From now it will be possible to talk of full human intercourse: in the past all has been but racial and partial. Only now do we begin to hear the music of humanity.

This new condition of things has been brought about partly by extended exploration, still more by the progressive improvement of our means of communication, but, most of all, through the extension of good government over large parts of the earth's area and the effective policing of the waters of the ocean. Without peace on land and sea, our knowledge of the earth's surface and our means of communication would be comparatively valueless. Peace on earth brings goodwill amongst men.

Every one can already see large results arising from this world-wide intercourse. All the civilized peoples are learning from each other. There is a rapid process of assimilation going on, in industry, business methods, education, science, art, literature, morals, and religion, in part most peacefully, but here and there with a good deal of strife and friction.

What the final outcome will be, no man can yet say; but one does not risk much in prophesying that the results are certain to be very great, since the rate of human progress is likely to be indefinitely accelerated under the new conditions.

The evolution of our human life has entered upon a new stage, and incalculable benefits are likely to arise. Only now have human knowledge and skill a chance of doing their best. Only now have the greatest forces an opportunity to act. Much of our past history may be put down under the head of the removal of hindrances to progress. From now onwards a man's work, when it is really valuable, will tell all over the world; while in past ages the best work has often been restricted in its influences for a long time to a small group of peoples or to a single nation. We are very rapidly approaching the moment when every piece of new knowledge will be absorbed by every nation as soon as it is acquired, and when the experience of any one nation, whether in industry, in art, in morality, or in religion, will be at once appreciated, caught up, and used the world over.

Here we restrict ourselves to the results produced on religion by the arrival of the new period. All the religions of the world that are of any importance have already been brought into effective contact the one with the other, and, in consequence, have begun to display to the utmost the treasures they severally possess. Each is driven by the instinct of self-preservation to seek to win other men to its fold.

Another most important fact in the situation is the rise of the Science of Religion. The scientific consciousness which recognizes the unity of the religious life of man, the evolution hypothesis through which the most varied and seemingly most contradictory phenomena are ranged in intelligible order within the bounds of that unity, and the eager passion to know how the early tribes of men thought about God and sought to approach Him, provided the intellectual conditions required; while the necessary material, viz. information about the religions of the world, became available through the unveiling of the ancient languages of India, Persia, Babylonia, Assyria, and Egypt, and through the opening of communications with all the inhabited lands. Our knowledge is still far from complete; and there are many lines of reflection which have as yet been scarcely thought of; yet the science has reached great proportions, and the results already attained are of inestimable value for thought.

The first outcome of this great accumulation of fresh religious material has been a feeling of deep surprise at the riches of the heritage of some of the great religions, especially in philosophy and in art. Hence an immense interest has been created in them, not only among students of religion as such, but among the cultured public in general. The growth of this interest these last ten years has been very remarkable. It is reflected in the publication of a large number of popular books on various aspects of Eastern religions. This deepened interest has given birth to a new feeling of brotherliness in religion, a sympathy with men of other faiths, which is most precious and fraught with future good. There is a keen desire for interchange of thought, for increased knowledge, for scientific consideration, and as keen a distaste for controversy. There is a deepened consciousness of the sacredness and intimacy of religion. Certain common elements in the chief religions have been welcomed with enthusiasm. The mere realization that such things exist has produced much sympathy. There is an inclination to regard the great religions as a group of noble peers, worthy of the utmost mutual respect, and a hope that it may be possible for sincere religious men of every race and faith to unite and work together.

Yet it must be confessed that, apart from those who have set themselves to the laborious study of the religions of the world, the new movement is still marked by curiosity rather than by knowledge, and that it is romantic and dilettante rather than scientific or religious. Those who are carried along by the new current and are most ready to talk enthusiastically about religious philosophy, literature, and art are often the very people who are most impatient of the real heart of all true religion. Men and women who have lost hold of their own religion, and miss the warm glow of faith in their lives, are caught by a fancy for some curious or attractive element in another faith; and, without waiting to consider what its practical worth may be, snatch at it and sing its praise. There is thus a good deal that is foolish and unreal in the movement.

Yet these things are on the surface. The new attitude is a prophecy of much better things to come. As knowledge increases and study becomes deeper, many of those who are now triflers will come to realize the dominant place which religion holds in national life, its primacy as the creative power in morality, society, and the family, and the vast results which the centuries work out in the life of a people from a single religious principle. They will begin to see what serious religion is in the life of an individual, and the incalculable value of the truly religious man to his people.

II. The progress of the Science of Religion has brought great gains to several departments of scientific inquiry, especially to theology. Among the more notable services rendered by the science are its proof that every race of man is religious, its convincing demonstration that religion is one of the practical activities of man as man, and that it has a great deal to do with the building of human society, the creation of institutions, and the laying of the foundations of morality. It has transformed all studies of individual religions by showing the importance of worship and explaining the purpose of ritual. It has made the function of belief and the position of literature in religion far clearer than before. It has shown us how frequently parallel beliefs and practices have been developed in different nations quite independently, and has thus made us chary of declaring that there has been borrowing, unless there be unmistakable evidence. The anthropological side of the study has thrown a flood of light on the earlier forms of religion, making much comprehensible which was obscure before, and has enabled us to detect many a survival from early times in the religions of civilized peoples.

A. But there is one aspect of the religious problem which has been scarcely touched by the science as yet, namely, the relative value of the different religions. Only when we have a calculus for determining the practical value of each religion shall we be able to set them in their true relationship to one another. To the present writer at least it seems that students of the science have as yet scarcely thought of this as one of its tasks. There are, it is true, many observations scattered up and down the books which have a bearing on this question. The very classification of religions as tribal, national, and universal, as natural or ethical, as ritualistic or spiritual, and the recognition that the low religions appear to be in many respects a parody of the higher faiths—these all suggest practical judgements. Here and there, also, a writer strikes a clear note, definitely declaring one religion to be of far greater value than others, or pointing out the practical difference between two faiths; yet even he usually writes in such a way as to show that he regards this part of the subject as outside the legitimate work of the science and belonging to the domain of personal opinion. No author is at his ease in giving expression to his convictions: the Christian expresses himself either dogmatically or tentatively, while the anti-Christian is apt to assume a defiant tone. There is seldom the quiet, assured attitude of science; and one meets no attempt to treat the subject in large, orderly, sober fashion.

Yet, after all, is not this the one living issue involved in the study of the science? How does the science impinge on life, if it has no answer to the practical question?

B. Meantime the need of a clear statement of the practical relationship of Christianity to the other great religions has become urgent.

1. The need is seriously felt from the inside.

(*a*) The coming of the Science of Religion and the universal interest in non-Christian systems have made it most necessary, for both the clergy and the people, that the real relationship of Christianity to other religions should be thought out and clearly expressed. The altered courses of most Theological

Colleges prove that attempts are already being made to meet this need in the education of preachers; but for the man in the pew comparatively little has yet been done.

(*b*) The missionary movement is steadily growing in strength, influence, and self-consciousness. Its large importance is now clearly perceived and frankly acknowledged by Governments and by scientific men.[1] The work is everywhere making progress. The latest census results in India are in complete accord with the growth of the Church elsewhere. Christians consequently want to understand more clearly the aim and the work of the movement. The World Missionary Conference held in Edinburgh in 1910 is the most prominent expression of this desire. But, meanwhile, a method of considerable significance and promise has arisen within the churches. Courses of Mission Study, which deal in scientific fashion with non-Christian religions and with the aims and activities of Missions, are written annually, and are studied by groups of young people in Mission Study Circles.

(*c*) Missionaries feel far more keenly than ever before the need of stating clearly how their work and their faith stand related to the systems they are face to face with; and they are in great perplexity as to how to put things. In many fields there is a divergence of opinion as to the attitude which the Christian ought to adopt to the non-Christian religions. In India there is a party, small or large, who distinctly disapprove of the attitude adopted towards Hinduism by the Commission of the Edinburgh Conference which dealt with the Missionary Message. See Dr. Cairns's masterly summary in the fourth volume of the Report of the Conference.

(*d*) For the sake of the young churches now growing up in the various Mission fields a sane estimate of the old religions in relation to Christianity is most necessary. The churches will inevitably be influenced by the faiths which form part of their environment. It is therefore of extreme importance that the leaders should understand the forces which are round

[1] *I. R. M.*, July, 1912, pp. 526–528.

about them, in order that they may set themselves to resist the evil and may be ready to welcome all that is good.

2. On the other hand, Christians are compelled to seek an understanding of the relation of their religion to other faiths in order to meet objections from the outside. The world-changes to which we have made reference have necessarily led to great changes in religious thought and belief. It was inevitable that Christianity should be deeply affected. Each of its fundamental ideas has reference to all men. Whoever holds the religion with conviction and intelligence necessarily looks forward to its becoming the cherished possession of every human being. Missionary work is the most vital activity of the faith. The Church must expand, or perish of unbelief. Hence new thought about the religious life of the world necessarily reacts with immeasurable force upon Christianity. Every universal principle stands in similar hazard. The new period has thus quite naturally brought with it new forms of opposition and criticism.

There is a far deeper cleavage of opinion upon the missionary question in Europe and America than there was twenty years ago. While the central party in each church which supports Missions is more convinced and more active than ever; and more money and men are available than at any earlier period; the dull, dead indifference of former years has now formed a conscious centre and expresses itself in demands for the restriction of missionary effort. Formerly one frequently heard the work of Missions depreciated, jeered at, and the results put down at nil. That is in the main a thing of the past. Only where extreme ignorance prevails is such an attitude possible. But there are now many who frankly say that Missions are unnecessary, and some who demand that there shall be no more attempts to win converts, at least from the great religions. The opposition of educated non-Christians to Missions has probably become accentuated in recent years. It certainly has become much more articulate, and much more definite in its condemnation of missionaries. There is a loud demand, at least in certain countries, that Missions should desist from making converts.

Now this attitude to Christianity, whether at home or on the Mission field, clearly implies a certain estimate of the position of Christianity with reference to other religions. When a man says that it is wrong to seek to persuade a Hindu, a Buddhist, or a Muḥammadan to become a Christian, he must have some idea in his mind which limits the rights of the Christian faith in relation to those religions.

From this point of view, then, it is of the utmost consequence that Christians should realize and state frankly the relation of their religion to others. If we cannot justify Missions to the minds of thinking men, we must confess defeat; and it is clear we cannot justify them in present circumstances without a clear exposition of the relation of Christianity to the religions of the world.

But, in order that our exposition may keep in close touch with facts, it will be well to realize first of all what the theories are which are put forward as reasons why the Christian Church should not seek to make converts. We begin with two which are so manifestly unsatisfactory as to be scarcely worthy of consideration; yet, since they influence public opinion, it will be well to take a look at them.

(*a*) There are, first of all, those who urge that the differences between religions are superficial and of no consequence, that, when you look down into the depths of reality, you find that all men really believe the same things. This would reduce all religions to a dead level, and would make the attempt to think out the relationship between any pair of faiths altogether useless. There are comparatively few people who would subscribe to this bald statement; yet it is sometimes urged. In one of her recent books Mrs. Besant states first the fundamental principles of Theosophy, and then proceeds:

> Its secondary teachings are those which are the common teachings of all religions, living or dead: the Unity of God; the triplicity of His nature; the descent of Spirit into matter, and hence the hierarchies

> of intelligencies, whereof humanity is one; the growth of humanity by the unfoldment of consciousness and the evolution of bodies, i.e. reincarnation; the progress of this growth under inviolable law, the law of causality, i.e. karma; the environment to this growth, the three worlds, physical, astral, and mental, or earth, the intermediate world, and heaven; the existence of divine Teachers, superhuman men.[1]

Here we are told that all religions, living or dead, teach this long list of doctrines. What do anthropologists think of the claim that savage religions contain this great catalogue of ideas? What do Christians think of the assertion that Christianity teaches reincarnation? What do Muḥammadans think of the assertion that Islam teaches that God's nature is triple? Clearly thinking men can only express their utter amazement that such baseless statements could ever be seriously made.

(*b*) The second group are both more reasonable and more numerous. They are quite ready to admit that religions differ very deeply in their doctrines, and also in their modes of worship, but they argue that, since religion is a practical thing, these differences do not matter. Even in the lowest religions each man knows that he ought to do his duty both by God and man. All religions seek the same God, consciously or unconsciously. Hence it is quite unnecessary to change any one's religion. Frequently the thought is added that each man's religion is the best thing for him. This idea was expressed by a Hindu ascetic named Rāmakṛishṇa Paramahaṁsa:

> Every man should follow his own religion. A Christian should follow Christianity, a Mohammedan should follow Mohammedanism, and so on. For the Hindus the ancient path, the path of the Aryan Ṛishis, is the best.[2]

Clearly this statement has only to be looked at to be rejected.

[1] *The Riddle of Life*, pp. 1–2.

[2] *Rāmakṛishṇa*, 177. It is most interesting to realize that this was the attitude of Celsus, the second-century opponent of Christianity. 'Over and over Celsus maintains the duty of "living by the ancestral usages", "each people worshipping its own traditional deities."'—Glover, 254.

Such a line of argument would justify the foulest religions on earth, systems which inculcate cannibalism, human sacrifice, promiscuity, incest, and every other abomination and cruelty.

(*c*) But serious people do not seriously believe that all religions are the same, or that it is wrong to try to make a cannibal a Christian. The truth is that these two statements are merely blundering attempts to put into universal form the instinctive feeling, present nowadays in thousands of minds, that the great religions of the world, Muḥammadanism, Judaism, Buddhism, Hinduism, Jainism, and Zoroastrianism, are so noble, and produce such good results, that it is a shame to attack them and disturb those who profess them.

This is the foundation on which Theosophy has built itself. The theory is that all the great religions are reconciled in its ample bosom, that there is no longer any need for controversy or for propaganda, but that each faith may live its own life in love and harmony with its neighbours. Many people all over the world have been greatly attracted by this statement, and also by the summons of the Theosophical Society to join in forming a brotherhood of men. The teaching of the Society has been welcomed by many who were without definite religious belief of their own; and in India, Burma, and Ceylon multitudes have acclaimed it as the means that is destined to re-establish the ancient religions.

But, though the programme of love and unity is a most attractive one, and though the summons to brotherhood and human service is something which every Christian must rejoice to hear, yet Theosophy itself is no safe refuge for the present distress. So far from providing a means of reconciling the great religions, Theosophy creates another religious system. It is simply a new doctrine with a crude mythology. Mrs. Besant, who is President of the Theosophical Society, in her *Theosophy*,[1] in Jack's series, 'The People's Books,' puts forward as the central doctrine of the system the statement,

[1] p. 14.

that the community of religious teachings, ethics, stories, symbols, ceremonies, and even the traces of these among savages, arose from the derivation of all religions from a common centre, from a Brotherhood of Divine Men, which sent out one of its members into the world from time to time to found a new religion, containing the same essential verities as its predecessors, but varying in form with the needs of the time, and with the capacities of the people to whom the Messenger was sent.

Christianity teaches that the Father sent the Son to be the Saviour of the world; Muḥammadanism teaches that Allah sent Muḥammad as the final Prophet; Hinduism has its avatāras, but they are no brotherhood of men, but are each an incarnation of the supreme Vishṇu; while Mahāyāna Buddhism also has its incarnations, but they come from the Supreme likewise. It is quite easy to say that Christ, Muḥammad, Kṛishṇa, Gautama, and the rest are all members of the brotherhood, and that that reconciles the religions. The reconciliation is effected by cutting the heart out of each, and substituting this new mythology. The truth is that, so far as their central theological ideas are concerned, Hinduism, Buddhism, Judaism, Muḥammadanism, and Christianity stand much nearer to each other than they do to this new dogma. Certainly no sincere Christian, Jew, or Muḥammadan can accept a system which detaches religion from God. It stands nearer Hinduism than any other faith; yet many Hindus already protest loudly against the identification of their religion with the system; and as time goes on its true nature will become clear to many who now trust in it. The great success of the propaganda in India is almost exclusively due to its defence of caste and idols. What sort of 'reconciliation', then, does it offer to Christians and Muḥammadans?

(*d*) But the vast majority of those who have come under the sway of the new thought are not at all inclined to adopt the fanciful theories of Theosophy. They have no reasoned statement of their position ready to give to the inquirer, yet both their feelings and their convictions on the question are deep and serious. They fall into two distinct groups.

i. The first group consists of people in Christian lands, many of them genuinely Christian people, others men and women whose faith has been partly shaken, but all impressed with the importance of the faiths of the East and the obligation lying upon us to treat them honourably. They show an immense interest in these religions. They are hungering for information, eager to listen to a competent teacher, sometimes ready to struggle through hard books. Even if they know but little, they are keen and enthusiastic. They are all inclined to say: These great religions are all so good, they contain so much that is noble, and they train so many good men, that it seems a shame to disturb them in any way. Ought we not rather to be thankful for them and to seek to learn from them?—These ideas have come to them from a variety of sources.

European administrators, judges, army officers, educationalists, and business men come into close personal contact with educated Hindus, Buddhists, and Muḥammadans, and find a large number of them men of high moral character, of keen intellect, and of real religious feeling. They frequently appear to be as good men as Christians of the same condition of life are. It is perfectly clear that they get a great deal of help from their religions. They have large joy and deep confidence in them. The question therefore naturally arises, Why should they be teased into becoming Christians?

A few Europeans also come into contact with the quiet population of the villages of Eastern lands and learn to admire their industry, patience, endurance, and charity. These people live a quiet settled life. They are happy in their own way, and there are many beautiful points in their intercourse with one another and in their religion. Quaint touches of spirituality and religious insight flash out in their conversation now and then.[1] Their ideas and their practice

[1] Two Hindu women fell out in the street. One became very violent. The other turned to her and said solemnly, 'Hush, you will hurt the Brahman in you.' For the Brahman see Chap. VI.

seem to fit very well into their circumstances. On the whole they do very well with their religions. Why should they be disturbed? On the other hand, some of those who have become Christians in those lands seem to have lost their good old manners and to have become a travesty of European civilization. Is it worth while doing so much to produce this result?

The practical man is usually quite satisfied with Asiatic lands as they are. These people make good material for governing, and for drilling as soldiers. Business amongst them pays the business man. Things on the whole go very well. From this point of view there does not seem to be any need for a great change. Hence many an Indian civilian, doctor, army officer, and business man tells his friends when he is on furlough that he knows the people of India and he sees no reason why they should become Christians at all.

The revival of Hinduism and the swift rise of the National Movement have made the Indian express himself very forcibly both in speech and in literature. There can be no question that educated India has deeply influenced the opinion of Europe and America these last few years.

The publication of large numbers of translations of sacred texts from the East and of innumerable articles and books expounding the great religions, the loud protests of a few European scholars who, having laid aside Christianity, are favourably disposed towards Eastern religions, the Parliament of Religions in Chicago, and the visits of Hindu and Buddhist teachers to Britain and to America, have all helped to produce a much higher appreciation of these religions and a deep sympathy with those who profess them.

General considerations have also come in to strengthen this mass of kindly feeling. People are inclined to reason as follows: We do not really know the other world: why should we dogmatize about it? Let us live good lives ourselves and leave others to do the same. Why should we raise religious strife?

Racial and national questions have also their influence. Race is deep and national differences go far. As rulers, we find it necessary to tolerate much, to make large allowances for race: may not the religions of these strange peoples be related to their racial qualities? Here we come very close to Rāmakṛishṇa's idea. The adaptation of these Eastern systems to the peoples and their civilizations is certainly insisted on by many; and the idea is buttressed by the recollection of the fierce character of religious passion when once roused, and by the belief that it is altogether impossible to separate these people from their religions.

There are large elements in these Eastern faiths which attract a certain type of mind. The doctrine of transmigration is most interesting and suggestive. Mystic pantheism draws many more. The great toleration of these religions seems to many minds a most admirable feature. Since they only ask to be left alone, since they are quite willing to tolerate Christianity, why should we not accept the policy?

But, while all this mass of honest thinking and noble feeling is present in the movement, it would be foolish to ignore the fact that in many minds there lies also the idea that religion is not a matter of such importance as to justify the machinery of Missions and the disturbance they cause. This fruit of religious indifference and rank ignorance ought to be clearly distinguished from other factors by all those who are interested either in practical religion or in the advance of religious science.

ii. The second group consists almost entirely of non-Christians who have had a Western education. They admire Western thought, science, and social life, and there are but few of them that have not adopted Western habits in some degree. Many of them regularly use English in talking of the things of the mind and the spirit. They usually know something about Christianity. But they are men who have felt in their own lives and in their own community the power of their own religion. They have been created by it. The soul-windows through which they look out upon the world have been made by it. The past lives in them. Every aspect of their religion, its thought, its philosophy, its cult, its home-life, even what seems absurd to the outsider, is sacred to them. They see the glint of the spiritual world on every part of it. They are quite content with it. Like Plutarch they say,

> The ancient faith of our fathers suffices.[1]

Jesus knew them and described them:

> And no man having drunk old wine desireth new: for he saith, The old is good.[2]

Others, more conscious of the danger, go a step further and say, 'Our religion is as good as Christianity. We do not set up our religion to be the only religion for mankind, but we do maintain that it is pure, spiritual, stimulating, and satisfying. It pleases us more than any other religion ever could. Therefore we believe it to be as good as yours.' Thus Hindus, Muḥammadans, and Buddhists are not only up in arms in defence of their religions, but urge that the missionary in seeking to bring men into Christianity is actually doing wrong. A few extremists would like to see the missionary sent home bag and baggage; but the majority of educated men protest that the educating, civilizing, uplifting work of Missions is far too precious to be dispensed with. Their one objection to Missions is the baptism of converts, the planting of the Christian Church. That, they contend, is not only unnecessary, but is an act of unjust aggression upon the existing religions.

In face, then, of this large body of serious and moderate opinion, it is clear that the Christian must either transform his missionary methods or else justify what he is doing in the face of all the world. This he can do only by setting out clearly how he believes Christianity is related to other religions.

[1] Glover, 89. [2] Luke 5, 39.

There is all the more reason for so doing, because here we have to deal, not with a single reasoned opinion, but with a very large mass of powerful and noble feeling, shot through and through with many lines of thought, clear and inchoate, strong and weak.

III. The position which the thoughtful, modern Christian takes up towards other religions may be expressed under the following four heads.

A. There is a certain underlying unity in all religions as there is in the manifestations of every other human function. The human heart and mind are the same everywhere. Hence there is something which links the lowest religion to the highest. There are gleams of light, suggestions of truth, in the most degraded faith. There is an identity which persists throughout the myriad forms which religion takes.

Further, each religion has been of value to the men who have professed it. Every religion has given its followers at least the idea of duty and of the community, and usually also the idea of God and of worship. There has never been a religion that did not uplift men, that did not bring them nearer God.

Yet even that does not express the whole truth. The religion of a savage is the very highest thing he knows, however gross it may be. In its activities his soul reaches its highest exercise. Hence we must recognize that, through his gross religion, the savage can reach God—

> That the savage hands and helpless,
> Groping blindly in the darkness,
> Touch God's right hand in that darkness
> And are lifted up and strengthened.

As the writer once heard a good man say in a public meeting, 'Religion must be a very simple thing in God's eyes; otherwise the simple folk of the world would have no chance at all!' We must believe that it is possible for every human being, no matter what his circumstances may be, to find his way to God, if he truly use all the light he has.

Otherwise, the relation of Father and child does not exist in his case. So the very foundation of Christianity demands this acknowledgement. Our belief in Christ leads to the same truth; for we hold Him to be

> the light which lighteth every man;[1]

and we believe that even in savage minds God

> left not himself without witness;[2]

and that the very lowest men

> show the pith of the law written in their hearts.[3]

Thus through the grossest religion there is a path to God.

Christianity frankly acknowledges that a man may be acceptable to God in any religion. This is stated in the clearest possible language by Peter:

> Of a truth I perceive that God is no respecter of persons: but in every nation he that feareth him, and worketh righteousness, is acceptable to him.[4]

The ladder from earth to heaven is there for the lowest savage as well as for Jacob and the modern man.

B. The condition under which a man reaches God is utter sincerity, the turning of his whole soul toward the light, the frank acceptance of truth into his heart, straightforward obedience to the very highest he knows. It is this pose of the soul that opens it to heavenly influences, that makes it possible for our Father to enter into personal fellowship with His child. Without this attitude, there can be no true religion anywhere. Beyond this no man can go, however narrow or however wide his knowledge, experience, and opportunities may be. This law then applies to men in every religion.

Take the case of a savage who has been living a faithful life, in accordance with his light, in a coarse cannibalistic religion. He hears Muḥammadanism preached, feels the

[1] John 1, 9. [2] Acts 14, 17. [3] Romans 2, 15.
[4] Acts 10, 34, 35. Cf. also Paul's words, Rom. 10, 12.

reasonableness of monotheism, the pressure of the doctrine of judgement on his conscience, the high moral value of the ethics of Islam. But, for various reasons, he continues his old life and the practice of cannibalism. What is the inevitable result? The religion through which he formerly received help is no longer of any use to him. He has seen truth and has refused to obey it. He is no longer a religious man.

So, when a polytheist, coming in contact with Christianity, realizes the folly of idolatry, and feels that the cross and the love of Christ are just what he needs for the transformation of his sin-stained soul and life; if he fail to confess Christ publicly; if he shrink back from acting upon this revelation of religious truth in his inner life; if he continue to bow down to idols; his old faith, however valuable it may have been to him formerly, can never be for him a door into fellowship with God again; for he has turned his back upon the highest, and has made the great refusal.

C. Christians acknowledge fully the great and good work that has been done by each of the great religions. We gladly recognize that, in them, many saints have been trained, thousands of homes have been purified and uplifted, and multitudes of men and women have found God. We rejoice in the true and fruitful religious experience of these good men. We also recognize that in each of these religions men and women are still being trained in goodness and lifted nearer God. These are the facts on which people in Europe and America and educated non-Christians insist, when they demand that missionaries shall cease to make converts to Christianity. We acknowledge them and thank God for them.

We go still farther: we gladly confess that these great and good results prove the presence of truth in each of these systems:

> By their fruits ye shall know them. Do men gather grapes of thorns, or figs of thistles?[1]

[1] Matt. 7, 16.

When, however, certain of our friends go one step farther and say, 'Thus, all these religions are true,' we call a halt, and ask them to state more definitely what they mean. Do they mean to say that each is true in part, or that each is wholly true? that each contains a considerable amount of truth, or that each is the very truth of God? Clearly it can be only the former; for these great religions contradict each other very seriously on many points. Thus we agree with our friends completely, when they say, 'All these religions are good and helpful because each contains much truth.'

D. It is now necessary to take a look at the points on which the great religions contradict each other; and, in order to make our exposition as clear as possible, we shall restrict ourselves to the great quaternion, Hinduism, Buddhism, Christianity, Muḥammadanism. These will provide quite sufficient material and illustration. Hinduism teaches that every soul is born and dies many times; Christianity says,

> It is appointed unto man once to die, and after this cometh judgement.[1]

Buddhism agrees with Hinduism on this point, but condemns Hindu literature, priests, and sacrifice, and sets forth the Buddha as the omniscient and infallible teacher for all men. Christianity teaches that God is the Father of men, that His Son became incarnate to reveal the Father and to die for the sins of the world, that He is the ideal for all men, and that His moral and spiritual teaching is necessary for all men. Muḥammadanism, agreeing with Christianity that men are born and die once, denies all the affirmations of Christianity, and proclaims Muḥammad as the last and greatest Prophet and the Koran as the eternal utterance of God. These oppositions and contradictions are as abrupt and definite as they can well be, and there are many more, quite as clear-cut and irreconcilable. The differences between the great religions are by no means small.

[1] Heb. 9, 27.

Let us now place beside these facts the contention that the great religions are all so noble and so great that we ought not to make odious distinctions among them, but should recognize them as a band of brothers. Clearly this contention can be maintained only on the ground that the differences between the religions are negligible. They may be regarded as negligible from different points of view. The atheist and the agnostic, acknowledging the value of the moral teaching of the various systems, put aside the differences between them as so much mythology. Many a humble man says, 'I believe my own religion is true; but I recognize that a Hindu or a Muḥammadan feels in the same way; and so I think it best not to meddle with questions which I cannot settle, when there is so much good in each system;' some few plead for peace on the ground that the inner spirit of all the great religions is the same; while many a modern student is inclined to say, 'I cannot see into the other world: I do not know the truth on the great subjects of the nature and character of God, the coming of men to birth, and their destiny after death. Why should we dogmatize? Let each religion do all the good it can. We shall study all and sympathize with all.' The point of view varies; but, whatever the point of view may be, the demand that we should recognize these religions as equals and should not seek to make converts rests upon the idea that the differences are negligible.

Now there is only one point here which the Christian challenges. He acknowledges to the full, as we have already seen, that the great religions are of extreme value as compared with lower faiths, that each contains a great deal of truth, and that each produces precious results: thus far we are all agreed. The Christian simply goes one step beyond the others. He says these differences which so many people regard as negligible are of large importance.

Things are not as they were fifty years ago. The nations of the world are much nearer each other than they were;

immense masses of information about all the peoples and all the religions have been gathered together; and the Science of Religion has escaped from the period of stumbling experiment and come into an assured kingdom. Meantime, the Christian Church has been in closer relations with each of the great religions than ever before, has studied their literatures and their practice, and by daily companionship with their educated men has entered into their thought and spiritual experience. In this matter Christians occupy a position of supreme advantage. No other body of men and women have had the priceless opportunities which Mission work among educated Buddhists, Confucianists, Hindus, Jains, Muḥammadans, and Zoroastrians has brought them. It is on the basis of these accumulated stores of knowledge and of all this practical religious intercourse with non-Christian nations and individuals that the Christian dares to say that the differences which sever the great religions are by no means negligible, but are of extreme importance. He believes, as a result of his study and his experiences, that the matters in which Christianity differs from the other faiths are of supreme practical value and significance for the life of man. Every thinking man sees clearly the superiority of the great religions over the lowest faiths. The Christian sees as distinctly the superiority of Christianity to the rest of the great religions; and he believes the evidence can be set forth with overwhelming force.

The savage gets on, one way or another, with his savage religion; and, as we have seen, it really helps him, does him good. But now, let Muḥammadan civilization reach his village. He and his gradually pick up the elements of a higher culture; and, as the years go by, their thoughts are widened. Will his ancient savage faith still suffice? Will it now be able to do him good, to stimulate him to the best he is capable of? Clearly, it cannot; for it belongs to the lower stage of knowledge and thought which he has left behind. He must get a higher faith or live an atrophied religious life. This principle holds good universally. A religion is of value to a people only so long as it is the very highest the people know. Nor is the reason hard to see. Religion is the creative, organizing, stimulating, kindling power in human life: how can it lead men on, if it is not in advance of them? When most of the leading ideas of a religion have become incredible to its people, they may continue to observe its ancient practices, but clearly it cannot exercise the old influence over their minds and hearts. The harvest which was reaped from the faith when it was alive will not spring up from it now that it is dead.[1]

The whole world has entered upon a new stage of existence, the stage of universalism. We are now compelled to think in terms of the human race. Nations whose horizon until recently was bounded by their frontiers now find themselves talking of all the continents. It is not merely that we are interested in world-politics. Moral questions have become interracial and international: the treatment of Indians in South Africa is a case in point. All the civilizations are now clashing; all the religions have met face to face. The villagers of Bengal, of Shantung, of the Tokaido have been transformed into citizens of the world. Hence the proportions and the relations of things have changed. New ideas forcibly take possession of whole populations, and change the face of things in a day.

These things are of the utmost significance to the Christian. He believes that, in the light of the new circumstances of the nations, the practical differences between Christianity and the other great religions now stand out in startling vividness. The new age, with its world-wide relations and world-wide thought, subjects every business method, every moral rule, and every religious belief to a terrific strain and test. Customs and laws which for centuries have proved equal to the ordinary demands of a people's life are now creaking, crashing, and falling to

[1] An educated Jain said to a friend of the writer the other day, 'My religion is just a dummy religion.'

pieces like the spars of an old ship caught in a cyclone. The needs of the new time, so far as we can see, can be met only by Christianity. Not in arrogance, not in partisanship, do we say this, but with wide open eyes and with full consciousness of the stupendous character of the claim we make.

In this volume an attempt is made to substantiate in some degree this tremendous claim in the case of Hinduism. The phenomena of religion are so varied, and require to be stated with so much precision and care, that a single study is much more likely to be useful than a scamper over the whole vast field would be. The rest of this Introduction will state the way in which the relations between Christianity and Hinduism present themselves to the writer, and the method which will be followed in bringing the two religions into comparison in the chapters of the book.

IV. We shall keep in closest touch with facts and also find an excellent starting-point for the development of our position, if we begin with an objection which is frequently urged against Christian Missions in India to-day. Educated Hindus regard the missionary propaganda as an unjustifiable attack on the national genius and spirit. Christianity is objected to not as being untrue, but as being destructive and denationalizing. The following quotation from a Hindu writer puts the charge quite forcibly:

> The missionary is the representative of a society, a polity, a social system, a religion and a code of morality which are totally different from our own. He comes as a belligerent and attacks our time-honoured customs and institutions, our sacred literature and traditions, our historical memories and associations. . . . He wishes to destroy our society, history, and civilization. . . .
>
> He is the arch-enemy who appears in many guises, the great foe of whatever bears the name of Hindu, the ever-watchful, ever-active, irreconcilable Destroyer of the work of the Rishis and Maha Rishis, of that marvel of moral, intellectual, and civic achievement which is known as Hindu civilization. Let us labour under no delusions on this point. You may forget your own name; you may forget your mother. But do not for a moment forget the great, all-important fact that the missionary

is the most dreadful adversary you have to meet . . . the greatest enemy of dharma and Hindu national life in the present age.[1]

There is no mistaking the meaning of these sentences. They are clear and to the point. We believe also that the words will create sympathy in every heart. The modern mind makes a deep response to the national spirit.

It is quite true that the destruction to which the writer refers is going on. Serious havoc is being wrought in the ancient structure of Hinduism. It is also true that Christianity is one of the forces that are disintegrating the religion; but it is only one of several; and the destruction would go on almost as rapidly as ever, even if every missionary were deported from India to-morrow.

The missionary's power of destruction is subject to a very effective automatic check, and his will to destroy is limited by the very nature of the aim he has in view. Many people imagine that the missionary's addresses are a tissue of exposures and condemnations. Nothing could be farther from the truth. Destruction is of no service to the Christian cause. Total loss of faith does not make a Hindu a Christian. A Christian is made only by personal submission to Christ and spiritual union with Him. Hence Christian addresses must be filled with spiritual wisdom and power if they are to do any good. I have listened to hundreds of addresses delivered to educated Hindus, Muḥammadans, and Buddhists by men of different nationalities and churches; and I believe at least eighty-five per cent. of all the matter has been pure Christian teaching, uttered without reference to any other religion. About ten per cent. of the addresses, I should think, have been comparative studies, dealing with some aspect of Christianity and Hinduism, or some other faith. Even this small number of mixed addresses would not have been given, were it not that non-Christian audiences are very eager to hear such comparisons. Missionaries would have larger

[1] Prof. Har Dayal. The passage is quoted by Coomaraswamy, *Essays in National Idealism*, 156.

audiences if they were willing to deal more with the religions, but they prefer to give Christian teaching to smaller numbers. In all the hundreds of meetings I have attended, I have scarcely ever heard a disrespectful sentence used with regard to any non-Christian faith. Even if a missionary were unwise enough to wish to attack Hinduism with hard words, he would not dare to do it; for no educated audience would stand it. In Mission schools and colleges the teaching is almost purely Christian. One hears only an occasional reference to Hinduism.

The case is somewhat different with missionary literature. A much larger proportion of books deal with Hinduism and the other religions. And here the writer readily confesses that the missionary record is not clean. Down to some ten or twelve years ago a considerable number of Christian books published in India contained harsh judgements, denunciatory language, and, here and there, statements that were seriously inaccurate. But that is now almost altogether a thing of the past. The men who write to-day have a far more competent knowledge of the religions they deal with, and the publishing societies will have nothing to do with harsh language and denunciation. But the main point to be noticed is this, that such wrongdoing brings its own penalty and corrective with it. Hindus simply will not read such material, and they mark the man who is guilty and will have nothing to do with him.

Thus the direct destructive power of the missionary is very strictly limited. But Christian teaching by itself introduces new ideas into the Hindu mind; and, in so far as these are wider, deeper, more ethical, more spiritual than the ideas of Hinduism, they do undoubtedly weaken Hindu faith. But here once more there is the double safeguard: the Hindu need not listen unless he choose to do so; and the new teaching can find entrance only if it be very distinctly superior to the old.

The forces that are in the main destructive of Hinduism stand out quite clear. Everything Western brings with it an atmosphere which is most inimical to the old faith. Modern education tells with incalculable force on every student's mind. English literature, modern science, modern inventions, European business methods and the principles of Government action in India, are all disintegrating agents of great efficiency.

But there is another force which must not be forgotten: no one delivers such direct or such deadly attacks on Hinduism as the educated Hindu does. The following are extracts from an article by the very writer whose condemnation of the missionary as the arch-enemy of India we have just read:[1]

> Metaphysics has been the curse of India. It has blighted her history and compassed her ruin. It has converted her great men into miserable quibblers, and led them into useless channels of inquiry and effort. It has been the dangerous will-o'-the-wisp of Indian intellect during many centuries. It has elevated sophistry to the rank of an art, and substituted vain fancies for knowledge. It has condemned India's intellect to run in the same old groove for hundreds of years. It has blinded her seers and led them to mistake phantoms for realities. . . . Arrogant, pretentious, verbose and purblind, it has taken its cackling for an oracle and its fantastic word-towers for solid piles of thought-masonry. . . .
>
> While so much transcendental nonsense is being perpetrated, famines are desolating the land, pestilence and malaria hang like a pall on town and country, and there is not a single decent representative institution, technical institute, laboratory or library in the whole country. Science, economics, and politics are anathema to the enlightened men of India. They love only the eternal verities and the deep secrets of theosophy or brahmavidya! My friends, while you are going into ecstasy over the intolerable twaddle of many of your Shastras and quoting Schopenhauer and Max Müller in their praise, the world is stealing a march on you by scientific research, economic reforms, and political progress. While you are explaining to your people the ineffable joys of trance or 'samādhi', another trance is already upon them—the trance of starvation and the deadly pest. The Upanishads claim to expound 'that, by knowing which everything is known'. This mediaeval quest for 'the absolute' is the basis of all the spurious metaphysics of India. The treatises are full of absurd conceits, quaint fancies, and chaotic specula-

[1] Prof. Har Dayal in the *Modern Review*, July, 1912. Another article by the same writer containing similar statements with regard to other aspects of the religion appeared in the same magazine in November, 1912.

tions. And we have not learned that they are worthless. We keep moving in the old rut; we edit and re-edit the old books instead of translating the classics of European social thought. What would Europe be if Frederic Harrison, Brieux, Bebel, Anatole France, Hervé, Haeckel, Giddings, and Marshall should employ their time in composing treatises on Duns Scotus and Thomas Aquinas, and discussing the merits of the laws of the Pentateuch and the poetry of Beowulf? Indian pundits and graduates seem to suffer from a kind of mania for what is effete and antiquated. Thus an institution, established by progressive men, aims at leading our youths through Sanskrit grammar to the Vedas *via* the Six Darshanas! What a false move in the quest for wisdom! It is as if a caravan should travel across the desert to the shores of the Dead Sea in search of fresh water! Young men of India, look not for wisdom in the musty parchments of your metaphysical treatises. There is nothing but an endless round of verbal jugglery there. Read Rousseau and Voltaire, Plato and Aristotle, Haeckel and Spencer, Marx and Tolstoi, Ruskin and Comte, and other European thinkers, if you wish to understand life and its problems. . . .

India has hundreds of really sincere and aspiring young men and women, who are free from all taint of greed and worldliness, but they are altogether useless for any purpose that one may appreciate. They have established monasteries in remote nooks in the mountains in order to realize the Brahman. Instead of bearing the heat and burden of the day along with their fellow men, they aim at reaching a superior stage of illumination by practising all sorts of mysterious postures and other funny devices of a crude mysticism. . . .

'Samādhi' or trance is regarded as the acme of spiritual progress! How strange it is that a capacity for swooning away should be considered the mark of wisdom! It is very easy to lose consciousness if one has strong emotions and a feeble intellect. That is why ladies faint so often on the slightest provocation. But in India samādhi is the eighth stage of yoga, which only 'paramahansas' can reach. These be thy gods, O Israel! To look upon an abnormal psychological condition produced by artificial means as the sign of enlightenment was a folly reserved for Indian philosophers.

This type of writing is by no means uncommon to-day in Indian journalism. The following appeared as a leading article in the columns of the *Bengalee*,[1] the leading Hindu paper in Calcutta, the editor of which is Mr. Surendranāth Bannerjea, the noted nationalist:

[1] Reproduced in the *Statesman* of September 28, 1911.

We have referred in our previous issues to the fact that Hindu India is at present divided into camps—the camp of the orthodox who hold that salvation lies in every Hindu conforming rigidly and scrupulously to the rules and observances of social life handed down from the past, and that of the unorthodox, men who under the inspiration of Western culture and Western ideals have been dreaming of building up a new India by transplanting into their country the spirit of the social, industrial, and political institutions of Europe. It requires little reasoning to convince oneself that the extreme conservatism of the orthodox section of the Hindu community which finds itself fulfilled in an unswerving adherence to existing institutions and looks upon the least modification of, or innovation upon, them as a profanity and a desecration, is necessarily the negation of progress. It is born of the conviction that every practice and every custom at present current in Hindu society has had a divine origin, and that it is consequently no less a sacrilege to depart therefrom than it would be to deny the inspiration of the Vedas.

But it is clear that the community committed to such a creed is doomed to stagnate, and must eventually go under in the modern struggle for existence into which all the nations of the world have been forced by the annihilation of time and space through steam and electricity. Not a people in the world but is revising and readjusting its institutions, its traditional ideas and ideals to the new conditions, to the stern circumstance that the nation that aspires to occupy a place on the stage of progress has now for its competitors not only its neighbours but all the peoples of the world. What chance has India to keep abreast, or even to be within a measurable distance, of the sister nations in progressive advancement, with her sworn allegiance to a pattern of society which was suited to the conditions of a thousand years ago?

Let us take a few instances. We have worshipped the Goddess of 'Sakti' (i.e. energy) for centuries; how is it that through those very centuries we have remained so weak and helpless as a nation? We are the devout worshippers of 'Sarasvatī' (the goddess of learning); and at the same time have received a scant share of her blessings. The priests who are the monopolists of the religious rites and ministrations are for the most part as innocent of Vedic knowledge at the present day as the 'Sūdra' was in the days when the gates of knowledge were shut against him by the iron rules of castes. We offer our devotions to 'Lakshmī' (the goddess of wealth) every recurrent year; and we remain none the less a nation of paupers.

The orthodox Hindu makes a fetish of certain rules of hygiene formulated by his ancestors in the dim past; he regards it as sin, for instance, to take his meals without bathing, or to remain in unwashed clothes for more than a day; but, with all his religious devotion to the traditional rules of cleanliness, he betrays a strange indifference to the principles of sanitation evolved by modern science, though plague and cholera and all the other diseases that are generated in filth are decimating thousands of his fellow men year after year. One has only to be in a Hindu's house for a day to discover his ignorance of elementary sanitary principles in contrast with his particular conformity to the few rules of sanitation enjoined upon him by tradition. One would go grievously wrong in persuading oneself that the Hindu is apathetic to the rules of sanitation and the other life-saving injunctions of modern science, because he had transcended, by virtue of a strenuous spiritual discipline, the human craving for life. He loves life no less dearly than the passionate worldlings of the material West, as he calls Europeans.

The Hindu father blesses his son's wife with the invocation 'May she be like Sabitri'. But was there room in ancient Hindu life for the Philistinism which actuates the modern Hindu father to huckster and chaffer over the price of his son with the unfortunate person in search of a bridegroom for his daughter? It is evident even to the casual observer that extreme orthodoxy is without a soul to save it from the destructive influences that impend over it from all sides.

The orthodox Hindu clings, in the name of religion and morality, to dead forms and mummied institutions from which the informing spirit has long departed. Is not the practice of worshipping God at prescribed intervals of the day and the year, in a language which the worshipper in many cases does not understand, as mechanical as the automatic working of a machine? Is there the least trace of life in a system of rites which demands the punctilious performing of a number of ceremonials on the sole ground that these have been performed through the preceding centuries? Ask the Hindu why he wastes his substance and gets into debt over the celebration of his daughter's marriage; his honest answer will always be 'because his forefathers have done so'. Inquire of the bridegroom what he has understood of the sacrament he has gone through, what he has understood of the Mantras (Vedic texts) he has uttered at the dictation often of an ignorant and mispronouncing priest; he will tell you he has not understood much or perhaps anything at all. But to his mind that is of no moment, for has he not fulfilled his duty by conforming to the directions laid down in the Shastras (Hindu laws)? But surely, in the days when Hinduism was living, the Hindu who said his prayers to his God did so in full consciousness of what he was saying; the young bridegroom uttered the sacred Mantras in full cognizance of their purpose and purport.

> We will not multiply instances. But this much is clear, that when a people's religion and rites have sunk into soulless formulae they can exercise no corrective or controlling influence over, they must cease to be in intimate relationship with its daily thought and life. And so it is in our country. The champion of orthodoxy, conforming as he does to the fossilized forms of a religious and moral code which have long ceased to embody the living spirit, is most un-Hindu in the family affairs of his life.

We may also quote a few paragraphs from an article which appeared in the *Madras Christian College Magazine* in April, 1912, from the pen of a Hindu, Mr. V. Kunhikannan:

> Probably few nations in the world, ancient or modern, have been more superstitious, more credulous, more gullible than the Hindus. It is a most significant and noteworthy fact that even at this distance of time, even in this budding twentieth century, in an age of triumphant intellectual and scientific advance unparalleled in the history of the human race, many things which have been burnt to ashes under the all-embracing fire of modern science and modern thought, are still piously retained by the vast majority of the Hindus.
>
> Whosoever has eyes to see and uses them cannot deny that a marvellous religious revival has actually set in among the Hindus within the last few years. . . .
>
> But, however pleasant it may be to contemplate this aspect of the revival, no one can shut his eyes to the all too visible recrudescence of ancient superstitions which has accompanied the more truly religious revival. It is most deplorable that, with the luxuriant growth of the corn, much weed has also sprung up to hinder the ripening of the true grain.
>
> It is very painful, but nevertheless true, that the Theosophical Society is largely, if not mainly, responsible for this state of affairs at the present time. It is not a little amusing to find learned Theosophists defending and popularizing even the worst superstitions of the Hindus and trying to find an occult meaning for every tradition, rite, and ceremony which we have outgrown by the evolution of the intellect and the increasing knowledge of Nature and her laws. No doubt Theosophy has contributed not a little to the present religious revival of the Hindus. But if it has done much that is good and noble, it has also done harm through attempting in these modern days to make us believe that all the stories of the Puranas are historical facts; that behind every physical phenomenon a God is at work; that idolatry and the worship of the many gods is right; that when a man dies the bodies of his nearest

relations are literally polluted ; that there is an occult use and purpose in the meaningless ritual and ceremonies of the Hindus, and so on. It is absolutely useless and futile to teach such things in this age in which reason and intellect predominate. . . . Every critical observer sees that modern thought has almost completely undermined the peculiar Hindu ideas and customs. The framework of that mighty system of religious and social organization has well-nigh broken down, and it needs no prophet to say that at no distant date a complete re-arrangement of things will be the result. . . .

It is quite surprising to find even to-day Hindus who abhor the idea of foreign travel on the strength of the supposed injunctions of the Shastras against it. The practice of excommunicating transgressors of this rule is still prevalent among the higher castes. Upon a superstition so glaring comment is needless.

Again, I have often noted with pitying interest how even educated Hindus stand up in reverential awe and bow down with clasped hands before the lamp lighted at dusk and shown upon the verandah in every Hindu home. They are bowing to the fire-god, it appears! It is intelligible that in times of primitive ignorance men should have personified the forces of nature and worshipped them as gods, being wonderstruck at the mysteries of Nature. They saw the glorious sun and thought it was a god and began to worship the same. But what is to be thought of the modern Hindu who follows suit, in spite of the advancement of knowledge of Nature and her secrets ?

Again, it is a sorry spectacle to witness Hindus still worshipping the village gods and goddesses in the most hideous and superstitious manner. In my own place there is a 'kavu' (temple) where thousands of fowls and sheep are every year butchered for the propitiation of the supposed god and goddess. The sacred temple is literally transformed into a slaughter-house. Can any man conceive a more horrible and degrading way of worshipping the Supreme Father of the universe ?

Another superstition is the belief that our sins will be washed away by bathing in the water of the Ganges and other sacred rivers and by visiting sacred (?) cities like Benares. For this purpose millions of Hindus spend all their hard-earned money in visiting such places and bathing in the waters of such rivers, thinking that thus their sins will be forgiven. Could any idea be more primitive? If we can commit sins and wash them away by bathing in the waters of certain rivers, how easy have things become! Such ideas are most dangerous to man's moral evolution. They encourage the commission of sin by holding out the hope of cleansing through the holy water of the Ganges.

Once more, Hindus waste a lot of money by performing the sheshakriyas (after-death ceremonies of the dead, such as the pinnam, shraddha, &c.). We have absolutely no evidence to show that the dead derive any benefit at all from such ceremonies, and, if the doctrine of karma be true, it is clear that a man's suffering after death will be exactly according to the evil deeds done by himself in his mundane existence, and he will have to pay the debt to the last farthing. How then can shraddha afford him any benefit? It is as yet unexplained how certain rites performed here in the physical world can affect those who are supposed to be in some other spheres which are anything but physical. Unless and until a clear explanation is forthcoming, no rational man has any right to perform acts the use of which is entirely unknown to him.

Another startling superstition is that small-pox and cholera are due to the visitation of certain goddesses. The goddess is angry, for some reason or other, and hence the outbreak of the epidemic. Although Western science has opened our eyes to the real cause and prevention of these fell diseases, yet the vast majority of Hindus piously retain the old belief to their eternal shame and degradation. Again, if any disease occurs in a house an astrologer is consulted before the physician is called in.

Every one will realize what a potent destructive influence such writing as this by Hindus must exercise on the young Hindu mind. What missionary would ever dare, or wish, to write in such a strain?

Perhaps most readers will now agree that, whether missionaries are to be condemned as the arch-enemies of India or not, a far more important matter has come in sight, namely this that, whoever may be to blame, Hinduism is being disintegrated. This is the great fact which has to be realized. The ancient religion of India is breaking up. The following chapters will give abundant proof of this fact. Each of its great old religious ideas is fading out of the minds of her educated men. They are steadily decaying, and there are but few signs of fresh integration.

It is also clear that the cause of the break-up of the old faith is the coming of the new era. The thought of the West creates a new climate which is fatal to Hinduism. The air is too rarified. Its fundamental principles shrivel up in the new atmosphere. Those who have entered the world of Western culture simply cannot hold them. Many proofs of this will appear as we proceed. The third article quoted above states the fact very clearly in two sentences: [1]

> Every critical observer sees that modern thought has almost completely undermined the peculiar Hindu ideas and customs. The framework of that mighty system of religious and social organization has well-nigh broken down.

Thus Christianity, so far from being an intruder at this time, is most seriously required to sow the seeds of spiritual religion and healthy moral life. Thoughtful Indian leaders frankly recognize that the ethical and religious influence of missions is of extreme value in this time of trial; and every one who has been in close touch with the educated classes realizes that they need moral help most seriously. But we may go farther. If 'the framework of that mighty system of religious and social organization has well-nigh broken down', is it not high time to bring to the mind and heart of India a new system, fit to stand the strain and stress of the age, and equal to the task of stimulating the Hindu people to the noblest spiritual activity? This supreme need will steadily become more apparent as the decay of Hinduism proceeds.

It will now be well worth our while to return to the charge, that Christianity is a destroying and denationalizing force, and try to see what is behind it.

A. The first point to be realized is that this is an indictment which has been laid against the religion at many points in its history from the very beginning. At a meeting of the Jewish Council, the case of Christ was discussed, and the talk was,

> What do we? for this man doeth many signs. If we let him thus alone, all men will believe on him: and the Romans will come and take away both our place and our nation.[2]

[1] See p. 41. [2] John 11, 47, 48.

But the high priest said,

> Ye know nothing at all, nor do ye take account that it is expedient for you that one man should die for the people, and that the whole nation perish not.[1]

In consequence they handed Him over to the Romans and had Him crucified. When Paul and Silas preached in the Roman colony of Philippi in Macedonia, they were brought before the city magistrates, and what their accusers said was,

> These men, being Jews, do exceedingly trouble our city, and set forth customs which it is not lawful for us to receive or to observe, being Romans.[2]

The authorities of the Roman Empire considered the religion so inimical to the customs and laws that regulated civilized society that they made the very profession of Christianity a crime; in the eye of the Roman law Christians stood on a level with robbers; and from time to time during the first three centuries fierce persecutions broke out in which countless thousands of men and women suffered death for their faith.

History has repeated itself in modern times. In the sixteenth century Christianity was introduced into Japan, and a considerable section of the people became Christian; but in the seventeenth century the Government became afraid that the movement might prove disloyal, and in consequence they forbade the profession of the religion, and stamped it out in such a fierce persecution as has seldom been witnessed.[3] It was a similar idea that led to twenty-six years of persecution in Madagascar. Finally, the Boxer rising in China, only thirteen years ago, in which thousands of Chinese Christians laid down their lives for Christ, sprang from the idea that it was a foreign and denationalizing faith.

It is thus clear that there is some feature of the religion which inevitably excites suspicion in this way. It is not

[1] John 11, 49, 50. [2] Acts 16, 20, 21.

[3] See below, p. 291.

at all strange that Hindus should think and speak as they do.

B. But let us look at the subsequent history.

1. Is there any thinking man to-day who believes the Jews acted wisely in getting Christ crucified? No; all men now acknowledge that the teaching and the life of Jesus were the healthiest and holiest influences of the time; and that, so far from being a danger to nationality, He was the only wise friend the nation had. If the Jews had accepted Him, they would have retained the nationality which within forty years they flung away in war with Rome. So far from destroying the Jewish religion, Jesus has made the God of Abraham, the Scriptures of Israel, and the history of Israel the heritage of the whole human family.

2. Turn to the Roman Empire. What has the course of history shown? It is now plain that in the early Christian centuries the ancient religions were dying, inevitably passing away. The Roman emperors, conscious of the danger, sought to prop them and revive them; and they believed that in Caesar-worship a new living centre had been found for the old faiths; but it was all in vain. Christianity, so far from being a dangerous foe, was precisely the friend the great Empire needed. Constantine realized the truth and acted on it. Not only the safety of the old Empire, but the life and health of Europe, nay the promise and possibility of the whole modern world, were aboard that frail bark which the emperors sought so industriously to wreck.

3. It is also most significant that it is in Europe and America, where civilization has felt the influence of Christ most deeply, that the modern self-governing peoples have appeared. Autonomous nationality, the ideal towards which the Muḥammadan powers and the ancient peoples of Asia are now straining, is the product of a Christian atmosphere.

4. Commodore Perry appeared in Yedo Bay in 1853; in 1854 the Japanese Government signed the treaty which opened Japan to the world; and in 1858 missionaries entered

the country. But the profession of Christianity was still interdicted. In 1868 a fresh edict was placed on the public edict-boards, which ran:

> The evil sect called Christian is strictly prohibited. Suspicious persons should be reported to the proper officers, and rewards will be given.[1]

The representatives of the foreign powers protested against the edict, but the Government persisted until 1872, when the edicts were removed, Christians in prison were released, and those in exile were allowed to return home. Thus it is only forty-one years since Japan gave up the persecution of Christians.

Yet on February 25, 1912, the Japanese Government held a Conference in Tokyo with the express purpose of strengthening the moral forces at work in the country; and to that Conference not only Buddhists and Shintoists, but Christians were invited. There were present, by Government invitation, thirteen Shintoists, fifty-one Buddhists, and seven Christians.[2]

Clearly the Japanese Government had learnt a lesson in the course of these forty years.

5. The Boxer rising, in which many missionaries and many thousands of Christians were murdered as enemies of the national life, took place in 1900. Yet Sun Yat Sen, the leader of the Revolution which made China a Republic, is a Christian; many of the most prominent nationalist leaders are Christians; Yuan Shi Kai, the President of the Republic, is a personal friend of missionaries, and had a missionary's daughter to educate his children; and on the 17th of April last the Chinese Government requested that prayer should be offered for China in all Christian churches throughout the Empire.

6. Even in India to-day we believe the real character of the religion is steadily become clearer. It is quite true that

[1] Murray's *Japan* (Story of the Nations Series), 379.
[2] *I. R. M.*, July, 1912, 552.

the infinitesimal Christian communities, mere pin-heads amid the vast masses of the Hindu and Muḥammadan population, have, in the past, felt it necessary to keep very much to themselves, in order to preserve in purity the precious truth committed to them; but the iron necessity of that hour is now passing away; and Christian men and women will henceforward take a rapidly increasing share in the national life.

Even now the signs are clearly visible to every one who has eyes. Is Christian work among the Outcastes denationalizing? Let the Brāhma, the Ārya, and the Hindu answer, who imitate the missionary to the limit of their power. Are Christians denationalized when they sit on the bench as Magistrates, or serve as members of District Boards or Municipalities? How would women's hospitals in India be staffed apart from Indian Christian girls? How many Hindu schools for girls employ Christian women as teachers? Do educated Hindus become denationalized when they become Christians? Was there a truer Nationalist in India, from Kashmir to Cape Comorin, than Kali Charan Banurji? He was a prominent member of the Indian National Congress from its inception to his death; he was elected by the graduates to represent Calcutta University on the Council of the Lieutenant-Governor of Bengal; and he was a personal friend of every prominent Indian of whatever creed.[1] Or is Christian education denationalizing? We venture to think that the following vignette from the pen of a Hindu [2] will become classical:

> Though cut off from the parent community by religion and by prejudice and intolerance, the Indian Christian woman has been the evangelist of education to hundreds and thousands of Hindu homes. Simple, neat, and kindly, she has won her way to the recesses of orthodoxy, overcoming a strength and bitterness of prejudice of which few outsiders can have an adequate conception. As these sentences are

[1] See his life by B. R. Barber, published by the C. L. S. I.

[2] From *I. S. R.* The passage was quoted in the *Christian Patriot* of March 28, 1903.

being written, there rises before the mind's eye the picture of scores of tidy, gentle girls, trudging hot and dusty streets barefooted, under a scorching sun, to carry the light of knowledge to homes where they will not be admitted beyond the ante-chamber, and where they cannot get a glass of water without humiliation, yet never complaining, ever patient. To these brave and devoted women wherever they are, friends of female education all over the country will heartily wish 'God-speed'.

It thus seems to be clear that the suspicion that Christianity is a destructive and denationalizing force, despite its strength and persistence, is, at least, in large measure, a mistake.

C. Can we then specify what element in Christianity it is that leads men in every land to think that it is destructive and denationalizing?

Jesus comes to each individual, saying,

> Follow me.

He then explains what is implied in this invitation:

> If any one wish to come after me, let him renounce himself, and take up his cross, and follow me.[1]

This most serious act, in which a man renounces himself and accepts Christ as the Lord of his life, necessarily involves the giving up of the worldly life, and also the renunciation of any other religion he may have been living by. If he is a follower of one of the great old national faiths, this demand usually seems to him a most unreasonable thing. A national religion has a mass of national ideas, customs, and forms of life associated with it. Religion and patriotism are in it intertwined. In most of the ancient nations, the man who did not recognize the national gods was regarded as a bad citizen. That was one of the counts in the indictment against Socrates. Thus to men trained in such a faith Christ inevitably appears to be an enemy not only of the national religion but also of the national life.

Christianity thus seems bad enough in its relation to the

[1] Mark 8, 34.

individual at the very outset. But things assume a far worse aspect when a number of men leave the national religion and become Christians. It then seems that the very existence of the national religion is threatened. Christianity is a new, unheard-of sort of monster in which nationality seems to be swallowed up. Another portent usually appears at the same time. As Christian thought and teaching spread, many of the doctrines and practices of the old faith begin to look unreal and paltry. Hence the popular cry arises, 'Let us get rid of this intruder. We do not need it. We did very well without it.'

The Christian idea, that the individual should renounce his old national religion, is not an excrescence, but belongs to the very heart of Christ's system. The truth He teaches is for all men; and we cannot get the benefit of it except by complete submission to Him and faithful obedience to His laws. That His call, 'Follow me,' should lead to the surrender of the old religion on the part of the individual, and in the end to the death of the old religion, is in full accordance with the leading principles of His teaching.

Christ demands a serious change from every one who seeks to follow Him: 'Repent of your sins; lay aside your old life; deny yourself; surrender yourself to Me; and die to all your old passions and desires.' It is only through death that Christ promises life to us. The great statement,

> If any man wish to come after me, let him renounce himself, and take up his cross, and follow me,[1]

is immediately followed by the explanatory sentence,

> For whosoever would save his life shall lose it; and whosoever shall lose his life for my sake and the gospel's shall save it.[2]

This is Christ's constant attitude to the individual: eternal life springs up through the death of the old self.

The same principle applies to each of the national religions as well. Each is prevented by its national character and

[1] Mark 8, 34.

[2] Mark 8, 35.

organization from working out its own noblest thoughts practically and making them available for other nations. Each must therefore die before it can bear fruit in all the world and find its highest aspirations truly fulfilled. Just before the death of Christ a group of Greeks came to speak to Him in Jerusalem. It is a matter of the utmost interest and significance that, when the representatives of Greek religion, philosophy, and art stood before Him, it was this great lesson of life through death that He sought to teach them. His words were:

> The hour is come, that the Son of man should be glorified. Verily, verily, I say unto you, Except a grain of wheat fall into the earth and die, it abideth by itself alone; but if it die, it beareth much fruit. He that loveth his life loseth it; and he that hateth his life in this world shall keep it unto life eternal.[1]

This law, which was about to be fulfilled in Himself, He pressed home upon the Greeks as necessary for them also; nor need we doubt that He saw clearly that the system under which the Greek people were living would have to die before it could become of the highest service to the whole world.

This principle received its highest illustration in Christ Himself. He gained His victory through death. His own resurrection and the birth of the Christian Church were both fruits of His death on the cross. It was Calvary that created Christianity. The living principle of the faith was expressed once for all in the self-devotion and death of our Lord. Like the grain of wheat He fell into the earth and died, in order to bear much fruit.

Thus, when Jesus says, 'Follow me,' He means to say 'Follow me in the surrender of everything; follow me, if need be, even to the cross'. This dying to all that impedes the work of God in the soul includes for the Hindu a dying to Hinduism, which is no easy or pleasant duty.

In the philosophy and theistic theology of Hinduism there

[1] John 12, 23-25.

are many precious truths enshrined; but, as we shall see, the ancient Hindu system, within which they appeared, effectually prevents them from leavening the people. This hard, unyielding system must fall into the ground and die, before the aspirations and the dreams of Hindu thinkers and ascetics can be set free to grow in health and strength so as to bear fruit in the lives of Hindu villagers. Hinduism must die in order to live. It must die into Christianity.

D. How then does death issue in life?

By His life, death, and teaching Jesus founded a new religion. He thus takes His place, in one sense, beside other founders of religions. Yet the way in which He did it separates Him from all others. We shall understand best if we compare Him with the great Buddhist leader. Gautama cut himself adrift completely from Hinduism and denounced the Vedic sacrifices, the Vedas, and all the works of the Brāhmans. He made a clean sweep and a new beginning. Jesus, on the other hand, acknowledged that the faith of Israel was from God, yet declared that He had been sent to transform it into a new religion. This was possible, because He knew that God's method of revelation is not the presentation, once for all, of a complete system of truth expressed in a book from all eternity, but a gradual and historical process. The simple beginnings of the faith of Israel are laid before us in the Book of Genesis; they grow before our eyes in the narratives of the other books of Moses; and they find still richer development in the Prophets and the Psalms. But even in them God's will is not completely revealed. Hence, to Jesus, the religion of Israel was given by God, but not given in permanency. It was God's instrument for the training of Israel. He came to crown it by transforming it into the religion for all men, and to crown its knowledge of God by revealing Him as the Father of men.

The contrast between Christ and Buddha in this relation comes out most clearly when we compare the Buddhist books with the Bible. There is no hymn from the *Ṛigveda*, no meditation from the *Āraṇyakas*, no glowing passage from the *Upanishads* in the Pāli *Tripiṭaka*; while the whole of the Jewish Scriptures reappear in the Bible as the Old Testament. Thus the principle of living growth, of progress and development, is set before us in visible form in the Christian Scriptures. The Old Testament is the bud; the New Testament is the flower.

But, though the whole of the Jewish Scriptures are contained in the Christian Bible, they are not used by the Christian as they were used by the Jew. The whole of the Old Testament is retained, but it is read through Christ. For the Jew the whole is binding; for the Christian it is binding only in so far as it is in consonance with the Spirit of Christ. The Christian does not obey the Laws of Moses, though these are all contained in his sacred book. He does not offer animal sacrifice, nor abstain from the unclean foods of the law, nor circumcise his male children. The institutions of the old law were necessary for the childhood of the world. They are pictures, symbols, prophecies, but the reality is Christ. To the man who knows Christ these external rites are unnecessary. Yet the whole of the Old Testament is of very great value for the religious life; and a very large part of it is filled with the highest moral and spiritual truth, and is accepted as such by the Christian, as it was accepted by Christ.

Christ regarded the Old Testament as pointing forward to Himself. Here is a most instructive scene, His first sermon in the synagogue of His own city Nazareth:

> And he came to Nazareth, where he had been brought up: and he entered, as his custom was, into the synagogue on the sabbath day, and stood up to read. And there was delivered unto him the book of the prophet Isaiah. And he opened the book, and found the place where it was written:
>
> The Spirit of the Lord is upon me,
> Because he anointed me to preach good tidings to the poor:
> He hath sent me to proclaim release to the captives,

> And recovering of sight to the blind,
> To set at liberty them that are bruised,
> To proclaim the acceptable year of the Lord.
>
> And he closed the book, and gave it back to the attendant, and sat down: and the eyes of all in the synagogue were fastened on him. And he began to say unto them, To-day hath this scripture been fulfilled in your ears.[1]

In His coming, teaching, life, death, resurrection, person, the whole of the old religion is summed up, and makes a new beginning, no longer merely for Israel, but for the world. He is the Messiah of the prophets; He brings in the Kingdom of Heaven promised by them; and His teaching sums up the Law and the Prophets. In Him all the old lines meet, and again stretch out to all the world. He sums up His whole relationship to Israel in the words:

> I am come not to destroy, but to fulfil.[2]

The religions of Greece and Rome could not be the starting-point for the religion of the world, like the religion of Israel. Yet in them also much broken spiritual light was visible; and every type, symbol, and shadow found itself reproduced in spiritual reality in Christ. He did not destroy the old civilization, philosophy, literature, and art. Everything of value that the old world contained has been preserved and has flowered once more in Christianity. Our modern education, thought, science, and art rest on the ancient foundations. It is most significant that Greek philosophers at first regarded the crucified Jew with unspeakable disdain, but later realized that Greek philosophy was but a preparation for his teaching. Clement of Alexandria writes:

> Philosophy tutored the Greeks for Christ as the Law did the Hebrews.[3]

Thus it will be with India. Missionaries do not 'wish to destroy' Hindu 'society, history, and civilization', as Prof. Har Dayal imagines they do.[4] The Muslim came, smash-

[1] Luke 4, 16–21.
[2] Matt. 5, 17.
[3] *Stromateis*, i. 28.
[4] See p. 33, above.

ing temple and image, killing priest and scholar, confiscating temple and monastic lands. Christ comes, not to steal, and kill, and destroy, but to give life and to give it abundantly.[1] Under the spell of His influence modern India has already awaked to new and wondrous life. Here is the testimony of one who is not a Christian, Sir Narayan Chandavarkar, Vice-Chancellor of the University of Bombay and a Justice of the Bombay High Court:

> The ideas that lie at the heart of the Gospel of Christ are slowly but surely permeating every part of Hindu society and modifying every phase of Hindu thought.[2]

Christ is already breathing life into the Hindu people. He does not come to destroy. To Him all that is great and good is dear, the noble art of India, the power and spirituality of its best literature, the beauty and simplicity of Hindu village life, the love and tenderness of the Hindu home, the devotion and endurance of the ascetic schools. Paul gave perfect expression to the Christian spirit in this regard:

> Finally, brethren, whatsoever things are true, whatsoever things are honourable, whatsoever things are just, whatsoever things are pure, whatsoever things are lovely, whatsoever things are of good report; if there be any virtue, and if there be any praise, think on these things.[3]

True, Christ passes everything through His refiner's fire, in order that the dross, which Hindus know so well, may pass away; but the gold will then shine all the brighter. What He cannot endure is that fine art and high literature and lofty philosophy should be used to enslave the poor of the people to superstition. All must be purged for their sakes. Hindus, like His own people, imagine Him a destroyer; but, when the period of pain and strife has passed, they too will see that He is not the Destroyer but the Restorer of the national heritage, and that all the gleams of light that make Hindu faith and

[1] John 10, 10.
[2] From an address delivered in the Y. M. C. A., Bombay, on June 14 1910.
[3] Phil. 4, 8.

worship so fascinating to the student find in Him their explanation and consummation. It is one of the chief aims of this volume to show that Christianity is the Crown of Hinduism.

E. The Churches of the West and the missionaries they send must obey this spiritual law of seeking life through death.

1. In relation to those they seek to win to Christ. The missionary's life must be a daily death to self in every aspect of his behaviour, if he is to exercise his full influence for Christ. No words are sufficient to tell how meek and lowly in heart the winner of souls must be, what humility of speech, what quietness of manner, what superlative self-effacement are necessary, in order that the light of Christ may shine through him into Hindu eyes. The peculiar circumstances of India give three aspects of this duty special prominence.

There is, first, race feeling. The fact that India is under Britain complicates matters for the Christian rather seriously. The missionary is presumably quite incapable of the extreme insolence not infrequently shown to Indians by individual Europeans, when the swaggering British private, the shop assistant, the mill mechanic, the army officer, and, occasionally, even the Indian civilian, display their common lack of breeding and of the imperial instinct. Yet there is extreme danger even for the missionary. He comes to the Indian because he believes him to be his brother; but the glories of his race and of its imperial position still live in his thought; and the simple fact that, for the present, a much larger percentage of effective men are found among Europeans than among Indians, is apt to assume exaggerated importance when one comes to practical work; so that the brotherhood which Christ teaches us tends to become qualified by other considerations. The danger is that these ideas will colour his behaviour, and that the Indian will be only too conscious that he is regarded as an inferior creature. We must therefore be most careful to treat every man with the supreme courtesy which Christ would show him, lest we cause one of these little ones to stumble. It is also right and wise to seek the closest social relations possible. Christ's example is here decisive. The extreme difficulties which Indian society presents should only stir the Christian to greater wisdom and inventiveness. In this as in other things love can see ways at first invisible. The missionary must also check the tendency, so noticeable in certain Indians, to become subservient to the European. Our noble King-Emperor has shown the right spirit: a Punjabi was about to prostrate himself at his feet, but the king caught him ere he fell. The Christian must refuse to allow the Oriental to do otherwise than play the man.

The sensitive Indian spirit is often repelled by our too self-conscious culture, by our society manner or university tone. For culture itself the Indian has unlimited respect; but the man who makes a shibboleth of the trifles of behaviour and the lady with a society sniff grate on his very soul, and make him shrink into his innermost reserve. There is surely no excuse for the man who follows Christ and studies St. Paul if he fail in this matter.

The rule for the behaviour of the monk, Buddhist as well as Hindu, which is dealt with below,[1] has given the Hindu a high ideal of how the religious teacher should live and act towards others. He readily grasps the point that Christ does not bid His followers live as monks; yet he expects them to show the meek, patient, unworldly temper demanded of the monk—no anger, no fuss, no overbearing words. Our Western temper, eager to act, impatient of laziness, crookedness, scamped work, and fecklessness, is apt to rise in indignation in practical relations with Indians. The Hindu may not behave better himself, but he holds that the missionary has not behaved rightly; and Christ agrees with him.

2. The same law must rule our conduct in relation to Hinduism. There is so much that is immoral and cruel in the laws and practices of the religion that the first impulse

[1] p. 256 f.

of the healthy Christian is to denounce these things in the frankest possible terms, as they are denounced by Hindus in the articles quoted above;[1] and it must be confessed that, at first sight, it seems as if such denunciation were fully justified from the practical standpoint of the welfare of the people of India. But there is a further fact which the practical missionary usually fails altogether to notice. No matter how gross, superstitious, cruel, or immoral a law or practice may be, there is always a glint of higher light upon it. This is shown at length in our last chapter. Even if it be a jewel in a swine's snout, it is there, and it is the secret of the reverence in which the rite or custom is held by the Hindu. Hence it is neither just nor wise to denounce the practice without reference to that which touches the sensitive Hindu spirit. Indeed the full scientific truth is not told unless both elements are recognized and the way in which the spiritual gleam comes to fall on the vicious act is set forth. Thus in dealing with every detail of Hinduism the utmost self-restraint is required. There must be a dying to self in this matter also. The writer here wishes to make public confession that during the first years of his life in India unguarded expressions fell from him in teaching, in public addresses, and in literature, of which he is now heartily ashamed.

Many a Hindu who is in the main friendly towards the practical work of missions and also towards the spread of the teaching of Christ in India complains that missionary literature very frequently judges Hinduism by the worst parts of Hindu practice, and sets forth, in contrast, the highest ideals of Christianity. It must be confessed that there is some truth in this serious charge; and the writer of this volume wishes to disassociate himself altogether from such writing. Christian criticism is unchristian unless it be impregnably just and truly Christlike in tone. Unsleeping watchfulness requires to be exercised in this regard. Strenuous efforts have been made

[1] See pp. 36–42.

in the following chapters to be scrupulously fair, and to interpret Hindu teaching with as much imaginative sympathy as a Christian would wish a Hindu to bestow on the religion of Christ. Special care has been taken not to violate the great canon, that a religion must not be judged by the conduct of those who refuse to obey it. The crimes and immoralities of a country can be attributed to its religion only in so far as it commands or condones them. As the sexual vice of Europe exists in defiance of Christ, so, much that is deplorable in Hindu life arises in flat disobedience to the precepts of Hinduism. Hence the only sane rule is to judge a religion by its principles, its laws, and its institutions, and not by the excesses of certain groups of the population.

3. There must be the same readiness to die to self in relation to certain aspects of our own Christianity. When we say that Christianity is the Crown of Hinduism, we do not mean Christianity as it is lived in any nation, nor Christianity as it is defined and elaborated in detail in the creed, preaching, ritual, liturgy, and discipline of any single church, but Christianity as it springs living and creative from Christ Himself. Christ is the head of the whole Church, not of any one denomination. Christ is human, not Western. Far less is He English, Scottish, American, or German.

Only in this way can we be true to Christ. For He set forth no detailed laws for the Church, for the moral life, or for the State. While Hinduism, Muḥammadanism, and other religions have laid down detailed rules for human conduct in the matter of the family and other institutions, Christ deliberately refused to do so. In all these things He taught merely the spiritual principles which are necessary for our human life and left us to apply them in detail ourselves. The contrast between the Old and New Testaments in this regard is so striking as to leave no room for doubt. The Law of Moses differs very seriously in many ways from the Law of Manu; yet both bring every aspect of human life under religious law; both mix up religious, political, moral, and sanitary regulations in a way that is most disconcerting to a modern mind; and both contain numerous rules for man's guidance in social matters. Thus, in their general form, the Hindu Law and the Jewish Law stand on a par. But there is no law in the New Testament. Jesus left no detailed social and religious regulations for His followers. Instead of a multitude of commands and prohibitions, He left them His own principles and the divine freedom of sons of God. In this way He gained two most valuable ends.

First of all, His system is truly universal, applicable to all races of men, to all countries, and to all times; while every detailed system of laws, however wisely drawn up, necessarily becomes obsolete as civilization advances. Hindus are now beginning to discover that this is true with regard to all the social institutions of their religion, and they are casting about for wise means of reform. It is the same thing that is wrong with Muslim institutions; but very few Muslims have as yet realized the fact. They do not yet see that it is impossible to secure a healthy society and nation by applying the institutions of the Arabia of the seventh century to modern life. Such difficulties cannot arise where Christianity is understood; for Christ gave us principles which can be applied in innumerable forms to the detailed needs of men in all circumstances.

Secondly, the method of Christ gives each people freedom, allows them to build up the fabric of their social life according to their national genius. The systems remain Christian, so long as they are guided in every detail by the spiritual principles of Jesus. But that is not all. The complement to the freedom of the Church is the constant presence and activity of the Holy Spirit:

> He will guide you into all truth.[1]

The Church, in freedom, faithfully seeking and following the guidance of the Spirit of Christ in applying the universal

[1] John 16, 13.

truths taught by Jesus to the details of life, thought, and worship, finds her way into health and righteousness.

The sheer originality of the method of Jesus in these matters is unparalleled. No other teacher approaches Him. Students will note how consistently He maintained this attitude: in all circumstances He remains the universal religious teacher; He refuses to become a mere legislator. In full conformity with this position, He also refused to act as judge. In the case of the man who asked Him to adjudicate in the matter of the family property between himself and his brother, He said,

> Who made me a judge or a divider over you?[1]

and in the painful case of the woman brought before Him for adultery He so acted that her accusers, accused by their own consciences, slunk away; and the woman found in Jesus not a judge to condemn her, but the Saviour of both her body and her soul.[2]

The New Testament itself presents us with a practical example of the out-working of these principles which may be of service to us. The original disciples of Christ were all Jews; but soon the Good News was told to Gentiles and many responded. The first impulse of the Christian leaders was to make these converts into Jews and to impose the whole Jewish law upon them. But some protested; and finally the whole Church was led, in part by Peter, but in the main by Paul, to see that Christ Himself was all-sufficient for them without the law.[3] Hence the perfect freedom we have in Christ.

What was sufficient for the infant churches of Syria, Asia Minor, Greece, and Italy will assuredly prove sufficient for India, China, and Japan. We need not impose on them our elaborate theologies, our detailed canon law, or the particulars of our ritual, or the forms of our society. It is a hard

[1] Luke 12, 13, 14. [2] John 8, 1–11.
[3] Acts 15, 1–31.

task to distinguish in full wisdom the vital spirit from the phenomenal dress; but the will to die to all that is only our own will enable us to hear the voice of the Spirit of Jesus and to recognize what is merely racial, national, sectional, local, or temporary in our conception of Christ and His gospel. It is far easier to work this out in practice than in theory. Indeed it has been already done in many a community. Then, the more progress Christians make in co-operation, federation, and union, in conscious loyalty to Christ's principle of freedom,[1] on the one hand, and to His dying prayer for unity,[2] on the other, the more easy will it be to make this difficult yet altogether necessary distinction. Hence, in seeking to transfuse the life of Christ into the Hindu people, Christians must be constantly on their guard, laying aside all that is merely Western or temporary, and offering only the Bread of Life Himself.

F. We would invite the Hindu also to distinguish and discern. People sometimes write and speak as if it were the policy of missionaries to impose imperiously the whole of their own religious, civil, and social life unchanged upon the people of India. Such a policy would be downright tyranny, and if successful would be seriously subversive of national life. But such a thing is neither possible nor desirable. Serious Christians, above all, do not dream of doing such violence to the spirit of man. We are very fully conscious of the imperfections of the Christianity of England and of every other country of the West. We do not imagine that we or any other group of men have 'attained'; but we do hold most seriously that in Christ we have something which the nations need. The education and the science of England or of Germany are not perfect; yet India, China, and Japan are adopting Western education and Western science as fast as they possibly can. The Government of Britain is by no means perfect, yet every awakened nation of the East, Muslim, Hindu, Buddhist, or Confucian, is panting after British freedom.

[1] Matt. 17, 24–26. [2] John 17, 20–23.

Spiritual religion can be absorbed without loss of nationality, as truly as these other activities of the human mind. If the intellectual life of the West is necessary for the welfare of the East, much more are the principles of Christ necessary for the healing of the nations.

There can be no such thing as a national acceptance of Christ. He cannot be received by men *en masse*. Each soul must turn in its bare individual personality to find union with Him. The only cry possible is:

> Rock of Ages, cleft for me,
> Let me hide myself in Thee.

Hence, no existing nation is anything like fully Christian. A certain percentage of the population surrender to Him; others yield only a partial allegiance, and some even consciously oppose Him. The moral and spiritual standard which Christ lays upon the human soul is so high and so exacting that the worldly man rebels, and many seek to belong to Him and yet to escape the more serious aspects of His Lordship. Hence no Christian country fully represents Christ. His power must not be measured by any land. We make fullest confession of all the evils visible in the life of Christian countries in the West. Hindus often write and speak of these things, but they are far more painfully present to the Christian mind. Yet these things do not prove that Christ has failed.

The example of Israel is sufficient to prove that a nation may possess truth of the highest value to all the world, and yet a large part of the people may fail to use it in their lives. The Old Testament is the record of the supreme religious revelation of the ancient world, yet the disobedience of the bulk of the people is the most constant feature of their history. On the other hand, the core of the nation was true to Jahveh; and in them, above all, but also in the whole people, the wonderful work of God is manifest. So in the West. Despite our pitiable failure, there is abundance in our life to show the supremacy of Christ. The West surpasses all the world in practical philanthropy, in eager endeavours to serve men, in the uprightness and purity of its government, and in general efficiency. This last quality which the East longs so vehemently to possess is largely the result of two Christian forces, the position of woman in the family and society, and the general purity of public administration; both of which spring from the depth and clearness of Christ's ethic. The mere fact that all the nations of the East now wish to copy the West is proof of the mighty dynamic at work there. But the thoughtful man will test Christ not by the Western world as a whole but by its Christian core, and there he will recognize the constant presence of a high and great type of character, distinguished chiefly by heroic service of mankind and by the full reconciliation of the highest culture the world knows with full faith in Christ.

But there is another point to be noticed. However faithful any single country might be to Christ, it could not interpret Him fully. He is human; and the riches that are in Him can be set forth only by the united efforts of the whole human family. There are many elements in His life and teaching which are acknowledged by the Church, yet have never been fully worked out in thought or in life:

> We are but broken lights of Thee.

But a new age is dawning. We see Jesus already crowned with many crowns; but we do not yet see all things put under Him. But in this new age on which we have entered His Kingdom will continue to extend rapidly, until

> All kings shall fall down before him:
> All nations shall serve him.[1]

Then much that is now but promise will find concrete exposition and embodiment, and the glory and universality of our Lord will be placed beyond cavil. How much will be possible, when the whole world acknowledges, even with meagre intelli-

[1] Ps. 72, 11.

gence, the Lordship of Christ? How many reforms will inevitably come? How much uplifting of the fallen, whether individuals or peoples? How many forms of change will then come within the range of possibility?

Then will the wonderful religious genius of India reveal its power anew in its interpretation of Christ. Aspects of His example and of His message which are latent in the West will in India find free and full expression. May not Christ's attitude to poverty find glorious illumination, His deep sense of the meaning and the sacredness of society be exhibited to the world by a people set free from Caste indeed, yet reaping its fruits as never before, and the prayer and communion with His Father to which Jesus so often gave His nights be turned to priceless account by the descendants of the ṛishis and yogīs? Aspects of Christ which the hard practical West has failed to utilize will prove fruitful beyond our dreams in the Christian experience of the richly dowered Hindu race.

Hence, in this volume, in setting forth Christianity as the Crown of Hinduism, we shall restrict ourselves to Christ Himself, drawing our evidence only from His own life and teaching, and from those parts of the Old Testament which He accepted without alteration. If we use a sentence here and there from the Apostles, we do so only to further illustrate the meaning of Christ.

* * * *

It has been rather difficult to decide in what order the various aspects of Hinduism ought to be reviewed; for each has influenced the others in turn. But, since karma is the one principle which has leavened every part of the religion, it necessarily had to be dealt with early. On the other hand, it is clear that the chief religious ideas behind the Hindu family took form before the rise of the karma theory; and, in the main, they have continued to act as if there were no such doctrine. Hence the family is taken first and karma next. There is one other fragment of the religion which has come very little under the influence of karma, namely the life of the *vānaprastha*; but, as that is bound by so many ties to the life of the *sannyāsī*, it seemed better to take them together and simply to point out the historical circumstances in which the rule arose.[1] The reasons for the order of the other chapters lie on the surface.

[1] See below, pp. 249–253.

CHAPTER I

THE INDO-ARYAN FAITH

I. IN the darkling cave of prehistoric time we are beginning to make out faintly the outlines of the religion by which the parent Aryan people lived before they spread abroad and gave birth to many nations. Their original divinities were a vast number of petty spirits, each supposed to have only a single function; but they learned rather later to revere a number of the greater phenomena of nature. They worshipped these heavenly powers by means of sacrifice and prayer and with the aid of priests. They also laid great stress on the worship of their ancestors; and this ritual formed the foundation on which all the institutions of the Aryan family were built.[1]

II. One of the great swarms that hived off from the central body found its way into the lands to the south of the Oxus, and gradually took possession of the country to the west, east, and south. This people may be designated Indo-Iranian at this stage; for, in the course of their slow expansion, they gradually became divided in two, the eastern half entering India and creating its civilization, the western populating Iran, and giving birth to Zoroastrianism and the ancient Persian Empire. By inference from the *Vedas*, on the one hand, and from the *Avesta* and other Zoroastrian documents, on the other, we are able to realize in outline what the religion of this prehistoric people was like.

Clearly considerable advance had been made in conceiving the heavenly gods; for there is now quite a group of persona-

[1] Art. 'Aryan Religion', *E. R. E.*

lized divinities with definite names and lofty functions. It seems clear that the following at least were fully recognized: Varuṇa, Mitra, Aryaman, Bhaga, and Indra, and along with them Yama and Soma. Theology had made a good deal of progress; for the gods are thought of as spiritual beings, and the natural phenomena from which they originally sprang are now but the medium of their manifestation.

The sacrifice, meanwhile, had been greatly elaborated. A ritual had been established, and hymns as well as prayers accompanied the stated acts. The home of the gods being now believed to be in heaven, it was the common practice to send the sacrifice to them on the flames and smoke of the altar fire. The drink of the gods offered in sacrifice was the juice of a plant called *soma* in Sanskrit, *haoma* in Zend, the language of the *Avesta*. A special ritual for the offering of this divine drink had appeared and the drink itself had undergone apotheosis. *Soma* was already a god. The priests, too, had far fuller functions than before and were called by special names.

The belief about the dead had also made considerable progress. Burning had almost universally taken the place of burying, probably from a wish to release the soul as completely as possible from the body and to bear it away on the flame of the pyre to the heavenly regions. When men die, they are believed to go to heaven, where they join the company of glorified ancestors and enjoy immortality with the gods. They are invited to the sacrifice in the same way as the gods. They are believed to be very powerful.

But the most interesting fact about Indo-Iranian days is that there was a movement which, had it not been checked, might have culminated in an ethical theism; and it is clear that ideas of considerable worth were pressed forward in the reformation. The god who held the supreme place was Varuṇa. Scholars now agree that Asura Varuṇa of the *Ṛigveda* is Ahura Mazda of the *Avesta*. Varuṇa is called *khā ṛitasya* in the *Ṛigveda*, while Ahura Mazda is called *ashahe khao* in the *Avesta*. These are merely dialectic forms of the same phrase, signifying 'source of divine law'. This noble conception of supreme law, Sanskrit *ṛita*, Zend *asha*, covers the unchanging order of nature as well as the moral law. It is clear, however, that the reform had not been carried through when the moment of unconscious separation arrived.[1]

III. If our knowledge of the primaeval Aryans, and even of the Indo-Iranians, is a matter of rather hazy inference, the life which the Indo-Aryans lived in the morning of history stands out before us in the *Ṛigveda* clearly defined and rosily beautiful, like the snows of the Himalayas in the sparkle of dawn. Since the *Ṛik* became known to Europe, innumerable scholars have made it the centre of their researches; so that the religion represented in it is now well understood, and its beliefs and its practices have been carefully analysed and brought into relationship with similar phenomena elsewhere.[2]

Their home was at first the Western Panjab and certain districts of Afghanistan beyond the Indus, but they gradually spread eastward, subduing or displacing the aboriginal tribes, and thus steadily adding to the territory under them. They were a simple people, organized in tribes, each ruled by its own chieftain. They lived in villages, getting their livelihood by cattle-feeding and tillage, and therefore were dependent upon sunshine and soil, rain and river, for their wealth. Yet they were as well used to the sword as the plough, and were always ready to fight the dark barbarians around them or to dispute a piece of territory with a neighbouring Aryan tribe. They knew but few of the arts; they had no writing and no coinage. They ate beef and drank intoxicating drink.

The father, as in the early Aryan age, had the ancestral rites in his hands, and, in consequence, had all the authority of the family in his power. Marriage was universal, and parents prayed for sons to take over the rites from the father. Girl

[1] Most of the details are from Bloomfield's *Religion of the Veda*.
[2] Kaegi gives a good summary of what is known.

children were sometimes exposed as in earlier days. But although the patriarchal system placed great power in the hands of the father, it had not yet developed its evil tendencies. Women had a great deal of liberty. Young men and maidens formed acquaintances at festal and other gatherings, and marriages were usually arranged according to their wishes. There was no child-marriage and no life of seclusion behind the purdah. A widow was not expected to burn herself on her husband's pyre, and there was no rule forbidding her to remarry. Polygamy was known, but was little practised.

There was no caste, although the three classes—warriors, priests, farmers—which at a later date became the three twice-born castes, can already be traced among them.

Strangely enough, not one scrap of anything material that can be with certainty ascribed to this age has ever been found. Even pottery seems to fail, probably because of the semi-migratory life they were still living. Had it not been for their religion, we should be absolutely without direct evidence about this most interesting and gifted people. But, thanks to that, there remains to us to-day the most stately and most significant memorial that exists of any early people.

The *Ṛigveda* is a work of surpassing interest. While in the strict sense it is not true to say that the religion and the civilization which gave birth to the hymns are primitive, it is true that no other people has bequeathed to us a body of lofty literature representing such an early stage in the development of civilization. Clearly the people who created the *Ṛik* were a race of remarkable gifts. The high qualities which produced these hymns are as conspicuously revealed to us in the character of their language. While ancient Sanskrit is one of the great group of Aryan languages, all of which show many common features, yet it is the only member of the family which has preserved its words in such form as to make their origin quite plain to the philologist. The linguistic consciousness of the people who developed Sanskrit must have been delicate and analytic far above the average. The religious conquest of the whole Indian Peninsula by the Brāhman race, and the remarkable qualities of the philosophy and the literature which they produced, are sufficient titles to a very high place in the aristocracy of humanity.

The heavenly gods whose rise we noted in the Aryan period have now reached the summit of their glory, and have either eclipsed all others or drawn them into the shining circle of the Celestials. The Indo-Aryan gods are all *devas.* What gives them their unrivalled splendour and interest is the fact that they are still identified with the most glorious natural phenomena, the all-encompassing Sky, the flashing Sun, the Thundercloud, gigantic, omnipotent, the Dawn divinely beautiful, the roaring Storm ; so that no such thing as temple or image is ever dreamt of; yet they are so far personalized that they not only receive sacrifice and listen to prayer and hymn, but have their own high home of unapproachable light beyond sun and stars, where they live in immortal joy.

The greatest of all the gods, Indra, the Thunderer, whose primal function is to bring rain to the parched fields, goes out armed with thunderbolts, flanked by wild winds, *Maruts*, and smites *Ahi*, the demon Restrainer, who would keep the living waters from the dying land. The fighting Thunderer naturally became War-god and Leader to the forward-marching, conquering Aryans. Whence the transition to Sustainer, Creator, and omnipotent Lord was not difficult. *Agni*, Fire, the high priest of gods and men, holds the second place. Along with him comes *Soma*, originally the intoxicating juice of a plant, drink divine for both men and gods, now a great god, to whom sacrifice and song are offered. *Sūrya, Vishṇu, Savitar, Pūshan*, are different forms of the Sun ; *Ushas* is the Dawn ; and the *Aśvins*, sons of the Mare, are the Dioskouroi, swift light-bearers of the morning sky. They had added functions as Healers and Helpers in distress. *Rudra*, the Roarer, is a storm god ; *Vāyu*, the wind ; *Dyaus* Heaven and *Pṛithivī* the Earth ; but these two ancient divinities have fallen far into the background. *Yama* is honoured as a god, but is described as the first man, and as having discovered the path by which the righteous dead go to heaven to join the company of their ancestors and the gods.

But by far the most interesting group are the *Ādityas*, the seven sons of the great mother *Aditi*, Eternity. The seven names are not all given. We hear only of *Varuṇa*, *Mitra*, *Aryaman*, and *Bhaga*. These are the highest of all the gods. *Varuṇa* and *Mitra* especially are conceived as powers behind the other gods, rulers who have marked out the path for other gods to tread. The origin of this group of divinities is still wrapped in obscurity.

The figure of Varuṇa is by far the noblest in the *Ṛigveda*. He was the centre of the theistic movement of the Indo-Iranian age, as we have already seen.[1] In the *Ṛik* he represents all the loftiest thoughts connected with the Ādityas. He stands out in a lonely grandeur which, to us, has in it something of solemn sadness; for the group of noble conceptions with which he is connected is the one segment of Ṛigvedic theology which is not carried forward and used in the great culmination of Indian thought which characterizes the next age.

His name suggests that he was originally 'the encompassing heaven', but he scarcely appears in the hymns in that character at all. He is the Creator and Sustainer of all things, the omniscient Ruler who watches the whole universe with all-seeing, unsleeping eyes, the compassionate Protector and Helper, the Holy One, from whom Law and Right (*ṛita*) proceed, who blesses the righteous, sternly punishes the sinner, pardons the penitent, and confers immortality on the faithful dead. Serious sickness and sudden danger seem to have been usually interpreted as the outcome of Varuṇa's anger over a breach of his laws. There are quite a number of hymns in which the singer prays to him for pardon and release from punishment. The petition usually runs, 'Whether

[1] See above, p. 67.

we have sinned consciously or unconsciously,' or 'Whichever of thy laws, known or unknown, we have broken'. There is more ethical feeling in the hymns addressed to Varuṇa than in any other group. He is the only god of the *Ṛik* who is consistently holy.

But this gracious, righteous, omniscient Lord is already fading into the background in the *Ṛigveda*. Indra, the bold warrior, stands out as the national god. For him the greatest sacrifices are held; for him the singer makes his hymn. To Varuṇa no great hymn occurs among the latest hymns of the *Ṛigveda*. The lofty ethical god has passed out of sight. Henceforth he is only a minor divinity, the god of the waters. Along with Varuṇa there also disappeared the splendid conception of *ṛita*, divine law. The magnificent ethical promise of this early idea was never fulfilled. India lost it, along with Varuṇa, the fount of righteousness, and never clearly rose out of the common ancient point of view, that the gods are above morality.

Though the Aryans of the time of the *Ṛik* were polytheists, yet they were far enough advanced in thought and religious feeling to be frequently led by their higher instincts to ideas and expressions which are scarcely consistent with a belief in many gods. We have already seen that Indra is revered as the Creator, the Sustainer, the omnipotent Lord, and that Varuṇa also receives all these epithets and is recognized as the source of Law besides. The worshipper is frequently carried forward, in the fervour of his feeling for the god who is the object of his adoration at the moment, to think of him as supreme, as the only possible object of adoration. The right way to interpret these facts is to say that the only really rational form of religion is the worship of one God, sole and supreme; that early men very seldom, if ever, reached the full perception of that truth; but that the more open they were in mind, and the more reverent and moral they were in life, the more were they unconsciously drawn towards belief in one God only. The *Ṛik* is polytheistic, but contains numerous phrases which show in what direction the minds of the worshippers were tending.

The worship of the *Ṛigveda* is summed up in the sacrifice. The priests, the householder and his family gathered in the open air where preparations had been made. The altars were shallow trenches cut according to rule and filled with sacrificial grass. Close by were the three sacred fires, and the sacrificial posts to which the victims were tied. The priests pressed the soma, and set it out in cups. They killed the animals, poured offerings of butter, milk, and grain on the fires, and laid out food on the grass-covered altars. All the while they recited, chanted, or muttered portions of the hymns, inviting the gods to the sacrifice and asking for their favour and help. The extremest care was taken that no slip should occur either in the ritual or the liturgy.

The worship is distinctly ignoble. It is frankly a method of bargaining with the gods and persuading them to give the sacrificer and the priest the large material and earthly boons which they desire. The beauty and dignity of the hymns are means towards this end. There is little real religious feeling manifested in the whole elaborate cult.

The worship of ancestors, now known as 'the fathers', stands out in great clearness in the hymns. Burial has not altogether passed out of use, but cremation is the regular method of disposal of the dead. The hymn sung at the funeral bids the soul go without fear and follow Yama, who has found the path to the home of the righteous 'fathers' in heaven, where he will enjoy a blessed immortality, in the company of those of his loved ones who have gone before him. Then a funeral feast is held; and annually afterwards it is repeated. 'Then with Yama and Agni all the "fathers" who are known and who are not known are summoned to the funeral feast, to the food on the sacrificial straw and to the prized *soma*.' The 'fathers' have their home in heaven, but they move freely through the wide spaces of the air, bringing blessings to their posterity and helping them in all trouble.

They are righteous, and eagerly distinguish between those who do right and those who do wrong. It is most noteworthy that in those days men were believed to die but once, and thereafter to enjoy immortality. No thought at all resembling transmigration occurs in the hymns.

Indeed rebirth was too gloomy a thought for those days of sunshine. The whole outlook of the people was bright. The world was no illusion to them, and life was good: they prayed that they might live a hundred years; and they looked forward to meeting their loved ones and enjoying unending happiness with them in heaven. It is also rather remarkable that there is no sign of asceticism among them. Austerity, *tapas*, occurs in some of the later hymns; but there is no ascetic idea connected with it. It is simply a method, parallel with sacrifice, of getting what one wishes.

There is another element in the *Ṛik* which must not be neglected. The beginnings of religious philosophy appear in some of the later hymns. There is no system taught. Rather is the material in the form of hard questions and mystic suggestions. But already one of the characteristic ideas of Hindu philosophy finds expression, the One behind the many gods, he who is the unseen source and supporter of all that is.

It seems to be clear, however, that the *Ṛigveda* does not give us a complete picture of the religious life of the time. Except in the matter of ancestor-worship, the domestic and the private observances are scarcely represented in the hymns. Simple domestic rites there must have been which developed later into the sacraments described in the legal literature. We have also the evidence of the *Atharvaveda* to prove that the people were accustomed to use magic rites and spells to save themselves from dangers and enemies of many kinds, and to bring evil upon those whom they hated. Such practices date from the early Aryan period and have survived in India until our own day. The *Atharvan* was compiled at a later date than the *Ṛik*, but many of its hymns and incantations belong to the same period as the sacrificial hymns; so that its evidence is of undeniable value.

The priests were already very powerful. The greatest of all was the Chief's chaplain, the *purohita*; but all were revered for their sacred knowledge and skill, and for the power they wielded over the gods. Already they were divided by function into three groups, the *hotṛis* or reciters, the *udgātṛis* or chanters, the *adhvaryus* or sacrificers. There were six priestly families of great celebrity and capacity, each of which treasured a group of hymns which had been produced by its members, and which were believed to be of priceless worth for their influence over the gods. Towards the end of the period we find evidence of the existence of schools in which young priests were trained. The education was necessarily oral, and the one subject of study was the hymns used at the sacrifices. It seems likely that it was in the six great families that these schools first arose, and that the head of one of them succeeded in learning the hymns belonging to the other five, and was thus able to teach six distinct sets of hymns to his pupils. In this way we account for the bringing together of the six groups of hymns, each attributed to one of the great families, which now form Books II and VII of the *Ṛigveda*, and which are recognized by all scholars as being the nucleus of the whole. At later dates other groups were added, until the contents of the ten books as we have them were gathered into a single collection.

IV. The religion of the *Ṛigveda* is held by no Hindu now. It was transformed, in the course of the subjugation of India, into a very different religion. How this great change came to take place, and what the forces were which produced it, will appear in the following chapters.

Hindus often speak in high praise of the religion of the *Ṛigveda*; and there is abundance of justification for their so doing. Perhaps they scarcely realize, however, that this early faith stands much nearer to Christianity than it does to Hinduism. A transition from the religion of the *Ṛik* to

Christianity would be much simpler and more natural than a transition to Hinduism. How easy it is to step from a simple, external, sacrificial polytheism, such as we are dealing with here, to Christianity, is proved by numerous examples. Those who have leaned on animal sacrifice turn with deep religious joy to the perfect moral sacrifice of the death of Christ, once the thirst for a spiritual faith has made itself felt. We have seen how for a time men prayed to Varuṇa, the righteous and omnipotent Lord, the source of *ṛita*, i.e. Law both natural and moral, who punished the guilty and forgave the penitent. This beautiful but short-lived faith finds full justification for itself in the Heavenly Father, whose nature is love and holiness, whose will is expressed in the regularity and impartiality of nature as well as in the moral law, who gave up His only Son to death, that we might have forgiveness. Further, Christ's doctrine, that those who know the Heavenly Father on earth will spend eternity in close personal fellowship with Him in heaven, is the direct spiritual culmination of the Vedic faith in one life and one death, followed by an immortality of happiness; while transmigration and karma is an altogether alien conception. Finally, think of the bright, hopeful outlook, the joyful acceptance of the world as good, and the healthy social and family freedom which the Indo-Aryans enjoyed—no caste, no child-marriage, no child-widows, no enforced widowhood, no *satī* and no zenāna. How near all this is to the spirit of Christianity!

The members of the Ārya Samāj revere the *Ṛik* and the other three Vedas as the only true Revelation, on the ground that they are 'God's knowledge' (*Veda* is the Sanskrit word for knowledge). They contend that, being God's knowledge, the four Vedas contain all the truths of religion, and also all natural science. The truths of religion which they find there are the doctrines taught by the Samāj, notably, that there is one personal God and no other, that transmigration and karma are the laws that govern human life, and that forgiveness of offences is for ever impossible. They deny the existence of polytheism in the Vedas and stoutly maintain that they teach monotheism and transmigration. They as confidently affirm that every truth already discovered by Western science occurs, at least in germ, in the fourfold canon. These are most astounding contentions; for the *Sāman*, *Yajus*, and *Atharvan* exhibit the same polytheism, and the same doctrine of life and death, that we have found in our study of the *Ṛigveda*; and there is no more natural science in them than there is in the Homeric poems.

The maintenance of a living connexion with the past is not merely a healthy, but a necessary, element of modern religion; so that it was a sound instinct which led the founder of the Ārya Samāj to seek to link his faith to the Vedas; but to attempt to establish a connexion by means of assertions which scholarship is compelled to repudiate, is to build upon a quicksand. The position of the Ārya Samāj is absolutely indefensible.

How then can a modern religion be related to an early faith? We need not pretend that our thoughts and knowledge are the same as those of the naïve minds of primitive ages. We are bound to acknowledge frankly the vast differences which sever the old from the new. But if the beliefs we now hold are the true spiritual successors of the simple ideas found in the primitive religion, then we may well claim that to us has descended the heritage of the early faith. In this sense, then, the religion of Christ is the spiritual crown of the religion of the *Ṛigveda*.

CHAPTER II

THE HINDU FAMILY.

I. ALMOST all primitive peoples hold that the human soul is distinct from the body and separable from it. Along with this there usually goes the belief that the soul survives death and lives a new life apart from the body, either in close proximity to its old haunts, or in some other place. But early man, not having been able to reach the idea of spirit as distinct from material substance, conceives the soul as a material thing, and believes that after death it is dependent for its continued existence on food and drink precisely like a living man. In consequence of this, nearly all primitive races have been accustomed to provide food and drink for the departed souls of members of their own families. The food is laid out as for a feast, and the souls of the dead are invited to come and eat and be nourished thereby. These ideas are the origin of all feasts for the dead. The observances have taken many forms in different times and places. Some people feed the dead daily; others monthly, or annually; and there are many modes of preparing the food for them. We must note carefully that this practice, which is all but universal among the simpler peoples, is a service of souls and not a worship. The dead are dependent on the family for their nourishment. The belief usually is that, if they do not receive this attention, they become wandering and harmful ghosts.

But these beliefs have passed among many peoples into a more developed stage, where the dead are conceived as being powerful beings, controlling the welfare of the family.

When this idea arises, the old service of the dead becomes a worship. The family pays them great reverence, not merely because they are relatives, but in order to secure their loving care over the family. Ancestor-worship, though not so common as ancestor-service, is yet a very widely prevalent cult. It has been found in many parts of the world and in many forms, but appears most distinctly in the various peoples of the Mongolian race and the nations that form the great Aryan group. Seemingly, ancestor-worship had been developed by the original Aryan race before it split up into many groups; for traces of it are found among every Aryan people. The general features of the worship are the same in all branches of the race, but the details vary considerably. The dead are everywhere distinguished from the gods; and yet they are conceived as their companions; and their worship is very similar to the worship of the gods. They are believed to possess great power and to bring blessing to their righteous descendants.

Now consider the way in which this worship modified the organization of the family. The father was the family priest, and controlled the worship of the ancestors of the family in all details. He alone knew the peculiar ritual which was traditional in his family, and which had to be maintained unchanged, if the favour of the dead was to be retained. He alone had the power of passing on the rites to his son. As the high priest of the ancestral rites, he was the acknowledged head of the family. The reverence and the power which his priestly position brought him made him supreme in the home. In this way the patriarchal family took shape. In earlier times there was a looser organization, or the mother might be the head of the family; but with the establishment of ancestor-worship the father became supreme. He had full power over his wife and his young children, and in most nations his grown-up sons also were completely under his authority. The property of the family was altogether in his hands. This is the source of the *patria potestas* of Rome, and of the prominent place held by the father in Greece, Persia, India, and among Teutonic and Slavonic peoples as well. This type of family is called patriarchal because the father has so much power.

There can be no doubt that the family reached its strong position in ancient society through the power vested in the father, and that the worship of ancestors, through its influence on the family, produced moral results of very great value. The sacred rites, binding together the living and the dead, led the members of the family to think more of their unity. They became conscious of the family as an organism, part of which had already passed into the other world and part of which was not yet born. They thought of it as a living, constantly growing unity, and the thought filled them with deep reverence and pride. To act worthily of the family, to bring no disgrace upon one's ancestors, to do everything to build up and strengthen the heritage of the family, became a motive of superlative strength. Since ancestors were conceived as displeased, or even injured, by an act that injured the family, the motives for right behaviour were greatly strengthened. Marriage became more sacred than it had ever been thought of before; for the welfare of all the members depended upon the family being kept pure. The chastity of the mother thus became a matter of the greatest possible importance. The position of the father drew great reverence to him, and both son and father were thereby led to think, feel, and act more worthily towards each other. From ancestor-worship also arose the sacredness of the hearth. For, since the ancestral protectors were honoured at the hearth, the wedding ceremony and other domestic rites were celebrated there too. All the holiest and most touching scenes in the life of the family were connected with it. It was the focus of the joys and sorrows of the home.

The importance of carrying on the rites was so great that it was conceived to be the duty of every man to marry, in order that he might have a son to follow him in his priestly work. Marriage, therefore, became universal wherever ancestor-worship prevailed. As only a son could take over the rites from a dying man, the birth of a boy was most ardently desired; and if marriage failed to provide a son, it was a man's duty to have recourse to adoption. In all the ancient Aryan nations, the adopted son held completely the position of a real son.

Only those who were allowed to share in the family worship and to taste the food offered to the ancestors were recognized as belonging to the family. If, for any reason, a man was interdicted from the feast in honour of the dead, he was counted an outcast. Only those who shared in the worship of the ancestors of the family could share in the division of property on the death of the head of the house.

It is thus clear that ancestor-worship, through its creation of the patriarchal family, has done civilization a very large service. That stage in the evolution of the family produced changes of extreme value.

We must acknowledge, however, on the other hand, that the system has two inherent weaknesses, which in certain parts of the world have led to serious results. Races have varied greatly in the completeness with which they have developed the patriarchal family. In some places it remained rudimentary; in others it was developed to its utmost implications. (1) Wherever the father's power grew so large that all his male descendants of whatever age were completely under his authority, there, necessarily, the family bulked large in the minds of men and the individual became weak. (2) Another result of the father's power has been the depreciation of the value and the capacity of women. As we have already seen, the patriarchal family naturally created a desire for sons. Man was exalted and woman was regarded as very inferior. When a daughter was born, she received a very poor welcome. She brought no strength to the family: at best she would by marriage pass out of her father's family into another. Consequently, female infanticide was found everywhere in the ancient world alongside of the patriarchal family. The wife also tended to have no rights as against the husband; but the variation in different races on this matter was very great.[1]

II. We may now leave the general question and turn to the ancestors of the Hindus.

A. Amongst the Indo-Aryans in the Panjab, as we find from the *Ṛigveda*, the blessed dead were spoken of as the 'fathers' (*pitṛis*). They were believed to move through the earth's atmosphere, bringing gifts to those who sacrificed to them, rewarding the good, punishing the evil. Their descendants honoured them at the funeral feast: they were invited to come and eat the food laid out on the sacrificial straw, and to drink the *soma* prepared for them. Thus, ancestor-worship was fully organized amongst the Indo-Aryans, as amongst the other Aryan peoples; and the family was patriarchal in its organization. The system, however, was not yet far developed. The state of affairs was very similar to what we find in early Greece. Female children were exposed, but women still held a good position.

When the Brāhmans succeeded in winning for themselves an authoritative religious position, and when the conquest of North India was begun in real earnest, the whole religion of the Aryan people began to change. The worship became much more elaborate, and stringent rules were laid down for every detail of every sacrifice. This applies to the worship of the *pitṛis* as well as the worship of the gods. The *Śatapatha Brāhmaṇa* contains a chapter[2] which ordains that the pious man shall worship the *pitṛis* every month, and gives detailed rules for the observance. Here for the first time we meet with the *piṇḍa*, the word used throughout the history of Hinduism for the cake or ball of rice offered to ancestors. It is well worthy of remark that in this passage there occurs several times the phrase, 'The Fathers have passed away

[1] Art. 'Ancestor-worship', *E. R. E.*, and Bosanquet, *The Family*.
[2] II. vi. 1.

once for all': transmigration has not appeared as yet. Another noteworthy matter is this, that the help of a Brāhman is already required for this monthly worship of the Fathers. Even at this early date the priestly caste had begun to usurp the father's rights in the religion of the family. A Brāhman's help is required to-day in all the *śrāddha* ceremonies, i.e. the worship of ancestors. A similar but later account occurs in the *Gobhila Gṛihya Sūtra.*[1] In both these books the old idea that the 'fathers' come and eat the sacrificial food remains unchanged. The blessed dead are conceived as requiring ordinary food and drink and as dependent upon their descendants for it.

A little later, as we find from the Upanishads, the theory of transmigration arose among the ancient Hindus. This is a totally new conception of man's destiny after death; for the belief is that a man is born and dies many times. It is therefore impossible for a man after death to join permanently the ranks of the blessed dead, as the conception is in the earlier literature. Even if after death he goes to heaven, his stay there is necessarily limited; for he must return to earth to be born again. Thus the new idea was quite inconsistent with the basis of the worship of the *pitṛis.* Yet the practice went on without a break, and with little change.

The worship has continued among Hindus down to the present day. There has been little essential alteration in the ceremonial, but one very important change has arisen in the conception. Originally there was no idea of the spirituality of the soul. Since that conception laid hold of the Hindu mind, a new theory about the use of the *piṇḍa* has been formed. The idea is that each soul at death carries with it into the other world a subtle body, but that a gross body is also required, which can be got only through the *piṇḍas* offered by the surviving relatives. When a Hindu dies, his body is burned. At the burning, and during the next nine days, funeral rites are performed for him, his son taking

[1] IV. iv.

a prominent place in the ceremonial. The essential point in the ritual of each of these days is the offering of a *piṇḍa*, that is, a ball of kneaded flour, with water, milk, rice, honey, &c., to the spirit of the dead man. The belief is that the spirit remains a *preta* (i.e. a wandering ghost), unless it receives this food. But the soul that receives the *piṇḍa* daily during these ten days gradually develops for itself a gross body. It is thus transformed into a *pitṛi*, and is received into the company of glorified ancestors in heaven. On the eleventh day after the man's death the first *śrāddha* (literally 'act of faith') is held, and this has to be repeated monthly during the first year, and once a year afterwards. Although the ceremony is carried out primarily for one person, yet a large group of other ancestors are also benefited by this and by all other *śrāddha* ceremonies. The food offered to the *pitṛis* is again in the form of a *piṇḍa*. Libations of water, called *tarpaṇa*, also are poured out for the refreshment of the *pitṛis* at these services. The person holding the service has to invite to it all his relatives, on both his father's and his mother's side, for three generations upward and three generations downward. These relatives are called his *sapiṇḍas* as sharing the *piṇḍa*-ceremony with him. This group of people is of considerable importance in family matters. The offering of water to the 'fathers' is also a part of the stated daily prayers.

According to Hindu thought the *śrāddha* ceremonies are not merely acts of loving remembrance, but are absolutely necessary for the welfare of those who have gone to the other world. The offering of the *piṇḍa* at the funeral ceremony is needed to transform the soul of the departed into a blessed spirit; and all *śrāddhas* thereafter performed are required to enable him to retain his position in heaven. Then, in turn, the welfare of the family is dependent on the welfare of the ancestors. If the ancestors fall from heaven to hell, the whole family will be destroyed. Here is a couplet from the *Gītā*,[1] than which there is no better authority:

[1] i. 42.

> Confounding of caste brings to hell alike the stock's slayers and the stock; for their Fathers fall when the offerings of the cake and water to them fail.[1]

What an influence such a belief as this was bound to exercise! To the ancient Greek or Roman burial was an absolute necessity: the ghost of the unburied man flitted about in utter misery until some pious soul flung a handful of dust on the uncovered body. To the Hindu, the offering of the ball of rice and of the water is similarly of the last importance. To omit the rite is not merely to show disrespect to the dead, but to deprive him of the peace and blessedness of heaven; and then, in turn, the man who is guilty of the neglect is doomed to hell, and his family to utter destruction.

B. It is from ancestor-worship that the chief principles of the Hindu family have arisen.

1. The first of these is that every man must marry and beget a son. If he fails to do this, he fails in his duty to his ancestors.[2] Their welfare in the other world depends upon his having a son to take over from himself the *śrāddha* ceremonies. No poem is so much read in Hindu homes as the *Mahābhārata*. One of the earliest stories in that great repository tells how the ascetic Jaratkāru wandered about, refusing to marry, until one day he came upon his ancestors suspended head downwards over a hole by a rope which was being gnawed by mice. He asked the reason and was told it was because he had no son. In consequence, he went off at once to look for a wife. Thus, to the Hindu, marriage is a religious duty, not merely a comfort or a convenience. On the other hand, the birth of a son brings great blessings to his parents.[3]

We had better notice here a very healthy rule which arose

[1] Barnett's translation is usually quoted, as here.

[2] The debt which a man owes to his ancestors is an idea that occurs very frequently in Hindu literature. The debt is paid by begetting a son. *Vasishtha*, xi. 48; xvii. 1; *Baudhāyana*, II. vi. 11, 33; *Manu*, ix. 106.

[3] *Āśvalāyana*, *G. S.*, I. vi. 1–4; *Āpastamba*, II. ix. 24, 3; *Baudhāyana*, II. ix. 16, 10.

among the three highest castes probably in the seventh century B.C. Away in that early time it became customary to send every Brāhman, Kshatriya, and Vaiśya[1] boy to a Brāhmanical school to receive a religious education. He underwent the ceremony of initiation (doubtless a primaeval puberty ceremony), received the sacred thread and immediately went to school, where he spent several strenuous years. Every student had to live a chaste life during his education. When that was ended, he returned home, and a ceremony, the home-coming (*samāvartana*), was performed. Then the young man could marry, but not till then. Most young men would be twenty to twenty-four years of age. Clearly the leaders in those days were deeply impressed with the necessity of preparing a man carefully by a religious education for his duties in life. Thus the young men of the three highest castes, at this time, had the priceless ideal of a chaste adolescence held before them, and doubtless many lived up to the rule.

But this rule of universal education for the males of the Aryan castes fell, at a later date, into disuse, and multitudes of Brāhman, Kshatriya, and Vaiśya youths did not go to school at all. Yet the ancient ceremonial was kept up. About the age of puberty, or earlier, each boy underwent initiation and received the sacred thread. Then, since he did not go to school, there was nothing in the way of marriage. Hence arose the evil custom, which has long been prevalent in Bengal and elsewhere,[2] to marry mere boys. The competition for eligible husbands is so keen that the parents of sons are usually approached early, and there is great temptation to hurry on the match. Hence, boys may be found in High Schools to-day who are not only husbands but fathers. The influence of the Social Reform Movement is very valuable in this matter.

[1] See below, p. 163.

[2] See Ranade, pp. 315, 316, for examples of boys married at eight, nine, or ten in the family of the Peshwas.

2. The second principle is that a man must not marry a woman who is a *sapiṇḍa*.[1] This rule corresponds to our law of prohibited degrees. The other rules which guide a man in selecting a wife are that he must marry *within* his caste, but *outside* his own clan subdivision of the caste.[2]

3. The third principle is that the authority of the husband in the family is absolute.

First, he has full authority over his wife. One of the most touching passages in Kālidāsa's *Śakuntalā* is the scene[3] in which King Dushyanta her husband, failing to remember her, refuses to acknowledge her as his wife, and her own friends who have pled her cause so eagerly leave her standing disowned and dishonoured before the king with the words,

> Śakuntalā is by law thy wife, whether thou desert or acknowledge her; and the dominion of a husband is absolute.

Śakuntalā wishes to return with her friends, but one turns to her and says angrily,

> O wife, who seest the faults of thy lord, dost thou desire independence?[4]

and another asks her,

> If thou art what the king proclaims thee, what right hast thou to complain? But if thou knowest the purity of thine own soul, it will become thee to wait as a handmaid in the mansion of thy lord.

Since, then, the husband's authority is absolute, it is the wife's duty to be absolutely obedient to her husband:

> Him to whom her father may give her, she shall obey as long as he lives.[5]

He is her sole authority. Tiruvalluvar, the Tamil poet, says of a good woman,

> Bowing not before the gods but before her husband.[6]

Whatever his character may be, her duty is to be utterly loyal to him and to worship him as her divinity:

[1] See p. 84 above. This rule varies in its practical meaning in different parts of India. See Trevelyan, 34-37.
[2] Trevelyan, 32-34.
[3] Act v.
[4] See below, p. 90.
[5] *Manu*, v. 151.
[6] *Heart of India*, 105.

> Though destitute of virtue, or seeking pleasure elsewhere, or devoid of good qualities, yet a husband must be constantly worshipped as a god by a faithful wife.[1]

Sītā says,

> My husband is a god to me.[2]

If a wife obeys her husband, she will be exalted in heaven.[3] If disobedient, the law says she may be chastised:

> A wife . . . who has committed faults may be beaten with a rope or a split bamboo.[4]

This law would not be upheld in an Indian law-court to-day, but it still influences opinion. If she persists in opposition, she may be superseded:

> A barren wife may be superseded in the eighth year, she whose children all die in the tenth, she who bears only daughters in the eleventh, but she who is quarrelsome without delay.[5]

Secondly, as father, his authority is absolute over his son as long as he lives. Whatever he orders the son is bound to do, even if it be the greatest possible crime. This is a very serious matter in the case of the criminal tribes, which are found all over India. When they are Hindus, the son of a thief or a coiner is guilty of sin, if he refuses to obey his father and join him in his criminal occupation. Here is what Rāma, the ideal son, says on this point:

> I have no power to slight or break
> Commandments which my father spake. . . .
> Once Kaṇḍu, mighty saint, who made
> His dwelling in the forest shade,
> A cow—and duty's claims he knew—
> Obedient to his father, slew. . . .
> So Jamadagni's son obeyed
> His sire, when in the wood he laid
> His hand upon his axe, and smote
> Through Renuka his mother's throat.

[1] *Manu*, v. 154. [2] Griffith, II. xxix. [3] *Manu*, v. 155. [4] *Manu*, viii. 299. [5] *Manu*, ix. 81.

> The deeds of these and more beside,
> Peers of the Gods, my steps shall guide,
> And resolute will I fulfil
> My father's word, my father's will.[1]

Nearly all the remaining features of the Hindu family have arisen directly from the supreme position of the father, and the consequent depreciation of woman. As the Hindu family developed in the early centuries, its inner character manifested itself in institutions.

4. One of the earliest results was the establishment of the joint family. In this system a man's son brings his bride into the paternal mansion, and the daughter is taken by her husband to his father's house. Thus all the male descendants of the householder down to the third or even the fourth generation, if he happen to survive so long, and also the unmarried girls, live in the one house with him under his complete control. The landed property of the family and the income of any wage-earning members there may be are in the house-father's hand and are used by him for the needs of the whole family. Every member of the family owes complete obedience to the head of the family in all things. Thus, no matter how old a man may be, he is still a minor, if his father, grandfather, or great-grandfather is alive, and must obey him implicitly. Without his consent, he cannot marry nor undertake anything of importance. Here we have the patriarchal family in its most expanded form. Sometimes as many as seventy or eighty persons will be found under one roof, all of them lineal descendants of the patriarch, or wives or widows of such descendants. No wonder that the family consciousness is greatly developed among Hindus, and that the interests of the family bulk large in every Hindu mind.

Several fine results spring from this particular type of organization. The selfish individualistic motive gets little room to grow; for each contributes to the welfare of all the

[1] Griffith, II. xxi.

others; and if one son is peculiarly successful, his income brings extra comfort to the whole family. Every member of the family, no matter how useless or weak, is well taken care of. Each feels responsible for all the others. It is the family that counts, not the individual. Every woman in the house is the mother of all the children, and cousins feel as nearly related as if they were brothers. On the other hand, no one gets the opportunity of developing a self-reliant character of his own, except the head of the household.

This aspect of Hindu family life has begun to break down under the influence of Western thought and life, and very large changes are sure to come. In the childhood of the world a man could afford to live as a member of a family; but in modern times the individual counts for more and more.

But the most important results of the full development of patriarchal authority show themselves in the depreciation and complete subjection of women. While the family reached its strong position in ancient India through the power vested in the father, yet his supreme position made it impossible for the wife to receive adequate recognition. Nowhere else in all the world have things gone so far as they have in India. As we have already seen, the patriarchal family everywhere tends to exalt man and to depreciate woman. The full unfolding of the inner nature of that system in India reduced women to complete subjection, and led to the growth of a set of customs which have no parallel in the world elsewhere.

5. Hindu lawgivers unanimously declare that a woman is always in subjection, to her father, to her husband, or to her son; she can never have any independence:

> Let her be in subjection to her father in her childhood, to her husband in her youth, to her sons when her husband is dead; let a woman never enjoy independence.[1]

[1] *Manu*, v. 148. Cf. ix. 2–3; *Vasishṭha*, v. 1–2; *Baudhāyana*, II. ii. 3, 44–45; *Gautama*, xviii. 1.

There is a line in the *Rāmāyaṇa* which gives beautiful expression to the Hindu idea of wifely loyalty:

> As the shadow to the substance, to her lord is faithful wife.[1]

Yet how vividly it expresses also her hopeless inferiority. The idea is, not that the married relation places a woman in subjection to her husband, but that woman is essentially an inferior being. This is no mere popular prejudice, but a doctrine of Hinduism. In the *Bhagavadgītā*[2] we read that a woman is born such because of sin in a former life; and in the *Garuḍa Purāṇa* we read:

> Owing to my bad deeds in former lives I got a woman's body, which is a source of great misery.[3]

This belief in the essential inferiority of woman led to the Buddhist conviction that no woman can attain nirvāna until she be reborn as a man.

We shall take the other developments as far as possible in historical order, beginning with two which come from very early times.

6. Away in the far-back ages, before the Aryan people had split up, the establishment of the patriarchal family led to the universal desire for sons and to the custom of exposing a large proportion of the female children born. This custom, which, as we know, persisted throughout classic times in Europe until the influence of Christ put it down, seems to have been brought by the Indo-Aryans into India with them; and the practice continued in certain sections of the people unchecked until 1830, when the British Government began a long-continued crusade for its extinction. So ingrained was the habit in many Indian castes and tribes that the determination of the British Government to put it down was in many places baffled for years; and the best authorities are doubtful whether it does not persist in certain quarters to some extent even to-day.

7. Polygamy is another of the universal concomitants of

[1] R. C. Dutt's *Rāmāyaṇa*, I. vi. 10.

[2] ix. 32.

[3] *Garuḍa Purāṇa Sāroddhāra*, ii. 41.

the patriarchal family, inevitably arising from the idea that a man is of far greater value and importance than a woman. This custom also was brought by the ancestors of the Hindus into India with them. It was known, but little practised, in the age of the *Ṛigveda*. Yet, throughout Hindu history down to our own day, it has been recognized that kings and men of wealth or of social position have a right to marry several wives, and that no man is restricted to one. The number of a king's wives has always been a measure of his wealth and power. In the Law of Manu a Brāhman is allowed four wives, a Kshatriya three, a Vaiśya two.[1] Most of the Hindu gods are polygamous. Vishṇu and Brahmā, for example, have three consorts each.

In modern times, however, monogamy has become the rule for ordinary Hindus of all castes. The Kulin Brāhmans of Bengal, who until quite recently used to marry scores of women, were a lonely and ghastly exception. Down to some fifty years ago, however, the rule of monogamy was tempered by concubinism for all those who desired it and could afford it;[2] and, though public opinion is now seriously opposed to it, in certain parts of the country it seems to be still practised. Many princes are still polygamists.

Further, although monogamy is the usual practice, Hindu society holds firmly to the idea that the right to marry a second wife remains. Every Hindu marriage is *in posse* polygamous.[3] A Hindu marries in order that he may have a son. Hence, if his wife bears him no son, it is his duty to marry another in order to obtain a son. While these lines are being written, the newspapers announce that the daughter of the Gaekwar of Baroda is to become the second wife of the Mahārāja Scindia, because his first wife has not borne him an

[1] iii. 13; also *Baudhāyana*, I. viii. 16, 1-4; *Pāraskara*, i. 4, 8-11. For these castes see below, p. 163.

[2] *E. R. E.* V. 739. Cf. p. 395, below.

[3] Trevelyan, 29. Hence it is unsafe for an European woman to marry a Hindu.

heir.[1] Frequently the wife herself begs the husband to take a second wife. Yet many a Hindu is too loyal and too deeply attached to his wife to do so. Finally, if a man finds his wife stubborn and troublesome, Hindu law gives him the right to marry another, as we have seen above.[2]

8. But though in the times of the *Ṛigveda* infanticide and polygamy were both known, yet the patriarchal family was not far developed. Women had a great deal of liberty and a great deal of power; and the family was on the whole healthy. But at a later date the family began to change. Two innovations come from the times of the Brāhmaṇas. The first of these is the rise of the joint family, which we have already discussed. The other is the appearance of the rule that a man must not eat with his wife. This rule occurs in the *Śatapatha Brāhmaṇa*,[3] is repeated in all the law-books, and is in full force in every Hindu household to-day. The emergence of this extraordinary rule at this early date, the seventh or eighth century B.C., shows that already the power of the father was growing, and that woman was being relegated to a far lower place than that which she held in the times of the *Ṛigveda*.

9. Nor do we have to travel far to find further evidence of this tendency. As we saw above,[4] it became the rule, at a very early date, that every boy of the three twice-born castes should receive an education in one of the Brāhmanical schools. But girls were not admitted to the schools; the Vedas were forbidden to women as strictly as to Śūdras.[5] No provision was made for female education; and women were excluded from the noble culture which their fathers, brothers, husbands, and sons received.[6] A further result was

[1] The engagement has since been broken off. [2] p. 88.

[3] X. v. 2, 9; I. ix. 2, 12; *Gautama*, ix. 32; *Vasishṭha*, xii. 31; *Manu*, iv. 43. [4] p. 86. [5] *Manu*, ix. 18. For Śūdras, see p. 163.

[6] Want of school education does not necessarily make a man or a woman uneducated. In the ancient world very few children went to school, yet there were considerable numbers of cultured people, both men and women. There was very little school education in Homeric Greece;

that, with the exception of the marriage ceremony, every domestic sacrament was performed without *mantras* (i.e. Vedic texts) in the case of girls,[1] and a woman could perform no sacrifice without her husband.[2]

10. About the same time it became recognized as a Hindu religious law that a girl ought to be married before she reaches the age of puberty.[3] Here we get some light on the question of education; marriage in the case of girls took the place of Initiation, the religious ceremony which began a boy's education: the Law of Manu puts this quite clearly.[4] It seems certain that pre-puberty marriage was already recognized as the ideal in the sixth century B.C., for it is found in the earliest existing law-book, the *Dharmasūtra* of Gautama, which is placed by scholars before 500 B.C., and in all later treatises on law;

yet the heroes were men of judgement and taste. Akbar is a modern example. So, throughout the history of Hinduism, there have been illiterate men, and here and there also women, who have shown great capacity and considerable culture. Yet it remains true that for many centuries, Hindu women, whether of the upper or of the lower classes, have been uneducated, except in so far as their religion has given them wider interests. The facts which told against them most of all were child-marriage, their ignorance of Sanskrit—the language of science and culture—and finally the zenāna: what race of women could break through such barriers?

In the earlier periods of the history we occasionally meet educated women. Many of these cases occurred in communities where the Brāhmanic law was not yet rigorously enforced, and the others are mostly cases of individual women in peculiar circumstances.

Though the study of the Vedas and of the Sacred Law is absolutely forbidden to women, they are not without literature. The *Rāmāyaṇa* and the *Mahābhārata* in the original and in many vernacular adaptations are theirs, the *Purāṇas* also, and the whole range of vernacular literature, many parts of which are exceedingly rich.

Women have at various times taken a place in Indian literature. Some hymns of the *Ṛigveda* were composed by women; we meet them as interlocutors in the Upanishads; there is a volume of Psalms, the *Therīgāthā*, which is the work of Buddhist nuns; and a Rājput princess, named Mīrābāī, was a gifted poetess and religious leader.

[1] *Āśvalāyana*, i. 15, 10; *Manu*, ii. 67.

[2] *Gautama*, xviii. 1; *Āpastamba*, II. vi. 15, 17; *Manu*, iv. 205–206; v. 155; ix. 18; xi. 36.

[3] *Gautama*, xviii. 21–23; *Vasishṭha*, xvii. 69–70; *Baudhāyana*, IV. i. 11–12. Also *Manu*, ix. 4, 88, and all the later books.

[4] ii. 67.

but it was not generally practised among Hindus until several centuries later. For a long time it continued to be the Indian custom to marry a girl at the age of sixteen. This stands out quite clear in the literature, Hindu, Buddhist, and Jain, of the fifth, fourth, and third centuries. It was the steady pressure of the Brāhmanical law that introduced the change. By the beginning of our era at latest the change was complete. We may note here also that many Hindu princesses of the early centuries were allowed to choose their own husbands; the custom is known as *svayaṁvara*, self-choice.

But the matter does not end there; for parents (especially when the caste-group within which marriage is possible is narrow), fearing they may fail to secure a bridegroom at the right moment, marry their daughter when a suitable bridegroom is available, no matter how young the girl may be. This is how the practice of marrying little children or even infants arose. The child does not go to her husband's home until she is eleven or twelve; yet the marriage is absolutely binding. Hence, through the death of husbands in the intervening years, there are multitudes of Hindu widows who have never been wives.

We can only guess at the causes that led to the establishment of child-marriage; yet all inquirers are agreed that it is one of the clearest proofs possible that the Hindu woman was already in complete subjection. But though no one knows precisely what it was that led the Hindus to formulate this law, yet, in the earliest documents in which it occurs, a clear, comprehensible, religious reason is already suggested for the practice. The law appears in the *Dharmasūtra* of Gautama and in nearly all the later law-books. In each one we are told that the father who does not see that his daughter is married before the menses appear commits sin;[1] and in most of the books the sin is said to be equivalent to abortion.[2] Clearly

[1] See the passages referred to above, p. 94, n. 3.

[2] *Baudhāyana*, IV. i. 12; *Vasishṭha*, xvii. 71, and also *Bṛihashpati*, *Parāśara*, *Śātātapa*, *Vyāsa*, *Atri*, *Yājnavalkya*, *Hārīta*, *Saṁvarta*, *Aṅgirā*, *Vishṇu*, *Yama*.

the ancient Hindu believed that to fail to give a girl at puberty the chance of bearing a child was, so to speak, to prevent the birth which ought to come, and therefore was as sinful as destroying an embryo. This belief, in its sensitiveness to the claims of life, recalls the law of *ahiṁsā*, which arose about the same time, viz. that an ascetic must not kill animals, nor even break off a living twig.[1] Another rule, which rests on the same basis, runs that the husband who does not approach his wife after her monthly sickness commits sin.[2] Thus what makes child-marriage obligatory to the Hindu is the belief that to fail to give a girl at puberty the chance of becoming a mother is sinful.

11. The next downward step was the prohibition of widow-remarriage. Already by 500 B.C. only the childless widow was allowed to remarry,[3] but the law is first laid down for all widows in the great law-book of Manu.[4] As this code took several centuries to grow, it is impossible to fix the exact date of any law contained in it; yet we shall not be far wrong if we conclude that this regulation, that no widow may remarry, was already in force at the opening of the Christian era. Even a virgin child-widow is condemned to perpetual widowhood. Yet the very law which forbids the widow to take another husband expressly bids the widower remarry.

The origin of widow-celibacy is to be found in the Hindu idea of marriage. A Hindu woman marries, not merely 'for better for worse', but for this world and the next. There is marriage in heaven[5] amongst both gods and men, according to Hindu belief. The following words of Sītā in the *Rāmāyaṇa*[6] will make the matter plain:

> Still close, my lord, to thy dear side
> My spirit will be purified:

[1] See below, pp. 250, 256.
[2] *Baudhāyana*, IV. i. 17–19; *Manu*, ix. 4.
[3] *Gautama*, xviii. 4–17; *Vasishṭha*, xvii. 55–68, 74.
[4] v. 155–160. [5] See below, p. 297 f.
[6] Griffith, II. xxix; cf. *Manu*, v. 153–156.

Love from all sin my soul will free;[1]
My husband is a god to me.[2]
So, love, with thee shall I have bliss
And share the life that follows this.
I heard a Brāhman, dear to fame,
This ancient scripture text proclaim:
'The woman who on earth below
Her parents on a man bestow,
And lawfully their hands unite
With water and each holy rite,
She in this world shall be his wife,
His also in the after life.'

This belief gave point to wifely loyalty and faithfulness; for unless a wife proved a good woman and faithful to her lord, she could not expect to rejoin him in heaven.[3]

There is, then, another fact to be noticed. A girl is born a member of her father's family and belongs to him; but at marriage the father gives her to her husband and she becomes incorporated into his family.[4] Then, if her husband dies, she cannot again be grafted into her father's family:[5] it is impossible to play fast and loose with religious ties. Her closest relationship is with her husband, who is in the other world. So that, to the Hindu, she no longer quite belongs to ordinary society, but is in a way outside it, like the sannyāsī.[6]

Since Hindus thought in this way, we are not astonished to hear that at an early date it became customary that the widow who was a mother should not remarry. Then, later, the rule was extended to childless widows, and even to virgin widows who had never lived with a husband. A Hindu woman's virtue came to be summed up in life-long loyalty to the man to whom her father had given her, whether he was alive or dead.[7] If she was left a widow, it was her duty to set her whole heart on her coming reunion with her lord in heaven.[8]

[1] This is the sin which led to her birth as a woman. See above, p. 91.
[2] See above, p. 88.
[3] *Manu*, v. 161.
[4] *Āpastamba*, II. x. 27, 3; *Mahānirvāṇa*, *T.*, x. 1; Ranade, *Essays*, 34.
[5] Trevelyan, 62, 63.
[6] See below, p. 254.
[7] *Manu*, v. 156.
[8] *Manu*, v. 158, 160, 161, 165, 166; ix. 29.

Consequently, the noble Hindu woman, trained in these convictions from her babyhood, cannot bear the idea of a second marriage. To take another partner would be to be untrue to everything which she holds most noble and most sacred. The hard discipline and the long sorrow of widowhood are infinitely preferable to that.

This idea could never arise with regard to a Hindu husband, and that for two reasons. He was, at least potentially, a polygamist: the duty of loyalty to one woman could not emerge in his case. Then, if his deceased wife was his only wife, he had to marry again, in order to have his wife with him at the sacrifices.[1]

12. The next act in the tragic history of the Hindu woman is the introduction of the custom of *satī* or widow-burning. This notorious custom is not an ancient thing in Hinduism. Many savage tribes have the idea that a man will require in the other world all that he has enjoyed in this. So his horse and his wife are slain on his tomb, and his weapons are buried with him. The Indo-Aryans had given up this inhuman custom; for there is the clearest proof that it was not in use in the times of the *Ṛigveda,* nor for many centuries later. How it was revived, we do not know; probably through imitation of some of the aboriginal tribes. The rise of the practice among a civilized people like the Hindus would be altogether incomprehensible but for the peculiar constitution of the Hindu family. We find the first beginnings of the classical Hindu custom in the later portions of the *Rāmāyaṇa* and the *Mahābhārata.*[2] It came into vogue gradually, and the history is not known. Kālidāsa's *Birth of the War-god*[3] shows that it was already well known by A.D. 400; and it receives legal recognition in the *Vishṇusmṛiti.*[4] It is praised in the *Garuḍa Purāṇa,*[5] but is condemned in the *Mahānirvāṇa Tantra.*[6] It was but a permissive statute: the widow was allowed to

[1] *Manu,* v. 167–169.
[2] *Great Epic,* 81.
[3] Canto iv.
[4] xxv. 14.
[5] *Garuḍa Purāṇa Sāroddhāra,* x. 35–55.
[6] x. 79.

mount her husband's pyre, if she chose to do so. Yet the records prove that there were unwilling victims. Rām Mohan Rai saw his own brother's widow burnt to death despite her attempt to escape.

Akbar, the Mughal emperor, prohibited it, but failed to put it down. By the beginning of the nineteenth century the evil had reached colossal proportions; so that Bentinck's act of abolition required considerable courage and firmness.[1] It was in Bengal that the largest number of cases occurred, yet the practice was well known all over India. At certain courts at least, a great holocaust of women took place on the death of the king.[2]

The rise of such a custom seems at first sight inexplicable, almost incredible, but it is quite comprehensible when the Hindu ideal of wifely loyalty and the belief in the joyous heavenly reunion are taken into account. A woman who has been happily married and is deeply attached to her husband suddenly loses him. Overwhelmed with grief, she does not want to live. The hard asceticism and lonely misery of widowhood make the outlook all the darker. On the other hand, she has only to endure the pyre, and she will immediately have a rapturous reunion with her lord in heaven.[3] Even in these days, eighty years after Bentinck's orders, *satī* is not unknown. Quite recently, near Calcutta, a bereaved wife, in the exaltation of her anguish, determinedly burned herself in her own room at the very time when the body of her husband was being consumed on the pyre. When such a case occurs, the Hindu community thrills with sympathy and reverence. The old religious ideas have by no means lost all their force.

There is much here which we Westerns can understand. How many a wife, and husband too, who has lost a beloved partner, could never dream of a second union!

[1] *Imperial Gazetteer*, ii. 498.
[2] *Imperial Gazetteer*, ii. 94; cf. also Ranade, 317; Havell, *Benares*, 111.
[3] *Manu*, v. 165, 166.

And what to her shall be the end?
And what to me remains of good?
To her, perpetual maidenhood,
And unto me no second friend.

With the love and self-devotion of the *satī* we can deeply sympathize. How many broken-hearted widows and widowers have prayed for easeful death!

But what we can scarcely understand is how these tragic glooms and awful ordeals could be imposed as laws upon weak women, while men went their own way in comfort and freedom, and above all how the dark sorrows of widowhood could be laid on smiling infants and little toddling mites, equally innocent of love, marriage, and death.

13. Long before the practice of widow-sacrifice arose, it was regarded as a fitting thing that a widow should live a mildly ascetic life, enduring hardships and subsisting on a vegetarian diet.[1] When *satī* became common, the ascetic life became compulsory for those who did not mount the pyre. The original idea seems to have been that, with the death of her husband, the widow passed out of society, like the monk; and therefore it seemed right that she should practise his asceticism.

To-day every widow is condemned to perpetual mourning and austerity. In Bengal the rule is that a widow has to lay aside all her ornaments, wear a *sārī* without a border, subsist on a vegetarian diet, eat only one solid meal per day, and twice a month pass a whole day of twenty-four hours without eating and drinking; and this rule is applied even to girl-widows.[2] A woman's hair is her glory, the last piece of beauty she cares to part with. In large sections of India the barber shaves away the widow's glossy tresses and leaves her a tonsured nun.[3] It seems likely that a high religious purpose was once present in this ascetic life; but if so, the spirit of it has not been preserved. Were the widow a sort of stay-at-home nun,

[1] *Manu*, v. 156–158. [2] A child-widow is allowed a light supper.
[3] *I. S. R.*, Dec. 19, 1909, p. 185; Feb. 20, 1910, p. 296.

voluntarily renouncing the world, devoting herself to a life of prayer and meditation, one could understand the ideal; but, oh the pity of it! the widowed children of India are compelled to live a severely ascetic life, and are usually given a heavy share of the household drudgery as well. Finally, the doctrine of transmigration and karma is used to make the poor girl responsible for her husband's death: if she had not sinned grievously in a previous life, he would not have died. How strange that this religious inference is not used with similar effect in the case of the husband who loses his wife! The widow is driven away from scenes of happiness and rejoicing as a guilty thing likely to bring ill-luck. 'Her hard lot, her life-long misery and degradation, her endless fasts and privations,' are the words used by a Hindu to describe the widow's experience.[1] It is a relief to the heart to realize that, though the life of penance and drudgery is everywhere the rule, widows are not treated with equal harshness in all parts of India. It is not that Hindus are hard-hearted: it is the beliefs and the laws that are at fault.

14. The last downward step, fatefully possible because of all that had gone before it, was the acceptance of the custom of secluding the women of the upper castes in the women's apartments and cutting them off from all participation in public life. Surely a fitting climax to their seclusion from the noble education of ancient India! The custom arose among Hindus during the Muḥammadan period, perhaps partly in imitation of their masters, but partly also in self-defence. The practice does not affect in the same degree those provinces that came little under Muḥammadan influence, and the women of the lower classes usually lead a very free life. On the other hand, the zenāna system, like strict caste rules, child-marriage, enforced widowhood, and other characteristics of high-caste life, is copied, as a patent of nobility, by the lower castes so far as their means will allow.

[1] In *I. S. R.* Feb. 13, 1910, p. 283.

C. Yet, despite the crushing weight of patriarchal authority and all its pitiable results, the Hindu home hides some very beautiful things. The faithfulness, devotion, and love of the wife and mother, the humility and willing ministry of the broken-hearted widow, the obedience and affection of the sons and daughters, even when grown up, the subdued joy and shady retirement of the zenāna, the sacramental note present always and everywhere—these are things of real worth and beauty, exquisite as a bed of scented violets in an English forest-glade. There are Hindu mothers belonging to all castes whose place and power in the home show that human nature is often too strong for human law. They are treated with supreme respect by both husband and children, and live lives of great influence and usefulness. Yet they are but exceptions, and their position is altogether insecure. Further, high-caste women are to be met here and there who, though illiterate, are cultured, thoughtful, and capable. They know by heart large parts of the religious literature. Their practical and religious training has made them women of character and capacity. Their husbands rely on their judgement, and they wield great influence in their homes. The Hindu family has produced these rich fruits amidst ignorance, oppression, injustice. What may we not look for from this thrice-noble race of women, when they receive their rightful freedom, education, and position?

Then depreciation and subjugation are not the whole truth about Hindu women. According to Hindu law, the wife may accept and hold property of her own which even her husband cannot touch.[1] Social reformers complain that the law is frequently rendered nugatory: many a wife can be brought to surrender her property by the threat of a second wife.[2] Yet the law exists, and is frequently taken advantage of.

D. These regulations for the family are very widely

[1] *Manu*, viii. 28–29; ix. 104, 131, 192–198. For a modern statement of the rights of a Hindu wife see *I. S. R.*, Dec. 5, 1909, p. 162.
[2] *I. S. R.*, Sept. 10, 1911, pp. 16 ff.

followed by Hindus throughout the country; but they are by no means universal. While the laws of the Dharmasūtras and Dharmaśāstras are very generally revered and obeyed, there is a far greater law than any of them, the law of custom—

> Let him walk in that path of holy men which his father and his grandfathers followed; while he walks in that he will not suffer harm;—[1]

which overrides every other law. If a Hindu can prove that a custom has been faithfully observed in his family or caste for generations, then it is right and obligatory for him, no matter how immoral, anti-social, or revolting it may be. Hence the marriage laws of many castes do not conform to Hindu rule. The younger sons of the Nambutiri Brāhmans of Travancore practise polyandry; among certain South Indian castes the marriage of a man with his niece is permitted; some castes practise divorce; in others it is considered right to marry a daughter to an idol, a flower, a sword, or some other material object and to allow her to lead thereafter the life of a prostitute;[2] while in many temples there are *devadāsīs*, servants of the god, dedicated by their relatives, who do take part from time to time in the services, but whose real occupation is immorality.[3]

E. There are several points in the Hindu family that are inconsistent with the doctrine of transmigration and karma. The basis of the worship of the 'fathers' is the two ideas, that they have won immortality in heaven, and that the offerings enable them to retain their place there. But transmigration teaches that they must return to earth to be born again; and, according to the karma doctrine, nothing that any survivor on earth can do can alter their destiny by one hair's breadth: that is settled by their own karma and that alone; so that there is a double inconsistency. The law

[1] *Manu*, iv. 178. [2] See Lord Morley's Dispatch of March 3, 1911.
[3] See below, p. 313.

that a widow must remain faithful to her dead husband, and look forward to a happy union with him in heaven, clearly arose before the appearance of the doctrine of transmigration, and is scarcely consistent with it; for it is quite possible that the husband's karma may cause him to be reborn before his widow dies.

On the other hand, the karma hypothesis is used, as we have seen, to make the widow responsible for her husband's death. It also provides a justification for the belief in the inferiority of women: the theory is that they sinned seriously in a former life, and that their evil karma makes them women.

III. The Hindu family stood four-square for over two thousand years; for, although changes took place after the Christian era, in its main lines the structure was complete by 500 B.C. During all these long centuries its institutions scarcely underwent a criticism. Nay, they spread outside the Hindu community and affected both Muslims and Christians. But about 1800 A.D. Christian criticism began to make itself heard, especially in the writings of the Serampore missionaries. Here, as in every other department of Western influence, Rām Mohan Rai, the founder of the Brāhma Samāj, was the first Hindu to respond and to turn to practical action. He wrote against polygamy, and his share in the agitation which led Lord William Bentinck to put down *satī* in 1829 was not inconsiderable. Debendranāth Tagore, the next leader of the Brāhma Samāj, rebelled against the polytheistic and idolatrous character of the sacraments (*saṁskāras*) of the Hindu family, and prepared a purified manual for the use of Brāhma families, but did not recognize that he was acting under the influence of Christ. Keshab Chandra Sen saw far more clearly whence the light was coming and confessed it. His condemnation of child-marriage and other abuses led not only to real reform among those who followed him, but took shape in a Marriage Act passed by Lord Lawrence's Government in 1872. One of Keshab's contemporaries was Īśvara

Chandra Vidyāsāgara, a Calcutta pandit of great learning, who, realizing that in the earliest ages Hindu widows were free to marry, and also seeing clearly the grave evils which the prohibition leads to in modern life, spoke and wrote in favour of restoring the old freedom with so much power that Government agreed and passed the necessary Act in 1865. Mr. Justice Ranade, one of the leaders of the Prārthanā Samāj, founded in Bombay in 1867, is the next outstanding leader in family reform. To him we owe the organization of the social reform movement, which every year holds one national and several local conferences. Its organ, the *Indian Social Reformer*, exercises a most healthy influence. The only other name we need mention is Rao Bahadur Vīreśaliṅgam Pantulu, whose influence for good both in social reform and in literature has been very great, especially in the Telugu country where he has his home. It is worthy of notice that the members of the Ārya Samāj condemn child-marriage and permit widow remarriage. But the most significant fact of all is this, that the Theosophical Society, the Rāmakṛishṇa Mission, and the caste and sect conferences, although they defend the whole of Hinduism, yet advocate certain measures of reform, especially the postponement of the age of marriage and the education of girls.

It is also most noticeable that the progress of the national movement greatly strengthens the forces making for social reform. The loud demand of the Congress for progress, for economic change, for men and women of character to make the country great, helps the young student to realize that his sisters should be educated, that they should not be married until they have had an effective education, and that his widowed aunt should either be allowed to become a happy mother, or be trained to be a teacher, a nurse, or a doctor, in order to help in the uplifting of the girls and women of the country. Even the Hindu revival helps the cause of social reform. The Hindu school, the class for the study of the *Gītā*, the *Central Hindu College Magazine* and other revival literature, are all useful in making men think, in letting in the light, and so preparing the way for reform.

There are two fields of social reform in India, caste and the family. The latter has until now bulked most largely, and there the best results have been achieved. Apart from minor issues, there are four reforms which are demanded. These are the raising of the age of marriage for girls, education for girls, widow remarriage, and the suppression of polygamy. Opinion varies a good deal among the educated on these topics; yet all, or nearly all, recognize the need of the first two, the raising of the age of marriage and the provision of education for girls. On the subject of the remarriage of widows there are still many opinions; and, while most recognize that monogamy is the true ideal, a good many pleas are still heard in favour of a second marriage when the first proves childless. It is most significant that all the outstanding political leaders have declared most emphatically that, for the regeneration of India, the three reforms—female education, the raising of the age of marriage, and freedom for widows to remarry—are absolutely necessary. It is at first sight rather remarkable that one hardly ever hears a word raised against the pagan ceremonial of the funeral and the śrāddha ceremonies; but, when one looks more closely, the reason is plain, as we shall see.

A. The criticism directed against the Hindu family by Indian reformers is simply Christian criticism:

1. They point out that child-marriage robs the little wife of her adolescence and her chance of an education; that she has no girlhood, but passes at once from her childish years into the great strain of married life and premature child-bearing, whence come only too often an enfeebled physique, an impaired mind, and an early death; that the physique of the children suffers and in consequence the physique of the whole race; and that female education can make no serious progress until the age of marriage is altered. It is also stated that the moral results of plunging a little girl into all that

married life means are very serious; that her character never gets an opportunity of gathering strength and settling; and that, in consequence, hysteria and unbalanced feeling are painfully common among Hindu women.

One aspect of Hindu family life much commented on by reformers is a result of the combined action of child-marriage and widow-celibacy.[1] When middle-aged or old men remarry, they are compelled to take mere children as their wives. Hence all over the country, men of forty, fifty, sixty, or even seventy years are married to little girls of twelve, or even of more tender years; for no one pretends that Hindu society obeys the law of 1891 which forbids cohabitation before twelve.

It is also pointed out that, if no Hindu girl were married until she were, say, fourteen, there would be far fewer widows in Hindu society, and the whole class of virgin widows would be eliminated.

2. The education of girls is advocated by Hindu reformers partly as a right which ought not to be withheld, but mainly on the ground that it is absolutely essential if the family is to become healthy and the race is to reach real efficiency. The value of educated mothers is very clearly realized, and the most piteous waste arising from the present system is constantly set forth in the press. Women teachers both for schools and zenānas are wanted in large numbers; nurses and lady doctors are in great request, and cultured women to lead the ordinary Hindu woman to a higher life. The educated Hindu wants to marry an educated girl, but is seldom able to realize his wish.

3. The same pair of reasons are put forward in favour of giving the Hindu widow the right to remarry if she wish to do so. Reformers plead that it is wrong to refuse to give the widow the liberty which without question is conceded to the widower, and to compel her to live a life of severe asceticism

[1] See *I. S. R.*, June 19, 1910, p. 501.

and drudgery. The plea is made with increased emphasis in the case of virgin widows. But most Hindus lay stress on the expediency rather than on the justice of the reform. They set forth the very serious moral dangers to which the widow, and above all the young widow, is exposed; and they point out that, if widows were allowed to marry, widowers could readily find suitable partners.

4. Polygamy is not so often discussed in public, yet all the more thoughtful men feel very strongly about it. The chief conviction behind the agitation is the deep indignity and humiliation which polygamy brings to the first wife; but the moral results on the husband are also emphasized. On the other hand, so few Hindus have more than one wife that at first sight polygamy seems a small matter in comparison with other abuses. But another aspect of the question has recently been brought into public notice, namely the unlimited power which this right of polygamy puts into the hands of unscrupulous men and the very serious suffering many women undergo in consequence. Child-marriage usually secures the complete subjection of the wife to her husband. The little girl is brought into her father-in-law's home; and, being but a child, naturally and necessarily comes under the domination of her husband, who is at least several years older than herself. In domestic matters she is subject to her mother-in-law. The Hindu points out that by this means the wife is trained to complete obedience and perfect submission. But if a wife, despite this rigorous training, shows any signs of independence of spirit, the threat of a second marriage is at once used, and the poor child is cowed. The same threat may enable an unscrupulous husband to use his wife's private property.

B. The whole social reform movement is a most healthy influence in modern India. The changes it is producing on the Hindu mind and conscience are very precious. Yet, if its progress is to be measured by actual results in family life, it must be acknowledged to be very slow. The stalwarts constantly speak of the appalling contrast between the speeches and the actions of many of the leading reformers. How many leaders from Keshab down to the Gaekwar of Baroda have been pilloried in the press as 'backsliders'! But, though the actions of these men do stand out in painful contrast with their public protestations, yet the slowness of the advance of social reform cannot, in justice, be laid at their door: they are a symptom rather than the cause. Indeed it seems clear that social reformers have not at all realized what the mighty power is which thwarts their efforts.

The usual explanation given of the slow progress of social reform in the Hindu community, namely that it has to contend against all the forces of conservatism and stagnation, does not go to the root of the matter. There is an infinite difference between a reform which is in fullest consonance with the clear teaching of the religion of a people, and a reform which is diametrically opposed to the spirit, the law, the institutions, and the traditions of the national faith. The temperance movement, for example, is a comparatively easy crusade among Hindus. But the life of women is an altogether different matter. For more than two thousand years the Hindu people have been taught that a girl does not require an education, but that it is sinful not to marry her before puberty; and that a man may remarry as often as he is widowed, but that a widow who even thinks of remarrying is unfaithful to her husband and will suffer after death for her conduct. It is these deep religious ideas that retard the progress of social reform. The educated man is personally ready for reform, but his women-folk and all his relatives and caste-friends who have not had a modern education are still dominated by the old religious beliefs. This is the gigantic barrier that stands in the way of the re-creation of the Hindu family.

We may well ask whether in such circumstances the reforms ought to be seriously pressed. Should the women of a household be driven to consent to that which they do not think right, merely because the head of the house has become so emancipated by his education as to be ready to lay aside the religious scruples which still sway their simple hearts? Will not the true man's sympathy be with the women? Is it manly, is it honourable to drive them to act in flat disobedience to their consciences? If we are seeking to uplift the Hindu woman, shall we begin by doing violence to her religious convictions? May not the postponement of a wedding for a few years or the remarriage of a widow be too dearly bought at such a price? Does it not seem as if there were something wrong with the method of the social reformer?

One Hindu thinker has come very near a true appreciation of the present state of affairs. The following is a quotation from a paper read by Mr. V. Śrīnivāsa Rao, of Berhampore, before the Ganjam Hindu Reform Association:[1]

> Our present-day social practices are no doubt the natural outcome of certain religious beliefs. Unless such beliefs are shaken, the present social practices cannot be permanently shaken. If an attempt is made, as has till now been made, to shake the present-day social customs, without previously or simultaneously attempting to shake their foundations deep-rooted in religious beliefs, the result cannot be otherwise than what it is at present, viz. a creation of many halting and half-hearted 'sympathizers' of social reform, who accept one reform and oppose another, evidently being oblivious to the fact that the same root principles underlie all the reforms and are opposed to the principles that gave rise to the existing social customs. What are the principles that gave rise to the present-day social practices which are sought to be reformed? They may be many, but chief of them seem to be three, as shown below. The principles are so deep-rooted that they took the form of regular and essential institutions:
>
> i. Undue reverence to Shastras, which regards the Shastras to be supernatural, God-revealed, unchangeable, and the violation of their dictates, however violent to the conscience and reason, to be sinful; and which believes that the present-day social customs are based on them as interpreted by the old priestly class and tradition, however one may now try to prove that the Shastras do not advocate such customs. This belief is responsible for the prohibition against widow marriages, post-puberty marriages, &c. The father of a young virgin widow feels for his daughter's misery

[1] Reported in *I. S. R.*, Sept. 8, 1912, p. 16.

as much as anybody else, but he feels unable to go against the custom which he believes to be based on the dictates of the God-given Shastras.

ii. Ideas of caste system, which introduce and perpetuate invidious distinctions of privilege and status based upon mere accident of birth, and accentuate the spirit of pride and arrogance and of looking down upon some fellow beings with contempt, and which circumscribe the mental horizon in all respects. This idea of caste is responsible for the existing social practices of prohibition against foreign travel, inter-dining, inter-marriage, elevation of the lower classes, &c.

iii. Ideas of idol-worship, which harbour false conceptions of God, viz. that God is not One; that He has got all the idiosyncrasies of human beings; that He, like a tyrant king, enjoying all the sensual pleasures, demands bribes of vegetable or animal food in order to keep the devotee in good position; that there are different material heavens and hells for various kinds of souls, presided over by different gods and goddesses; that these should be propitiated by offerings made through a certain class of people on earth. Thus, by not presenting higher and spiritual ideals, the idolatry fetters the emancipation of the soul and narrows its horizon. A great thinker has once said, 'Show me your gods and I will show your men,' thereby meaning that our conceptions of God have much to do with our conduct in life. This is responsible for the low and barren state of the mental plane which is proof against the reception of all healthy and progressive ideas of social reform.

Whatever the apologists of the three old beliefs, who, having received liberal education, are anxious to reconcile them with the new beliefs which they imbibed by such education, may say—as, for instance, that all the Shastras are not taken to be supernatural, that the caste system is based on the good and scientific principle of 'personal magnetism', and that Idolatry is only keeping in view a concrete thing for concentration in worshipping the One True Spiritual God—the stern and incontrovertible fact remains there that all the Shastras, even the Puranas, are believed to have been written by god-inspired sages who are themselves supernatural, and whose dictates, established as the existing social customs, cannot be deliberately trampled upon without committing sin; that the caste system is not at present based on 'personal magnetism', but by mere accident of birth; and that the idolater does believe that some of the idols are the actual incarnations of God, called Archavataras,[1] and not mere symbols; that there is not

[1] See below, p. 320.

one God but many, quite independent of each other, one at Tirupati, the other at Chidambaram, and so on;[1] that one should be worshipped on a certain day with certain leaves; that the marriage and consummation ceremonies of one God should be celebrated on a particular day, and those of the other on another day, and so on.

Thus it is evident that the above three principles or popular beliefs of undue reverence for Shastras, caste system, and idolatry, as explained above, are strongly deep-rooted in the minds of the generality of Hindus, and are offering much obstruction to the implanting of liberal social reforms in the soil of the Hindu social economy, by stunting the mental expansion of their votaries, and thus making them impervious. If any one has outgrown, at least intellectually, these three beliefs, he alone is able to understand the righteousness and necessity of the several reforms proposed. There is a truth in the statement that only education can effect social reform, thereby meaning not that the education will directly introduce reforms, but that education will shake the above foundations of the existing social practices, and thus indirectly help the educated to grasp the reforms. However vigorously the seeds of social reform are tried to be sown on the soil of the Hindu social polity, it must be remembered that as long as the stones of the current popular religious beliefs are allowed to remain in the soil, so long will the effect be nil. The soil of the mental plane of the individuals must be cleared of noxious weeds and elevated with fertilizing substance, before we may expect to reap any harvest of social reforms. Such clearing and elevation can be effected by the processes of destruction and construction respectively; destruction meaning the shaking and removal of the rocky subsoil of the above three popular beliefs from their mental soil, and the construction meaning the substitution of the fertilizing soil of new, healthy, and progressive principles in their stead, without which the harvest will be equally if not more disastrous. It is true that education has so far been able to do the process of destruction and shake the old beliefs, but it has not yet equally been able to do the process of construction of offering substitutes which alone can give stability and permanence to social reforms when introduced. It was this want of constructive attempt on a sufficiently large scale that is responsible for the charge often made that some of the reformers are 'irresponsible, irreligious, dare-devil vagabonds' who, having lost all faith in the old principles, and having no substitutes for the same, have altogether abandoned all ideas of religion.

This is very incisive reasoning. Indeed, if carried one step farther, it would lay bare the whole truth.

[1] See below, pp. 324–6.

But the ordinary Hindu reformer has not realized what has taken place in his own mind. He has not noticed that, along with all other educated men and women, he has ceased to believe the doctrines which lie at the basis of the Hindu family. As we have seen, it is these beliefs that stand in the way of reform. The whole of the common people and all Hindu women, except the few who have come seriously under Western influence, are still swayed by these ideas. Educated men show that they are no longer bound by them by their advocacy of the reforms. If we look at each in turn, it will become abundantly clear that the foundation ideas of the Hindu family have already lost their hold over the mind of the educated Hindu.

First, the belief which forms the foundation stone of the whole structure, that, unless the *piṇḍa* be regularly offered in the memorial services and the water in the daily prayers, the 'fathers' will fall from heaven and the whole family be destroyed, is no longer held by educated men. If you talk to them about the *śrāddha* ceremonies, they will at once confess that they hold no such belief, that they do not consider that idea essential, but regard these ceremonies merely as a way of expressing their very deep respect for the dead. Thus, while it is quite true that the observance of these ceremonies continues among educated men, the beliefs which created the observances have already disappeared.

Secondly, the belief in woman's essential inferiority to man is rapidly passing away. The proof that this is so lies here that educated men now repudiate or explain away the practices which are the manifestation of the belief in the Hindu family. No educated man now defends infanticide; no one defends *satī*. The feeling is the same with regard to polygamy, as we have just seen; or, if a voice is now and then tentatively raised in favour of marrying a second wife when the first proves childless, there is no conviction in the tone. Concubinage, which in India used to be as common and as much recognized as in ancient Greece, is now universally condemned.

The agitation in favour of the education of girls is a further proof. Men are also steadily coming nearer a recognition of woman's right to freedom. The zenāna is not praised as it used to be. In this matter the attitude of the Hindu woman herself is of considerable importance. The progress made during the last ten years has been very remarkable. Finally, even those who oppose the reforms do not do so on the basis of the essential inferiority of women.

Thirdly, the belief, which underlies child-marriage, that it is sinful not to marry a girl before puberty, is dead among educated men and women. Very few educated men are now to be found who would defend child-marriage at all, although the vast majority, under the pressure of their women-folk and friends, still practise it. Yet, even if a minority among the educated defend the practice, no one now holds the belief which is the only foundation of the practice.

Fourthly, the distinctive Hindu conviction, that it is right for the widower but wrong for the widow to remarry, is also dead in educated circles. Men differ very seriously in their judgement as to what ought to be done. Some say that virgin widows should be allowed to marry if they wish to do so. Others demand that all widows should be given the option. Others, who hold that the ascetic life of the Hindu widow embodies a noble ideal and who are reluctant to give it up, urge various reasons for retaining it, especially the undoubted fact that the best Hindu women who have not come under Western influence have an intense dislike of the idea of a second union. A few have suggested that the true ideal is that neither widow nor widower should remarry. The significant fact, however, is this, that no one now holds that God's law allows remarriage in the case of widowers but not in the case of widows.

It would be quite possible to carry this farther, but it is unnecessary. There is abundant proof that the religious basis of the Hindu family is decaying among educated men. Nor can there be any doubt that it is the coming of the new era that has produced the decay. Through all earlier revolutions, whether political or religious, these beliefs have persisted. Buddhism did not perceptibly modify them. Except in the case of Akbar, Muslim influence, so far from waking the Indian mind in these matters, seems to have stiffened Hindu family usage all round. There is not the slightest evidence that any of the great Hindu thinkers of the past doubted these things. An occasional outburst from an atheist or from a free-lance[1] only makes the unbroken faith of the generations all the more impressive. But the forces of the new time have created an atmosphere in India in which these beliefs cannot live. Every one who enters the atmosphere loses the power to hold them.

From this point of view we can fully understand the position of the reform movement. The whole situation becomes clear when we realize that the reformers are no longer bound by the religious ideas which still hold the uneducated, and thus are ready for action, the very suggestion of which at once raises serious opposition on the part of those who are still held by them. We can also see that the contention of the more intelligent of the opposition party, that the acceptance of the reforms would be disloyalty to Hinduism, and would prove dangerous to the religion, is at least in large measure justifiable.

A most serious situation is thus disclosed. There is first the fact that the reformers and the orthodox mass stand face to face, and that it is not a social but a religious difference that divides them. But the tragic element lies here that the changes which the reformers demand are absolutely indispensable for the regeneration of India; and yet they cannot be carried out without abandoning the religious foundation of the Hindu family. The reformers have not realized what they were doing. It is probably the very word 'reform' that has misled them. They have all along imagined they were recalling the original form of the Hindu family, while, as a matter of

[1] *Heart of India*, 100, 112.

fact, what they have been seeking to reach is an altogether new structure. They are right in stating that the reforms are absolutely essential: their opponents are right in saying that these new proposals are alien and hostile to the Hindu family.

Thus the only satisfactory solution of the difficulty is the disappearance of the old beliefs. Every true patriot must wish to see them pass away; for, until they pass away, the reforms cannot be heartily welcomed by the people. Mr. Śrīnivāsa Rao comes very near the truth here.[1]

But we may go farther and recognize that disbelief of these things is bound to spread. No one can now stay the progress of Western education in India. It is not Britain that imposes it on the Indian spirit. The example of Japan and of China in this regard is final and conclusive. India must have Western education; and wherever that goes, belief in the potency of the *piṇḍa*, in the essential inferiority of women, in the duty of marrying a girl before puberty and in the sinfulness of widow-remarriage, melts away like snow under a rise of temperature. The only questions are, how soon, and under what agency, the change will take place.

IV. But a much more serious consideration has now to be faced. If the old beliefs are decaying and are certain to pass away, what is to be put in their place? The chief lesson taught by our study of the Hindu family is this, that every element in it rests on a religious basis. The same thing will be found true of every other form of family organization on the face of the earth. All are religious. Innumerable forms of organization were tried by our ancestors; and we have amongst us to-day only those that have succeeded in surviving. It is surely a truth of vast significance that every single surviving form is religious from top to bottom. Thus the thoughtful man will not attempt to rebuild the family of any nation without a foundation of religion.

[1] Supra, p. 112.

But have not the reform party been attempting to do so, consciously or unconsciously? They have steadily worked in opposition to Hindu family beliefs, but have proposed no new group of ideas to take their place. In many Hindu families the difficulty is seriously felt to-day. The emancipated son rebels against his father's authority. The daughter-in-law, having got a little education, believes she has rights of freedom and refuses to obey her mother-in-law. That is the new spirit uncontrolled by religion. The new wine of liberty needs new bottles to contain it.

The founder of the Ārya Samāj consciously attempted to rebuild the family on a religious foundation; but he used only materials provided by the Vedas, so that the attempt was foredoomed to failure. Already his own followers are making haste to repudiate one of his institutions, viz. *niyoga*, a form of temporary marriage which in his system is permissible for widows and widowers, and even for others.

What is needed is a strong, simple, religious doctrine which even the child and the illiterate woman can understand, a doctrine which will make the needed reforms inevitable, once it is understood and believed, and yet will at the same time place men, women, and children in the family under such clear religious obligations that individual liberty shall be restrained and the unity and purity of the family secured. Unity, purity, discipline, peace were secured in the far-away times for the Hindu family by the religious beliefs which are now crumbling to dust. Something of equal power but suited to modern times must be found now, else the modern Hindu family can never rise in beauty and power.

Mr. Justice Ranade had some inkling of this truth many years ago and gave expression to it:

> Our deliberate conviction, however, has grown upon us with every effort, that it is only a religious revival that can furnish sufficient moral strength to work out the complex social problems which demand our attention. Mere considerations of expediency or economical calculations of gains and losses can never move a community to undertake and

> carry through social reforms, especially with a community like ours, so spell-bound by custom and authority. Our people feel, and feel earnestly, that some of our social customs are fraught with evil, but as this evil is of a temporal character, they think it does not justify a breach of commands divine, for such breach involves a higher penalty. The truth is that orthodox society has lost its power of life; it can initiate no reform, nor sympathize with it. Only a religious revival, a revival not of forms, but of sincere earnestness, which constitutes true religion, can effect the desired end.[1]

Others[2] have said something similar more recently; but there has been no clear perception of the crucial fact that what is required is a group of fresh religious beliefs fit to form the foundation of the new family life desired by the reformers.

We have already noticed that the whole reform movement arises from the Western atmosphere now influencing India so deeply. It lays hold with strength only on those who have had a Western education. But we come nearer the real source when we note that these powerful ideas came in the first instance directly to Rām Mohan Rai and the other Brāhma leaders from Christian sources. We do not, however, reach the full truth until we recognize that every principle that controls the movement springs from Christ Himself; but, as that will become apparent at once to every one who will give careful attention to the work of the reformers, we need say no more about it. Since, then, Christ has inspired the movement so completely,[3] we shall do well to ask whether He does not also supply the ideas needed to provide the religious foundation for the new structure which we see taking shape before our eyes. What does He say about the basis of the family? In seeking to reach the answer to this question, we must begin with the fundamental principles of Christ, in accordance with what is brought out in the Introduction.[4]

[1] Quoted in *I. S. R.*, Sept. 8, 1912, p. 16.
[2] e.g. Mr. Justice Sadāśiva Iyer in *I. S. R.*, June 2, 1912, and Mr. V. Śrīnivāsa Rao in *I. S. R.*, Sept. 8 and 22, 1912.
[3] See Ranade's *Essays*, 23; Sastri's *History of the Brahmo Samaj*, i. 297.
[4] pp. 58–61.

It may be well, at the very outset, to say a word about a point frequently raised in Indian journals. When Christian teaching is offered as the solution of the problem of the Hindu family, Hindus are accustomed to object that the sexual immorality and the divorce of the West are as bad as anything found in India. We would ask our readers to recognize, on the one hand, that, in addition to all the injustice and weakness produced by its unhealthy family system, India suffers quite as much from sexual vice as Europe does, and, on the other, that such facts, even if they were more serious than they are, would not prove that the teaching of Christ on family questions does not form the final basis of healthy family life for all men. The ignorance of multitudes of people in the slums of European cities is no proof that Western education is unnecessary or unhealthy; and the millions of people who in many parts of the world live unsanitary lives do not constitute a disproof of the value of hygiene. Like Hinduism, Christianity must be judged by its principles, not by the vicious lives of those who refuse to obey it.

We turn, then, to the teaching of Christ.

A. The central message of Christianity is the Fatherhood of God. The word father has been applied to the divine Being in almost every land, but with great variety of meaning and feeling. In primitive religions it is quite common in the sense of physical parent. The savage believes that his clan is descended from his god. In much higher faiths, where a spiritual conception of God already obtains, He is called Father, as being the Creator, the Sustainer, and the loving Benefactor of His creatures. The word in that case is used metaphorically, just as it is when a king is called the father of his people. Such a use of the word 'father' implies nothing as to what man's nature is.

But Christ's conception of the divine Fatherhood is something quite different. To Him the Fatherhood is a personal relation between the supreme Spirit and every human being.

Three distinct yet closely related elements are contained in it. First, God created man in His own image; so that the spirit of man is a finite copy of the infinite Spirit. Man's spiritual nature, though finite and weak, is built on the same lines as the nature of God Himself. That which makes a man a man is likeness to God. Secondly, God made man like Himself, so that he might be fit for the immediate, personal, spiritual intercourse of a son with his Heavenly Father. The essence of humanity is thus spiritual kinship to God. Thirdly, having created man in His own image with a view to sonship, God loves every human being with the tender love of a father. Thus, God's relation to every individual human soul is truly that of Father, and nothing can ever break that bond or change the Father's heart. Every man, woman, and child has the peerless dignity of a child of the Supreme.

Since, then, man's nature and origin are such, we can see that every human being is of priceless value, both to himself and to God. Jesus said,

> For what shall a man be profited, if he shall gain the whole world, and forfeit his soul? or what shall a man give in exchange for his soul? [1]

Our kinship to God also fills us with infinite potentialities. Wrapped up in every human soul there are possibilities of moral and spiritual growth beyond our calculation. Christ's command is:

> Ye therefore shall be perfect, as your heavenly Father is perfect.[2]

Man's responsibilities are as great as his value and his dignity. Each of us will have to stand before the divine judgement-seat and give an account of his life. Jesus says,

> For the Son of man shall come in the glory of his Father with his angels; and then shall he render unto every man according to his deeds.[3]

[1] Matt. 16, 26. [2] Matt. 5, 48. [3] Matt. 16, 27.

1. From these quotations it will be clear that to Jesus the implications of the Fatherhood are so great that, in the light of that truth, all matters of sex, physique, birth, position, wealth, education, civilization, dwindle to nothing, and every human being is seen to be to God a child of priceless worth. Women are different from men, mentally as well as physically, yet they are as precious, as divine, as noble as men are, and as fully responsible to God. Woman's relationship to her Heavenly Father, and her mode of access to His heart, are the same as man's.

Only from this point of view can we understand the way in which Jesus spoke of women and dealt with them. They hold quite as high a place in His thought and in the Kingdom of God as men do. A woman who does God's will is Christ's sister, just as a faithful man is His brother:

> For whosoever shall do the will of God, the same is my brother, and sister, and mother.[1]

The Jews had not fully grasped the truth of woman's spiritual dignity, and she never received among them the same place as man. The disciples were astonished to find Jesus talking at Jacob's well with a woman;[2] and He had to defend Mary for sitting at His feet hearing His word.[3] It was His deep consciousness that a woman's spiritual dignity is as great as a man's that roused Him to indignation against the injustice of Jewish divorce.[4]

It was because Jesus received women as children of God, infinitely dear to the Father, that they crowded round Him, listening to His words, and turning away from the evil of their past lives. Therefore did the poor unfortunate stand behind Him, weeping in an agony of repentance,[5] and Mary poured the costly spikenard on His head,[6] and the Syro-Phoenician mother had courage to plead for her daughter,[7]

[1] Mark 3, 35. [2] John 4, 27. [3] Luke 10, 38-42.
[4] Mark 10, 1-12. [5] Luke 7, 36-50. [6] Matt. 26, 6, 7.
[7] Matt. 15, 21-28.

and Joanna and the other women ministered to Him,[1] stood round His cross,[2] and were the first to see the empty tomb[3] and to hear the Easter message.[4]

To one holding this high estimate of woman monogamy is the only type of marriage possible. Woman, being as noble and as precious a creature as man, enters on marriage as a full personality, and on equal terms. Her husband is wholly her own, as she is wholly his. So, when Christ deals with marriage, He says,

> Have ye not read, that he who created them from the beginning made them male and female, and said, For this cause shall a man leave his father and mother, and shall cleave to his wife; and the twain shall become one flesh? So that they are no more twain, but one flesh.[5]

Clearly, there cannot be three or four in this unity. Manifestly, then, in the doctrine that woman is a child of God as truly as man, an immovable religious foundation is laid for monogamy. The loose ideas which leave a Hindu free to marry a second, or even a third, wife while his first wife lives are altogether inconsistent with the Fatherhood of God. Polygamy places woman on an altogether different plane from man, while, in fact, she is as truly of infinite value as he is.

This principle of woman's spiritual equality with man will be found to be the secret of health in other aspects of family life also. Since woman is as precious as man, a girl has the same right to education that her brother has; widows and widowers then stand absolutely on an equality; and, in considering the right age for marriage, as much care must be given to considerations of the welfare of the wife as of the husband. The realization of the true dignity of woman makes the Hindu rule, that a husband must not eat with his wife, seem very unworthy; and, if woman is as noble a creature as man, why should she be shut up in a zenāna, if a man

[1] Luke 8, 1–3. [2] Luke 23, 49; Mark 15, 40. [3] Mark 16, 1. [4] Mark 16, 6, 7. [5] Matt. 19, 4–6.

is allowed his liberty? The principle of spiritual equality also demands that there shall be something like equality between a wife and her husband in age, in education, in culture, so that they may be fit companions for each other, that they may join harmoniously in bearing the strain of family life and may be equally ready to influence the children for good. This lofty principle thus raises a wife to her true place beside her husband, and releases the incalculable riches which lie hid in the heart, the will, and the intellect of woman, but can never be used so long as she is crushed down and refused the liberty which is her birthright.

2. The truth that every human being is a child of God, beloved and priceless, is as fruitful with regard to children. How very deeply Jesus felt the preciousness of a little child comes out clearly in the following words:

> Whoso shall receive one such little child in my name receiveth me: but whoso shall cause one of these little ones which believe on me to stumble, it is profitable for him that a great millstone should be hanged about his neck, and that he should be sunk in the depth of the sea.[1]

But to this pricelessness of the child Jesus adds another thought, that in their innocence and humility children are patterns to us of those who win the kingdom of heaven. These are the spiritual truths which lie behind the heart-moving scene:

> And they brought unto him little children, that he should touch them: and the disciples rebuked them. But when Jesus saw it, he was moved with indignation, and said unto them, Suffer the little children to come unto me; forbid them not: for of such is the kingdom of God. Verily I say unto you, Whosoever shall not receive the kingdom of God as a little child, he shall in no wise enter therein. And he took them in his arms, and blessed them, laying his hands upon them.[2]

Was it any wonder that the children loved Him?—He rode into Jerusalem, meek and lowly, upon an ass, cleansed the Temple of its profaning buyers and sellers; and there, in His

[1] Matt. 18, 5, 6. [2] Mark 10, 13-16.

Father's house, while He healed the blind and the lame, the little ones stood round Him singing,

> Hosanna to the Son of David.[1]

Thus, if we accept the divine Fatherhood, it is impossible to make an invidious distinction between boys and girls. Both must receive the very best training their parents can give them, secular, moral, and religious, in order that they may grow up to be worthy sons and daughters of God. The most serious responsibility lies on the father and the mother to train their children in the knowledge and the love of God, their Father.

The doctrine of the divine Fatherhood makes human fatherhood doubly sacred and worthy of honour. A true son cannot but love and venerate his father and mother all his life; and if at any time, whether through sorrow, sickness, or poverty, they require to be helped, it will be his greatest joy to come to their aid. Christ laid great emphasis on this duty and privilege.[2]

Necessarily, Christ's principle leads to the duty of complete obedience to parents on the part of children. He quoted with weighty emphasis the law,

> Honour thy father and thy mother.[3]

But, when children grow up and become men and women, then wise parents will no longer lay commands upon their sons and daughters, nor expect implicit obedience from them; for the grown-up child bears the same relation to God that his father does, and is as responsible to God for his actions. In almost every instance, it is true, the son would have no hesitation in obeying his father; but it is the father's duty to seek to develop his son's independence rather than to attempt to keep him in a state of pupilage; so that he ought not to exact obedience. There is then a further possibility which must not be lost sight of: the father may order the son to do

[1] Matt. 21, 15. [2] Mark 7, 9-13. [3] Matt. 15, 4.

something morally wrong, or may forbid him to do something which the son believes he ought to do. There is the case of the criminal tribes referred to above.[1] Christ, by both example and precept, taught that in these circumstances it is the son's duty to disobey. When His own mother sought to restrain Him from His work, He gently refused to be driven from His life-task:

> And when his friends heard it, they went out to lay hold on him: for they said, He is beside himself. . . . And there come his mother and his brethren; and, standing without, they sent unto him, calling him. And a multitude was sitting about him; and they say unto him, Behold, thy mother and thy brethren without seek for thee. And he answereth them, and saith, Who is my mother and my brethren? And looking round on them which sat round about him, he saith, Behold, my mother and my brethren! For whosoever shall do the will of God, the same is my brother, and sister, and mother.[2]

A young man, whom Christ had urged to follow Him, stated, seemingly, that his father was opposed to his doing so, but that he would certainly obey after his father's death. Jesus told him that it was his duty to obey at once:

> And he said unto another, Follow me. But he said, Lord, suffer me first to go and bury my father. But he said unto him, Leave the dead to bury their own dead; but go thou and publish abroad the kingdom of God.[3]

B. Jesus taught very distinctly that the children of God are free. The clearest piece of teaching occurs with reference to the payment of a religious tax:

> And when they were come to Capernaum, they that received the half-shekel came to Peter, and said, Doth not your master pay the half-shekel? He saith, Yea. And when he came into the house, Jesus spake first to him, saying, What thinkest thou, Simon? the kings of the earth, from whom do they receive toll or tribute? from their sons, or from strangers? And when he said, From strangers, Jesus said unto him, Therefore the sons are free.[4]

[1] p. 88. [2] Mark 3, 21, 31–35. [3] Luke 9, 59, 60. [4] Matt. 17, 24–26.

But the principle holds good throughout. The only ultimate authority in the life of children of God is their Heavenly Father. No one has any right to bind them. Men and women must therefore be left free to marry or to abstain from marriage, as they think best. It is clear that most people are better married; but some are better unmarried. The Christian principle does not command a widow to marry a second time; far from it; but it does leave her free to consider her own duty in the light of God's truth in this matter. No man has any right to forbid her to marry, if she wishes to do so. The children of God must be left free.

C. Jesus teaches us that marriage is a divine institution in which a man and a woman are united to each other more closely than they are to their own parents. We quote once more His words:

> He who created them from the beginning made them male and female, and said, For this cause shall a man leave his father and mother, and shall cleave to his wife; and the twain shall become one flesh.[1]

His conduct fully corresponds with His words. Invited to a wedding, He graced the occasion with His presence, and shared in its joy.[2] At another time He vindicated most forcibly the sacredness of the marriage bond;[3] and immediately thereafter took little children in His arms and blessed them, at the request of their mothers.[4]

1. Thus, to Christ, marriage is a most sacred thing, devised by God for our human help. Married life is in itself a perfectly pure relationship. The fact that it is necessary for the continuance of the human family ought to be sufficient to convince us that it is in accordance with God's will. It is the abuse of the sexual relationship which has filled the minds of multitudes of good men with suspicions of married life. Men and women have abused marriage to such an extent that multitudes have come to look upon it as merely a means

[1] Matt. 19, 4, 5. [2] John 2, 1–11. [3] Mark 10, 2–12. [4] Mark 10, 13–16.

for the gratification of passion. When so regarded, marriage is certainly degrading, irreligious, altogether unfit for the spiritual man. But when husband and wife enter upon it in the right spirit, and live together in prayerfulness and love of God, marriage is holy, and the family becomes a fountain of the purest joys and the most spiritual training for parents as well as for children.

2. Since marriage has these high ends in view, clearly a man and a woman ought not to marry, unless they are truly suited for each other, physically, mentally, and spiritually. Personal fitness is the one test which ought to be used in the selection of a woman for one's wife, or of a man for one's husband. But under that head how many things come! For the same reason child-marriage ought not to be tolerated. A child is not prepared for married life at all: body, mind, and heart are still immature, unready for the high tasks of marriage. On the other hand, no age can be fixed on as the right age of marriage for all. Some ripen much earlier than others; some need its help much earlier than others; some had better not marry at all. In thinking of these questions we ought not to neglect the guidance afforded by the experience of the human race, and of all that science teaches us as to the development of the human body and the time when men and women may most prudently mate.

3. This high conviction that marriage is a divine institution necessarily leads to that law which Christ expresses so clearly, that marriage should be dissolved only by death. Christ's words are:

> What God hath joined let not man sunder.[1]

Here, as elsewhere, He tells us our religious duty, but does not give us detailed legislation. No definite law of divorce can be drawn from the teaching of Jesus. What He does is to teach every husband and every wife to be absolutely faithful until parted by death.

[1] Matt. 19, 6.

4. The same principle gives us the Christian point of view, that there must be no sexual indulgence of any kind outside marriage. Every sexual act outside the marriage bond is a sin against our high dignity as children of God, and is a deadly enemy to the spiritual life.[1] Complete chastity is demanded of every unmarried person, precisely as complete truthfulness and justice are demanded. The rule proves its own rectitude by its splendid simplicity. Here we have no meritorious vow of chastity undertaken for a limited period, but an absolute law which knows no exception.

Modern inquiries have shown how natural and how healthy complete chastity is for the young. No young man or young woman, if properly trained, ought to find any serious difficulty in maintaining perfect chastity. There is no physiological reason for uncleanness. Nature and health both woo the young to purity. It is not natural but perverted instincts that lead us astray. We may go farther. Both biology and psychology prove the very great importance of the period of adolescence in our lives. The growth of the aesthetic faculty, the natural expansion of the emotions, the healthy advance of the intellect, and the spontaneous ripening of religious aspiration and feeling, all depend in a very large degree upon a healthy youth. The most precious fruits of this golden time cannot be gathered, unless chastity be preserved. The nobler aspects of manhood and womanhood arise largely as the result of the restraining of the sexual and emotional nature in the years immediately after puberty.[2] This is one of the great laws which the ancient Hindus were ignorant of. If they had known it, they would have never laid down the law that a girl ought to be married before puberty.

D. Marriage is a thing of this life only. There is no marriage in heaven. Christ's words are:

> Ye do err, not knowing the scriptures, nor the power of God. For

[1] Matt. 15, 19, 20.
[2] See Stanley Hall's *Adolescence*.

in the resurrection they neither marry, nor are given in marriage, but are as angels in heaven.[1]

Most religions have failed to conceive heaven in a truly spiritual way. They have thought of it, as the Red Indians did, as a repetition of this life, only with the sorrows of earth eliminated, and the company of the gods added. Such is the picture of heaven in the *Rigveda*; and such the idea remains throughout Hindu and Buddhist literature. In most countries a man is believed to rejoin his wife in heaven, it being impossible to imagine heaven as like this earth without the inclusion of marriage. The gods themselves marry and beget children.[2] In some religions, as for example Islam, sexual enjoyment is made one of the chief attractions of heaven. It is surely unnecessary to point out at this date that all such ideas of heaven make it impossible for any thinking man to believe in such a thing. The life of heaven is spiritual, or there is no such life at all. Christ made no such mistake. He knew too well how different the spiritual world is from this natural world; so He told men frankly that there is no marriage in heaven.

Since this is so, the reason given for not allowing Hindu widows to marry falls to the ground. Whether a man or a woman ought to marry a second time or not, must be settled in accordance with personal character and circumstances. In many cases a second marriage is best. In others perpetual widowhood is the only right thing to look forward to. The Hindu wife refuses to think of a second marriage, in order that she may have her own place beside her lord in heaven. The realization of the deep difference between this earth and the spiritual world makes such an idea incongruous. We shall know and love each other in heaven, but the old physical relationships will no longer obtain. Like all the best things of earth, married love will be raised to something better in heaven.

[1] Matt. 22, 29, 30. [2] See below, pp. 297–298.

E. Every one will realize what a strong religious foundation for family life this is which Christ lays down. The chief stone is the Fatherhood of God, which gives us the great truths of the priceless value and peerless dignity of every human soul, the spiritual equality of man and woman, and the essential freedom of every child of God. The second stone is this, that marriage is in accordance with the will of our Father, and therefore a sacred thing, a perfectly pure relationship, the only relationship in which sexual relations are moral, a bond dissoluble only by death. The third foundation stone is the truth that marriage is a thing of this world only, that there is no marriage in the spiritual world.

It will also be plain how perfectly these principles of Christ are fitted to form the religious foundation of the family which the Hindu reformers are seeking to build. The Fatherhood of God takes the place of the old-world belief that the 'fathers' guard the family, and creates the religion of the family; the spiritual equality of man and woman as children of the Father is precisely the law wanted to justify the four reforms, viz. a later marriage age for girls, education for girls, the possibility of remarriage for widows, and full monogamy for all; and the inviolable sacredness of the marriage union, which arises from its origin in God, gives family life that religious sanctity without which it cannot hold the heart and bind the conscience.

If these powerful truths were taught to the Hindu people, they would form such a basis of reliable conviction in their minds that it would soon become possible to begin introducing the much-desired reforms in a gradual way. There would then be no wounding of consciences and no serious dislocation of society. While women and girls would gradually be given greater freedom, independence, and knowledge, these new and somewhat dangerous gifts would be preceded, accompanied, and surrounded by the powerful religious truths of their personal relation and complete responsibility to their heavenly Father for every privilege, and their most weighty obligations to father, mother, sister, brother, husband, child, and every other relative.

The policy at present pursued by the party of reform is fraught with most serious danger on two sides. That policy is, Introduce the reforms as rapidly as possible, but let Hindu teaching and practice go on unchanged. On the one hand, then, children and young people are to grow up under the influence of the funeral and śrāddha ceremonies, the family sacraments, the various observances of home and temple worship, the ancient mythology and the teaching of gurus, priests, and the women of the family. It will be necessary to explain the ceremonies to them; so that in their most impressionable years their minds will be filled with belief in the value of the piṇḍa to the souls of their dead relatives, while the gods mentioned in the ritual of the sacraments will necessarily seem to them to have power over family life. They will be taught that all women are of sinful birth, i.e. that they are born as women because of sin in a former life, that parents are guilty of serious sin, unless they marry their daughters before puberty, and that a widow has an impure heart and sinful desires if she ever dream of a second marriage. Are these healthy influences for young people living in a reformed family?

On the other hand, they will be placed in the enjoyment of new liberties and in relationships not contemplated in the Hindu system; and yet no fresh religious obligations will have been created in their minds to prevent liberty from becoming licence, and to guide them in the unfamiliar circumstances of their new life. How many unsympathetic sons and revolted daughters-in-law will this policy necessarily breed, how many foolish actions and how many uncontrolled minds! Who can believe that such a policy is healthy?

V. But the most wonderful thing remains yet to be noted. The leaven of Christ, entering into the moral and intellectual life of India, has made the old beliefs on which the family is founded altogether incredible, and has roused the leaders of the Hindu people to an earnest campaign for the evolution of a new and stronger family; so that at first sight Christ seems to be antagonistic to Hindu thought and Hindu institutions. Yet, when we examine the master-lines of the family which He bids us build, we find, to our astonishment, that in it all the noblest ideals of the Hindu family reappear, but in completed form, while all that is unworthy and unhealthy has passed away. Christ thus crowns the Hindu family with a structure which is new, yet is in no sense alien, but is the natural consummation of the older and less perfect system. The following points are of the utmost interest:

(*a*) The sacred character which invests every aspect of Hindu family life is deepened by Christ; for He taught, not only that marriage and the family are institutions framed by the hand of God, but that God is the Father of all men, so that every human family is a miniature reflex of the family of God, and every home is meant to be a picture and a foretaste of heaven. Jesus revealed the heart of our Father towards the family when He took the little children in His arms and blessed them.

(*b*) Monogamy, which has always been the law for Hindu women, is the Christian law for men as well as women.

(*c*) The high ideal of loyalty and chastity which is set before the Hindu wife is demanded in Christianity of the husband as well as the wife.

(*d*) The lofty dignity of the Hindu husband and father is confirmed by Christ, but is conferred upon the wife and mother as well.

(*e*) Christ bids us treasure both sons and daughters as Hindu parents have been accustomed to treasure sons.

(*f*) In ancient India, education, religious and general, was the right of every boy of the twice-born castes: in Christianity, it is the right of every boy and every girl of whatever race or social position.

(*g*) The chastity which was so wisely demanded of the Hindu adolescent while a student is laid upon all adolescents without exception by Christian principle. The Christian law is that every unmarried person must observe complete chastity; and that, taken along with the Christian rule that only adults must marry, lays chastity upon every adolescent.

Thus the present weakness and unhealthiness of the Hindu family find their one remedy in the principles of Christ. The divine truths concerning man and woman which He revealed are needed to raise its best customs to their height, to universalize its highest laws, and to correct its glaring abuses. Christ will transfigure the Hindu family to glory.

CHAPTER III

THE ETERNAL MORAL ORDER

WE have seen what the religious system of the Aryans was when they entered India. Centuries later, when they were engaged in the imperial work of bringing all the peoples of North India under their political and intellectual domination, the great doctrine of karma and rebirth took shape. On the surface it appears to be essentially a doctrine of life and death; but we shall not be able to understand it unless we see that it is at bottom a theory of morality. The time was a period of serious reflection. It gave birth to the reasoned doctrine of the existence of the one unknowable God behind all the gods as well as the belief in transmigration.

I. We can see only in part what the origin of the doctrine was. The *outer* elements of the situation are not very clear. We can see that the time was the period of Aryan expansion over North India; and it seems certain that it was in the great intellectual activity provoked by the intercourse of the living Aryan mind with the many varied peoples of North India that the great theory was formed; but the few scraps of evidence which the literature affords us are not nearly sufficient to show how the conceptions were built up nor whence the various elements came. In the Brāhmaṇas we meet several fresh ideas on questions of eschatology. The old firm faith in a happy immortality spent with the gods and the 'fathers' has begun to give place to chilling fears about its being possible to die over and over again in the other world; and hell has become a more serious reality; but there is no hint of rebirth in this world, and there is no doctrine of karma.

It is certain that, among the many animistic tribes the invaders met on the broad plains of the North, there must have been some who held the common primitive belief that the souls of men may become incarnate in animals. There were probably totemistic clans who believed that at death a man became, like his totem, a tiger, an ox, a frog, or a snake. Whether the transmigration idea came from this source or not, it is impossible to say. But, even if the idea that human souls might undergo animal births came from the aborigines, that is but one element in the complex doctrine. That which gave the belief its power over the intellect, and also its value for the moral life, was the connexion of this fairy-tale idea with the powerful ethical conception of retribution; and we may be certain that that was the work of the Aryan mind. This seems to follow from the fact, which stands out clear in the literature where the doctrine first appears (viz. the earliest Upanishads), that it was among the cultured Aryans that the doctrine was first believed and taught. Educated men accepted it first; and it was then brought to the common people by the Brāhmans in the course of centuries of instruction. Even apart from this piece of evidence, one would be inclined to suspect that the idea of transmigration was borrowed from some primitive source, but that the conception of karma was thought out by the Aryans; for, while transmigration has been believed in many lands, the Hindu doctrine of karma is unique.[1]

The *inner* elements that went to the creation of the belief may be partly made out, but even they are far from clear. The fundamental thought clearly is the common human conviction that the heart of the world is just, that our lives are subject to moral law, and that both good and evil actions will receive a perfectly just recompense. The form which this conviction takes in the doctrine is that all the good and all the evil actions done in one life will be recompensed with an equivalent amount of happiness or misery in a later

[1] See Berriedale Keith's convincing paper, *J. R. A. S.*, 1909, p. 569.

life; but how the Indo-Aryans reached this particular combination of ideas, we do not know. It is easy to conjecture that the original form of the belief was that each man receives *in this life* the exactly measured recompense of his good and bad deeds in happiness and misery. There are a few incidents in the literature which would fit well into the conjecture. For example, when Daśaratha is compelled to drive his beloved son Rāma into exile, he recalls in his misery that, while out hunting as a young man, he rashly shot an arrow and thereby killed a young lad, the only son of hermit parents; and he concludes that the loss of his own son is the punishment for that rash act.[1] Here we have a sinful act punished in the same life in which it was done. This theory, that a man's health and fortune in this life are the recompense of his deeds, has been held by many other early peoples, notably by early Israel. But facts are too stubborn for such a theory: clearly it is not true. The stage in Israel's history when the old belief became incredible comes vividly before us in the Book of Job. We may conjecture that at the time when the transmigration theory came to the notice of the Indo-Aryans. they had by experience found the theory of material recompense in this life untenable, and that they seized on the idea of transmigration as a means of solving the problem. But all this is but conjecture. We know only that in the *Bṛihadāraṇyaka* and *Chhāndogya Upanishads* a few of the more advanced men teach, as a new and precious truth, the doctrine that as a man sows in this life he will reap in another.

From these passages it seems clear that the doctrine was first thought out and stated with reference to the future, and that it was some little time before reflection led to the further thought, that a man's present circumstances and experience are the recompense of his behaviour in past lives. Then this train of thought, carried farther both backward and forward,

[1] *Rāmāyaṇa*, II. lxiii.

would inevitably lead to the conclusion that the series of lives can have neither beginning nor end.

A definition of terms may be useful at this point:

The doctrine of *transmigration* is that souls are emanations of the divine spirit, sparks from the central fire, drops from the ocean of divinity; that each soul is incarnated in a body times without number; that the same soul may be in one life a god, in another a man, in a third an animal, or even a plant, and that the series of births and deaths goes on in a never-ending cycle, the soul finding no rest nor relief from suffering, unless it finds some means of release from the necessity of rebirth and returns to the divine source whence it came.

The word *karma* means literally action, but in the doctrine means the inevitable working out of action in new life. The idea is that a man's body, character, capacities, and temperament, his birth, wealth, and station, and the whole of his experience in life, whether of happiness or of sorrow, together form the just recompense for his deeds, good and bad, done in earlier existences. Every act necessarily works itself out in retribution in another birth. The expiation works itself out not only in the man's passive experience (*bhoktṛitvam*) but in his actions also (*kartṛitvam*). Then these new actions form new *karma*, which must necessarily be expiated in another existence; so that, as fast as the clock of retribution runs down, it winds itself up again, as Deussen remarks. The soul is also affected by its own acts. Every good action ennobles it in some degree and helps to loosen the grip of the sense-world, while every bad action degrades it and gives the world a greater hold; so that the man who persists in right action makes steady progress towards perfection, while continued vice plunges the soul in corruption ever deeper. No man reaches complete soul-health until he has spent many lives in strenuous well-doing.[1]

[1] The concept of inaction is not dealt with here: it arose only when men began seriously to seek immediate emancipation. It is dealt with below, p. 138.

In ancient times, as now, the transmigration theory was held in high honour because of the explanation which it gives of the appalling differences in human life. Is a man born blind, or deaf, or deformed? It is the result of *karma*. Does a man rise to imperial power and boundless riches? It is the result of *karma*. Every variation in natural capacity, in physical strength, in hereditary character, in social position, in wealth, in good fortune, is put down as the scrupulously measured requital of previous deeds. We thus get a seemingly satisfactory explanation of the extreme differences in the lot of men. Is God partial, that He should make one man a philosopher, a king, or a millionaire, another an idiot, a monster, or a sickly weakling? This thought more than any other accounts for the popularity of the doctrine.

To the Western man the theory is more noteworthy because of the wide sweep of its moral conceptions, the belief that every happening in the world is the outcome of some ethical act, and the idea that the perfecting of a soul is the work of many myriads of years and of uncounted lives. So hard a thing does the upward struggle seem to Hindu thought. Certainly the doctrine does not belittle the place of morals in human life, nor the difficulty of overcoming the world.

When reflection had made some progress, men began to regard these many lives as most undesirable, and to long for emancipation from the necessity of rebirth. When this unexpected change occurred, men began to deplore their own good deeds, because they led to rebirth as surely as their evil deeds; so, that which originally was the highest possible reward became hated.

II. To the careful student the most interesting aspect of this doctrine is the altogether immeasurable influence it has exercised on both the beliefs and the practices of Hinduism. It is not only the theory of the life of the soul, and the standing rule for the elucidation of every calamity, but is the explanation of all the phenomena of the natural world, the justification ot the caste system, and the reason why men obey the laws of caste, the family and religion. Above all, it was the source of the pessimism of India; and that, in turn, created the whole philosophic movement. We shall probably understand its bearing on the religion best if we consider it in connexion with the world, souls, and God.

A. *The world* is the realm of karma. The unending procession of unnumbered souls constantly passing through birth and death as plants, animals, men, demons or gods, is held to be not only the explanation of human sorrow, joy, and character, but of all that happens in the material world. Everything that is visible is the outworking of the action of the whole vast assembly of invisible souls. Karma is the law of the phenomenal world. Several results necessarily arise:

1. As every occurrence in the world is the effect of foregoing action, and as every action is followed by its retributive expression, it is clear that the process can have had no beginning and will have no end. *Saṁsāra*, as the process is called, is eternal. Hence the world is eternal, a constant concomitant of God. Human life, it is believed, with all its sorrow and sin, will go on for ever. Other elements of the system fit well into this idea. As karma is the moral system, it is necessarily conceived as eternal. As in each life a man's character and condition are the outcome of previous action, while his actions will inevitably lead to new life, the process can have had no beginning and will have no end. The soul is thus eternal, as eternal as God.

2. The world, though eternal, is completely dominated by karma. It is thus in every aspect transitory, and ever filled with birth and death, sorrow and suffering. Every soul in the universe is in bonds, chained by karma to birth and death, to pleasure and pain.

3. The process of retribution is so exhausting and the action of souls so disturbing that the world steadily degenerates. The age of full virtue (*kṛita yuga*) inevitably passes into the age of three-fourths of good (*tretā yuga*), that into the half-and-half time (*dvāpara yuga*), and that into the

age when only one-fourth of good survives (*kali yuga*). Thus, decline is the only possibility in worldly affairs. Progress is for ever impossible. We are now in the last evil age, hastening on to hopeless depravity.

4. The Hindu belief in the periodic dissolution and re-formation of the world is a reflection of the doctrine of the transmigration of the soul. The idea is that the whole phenomenal universe, after having degenerated through the four ages, passes into a formless, invisible, elemental state; souls leave their bodies; and elemental matter and souls repose in peace until the moment comes for a new manifestation. Then matter begins once more to evolve; inorganic things, plants, animals, men, demons, and gods come into being; the process of transmigration begins precisely where it left off; the castes are re-formed; the ṛishis see the Vedas; and the world comes to be as it was before. The period between formation and dissolution is called a *kalpa*, the period of repose a *pralaya*. Thus, the Hindu conception of the course of the world is an endless series of alternating periods of activity and rest. These changes result in neither progress nor decline; for the world is always the same at the beginning of each period of activity. Self-repetition is thus the characteristic of the process and not evolution. The one end of the whole process is retribution: there is no world-purpose to be worked out.

5. We turn next to caste. The Hindu believes that his caste is determined by his past life. Each man is born into that caste for which his former actions have prepared him.[1] If his former lives have been exceedingly good, so that he has become a truly spiritual soul, he is born a Brāhman.[2] If he is a step lower in spirituality, he is born a Kshatriya,[2] and so on. It is this that distinguishes the Hindu social order from every similar system that has existed in the world: a man's position in the social scale is held to be a clear index of the state of his soul.

[1] *Chhāndogya U.*, v. 10, 7. [2] See p. 163.

Thus, each Hindu is believed to bring with him into the world a certain accumulated store of spirituality which is the sole reason for his having been born into the caste to which he belongs. His caste-standing in future lives will then depend upon his behaviour during his present life. The caste into which he has been born is believed to form the one situation in which his soul can make true progress. Hence, he cannot form good karma unless he live as a loyal member of his caste, keeping all the traditional rules with complete faithfulness and fulfilling all his other obligations as a good Hindu.[1] These are in the main his family duties and his duties to the gods. A fuller account of all that is binding on Hindus will be given in Chapter V.[2] Here it is of importance simply to note that the doctrine of rebirth and karma reinforced the old religious sanctions of these duties by teaching that neglect of any duty ordained in Scripture would ripen to calamity and misery afterwards.

6. As all of joy or sorrow that happens to a man is the outcome of his karma, every calamity is set down as the direct result of some evil action in a former life. Thus when, through the machinations of Kaikeyī, Rāma, the eldest son of Daśaratha, king of Ayodhyā, is driven into exile, he thinks of his mother Kauśalyā's grief and says:

> Sure in some antenatal time
> Were children by Kauśalyā's crime
> Torn from their mother's arms away;
> And hence she mourns this evil day.[3]

In ordinary Hindu society, when a man dies, his widow is told that, if she had not sinned in a former life, he would not have died. Nay, the dogma goes farther still: the calamity of being born a woman is the punishment of sin.[4]

The same doctrine of calamity is used to explain the degraded and downtrodden position of the Outcaste tribes:[5] a man who lives a foul life, according to all Hindu authorities,

[1] *Gītā*, xviii. 45. [2] pp. 217-218. [3] Griffith, II. liii.
[4] See above, p. 91. [5] See p. 162.

is born a dog, a hog, or a Chandāla,[1] i.e. an Outcaste. The birth of other men as foreigners is explained on the same lines.[2] Consequently, Hindu compassion was not drawn out towards these wretched people living in their midst. They were the criminals of the universe undergoing a life-term of punishment. Who would waste pity on them? One might as well pity the soul that is born a worm or a beetle!

But the belief went still farther. Since the sufferings of these people were the justly measured requital of their past sins, no power on earth could save them from any part of their misery. Their karma was working itself out and would inevitably do so. Thus, Hindus not only shared the common conviction of the ancient world, that degraded tribes were like animals and could not be civilized. Their highest moral doctrine taught them that it was useless to attempt to help them in the slightest; for nothing could prevent their karma from bringing upon them their full tale of misery. Here is a very illuminating incident:

> Let me record another instance—It occurred at Madras during one of my visits there. One morning, as I was engaged in my studies in my lodgings, news was brought me that a remarkable Hindu widow had come with a peculiar mission to the house of a friend of mine. I went to the place to meet her. When there I found a young woman, a widow and an ascetic, majestically seated like a devotee and singing a Tamil song. They told me it was a psalm in praise of her deity. As she was singing with her hand on her little stringed instrument, big tear-drops were trickling down her cheeks. The psalm over, I began conversation with her through an interpreter. Her whole history was this—she belonged to a respectable middle-class family; after her widowhood she took the vow of attaching herself as a maid-servant to the Temple of Tirupati. She was still attached to that temple, and on that occasion had come to Madras to collect funds to give a new set of jewellery to her god. My mind at that time was being seriously exercised by the case of a number of famine orphans whom I had met in the streets. I opened to her the proposal of starting a shelter and an orphanage for these children, and asked her if she could be a mother to them. My proposal fell flat upon her mind. She did not look upon

[1] *Chhāndogya Upanishad*, v. 10, 7.

[2] See p. 164.

it as a religious act. As far as I remember, she observed, 'What have I to do with these children who have lost caste by taking food at the hands of all castes? they are suffering the consequences of their acts in a previous state of existence; who can help them? That is no business of mine.'[1]

It is most necessary to observe that, not in connexion with the Outcaste only, but in every other relationship, the theory of karma, through representing every weakness, defect, and calamity as punishment and as inevitable, checked seriously the natural flow of common human kindliness and put grave obstacles in the way of the rise of philanthropy. Beneficence could only act in spite of the law of karma.[2]

7. Since the world is the realm of karma and the gods are under its sway as fully as man, and since Brahman[3] is in no way connected with karma, the system is not under the control of any divine being, but is self-acting.

B. *Souls.* All souls are eternal, as we have seen.[4] Whether they be in gods, demons, men, animals, or plants, souls are under karma in consequence of their former deeds, good and bad; but there is this distinction between them and the phenomenal world, that for souls escape from karma is possible. In order to gain emancipation it is necessary for the soul to toil onward and upward through many lives. No forgiveness of the slightest fault is possible. Everything must

[1] Sastri, *Mission of the Brahmo Somaj*, 56-57.

[2] It is most instructive to note the teaching of the modern Hindu on this important point. In the *Manual of Religion and Ethics* published in connexion with the Central Hindu College, Benares, the difficulty is acknowledged, and the answer is made that, if I see a man in need of help, I ought to do all I can for him, even though I know my efforts are useless; for, if I make the attempt, I shall form good karma for myself, while if I abstain, I shall form evil karma. Clearly there is a serious confusion of moral ideas involved in such an utterance. If it is useless to help the degraded man, how can any one believe that to make a vain effort to help him can form good karma, if the world be wise and moral at core? The truth is that the idea that helping the needy is a good action comes from an akarmic atmosphere. Further, if my action brings my brother no real help, philanthropy is deprived of its only justification. It is no longer philanthropy but self-love which is the motive of what I do.

[3] See below, pp. 219-222.

[4] p. 139, above.

be expiated. It is only by living good lives that any progress can be achieved. Then, when through much good karma the soul is born as a man in a good Hindu family, if he is willing to renounce the world altogether and to live a life of inaction as a monk, he may achieve emancipation.

Transmigration cuts clean athwart the old faith in a happy immortality spent in heaven in the company of the 'fathers', Yama, and the gods. When reflection was turned to the point, the belief arose that souls spent the interval between two lives in heaven or in hell according to desert. So heaven and hell became places of temporary sojourn.

C. *Brahman.*[1] The unknowable One, the Source of the universe, is conceived as absolutely free from karma and rebirth. He is constantly spoken of as unborn and as free. The contrast between him and the world in this matter is frequently emphasized. Hence, since all actions, whether good or bad, necessarily create karma, he is conceived as altogether inactive. Had he been thought of as engaging in any kind of action, he would inevitably have come under the dominion of karma. So he is said to be without any desire or purpose that could stir him to action. He is altogether at peace, altogether indifferent, altogether passionless. This great thought, that Brahman is actionless, has produced very deep results upon Hindu theology. It cut Brahman away from morality and from every form of worship; it made it impossible to conceive him as a purposeful Creator; and it strengthened the tendency to think of him as impersonal. We deal with those points at greater length below.[2]

These paragraphs show what a commanding position the doctrine of karma holds in Hinduism. There is no aspect of the life of the people that has not felt its influence. It is karma that has given Hinduism its peculiar flavour.

It will now be plain that this doctrine is essentially a moral theory. Rebirth is its most noticeable and most picturesque

[1] See below, pp. 219–222. [2] See pp. 228–232; 244–246; 392–407.

feature; but the real heart of the whole is the conviction that every action works itself out in retribution. This retribution has two aspects. The more prominent of these is the pleasure or pain which the man experiences as the fruit of his action. But besides that, according to the doctrine, every act produces its result upon the man himself, either helping him onward to perfection or degrading him. Then, since the Hindu is taught that, if he is to make good karma, he must fulfil every detail of the laws of his family, caste, and religion, as these are laid down in the Dharmaśāstras,[1] the doctrine includes within itself a moral standard as well as a theory of retribution and of soul-progress. The doctrine of karma and transmigration thus forms the basis of the Hindu doctrine of morality.

D. We have now to notice that which has proved in history to be one of the most important aspects of the influence of the doctrine, namely its tendency towards pessimism. We must beware lest we exaggerate this tendency, for every observer must realize that the Indian outlook on life is far from being consistently pessimistic. Yet there can be no doubt that a shadow of considerable extent does fall upon Hindu thought. Some have sought the source of this gloom in race, others in climate. What the ultimate cause may have been, no one knows; but there can be no doubt what the proximate cause was: the shadow was cast by the doctrine of transmigration and karma. We shall see in a future chapter that this was the stimulus that roused the Hindu mind to its greatest effort, the effort which produced the philosophies of India.

We may approach the Hindu tendency to pessimism from several distinct conceptions. Each of these we shall find was formed under the influence of karma. It seemed a sad thing to be eternally chained to that which is transitory and full of suffering. Since all the world is under the dominion of karma,

[1] *Gītā*, xvi. 24.

men could not but regard everything phenomenal as leading to rebirth, and therefore as evil. The fact, too, that there was no means of escaping from the retribution due for any single act, nor any way in which a man might rise above his destined karma, proved very galling. Then the fact that it was not controlled by any divine being but acted automatically would also chill the human heart. Men felt they were caught in the teeth of a machine which was unerringly moral but as rigidly godless. Is it any wonder that the doctrine cast a shadow on the Hindu spirit, that men began to feel shut up in prison and weighted with clanking chains?

We are, therefore, not surprised to find that the conception had little more than taken form when men began to seek a way of escape. The very earliest statements of the doctrine of transmigration occur in the Upanishads, the literature of release. So soon as thinking Hindus realized how heavy their chains were, they began to inquire how the human spirit could find emancipation. This effort to win release can be traced in several distinct stages.

1. There is first the philosophical period, when the method by which all men sought release was knowledge and monastic renunciation, *vidyā* and *sannyāsa*.[1] Each leader declared he had found the one right way to emancipation, the necessary knowledge and the effective discipline. Philosophy was thus rather a practical science than anything else; though, dealing as it did with the constitution of the universe, it rose in certain systems to metaphysical theories of great interest. The thought on which all worked was this, that if men could break the ties which bound their souls to the phenomenal world, they would escape from the sway of karma and hence from the necessity of rebirth. In each system the theory showed how escape was possible, and those things which the theory declared had to be given up were renounced in the ascetic life prescribed. Whatever else was demanded, action had to

[1] See below, pp. 253 ff.

be given up; otherwise the man would continue to create new chains for himself by making new karma. At this stage in the history the monk alone could win release.

2. In all the later stages release is offered to the layman. The life of monastic renunciation is recognized as helpful and meritorious, but it is unnecessary; emancipation may be won in the lay life. The earliest theory of release for the layman probably appeared shortly after the Christian era. The theory is seemingly a reflection of the Buddhist doctrine, that desire binds a man, and that when desire is destroyed the bonds of karma are broken. The Hindu form of the theory is that release can be won without ascetic renunciation, if a man will do all the duties prescribed for him in the Hindu system without motive, without desire for reward.[1]

3. Very soon this theory took a slightly different form under the influence of a theistic theology. Here faith begins to believe that the Supreme conceived as personal can release one from the bonds of karma in certain cases. The thought is expressed in two ways. The first is that, if a man does all his duties in the spirit of renunciation to Vishṇu, i.e. renouncing in devotion to God all desire of reward for them, then these actions will produce no karma and will have no power to bind him. The other form of expression is: If a man will serve God with devotion, God will release him from all sins.

4. In the Śivaite sect matters did not proceed quite so far along these lines. But in the Śivaite theology of South India we find the belief clearly stated that Śiva chooses carefully such embodiments for souls as shall lead them most rapidly towards the spirituality that is necessary for release. Here again theistic thought is on the way to transform the closed system of transmigration and karma.

These four distinct developments all took place among those who held the transmigration theory most seriously and most intelligently. We have now to notice that, although the

[1] For a fuller statement of this movement see below, p. 365.

doctrine early found acceptance among Hindus of all grades, and still holds almost universal sway in the community, yet in most circles its full implications have never been known nor acted on. The average Hindu accepts the doctrine as an explanation of caste, of the inequalities of the lot of men, and of striking calamities, but he has never realized that, when rightly understood, it deprives the gods of all power to bless or to curse him. He has continued to worship his gods as his ancestors did before the doctrine of transmigration arose, offering them gifts and sacrifices and praying to them, in order to obtain health, wealth, and children, forgiveness of sin, deliverance from calamity, and all else that the average man wants. On the other hand, the hermit, *vānaprastha*, continued the severe austerities which had become usual in the hermitages before transmigration arose, and expected by means of them to win supernatural powers and other gifts altogether outside the closed circle of his karma. These large deductions from the sway of karma in two distinct provinces of the religious life have softened the influence of the doctrine very greatly for the masses.

III. This sketch of the efforts of the Hindu spirit to escape from the sway of karma shows how hard it has been for Hindus throughout the centuries to accept the doctrine in its entirety. The human spirit could not but beat its wings against the bars of such an iron cage. But in our days things have gone much farther. Educated Hindus still think the doctrine a brilliant speculative solution of the problem of the inequalities of human experience, and they glory in it as one of the greatest principles ever thought out by the human mind; but fresh ideas and aspirations have laid hold of them with extraordinary power, so that their thoughts and activities are turned in altogether new directions; and the institutions and practices to which karma and transmigration gave form are being more and more neglected or transformed. The doctrine in its practical application to Hindu life is rapidly dying out.

The life of educated India to-day is dominated by the future, by the vision of the brilliant, happy India that is to rise as a result of the united toil and self-sacrifice of her sons. The people are to be rejuvenated, to become intelligent, capable, wise, and good; the resources of the country are to be used; political freedom is to be achieved; education will stir the mind of India to such universal activity and such successful work as it has never done before; and India, possessing a wise, cultured, religious people, will take its place among the strongest, most honoured, and most progressive peoples of the earth. Thus, there seems to be a good deal of deflexion from the ancient ideal which bids each man live as his father and grandfather lived, and maintain the ancient polity unchanged in all its parts; and also from the ancient belief that the course of the four ages is a continuous process of deterioration. How is the new national life to be worked out, if we are now well on in the Kali Yuga? Clearly the Western idea, that human life is capable of indefinite progress, has laid hold of the Hindu mind with great force.

The political side of the national movement is responsible for much progress. Politicians have begun to realize that until the inhabitants of India are much more homogeneous than they are now political liberty is impossible. This is the conviction that has led all our most prominent Indian political nationalists, even Surendranath Bannerjea himself, to say that no serious political progress is possible until the people have full social freedom. The meaning of this dictum is that the caste system must be given up before the people can secure political freedom. Take along with this recent movement the long-continued agitation on the part of the Social Reform leaders in favour of the abolition of caste distinctions. Who will measure the significance of such an attitude on the part of Hindus? As we have just seen, the transmigration theory runs that men are drafted into castes according to their karma. Whoever sincerely believes this will inevitably uphold the caste system to the utmost. To what limbo of forgetfulness, then, do our politicians and reformers now propose to banish the doctrine?

Comparatively few educated men have yet reached the position held by the leading politicians and reformers, that the caste system should be given up; but many are ready for relaxation of the rules with regard to marriage between sub-castes, and most take large liberties in the matter of food. These changes in ordinary practice and the demands of the whole body of reformers, even when taken together, do not prove that caste is on the verge of passing away; but they do show most conclusively that the old beliefs, that a man's caste springs from his karma, and that the keeping of every caste rule is necessary to secure good karma, are passing away.

Nor is that all. Representation on the councils of the Empire is allotted to Hindus and Muḥammedans largely in accordance with the census returns. Hence the question whether the fifty millions of the Outcastes are to be reckoned as Hindus or not is a large State question. In the past Hindus have usually refused to acknowledge them as Hindus at all, on the ground that neither their worship nor their culture is worthy of the name; but the new circumstances have led to a new policy. Hindu leaders now speak of them as brothers, and invite them to take their place in the work of the regeneration of India. Some have even proposed to bring them into the religious community. Every one will rejoice that more humane language is being used about them, even if practice is as yet little altered. But one question obtrudes itself: Where has the karma theory gone? How can the unclean, untouchable Outcaste be the Brāhman's brother?

Christian missions have done brilliant work among the Outcastes. Thousands have been won from dirt, degradation, low morals, and superstition to cleanliness, civilization, education, and a Christian life. When missionaries began the work, Hindus scoffed, suggesting they might as well waste their energies over the monkeys of the forest. But the impossible has been accomplished; the degraded have been uplifted to decency and spiritual religion; and the ancient belief, founded on the law of karma, that such men cannot be reclaimed, has been proved false. In consequence, members of the Brāhma, Prārthanā, and Ārya Samājes have begun to follow missionaries in the attempt to uplift these people. Even Hindus have been found here and there to set their hand to the work. Could stronger evidence of the collapse of the karma doctrine be given?

All Indians are now summoned to join in earnest self-sacrificing toil for the uplifting of India. There is no longer the old fear of action. Unselfish work and eager philanthropy are commended to the utmost. The educationalist, the economist, the capitalist who starts a large industrial business, the scientist who introduces a new manufacture or a new industry into India, are everywhere praised. The spirit of the transmigration theory, which leads the reflective man to abstain from good as much as from bad action, or to perform actions without desire for results, has been left far behind. The ancient pessimism is felt no more; for men's hearts are now set on India's future, and they constantly see golden visions.

We have already seen how great the changes are which are being introduced into the Hindu family, especially with regard to the position of women. The old idea of the inferiority of women is rapidly passing away. Here, too, the old conception of karma is yielding; for the transmigration theory is that women are born women because of sin in a former life.

There is, thus, abundant evidence to show that the doctrine of transmigration and karma is dying out, even if most Hindus do not realize what is going on. The new thought from the West is stirring the educated class and rousing them to action; and, in consequence, the old transmigration ideas are everywhere being ousted from their places.

Can we see the reason why this powerful ethical system, which in the beginning gave every part of Hinduism its characteristic colouring, and which has dominated Indian thought in every century, is now crumbling to decay? We shall realize in later chapters, as we deal with the various aspects of the religion, what the proximate cause of decay is in each case; but we can already see the main defect in the system, which makes it altogether unfit to bear the pressure of a new type of thought dominated by a far more vital moral faith. The fundamental weakness of the Indian moral theory is that it stands apart from God. All the old gods are subject to karma, and hence no one of them can be the Lord of the moral order; while Brahman is conceived as the direct antithesis of karma, as free from all bonds, separate from all action; so that he cannot be the ruler of the Hindu moral system. Hence two most serious consequences at once appear. The moral order of Hinduism, having no divine personality at its centre, is a mechanical, automatic system; and the supreme God of the religion is non-moral. This fatal divorce is the cause of much of the weakness which is showing itself in decay of the religion to-day.

One cannot but look back with keen regret to the figure of Varuṇa in the *Ṛigveda.* He is conceived as an altogether righteous god, and as being the source of *ṛita*, that is, of all moral and natural law. Here is one who is truly Lord of the moral order. From that most profound conception a noble theistic moral order might have been developed. But, alas! from causes which we do not understand, the righteous Varuṇa was displaced by the mighty warrior Indra and sank down to the position of the god of the waters. Hence, there was no god left in the Hindu pantheon fit to become Lord of the moral order of the universe.

CHAPTER IV

THE DIVINE SOCIAL ORDER

I. Primitive men in ancient times were usually organized in clans or tribes of varying size; and the same is true of savage peoples to-day. There were many forms of social life, but in the type of organization which was most common the members of each tribe usually believed themselves to be of one blood, called themselves brothers, and looked back to some mythical being, human or divine, as their ancestor. Every other tribe was believed to be of distinct origin. Most primitive peoples have believed the different communities of men to be as distinct from each other as species of animals. Indeed the members of each group are inclined to regard themselves as men, and the members of every other group as something less than human. Even advanced peoples have usually regarded themselves as essentially different from others. The Greeks thought of themselves as freemen by nature while all other races were made for slavery. Hence, it never occurred to primitive men that the various tribes could be united and live together.

The struggle for life was exceedingly hard. Perpetual hostility was regarded as the only possible condition of affairs between tribes. Hence, the members of the tribe had to be faithful to each other, if the tribe was to survive. There were so many enemies outside that those inside were compelled to draw very near together. To fight for each other and to avenge each other was the only way to safety. Blood-revenge was the first of duties.

There was thus in the circumstances very little intercourse

with men of other groups; and, indeed, tribal customs seemed to be formed with the very idea of keeping each tribe in isolation. Men of different groups seldom hunted together, and barter was seriously restricted. Even temporary alliances for help in war were not often formed. Men of different tribes seldom took a meal together. To eat together was regarded as a thing possible only for those of the same blood. Indeed a common meal somehow actually had the effect of mingling the blood; so that, while it was right and natural for brothers, it was dangerous in the case of others. Marriage also was usually restricted within certain limits of blood, and, in many tribes, was the subject of the most stringent regulations. On the other hand, there were many tribes which allowed marriage by capture, while some permitted no other form of marriage. In such cases the woman was supposed to be absorbed into the tribe of her husband. There were scarcely any moral relationships with men of other tribes: why should a man have any regard for his enemies?

Amid innumerable differences there is one characteristic which is universally present in primitive society: the social organization of every tribe has a religious basis, and each people regards its own society as sacred.

Apart from its religious foundation, there are three points which are peculiarly noticeable with regard to tribal society. First, each group is exceedingly narrow, and there is no thought of widening society, far less any conception of the unity of mankind. Secondly, social life at this stage is subject to innumerable restraints. People imagine early men to be in all things free; scientific research has shown that the truth is exactly the opposite: the primitive man is everywhere in chains. He is bound to go through a large number of recurrent ceremonies; many kinds of food are absolutely forbidden; his choice in marriage is narrowed by many rules; to look at certain people at certain special times, or to taste their food, is believed to bring death: to look at a newly born child, or its mother, is forbidden; to touch a dead body is pollution;

to touch certain common objects is believed to be most dangerous. Early society is thus barred and restricted at every turn. Thirdly, there is little that is moral in the social conceptions of these tribesmen. While the innumerable prohibitions of their social life are the source from which later morality was born, there are few of these regulations that are themselves moral in the modern sense; and there is scarcely a trace of any moral relations between tribes. Thus very small groups, innumerable restraints, and rudimentary morality, are the leading characteristics of early society.

II. With the progress of civilization this particularist tribal organization has usually been transcended in various ways.

The introduction of agriculture leads to a settled life and a growing desire for peace. Thus, unconsciously, the old hostility dies down between tribes settled near each other, and various forms of intercourse spring up without interfering with the ancient tribal organization. This prepares the way for new forms of social life and the creation of a larger unity.

Military conquerors by destroying, separating, transplanting, enslaving, have frequently broken up the old tribal organization and laid the foundations of a larger political and social life. The great kings of Babylon, Egypt, Assyria, and China produced vast changes by their conquests. In these cases we see many distinct groups welded together by military pressure into a single nation.

Greece shows us higher forms of life and a new basis of unity. The various Greek states, while retaining each its old exclusive social laws, were so conscious of the rich deep culture which distinguished Hellenes from other races, that they formed numerous federations, which helped them in their struggles with outsiders, and yet left each city-state free to follow its own genius in religion, politics, art, and social life. To this is largely due the vital individuality and fruitfulness of Sparta, Athens, Miletus, Thebes, Corinth, and other cities.

But these loose federations were not strong enough to resist military pressure, as the Greeks discovered to their cost when brought face to face with Philip of Macedon. It was the Romans who produced the one form of organization which, while allowing all the old groups, great and small, to retain their own peculiar religious and social observances and exclusiveness, yet drew from them sufficient strength to render them full protection within the mighty Empire and so gave the germs of culture the opportunity of sprouting and bearing fruit. The principle of the Empire was toleration of all racial and tribal idiosyncracies, whether religious or social, so long as they did not endanger the common peace and the common safety; and the Romans themselves were as exclusive in social life as any other group, until the decay of the old stock compelled them to draw in outsiders for the maintenance of the Empire.

This stage in the growth of human society shows a great advance upon the earlier stage. Men now live in far larger societies; the hostility between individual tribes has been very largely overcome. The progress made along this line is very remarkable and of very great value. Yet it is well worthy of remark that even in the highest of these organizations, namely the Greek federations and the Roman Empire, the ancient idea, that different groups of men are of distinct origin and must live separate lives, survives as strong as ever. Each group believes itself to be a holy people of pure blood, regards its religion as its own exclusive possession, and holds that marriage and social intercourse are sacred and must be kept inviolate: the touch of outsiders is pollution. The spirit extends even to other spheres. Amongst the Greeks and early Romans political privileges were still restricted to the blood of the sacred race; and even the chief privileges of business were denied to aliens. All this is true, in spite of the larger federation under which men lived. The sacred character of each form of society, while of incalculable value, obstructs rather seriously every movement and tendency towards progress.

Considerable advance is also visible in the matter of liberty.

The Greek and the Roman, while still restricted by old prejudices in matters of religion, marriage, social intercourse, and such like, and still bound by many a rule which we should consider irrational, had much more freedom than primitive people have.

Thirdly, ethical ideas have made very large progress. They now have a far wider scope within the racial group, and have begun to influence men very deeply outside their own particular clan. Yet even so, the Greek or Roman of ancient times, if driven out of his clan, felt that he was a ruined man, practically expelled from human life.

In the case of each of these ancient peoples, Babylonian, Egyptian, Chinese, Greek, Roman and what not, there was a deeply rooted conviction that the social organization of the people had been created by the gods, and was therefore sacred and to be reverently and faithfully maintained. The persecution of Christians by the Roman Government arose from the belief that Christianity was essentially hostile to the constitution of ancient society. To resist this new society-wrecking force was held to be a high religious duty.

III. The *Avesta* and the *Ṛigveda*, when read side by side, enable us to form a picture of the common life lived by the ancestors of the Persians and the Indo-Aryans while they were still a single people. They, like so many other ancient races, were roughly divided into three classes, nobles, priests, and common people. By the time when the hymns of the *Ṛigveda* were being composed these distinctions had become if possible deeper, but the divisions were even then but classes.

During the latter part of the period of the *Ṛigveda* the priests made notable advances. The hymns themselves are very clear proof of their intellectual progress; ritual and sacrifice were becoming more and more elaborate; and schools had been established for the training of young priests. In such circumstances the priesthood naturally tended to become hereditary. The sacerdotal skill and knowledge which a man had acquired were too precious to be handed on to any one other than a son. Here we have one of several forces which combined to produce caste.

Meanwhile the process of fighting and conquering the aborigines was producing its inevitable results. The differences between the tall, white Aryans, with their advancing civilization and noble religion, and the short, black aborigines, with their coarse habits and degrading superstitions, were so great that cultured Aryans could not fail to shrink from close contact with them: intermarriage was unthinkable, and even social intercourse was impossible. The colour line was very noticeable and became the basis of all future distinctions: *varṇa*, colour, is one of two Sanskrit words used to indicate distinctions of caste. We see the elements of a similar situation before our eyes to-day in the attitude of the average European to Indians, or still better in the complete social separation of negroes from whites in the southern half of the United States. There is always this tendency when, along with a marked difference in culture between two races, there is a sharp 'colour' distinction as well. Thus, as the conquest of North India proceeded, and the various aboriginal peoples came under Brāhman authority, there was only one method of organization possible, namely, to make the distinction between pure Aryans and aborigines absolute, and to allow the old tribal differences among the latter to remain. This, then, the upper class of the Aryan invaders did; but it is perfectly clear that the rank and file of the Aryan invaders must have intermarried freely with the aborigines: the ethnology of modern India makes that perfectly evident.

Before the canon of the *Ṛigveda* was finally closed, a hymn found its way into the collection which declares that the Brāhman, the Rājanya, the Vaiśya, and the Śūdra had each a separate origin in God. The Brāhmans, the Rājanyas or Kshatriyas, and the Vaiśyas are the three old classes, the priests, the nobles, and the people; and the Śūdras are conquered aborigines. These four are now declared to be absolutely distinct races, each a separate creation. The passage speaks of Purusha as the great sacrifice, and goes on:

> The Brāhman was his mouth; the Rājanya was made from his arms; the being called Vaiśya, he was his thighs; the Śūdra sprang from his feet. *Ṛigveda*, X. xc. 12.

This is not caste yet, but it shows that men's minds were tending in the direction of caste, and that the three classes were becoming more distinctly shut off from each other and from the aborigines. We have here the basis of caste, the religious sanction for it rather than the thing itself. Events clearly were moving in the direction of the formation of a rigid social system. Doubtless intermarriages were still common; but the flowing tide ran towards caste organization.

The ancient belief in the separate origin of distinct groups of men, and in the necessity of an exclusive life for the preservation of purity both of race and culture, was the actual source of the conception; the verse quoted above gave the necessary religious sanction; the splendid rise of the Brāhmans and the Kshatriyas through their swiftly-growing culture and immense capacity created the political and social situation; while the absolute banning of the aborigines in marriage and social intercourse, coupled with their reception into the enlarged Aryan community, which was now taking shape, provided an example of a group, completely isolated socially, while included in the wider union, which could not but react on the classes within the Aryan people itself.

But all this would give us only such endogamous religious groups as were found among a number of ancient peoples, while Hindu caste is a perfectly unique form of social organization. What made the difference was the doctrine of rebirth and karma, as we saw above.[1] According to this theory each man is born into that caste for which his former actions have prepared him. If he is far advanced in spirituality, he is born a Brāhman; if he is a step lower, he is born a Kshatriya; and so on. Thus in Hinduism a man's caste is held to be an infallible index of the state of his soul. It was this reasoned

[1] P. 140.

conviction that laid hold of the Hindu mind and made the observance of all caste rules a matter of conscience and also of deep personal interest. Only by living as a faithful member of his caste could a man retain the spirituality his soul had won. To marry a woman of low caste, to eat with a man of low caste, or to touch an Outcaste, was to contract gross spiritual pollution, the result of which would be not merely some social slight, or even excommunication from his caste-fellows, but frightful punishment in hell, and then all the misery of an animal or Outcaste existence in his next life. Men sincerely believed that the occupation assigned to the caste was the best discipline for the soul of the man born in the caste:

> According as each man devotes himself to his proper work does he obtain consummation. . . . Better one's own caste-duty ill done than another's caste-duty well done.[1]

By the close of the sixth century B.C., as we may see from the *Dharmasūtra* of Gautama, the caste system had arisen in all its essentials. The supremacy and the religious authority of the priests form the basis of all the legislation of the Hindu people as stated in this law-book. The three highest castes stand quite apart from all others as the holy people for whom the Brāhman may sacrifice and whom he may teach. The religious education which each Brāhman, Kshatriya, and Vaiśya boy receives is held to be a birth into a spiritual life; so that these castes are called 'twice-born'. They alone wear the sacred thread. The position and the duties of Śūdras are clearly defined; and even references to unclean Outcastes and *mlecchas* occur.

But though the system appears full-grown in Gautama and other early law-books, it is perfectly clear from the rest of the literature—Hindu, Buddhist, and Jain—that the laws were far from being fully observed in actual life. The authority and the supremacy of the Brāhmans were by no

[1] *Gītā*, xviii. 45, 47.

means universally acknowledged; for the Kshatriyas still contended with them in many parts of the country for the first place; marriages between people of different castes were still common; and progress towards the faithful observance of caste regulations was a slow process. The prodigious religious ferment of the seventh and following centuries B.C. must have endangered the Brāhman position very seriously; for all the philosophic and ascetic movements were, at the outset at least, more or less hostile not only to Brāhmanic sacrifices and ritual but also to the exclusive pretensions and demands of the Brāhmans. Yet the process went on. The stars in their courses fought in favour of Brāhmanism; the Hindu people steadily came more completely under Brāhmanic rules and regulations: the social life of North India gradually settled in a fixed shape.

Yet it was several centuries before caste law assumed the rigid form which it has to-day. The Christian era may be taken as a mean date. The process, in the circumstances, was a most natural one. It was not the work of a master organizer, but the slowly evolved product of the inner mind of the people. We may speak of the religio-social empire of Hinduism, but we must carefully realize that it was created by no emperor and that at no time has it had a centralized organization. The Brāhmans have had much to do with the working out of the system; but there is no hierarchy uniting all Brāhmans.

Each of the three highest castes recognized in the verse in the *Ṛigveda* gradually expanded into a group of castes. Two processes contributed to this result, differentiation and foisting. Groups of Brāhmans, Kshatriyas, or Vaiśyas, through migrations or through gradual changes in culture, education, custom, and wealth, got differentiated into sub-castes which did not intermarry; and groups of people belonging to lower castes or even to other races were foisted into these castes and obtained recognition. The aborigines were not all made into one caste and named Śūdras: they entered the fold as separate groups, each of which gradually developed into a caste.

It is also clear that large masses of aborigines were shut out from the Hindu community as being too unclean for intercourse. Some of these have lived in secluded places and have retained their ancient religion and social life; while others have lived near Hindus, and in imitation of them have become organized in caste-fashion. These are the Outcastes, the Untouchables, the Depressed Classes of to-day. We must, however, note that, according to all Hindu authorities, some at least of these Outcaste groups arose from mixed unions among caste Hindus.

These people form one of the largest problems of modern India. Though they have lived beside Hindus for more than two thousand years, so that they have absorbed the spirit of caste and certain rudimentary religious ideas from Hinduism; yet they have been treated with such inhumanity that they remain to this day in the most piteous poverty, dirt, degradation, and superstition. They are not allowed to live in the same village with Hindus. They must not approach a high-caste man; for their very shadow pollutes. In South India they must not come within thirty yards of a Brāhman; and they are usually denied the use of public wells, roads, bridges, and ferries. They are not allowed to enter Hindu temples. Their religion is in the main an attempt to pacify demons and evil spirits. They number some fifty millions.

There is no country in the world that is without its submerged class: under every known civilization there is at least a remnant who fall behind, who fail to grip the necessary conditions of the times, who tend to become human wreckage. But where outside India is there a polity devised with the determinate purpose of creating a huge submerged class, of crushing one-sixth of the whole people down in dirt and inhuman degradation?

Throughout all the centuries since the caste system reached its full form changes have occurred. Groups of low-caste men have occasionally been able to secure recognition as belonging to higher castes. During the early centuries of our era many foreign tribes entered Hinduism and became organized as castes. Their kings were called Kshatriyas, while the commons received lower recognition. Even now the process of caste formation has not ceased ; and the modification of caste rules is still possible in any of the castes. Most scholars believe that Muḥammadan influence stiffened caste practice. Yet, in the main, the system itself has remained unchanged for two thousand years.

IV. The many castes of modern Hinduism are thus supposed to fall into four, or, if we include the Outcastes, into five groups as under :

Name.	*Caste occupation.*	
A. Brāhmans :	priests	The three twice-born castes, supposed to be of pure Ayran blood, and called twice-born on account of their education. They alone wear the sacred thread.
B. Kshatriyas :	rulers and warriors	
C. Vaiśyas :	business men and farmers	
D. Śūdras :	servants	Aborigines admitted to the Hindu community.
E. Pañchamas (i.e. fifth-class men), called also Outcastes, Untouchables, &c.		Unclean aborigines and progeny of mixed marriages.

We must note carefully, however, that, though this is the scheme of the caste system, it is very difficult to fit all the modern facts into it. In North India the three twice-born castes stand out quite distinct, but instead of two well-defined groups, Śūdras and Pañchamas, what we find is an immense collection of castes, the order of whose precedence it would be very difficult to settle, and which it would be rather hard to divide into Śūdras and Outcastes. The spirit of caste, i.e. the tendency to subdivide into closed groups, has worked so powerfully that it has broken through the ancient organization. In the South, on the other hand, there are very few Kshatriyas

L 2

and Vaiśyas, so that the bulk of the population falls into three clearly distinguished groups, Brāhmans, Śūdras, and Pañchamas.

The following are the essential elements of caste:

A. The whole system rests on the belief that mankind is not a unity but consists of a large number of species each of distinct origin, and that each man is born into that species or sub-species for which his karma fits him. If he is very far advanced, in virtue and spirituality, he is born a Brāhman; if less advanced, he is born a Kshatriya; and so on.

B. Since Brāhmans are born such because of their superiority in spirituality, to them all religious authority has been given by the gods. They alone, in virtue of their lofty spiritual nature, the result of virtuous action in many previous births, are fit for the highest spiritual functions, viz. giving religious teaching, deciding points of law, sacrificing and performing ceremonies.

C. There are an indefinite number of distinct species of men, but the three Aryan castes are far above all others. After them come the Śūdras, who are the descendants of those aborigines who were admitted into the Hindu fold; and then the unclean aborigines and the mixed castes. The last have arisen, according to Hindu theory, through intermarriage between the castes or through the commission of some sin. Foreigners are unclean and are called *mlecchas*.

D. Men vary in value according to caste, and therefore must be dealt with in all matters in accordance therewith. Thus:

(1) In education, the Brāhman alone has the right to teach; and since only the three twice-born castes are spiritual men, they alone are allowed to hear the sacred literature (*śruti*) and to receive the training of the Brāhmanical schools. All women are excluded.

(2) Consequently, the ministrations of the Brāhmans, the regular sacraments with the sacred texts prescribed for them, the Vedic sacrifices and the daily devotions (*sandhyā*) are restricted to the three castes.

(3) Men and women of the four castes are admitted to Hindu temples, but no others, except by special favour.

(4) If one man injures another, the heinousness of the sin depends upon

the caste of the sufferer: the higher the caste the greater the sin. Hindu law also directs that fines and punishments shall be imposed according to caste: the higher the caste of the criminal the lighter the punishment.

(5) Outcastes must keep at a distance from caste people, lest they should pollute by touch or shadow, the distance being roughly proportionate to caste status. They are not allowed to live in the same village with high-caste Hindus nor to enter Hindu temples.

E. Each member of a caste is bound to preserve his purity to the utmost. Pollution is dangerous not only to himself but to all the members of his family, dead, living, and unborn, and in less degree to other members of his caste.[1] Purity is preserved by the faithful performance of the domestic sacraments, the śrāddha ceremonies, and Vedic sacrifices, and the daily devotions prescribed, and by the avoidance of any breach of caste rules in the matter of marriage, food, social intercourse, or occupation. Only if a man faithfully obeys all these rules does he make good karma for himself and so secure a good birth in his next life. The chief of these rules are:

(1) No man may marry outside his own caste. Usually there are also a number of rules restricting a man's choice of a wife to certain subdivisions of the caste. In many parts of India sectarian differences are so acute that intermarriage and interdining are prohibited. This creates further subdivision of castes.

(2) Certain kinds of food are recognised as legitimate, while others are absolutely proscribed. There are stringent rules as to the caste of those who may cook for the members of the caste.

(3) No man may eat with a man of lower caste than himself. There are also strict rules as to the castes from whose hands one may receive water.

(4) There is in each caste one occupation which is regarded as fully legitimate. Among the lower orders the rule is usually very

[1] Confounding of caste brings to hell alike the stock's slayers and the stock; for their fathers fall when the offerings of the cake and the water to them fail.

By this guilt of the destroyers of a stock, which makes castes to be confounded, the everlasting Laws of race and Laws of stock are overthrown.

For men the Laws of whose stock are overthrown a dwelling is ordained in hell.—*Gītā*, i. 42-44.

stringent, but among the higher castes there is a wider choice. Even amongst the highest, however, there are definite limits to liberty; and the *Gītā* says it is better to keep to the caste occupation and do bad work than to adopt another and do good work.[1]

(5) No Hindu may cross the ocean.

All these regulations, except the marriage law, are at present undergoing considerable modification among certain groups of educated men, especially in the large cities. Among the educated the fifth is now inoperative in Calcutta, and is gradually becoming so elsewhere. For the mass of the people they remain as before.

F. If a man break one of the rules of his caste, some authoritative priest pronounces sentence on him, or a meeting of the members of his caste belonging to the neighbourhood is called, and his case is dealt with. If he is outcasted, he is driven from his home, is disinherited, and can never marry in his caste, nor eat with his relatives or any member of the caste. These liabilities will rest on his children and his descendants for ever.

It is to be most carefully noted that excommunication is imposed only on account of a breach of caste law, and does not stand in any relation to morality. A man may be guilty of gross immoralities and yet may be in good standing in his caste and his family; while a man of the noblest character who breaks a caste law, however absurd or inhuman it may be, will be outcasted. In Mysore, where Christian baptism still deprives a man of his property, there were two brothers. One was a man of high character, but he had become a Christian; the other was an orthodox Hindu, but was in prison undergoing a sentence for some crime. The Christian was disinherited, and the criminal got his property. This is in strict accordance with Hindu principle. The law-books contain many fine moral precepts, but they do not touch caste organization.

[1] See above, p. 160.

V. We may now try to estimate the work which caste has done for India.

1. The caste system was a great advance on the simple social arrangements the Aryans had when they entered India; for by it they were enabled to organize the great empire they had won, to live a peaceful and progressive life in close association with the aboriginal inhabitants, and to impart to these backward peoples some measure at least of their own higher civilization. There is no need of many words to show that it was an advance for the aborigines so far as they were admitted to the system: the Śūdras are to-day the middle-class people of the country. Thus to both partners the new arrangements were solidly beneficial. Let us, therefore, not criticize the conquerors, because they did not introduce into the Hindu religious empire ideas which did not become operative in the world until many centuries later. Caste was the best possible solution of the problem open to them. The old groups were retained in all their insularity and exclusiveness, but they were brought into some sort of relationship the one to the other and to the three classes of the Aryan people. The Hindu method of segregation did not lead to the wholesale destruction of aboriginals such as has occurred in many lands. Rules gradually grew up for regulating the intercourse of the groups with one another. Caste was thus really a very great conception, the greatest possible at that time. While in the circumstances of these modern days it more and more proves itself an anti-social system, it was social, and not the reverse, when it was instituted. The whole population was unified in some degree: common religious ideas and practices were taught them and took possession of them; and the aborigines necessarily admired and copied in varying degrees the social usages of the upper castes. Hindu society was on the whole healthy until caste became rigid somewhere about the Christian era.

2. Along with the institutions of the Hindu family, caste has preserved the Hindu race and its civilization. Apart from

this powerful protection, Hindu culture would have been overwhelmed by the terrific political storms of the centuries, and the race could have survived only in fragments. But, thanks to caste and the Hindu family, they have survived, and with them many other groups also have been preserved; for, embedded in the curious conglomerate of the Hindu social fabric, many a caste of strange ethnology and culture may be seen, clearly descendants of some invading force, who, flinging themselves violently on India and gaining a foothold there, were finally absorbed by the people they came to attack, and owe to their absorption their position to-day. Indeed, so powerful has the attraction been that the Hindu people have drawn into their federation all invaders, except monotheists.

3. Caste did for many centuries in India the work which was done in Europe by the mediaeval trade-guilds. The system springs from different ideas, yet worked on much the same lines. It preserved learning by isolating the Brāhman caste and throwing on them the exclusive duty and privilege of teaching. It preserved manual skill and knowledge of the arts and industries by compelling boys to follow the profession of their father. A permanent division of labour was also secured. By means of caste-guilds wages and prices were maintained at a moderate standard.[1]

4. Caste has also served to some extent the purpose of a poor law in India; for the well-to-do members of a caste fulfil, in some degree at least, the duty of providing for those members who have fallen into indigence.

VI. Caste retains to this day a powerful hold on the Hindu mind. To the average man, whether Brāhman, Śūdra, or Outcaste, caste life is not only society and respectability, race purity and religion, but comfort, personal safety, and culture. In caste a man believes he has behind him a pure ancestry to which the lineage of the kings of England is but of yesterday.

[1] Banerjea, *A Study of Indian Economics*, 37, 38.

Even the Pariah,[1] who to the Śūdra (not to speak of the Brāhman) is so low and unclean as to be untouchable, is in his own eyes a man of high birth and good ancestry, because there are so many groups lower still. To go out of caste is to degrade oneself to the level of coarse, ill-bred men. It is to go out of civilization.

Yet, in spite of all that caste has done, and in spite of its giant grip on the Indian spirit, educated Hindu society shows a number of anti-caste tendencies of very great importance.

As we have already seen, the early Buddhists and the other unorthodox schools of the same time withstood the pretensions of the Brāhmans; but there is no indication in the *Pāli Tripiṭaka* that Buddha or his followers condemned caste as such. The system had not then become rigid and harmful; so that it would have been strange if they had assailed it. Further, they held the doctrine of transmigration, which naturally expresses itself socially in caste. Nor was any idea incompatible with caste planted in the Indian mind by Buddhism. The same is true of Islam. Men simply did not feel that there was anything wrong in it. From the eleventh or twelfth century of our era, it is true, an occasional voice is raised against the system. In the writings of Kapilar, a Tamil, and of Vemana, a Telugu,[2] we find the system subjected to very acute criticism. Basava, in founding his sect, the Vīra-Śaivas or Lingāyats, appointed non-Brāhmans as priests and forbade his followers to recognize caste; and the same is true of the Kabīrpanthīs and the Sikhs; but the poison has crept back into each of these three bodies. Yet these were but sporadic protests. Never until now has there been any sign that the Indian mind was dissatisfied with the system. The facts we have now to deal with are therefore of great significance.

[1] The Pariahs are one of the large Outcaste castes of South India. The word is often inaccurately used as a synonym for Outcaste.

[2] *Heart of India*, 94, 100, 110, 112.

A. Educated men everywhere tend to seek certain forms of social freedom which are contrary to the rules of caste. This tendency, which is clearly a natural outcome of Western education, seldom touches marriage: the average educated Hindu keeps the matrimonial rules of caste with great care. It is in matters of food, social intercourse, occupation, and travel that freedom is desired.

1. The Hindu enjoys European food and wants to be free to use it from time to time. The average man keeps the rules of diet at home, but grants himself more or less liberty elsewhere. Many are so completely emancipated as to be quite ready to eat any European food, even beef, and to take Western liquor also; but most take only little liberties; and here and there one meets a man who is rigidly strict with his food.

2. The educated man wants to be free in the matter of social intercourse. Western education has been such a levelling influence that it is but natural a Hindu should want to dine with men of lower castes who sat on the same bench at College with him. When this feeling has grown a little stronger, he feels inclined to dine with Brāhmas, Indian Christians, and Muḥammadans. The great societies, religious, educational, social, and political, which sway educated men so powerfully, strengthen this tendency very greatly. If men work together for the highest ends, why should they not eat together? The student meets his European professor at a social gathering and finds it the most natural thing possible to take a cup of tea with him. When he goes out into the world, he enjoys dining with a few European friends at one of the Indo-European clubs which are now springing up. Wherever there are close relations, the desire for true social intercourse necessarily follows.

3. The educated man feels free to adopt any occupation. The sacredness of the cow and the feeling against the slaughter of animals have made Hindus look down very seriously upon all professions connected with hides. Yet one may find

Brāhmans dealing in leather, and many other anomalous facts. Almost anything is condoned to-day if it is believed to help forward the regeneration of India.

4. Until a few years ago a student who went to Europe or America to study had to undergo *prāyaścitta* (a ceremony of atonement) on his return to India or else suffer excommunication. In consequence there grew up in Calcutta a small community of highly educated men who had lost their standing in Hinduism for the sake of education. Most of them joined the Brāhma Samāj. But nowadays a Calcutta student of any caste is at once received back into Hindu society on his return. The law against crossing the ocean is not used against him. This procedure is spreading slowly among the educated classes in other parts of India also. Students, when in Europe, America, or Japan, do not attempt to keep caste rules about diet and interdining. This, too, is now condoned without a word.

These facts are most interesting and significant, but it would be very easy to exaggerate their importance. So long as the laws of marriage are rigorously enforced, the basis of caste remains. These changes in diet, in social intercourse, in occupation, and in travel are of considerable value to the community; but they rather prove that caste is a very elastic institution than that it is shaken to its depths.

B. The Social Reform movement is of great importance. While reformers have given their chief attention to family questions, caste in its various aspects has also been one of the subjects of their thought and agitation. It was from the side of religion that the movement started, but hygienic, moral, economic, and national considerations now play a large part in their literature.

1. Comparatively little has been written or said on the matter of food, but a few men have advocated the introduction of more nourishing diet, especially among certain races. Swāmī Vivekānanda thought Indians required to use less vegetables and more flesh, in order to develop both physique and

character. He himself, though he was such a stanch Hindu, ate beef. Dr. S. C. Mullick, a medical man of considerable reputation in Calcutta, is of opinion that the physique of the Bengali race suffers rather seriously because so little flesh is eaten.

2. Social reformers have done precious service in the way of advocating and practising interdining. The pages of the organ of the movement, the *Indian Social Reformer*, are often used for this good end. At their own annual conferences dinners are held at which Hindus of all castes, and now and then Indians of other religions, sit down together. So, after the Conference of the Aryan Brotherhood held in Bombay in November, 1912, a great company of Hindus of many castes dined together.

3. The Reform movement presses very seriously the wisdom of removing the barriers which at present prevent marriages between people of different sub-castes. The ideal aimed at is that all Brāhmans should be free to intermarry, that there should be no marriage barriers among Kshatriyas, or among Vaiśyas, or among Śūdras. This in itself would be a very large reform; for there are innumerable subdivisions and restrictions within each of the great castes. But the difficulties in the way are very great. The Kshatriyas of North India have now an annual conference at which they discuss matters relating to the welfare of the caste; and other castes and sections of castes have similar gatherings. At these meetings the great advantages that would arise from such a reform are often set forth in a presidential oration; but very little has yet been done.

4. It is only the leading reformers who propose what is called intercaste marriages among Hindus, i. e. that all barriers should be removed, so that a Brāhman might marry a Vaiśya or a Śūdra. This seems to most men a very far-away ideal, an almost impossible reform.

C. The third set of influences worthy of our study are those that centre in the Outcastes. During the past thirty-five years myriads of these downtrodden people have passed into the Christian Church ; and wherever Missions have been able to give them sufficient attention brilliant results have been won.[1] A distinguished Brāhman official writes of the work as follows in the *Travancore Census Report of* 1901 :

> But for these missionaries, these humble orders of Hindu society will for ever remain unraised. Their material condition, I dare say, will have improved with the increased wages, improved labour market, better laws, and more generous treatment from an enlightened Government like ours ; but to the Christian missionaries belongs the credit of having gone to their humble homes, and awakened them to a sense of a better earthly existence. This action of the missionary was not a mere improvement upon ancient history, a kind of polishing and refining of an existing model, but an entirely original idea, conceived and carried out with commendable zeal, and oftentimes in the teeth of opposition and persecution. I do not refer to the emancipation of the slave, or the amelioration of the labourer's condition ; for these always existed more or less in our past humane governments. But the heroism of raising the low from the slough of degradation and debasement was an element of civilization unknown to ancient India.[2]

Two points with regard to this aspect of Mission work require notice here.

Christianity and education produce marvellous results among these people, especially in the second generation. Many boys and girls prove quite bright students, and a small percentage proceed to the university and take degrees. In all the districts where these mass movements have taken place, you may find Mission schools in which the teachers are of Outcaste descent, while in every class a number of Brāhman boys study under them. The whole theory of caste is here proved by ocular demonstration to be radically false. The Hindu doctrine is that the unclean Outcastes cannot be raised : Christianity does raise them.

The great success which Christianity has met with in dealing

[1] See Phillips, *The Outcastes' Hope*. [2] Phillips, 81.

with the Outcastes has attracted wide attention in India.[1] Some have been stirred to deep sympathy; others have been roused to fury; but all have realized the great significance of the movement. In consequence the Ārya Samāj and the Brāhma Samāj have started Missions of their own to try to win the Outcastes; while a number of advanced Hindus, chiefly under the influence of members of the Prārthanā Samāj in Western India, have organized what is called the Depressed Classes Mission. This last body aims chiefly at education and encouragement. The Nationalist leaders call loudly for the education of the Outcastes and the betterment of the conditions of their life. One of these men remarked:

> After all, when it comes to practice, Christianity alone is effecting what we Nationalists are crying out for—namely the elevation of the masses.[2]

D. The main social result which has arisen from the activity of the political leaders is also well worthy of our attention. For twenty-five years the Congress leaders have been toiling to bring their ideal of representative government nearer. The experience they have gained in this very uphill struggle has, at last, convinced them that the divisions of caste are the most formidable of all the obstacles in their way. One after the other they have come to this conclusion. Surendranath Bannerjea, the greatest popular leader in Bengal, caused extreme excitement only last year by publicly declaring that complete social freedom was indispensable for the attainment of political liberty.

E. It will perhaps be well to give a few quotations from notable men on the general question of the influence of caste. The first is a sentence from a leading article in the *Mahratta*,[3] which is by no means one of the most advanced papers:

> No one now says or even thinks that the old water-tight compartments of caste should be perpetuated in future, even on the ground

[1] See *The Depressed Classes*, a booklet containing twenty-three essays by people of many faiths, published by Natesan, Madras.

[2] Phillips, 28.

[3] November 7, 1909.

that the caste system was a convenient method of securing division of labour in practice.

The others are from a more advanced position. The following comes from the *Times* report of an address delivered before the Indian section of the Royal Society of Arts by the Honourable Sir K. G. Gupta, a member of the India Council:

> The caste system had served useful purposes in the past, but it had not now a single redeeming feature. If the Hindu was again to lift his head and take part in the great work of nation-building, he must revert to the original Aryan type and demolish the barriers dividing the community.

Mr. Shridhar Ketkar, in his work on *Caste*,[1] says,

> The result is disunion of the people, the worst type the world has ever seen.

The next is from Lāla Lājpat Rai, the Punjabi leader:

> Caste . . . is a disgrace to our humanity, our sense of justice, and our feeling of social affinity . . . a standing blot on our social organization.

The editor of the *Indian Social Reformer* speaks of caste as 'the great monster we have to kill', and declares it to be 'utterly opposed to the modern idea of good citizenship'. But, instead of multiplying quotations, it will probably be more helpful if we read the words of Mr. Rabindra Nath Tagore, the author of *Gitanjali*, who is by far the greatest literary force at present in Bengal, and whose serious spirit and balanced character give his opinions very great weight:

> This immutable and all-pervading system of caste has no doubt imposed a mechanical uniformity upon the people, but it has, at the same time, kept their different sections inflexibly and unalterably separate, with the consequent loss of all power of adaptation and readjustment to new conditions and forces. The regeneration of the Indian people, to my mind, *directly and perhaps solely depends upon the removal of this condition of caste.* When I realise the hypnotic hold which this gigantic system of cold-blooded repression has taken on the minds of our people, whose social body it has so completely entwined in its endless coils that the free expression of manhood, even

[1] Vol. II. p. 133.

under the direst necessity, has become almost an impossibility, the only remedy that suggests itself to me is to educate them out of their trance. . . . Now has come the time when India must begin to build, and dead arrangement must gradually give way to living construction, organized growth. . . . If to break up the feudal system and the tyrannical conventionalism of the mediaeval Church, which had outraged the healthier instincts of humanity, Europe needed the thought-impulse of the Renaissance and the fierce struggle of the Reformation, do we not need in a greater degree an overwhelming influx of higher social ideas before a place can be found for true political thinking? Must we not have that greater vision of humanity which will impel us to shake off the fetters that shackle our individual life before we begin to dream of national freedom? [1]

These new movements of the Indian spirit are full of interest and suggest many questions. Yet it would be most unwise to jump to the conclusion that these yearnings and strivings are proof that the citadel of caste is about to fall. No one who has been in touch with the Hindu people, and who has realized the vitality, the pervasiveness, the grip of the system will be likely to minimize it or to imagine that it will be lightly overthrown. Caste has been not merely a vast organized system built upon the rock of religious belief, but a bodiless spirit, an overpowering contagion, which has overtaken and poisoned every Hindu sect that has tried to escape from it, and which has infected, at least in some degree, every community in India, numbing with its venom great groups of Muḥammadans, little circles of Jews, and even certain Christian churches.

It is also necessary to realize clearly that the immediate outlook in the matter of caste reform is not very hopeful. Social reformers are more sure of their position and wield greater influence than ever before; the political movement has now become an ally in some sense of the reform movement; and the slight changes visible in practice among educated men are all in favour of freedom. But during the

[1] The writer owes this quotation to Andrews, 184; but it appeared originally in the *Modern Review*.

past twenty-five years the revival of Hinduism has made enormous strides; and, as strength and confidence have grown, the leaders have plucked up courage to defend more and more of the ancient system. Between 1850 and 1890 very few educated men publicly defended caste or idolatry. The Ārya Samāj, the most vehemently anti-Christian body in India, was founded in 1875 by Dayānanda Sarasvatī: he denounced both caste and idolatry. But since then things have rather gone the other way. Rāmakṛishṇa Paramahaṁsa and his disciple Vivekānanda defended everything that is Hindu; the Theosophical Society, under Mrs. Besant's leadership, has taken the same line of policy; to-day every important sect and section of Hinduism has its own defence organization; and by arguments of the most amazing character, and principles and analogies drawn from everything in heaven and on earth, the Hindu undertakes to prove that caste is the most reasonable form of society possible, and that Hindu idols are channels of the purest spirituality. These movements certainly do not promise well for caste reform.

VII. But, while we must acknowledge that the agitation in favour of reform has as yet made very little impression on the mighty fortress of caste, and that the present policy of the leaders of the Hindu revival is a grave menace to the whole movement, there is one fact in the situation which has hitherto been very little noticed, and yet is of far more vital importance than all that the Social Reform movement and the Hindu revival taken together have been able to accomplish. The fact we refer to is this, that *the religious basis of caste has faded out of the minds of educated Hindus.* Articles and speeches which deal with the question, whether they plead for reform or seek to show the wisdom and the reasonableness of the ancient system, invariably take no notice of the mighty beliefs on which the organization rests. The leaders of the revival point out how much caste has done for the division of labour, for the preservation of skill and learning, and for the physique and the purity of the higher castes, and they frequently make the reckless assertion that there is as much caste in European as in Hindu society; but there is no attempt made to justify caste from the point of view of the old religious beliefs. Social reformers do not find it necessary to argue against the old doctrines. Who believes nowadays that the Brāhman is so much more spiritual than other men that all religious authority, teaching, and ritual ought to be in his hands? Who now holds that it is sinful to allow a Śūdra or a foreigner to hear the Veda? Who now subscribes to the doctrine of the *Gītā* that it is better for the Brāhman to be a bad priest than a good doctor or business man?[1] Who now believes that the Outcaste is a man whose former lives have been so foul that physical contact with him brings spiritual pollution to a high-caste Hindu? The truth is that the atmosphere of the new age makes the old ideas which lie at the basis of caste incredible. Let us consider them briefly, and the truth of this will become apparent.

A. The foundation of caste is the belief that the four castes had each a distinct origin in God. All serious scholars agree that in the society represented in the *Ṛigveda* there was no caste. The ninetieth hymn of the tenth book,[2] which is one of the latest hymns in the whole collection, shows that by the end of the period there was a desire for something like caste; but even then the four castes were still but classes. Throughout the whole of the period of the *Ṛigveda* there was free intermarriage between the various classes; and there was nothing to prevent a warrior from becoming a priest or a priest a warrior. Thus the whole *Ṛigveda* is evidence that the four castes are not races created separately by God. It is impossible to believe that even the Brāhmans are a race distinct from every other Indian race: even if certain Brāhman families have kept themselves pure from mixture since 500 B.C., when caste began to be strictly observed in certain quarters, or even since 700 B.C., what about the

[1] *Supra*, p. 160. [2] *Supra*, p. 159.

uncounted centuries before then? No one who studies the history of India sincerely can have the slightest doubt that the account given above of the origin of caste is the truth, and that the Hindu theory of special creations is merely a myth formed in order to give greater dignity and meaning to already existing divisions.

The study of ethnology and anthropology has convinced all scientific inquirers that there is no such thing as men of pure race anywhere. There has been immeasurable mixture in all races and in all parts of the world. Men of science are also in complete agreement on this, that the human family is a unity, that there are no species amongst men. Men are divided from the animals, which are their kindred, by an exceedingly deep distinction; but amongst men there is no serious difference at all. The race is one.

It is thus perfectly clear that a modern man cannot believe that the four great castes are distinct species, having each had a separate origin in God. The physical side of the theory of caste purity is altogether untenable.

B. But the Hindu holds that caste distinctions have another basis than physical heredity. He declares that each soul is drafted into that caste for which his spiritual progress has prepared him. A man is born a Brāhman because his soul is far advanced on the way to holiness. The Śūdra is born such because he is far behind the Brāhman, but far in advance of the soul that is born a Pariah or a *mleccha*. There can be no doubt that it is this idea which throughout the centuries has justified caste to the noblest minds of India. Transmigration is the Hindu doctrine of man. The belief that men rise through many spiritual stages to perfection is to the Hindu the deepest of all facts about the human spirit. Caste is thus the natural social expression of transmigration.

This claim, that the four castes are the divinely appointed expression of the progress of souls in spiritual things and, therefore, an infallible index of the religious value of the members of the castes, was criticized very effectively several centuries ago by a group of Hindu thinkers in South India. Here is a quotation from the Tamil poet Kapilar:

> In the various lands of the Ottiyas, Mlechchhas, Hunas, Singalese, the slender-waisted Jonakas, Yavanas, and Chinese there are no Brāhmans; but ye have set up in this land a fourfold caste-division as if it were an order distinguished in primal nature. By conduct are distinguished high and low degrees. The bull and the buffalo are unlike of kind; have male and female of these two classes ever been seen to unite one with another and breed offspring? . . . Who can see any unlikeness of form between men such as there is between bull and buffalo? In our life, our limbs, our body, hue, and understanding no difference is revealed. A Pulai-man of the south-land who should go to the north and unflaggingly study will be a Brāhman; a Brāhman of the north-land who should come to the south and be warped in his ways will be a Pulai-man. Vasiṣṭha, born of a lowly mistress to Brahmā, like a red water-lily springing up in mire; Śakti, born of a Chandāla woman to Vasishṭha; Parāśara, born to Śakti of a Pulai-woman; Vyāsa, born of a fisher-girl to Parāśara,—all these by study of the Vedas rose to high estate and are famous as holy men. I, Kapilar, with them that were born with me, who are the lineal offspring born to the austere and saintly Bhagavān by the good Pulai-lady Ādi of the great town of Karuvur,—we are in number three males and four females; and hearken to the brief tale of our nurture. Uppai grew up as a dweller in a Vannar household at Uttukadu town. Uruvai was reared in the home of Sanārs, in the toddy-drawers' village at Kaviripumbattinam. Auvai was reared in the home of Panars, in the village belonging to the viol-players. Valli grew up on the fair mountain-side where the lordly Kuravars gather their teeming crops. Valluvar was nurtured among the pariahs of pleasant Mailapur in the Tondaimandalam. Adhikaman was reared with a chieftain of Vanji, where blossom the tree-groves and bees swarm. I grew up nurtured by Brāhmans in Arur, the land of gushing streams.[1]

This is very penetrating reasoning even as it stands; but when we add to it the religious experience of the human race it becomes overwhelming. Confucius, Christ, Muḥammad were *mlecchas*: whence came their moral and spiritual capacity and power, if the karma doctrine be true?

But the real character of the theory becomes plain only when we set Hindu caste historically in its true place in the

[1] *Heart of India*, 100–102.

development of society in India and in the world. Caste is but one of many forms of social organization which the peoples of India have produced; and although from about 500 B.C. until to-day it has been the dominant form, it did not exist in the preceding milleniums, and is now clearly decaying. In the world-setting it is but one of many attempts—the most brilliant of all, doubtless—yet but one of many attempts made by oligarchies, whether religious or political, to eternalize their own position. To believe that this particular social scheme of all the hundreds which earth has produced is the one divine creation, and that its external relationships reveal with infallible truth the spiritual condition of souls, is altogether impossible for the modern mind. Kapilar's criticism has interested many a reader and raised many a smile, but it never endangered the Brāhman position. The arrival of Western thought, however, is a very different matter. The uplifting of the Outcaste by Christianity is in itself sufficient to overturn the theory.

Thus the doctrine of the spiritual basis of caste-life will not bear one moment's serious consideration any more than the theory of the distinct origin of the great castes in God.

C. It is a remarkable fact that nearly all the national religions of the world distinguished between clean and unclean food, and drew up lists of articles of diet permitted and prohibited. It was a serious religious duty to observe these regulations. Every violation was sinful, polluting the man religiously and rendering him unfit for his usual religious duties and social privileges.

It seems clear that such regulations arose largely in revulsion from the food used by neighbouring peoples. To the ordinary man there are always certain articles in the diet of any race other than his own which seem unclean and horrible, while he regards his own food as pure, healthy, and attractive in every way. Like all the other restrictions of early life, the food law was imposed to protect culture and religion by absolutely excluding what seemed impious, polluting, revolting.

Nor can there be any doubt that in the case of the Aryan people in India, surrounded as they were by innumerable tribes of barbarian aborigines, some such regulation was absolutely necessary. A glimpse at the food and the table customs of some of the Outcastes to-day will convince any one that the ancient leaders were quite right when they condemned the diet and forbade social intercourse with the ancestors of these people. Carelessness in these matters would have not only had a most deleterious influence on the culture of the Aryans, but would have probably produced loathsome and devastating disease among them. Prohibition was necessary in self-defence.

But if a prohibition had to be made, there was only one way possible in those days: it had to be religious. To all early races there is something mysterious in the eating of food through its connexion with life; and therefore it is a religious matter and under religious rule. Thus, everything that was felt to be injurious was necessarily regarded as religiously unclean. To eat such was a sin.

It was only gradually that men came to form the idea of healthy as opposed to unhealthy food; and, even when they had begun to use the idea, they still continued to avoid the use of what was regarded as unclean, since that was to them a serious religious duty.

In modern times, however, the distinction between the laws of health, on the one hand, and the laws of morality and of spiritual religion, on the other, has, under the teaching of Jesus, become perfectly clear; and there is no reason why any one should confuse them. While in certain climates and for certain constitutions fish may be a healthier food than fowl or meat, or an exclusively vegetarian diet than a diet of both vegetable and animal food, yet no food, whether rice, wheat, barley, or oats, fish, fowl, beef, or mutton, is either pure or impure from the point of view of morality or of spiritual religion. Food acts on the bodily tissues, and it is to be judged solely by its physiological results. It is my duty to keep my body healthy, and I do wrong if I neglect that duty; but I shall never do so by restricting myself to any particular list of foods as religiously clean, but solely by considering individual articles of diet in relation to the needs and the condition of my body. No food is unclean. Material things have no religious index. Religious pollution is a state of the soul, not of the stomach.

Thus the old Hindu rules of food are as much an anachronism to-day as charms for the cure of disease or the belief in witches. No modern man should countenance such regulations. They hamper the Hindu community in many ways and prevent its growth.

D. The rule that a Hindu must not eat with a man of lower caste than his own springs from the same causes as the rule against eating certain foods, and, like it, has overlived its time. It is literally a *superstition*; that is, a rule or belief which was natural and rational to men in an earlier stage of culture, but has survived into a time when there is no further justification for it. As we have already seen, most primitive peoples think it impossible to eat with men of other tribes. Besides this general reason for exclusiveness, it was probably necessary in early days in India, for reasons of health and culture, to prohibit all social intercourse with the aborigines. Any such prohibition in those days necessarily took the form of a religious law. Even if there were only a few customs that were regarded as dangerous and polluting, it was necessary to prohibit intercourse absolutely with the tribes who practised them, because all such customs were religiously binding.

But the inevitable result of the prohibition of all social intercourse with people of certain tribes is that men come to believe that those people are religiously impure and that it is a sin to eat with them; and this result we see before us in India to-day.

But modern men look at these things with other eyes. Science has taught us to be much more careful with regard to right diet, wise cooking, and absolute cleanliness in food than any ancient people possibly could be; but we have also learned that all such matters are questions of health, not of religion. It may be dangerous for me to dine with a man of a certain tribe, but the danger lies not in the man himself, nor in the fact that he belongs to that tribe, but in the food he offers me, in the unsanitary vessels in which it is cooked, or in the unclean dish, leaf, table, or floor on which it is served. The uncleanness of his food does not make him religiously impure. He may be a good man, though his food is bad. Men of the most degraded races may be civilized and taught to be cleanly in their habits and to use healthy food. Social intercourse then becomes quite possible with them. The uncleanness does not inhere in the race.

Thus the caste law against interdining is a survival from primitive times altogether irrational to-day.

E. We need scarcely say a word to prove that the old caste rule as to occupation is altogether indefensible. Through the action of this ancient law India has lost the services of a very large proportion of all the men of genius born in her families. In the higher castes there is a good deal of liberty, but elsewhere there is little or none. Except in the very occasional case when a boy's genius happened to run along the lines of his father's profession, every man of original gift has been forcibly deprived of the opportunity of exercising it. His spirit has been imprisoned, squeezed into the groove of the traditional occupation—like a Calcutta huckster, huddled up with his wares between two houses, his chink scarcely two feet wide by three feet high. How many thousands of gifted boys, born up and down the centuries in the lower castes and among the Outcastes, have been prevented, by the wasteful tyranny of caste, from serving India! Surely the uttermost stretch of human ingenuity would fail to create a system more fatal to initiative and originality, more calculated to turn men into listless, machine-like imitators, than this perpetual succession to the ancestral tread-mill. People complain that the ordinary Indian is unfit for anything but routine work. It is scarcely surprising. He has been at a single job for two thousand years.

The religious idea behind the occupation rule is that a man must do that work for which the precise stage of progress which his soul has reached fits him.[1] A low-caste man, being unspiritual, cannot perform the duty of a priest. A Brāhman, being by birth spiritual, cannot follow the occupation of a Śūdra or a Pañchama without loss of spirituality and the formation of bad karma. Manual labour degrades the spiritual man. This religious belief is no longer held by educated men. Indeed, the higher castes have never kept the occupation law. They have allowed themselves a great deal of liberty. Should not similar liberty be now proclaimed to the others? Behind the wonderful economic progress made by Japan during the last forty years there stands this freedom, necessarily granted when social equality was introduced. Surely, for the sake of India, educated men will not rest until the poorest and the most ignorant of the people have been told that religion does not demand that they shall allow their God-given capacities to run to waste. Let us go at least as far as Napoleon went, and proclaim 'les carrières ouvertes aux talents'.

There is another aspect of the occupation rule which must not be forgotten. In nearly every part of India there are criminal tribes, many of them Hindus. The Thags, whose profession was the strangling and robbery of wealthy travellers, were devout Hindus, and dedicated a percentage of all their plunder to Kālī. According to the rules of caste, it is the duty of boys to follow the occupation of their fathers. According to the rules of the family, the son sins if, when his father bids him follow the old occupation, he refuses.[2] How are these tribes to be reformed without a contravention of these Hindu principles?

Thus each of the leading conceptions of caste turns out

[1] See especially the *Gītā*, xviii. 41–48, and *supra*, p. 160.
[2] See p. 88.

to be an old-world idea which will not bear examination in modern daylight. The reason why educated men all over India are uneasily turning towards modification, reform, or abolition of the system is now apparent; and we can see with perfect clearness why it is that Hindu leaders do not urge the validity of these beliefs to-day. The religious ideas which created caste have faded out of the minds of the educated class.

It is this decay of the religious ideas behind caste that is the explanation of the otherwise incomprehensible fact, that Hindus have been found to declare that caste is a purely social and non-religious system. The modern educated man is so conscious that it is not a matter of religion to himself, but a mere social convention, that a few have actually been able to persuade themselves that it is essentially such.

We are now able to verify the statement made above about the transcendent importance of the decay of faith in the religious basis of the system. Caste spread throughout India and became an atmosphere which no one could escape, because of the power of these far-reaching religious ideas. No mind was beyond their dominance. No society could fail to yield to their influence. But a new and mightier force has now begun to act in India, a set of fresh ideas of overwhelming might; and whoever breathes this new air is unable to hold the old convictions. Nor is there any power on earth that can destroy this new atmosphere, or keep it from spreading through the Hindu community. It is affecting Hindu society at present most vitally at the top and at the bottom. The educated, at the top of the cone, hold by caste organization, but have lost the power to believe in its governing conceptions. The Outcastes, at the bottom, are quickly learning that the system, which for two thousand years has consigned them to dirt and the devil, instead of being the highest religious truth, is utterly false; and they are rapidly escaping from their hideous position. Meanwhile, the ordinary Hindu is listening more and more to what the missionary has to say on the subject of the dignity of man; and Western civilization, government, and education are steadily pressing the lesson home. One of the most sympathetic of observers remarks

> British rule and modern ideas are gradually breaking down the old social system and modifying the religious life of the Hindu.[1]

The religious basis of caste is clearly dying. But before we attempt to form a judgement as to what is likely to be the outcome of this decay and the changes we have been trying to understand, there are other facts to be taken into consideration.

VIII. These uncertain, uneasy, yet insuppressible strugglings of the Indian spirit towards social freedom are but part of a general uprising visible in many quarters of the world to-day. This widespread social unrest has three main aspects, distinct enough to be discussed separately, yet closely connected the one with the other.

The movement seeks first of all *human equality*. There is an impatience manifested with regard to the old race barriers, a distinct wish to see them broken down, in certain aspects of life at least. It appears in politics in India and in Egypt. The whole Congress movement in India and all the criticism of the British Government by the Egyptian press have for their sole justification the assertion of the political equality of the Indian and the European, or of the Egyptian and the Englishman. From the point of view of Hindu or of Muḥammadan thought the agitation has no right to exist at all; but Western education has filled thinking men in these countries with the ambition to enjoy the political privileges which Western nations have won for themselves. A similar phenomenon, only taking a different shape because of the different circumstances, has led to unprecedented changes in Turkey, China, and Japan, and in a less degree in Persia and Siam. In all these countries the movement is a democratic one; and, there being no foreign government to attack,

[1] Havell, *Benares*, 115-116.

political equality is demanded for all citizens of whatever race, religion, or social status.

The same spirit appears in another sphere in Turkey and Egypt in the eager agitation that all the different sections of the people may be equal before the law. Men demand that in the elections, in the Parliament and other assemblies, in the law-courts, in the schools and universities, and in the army, all classes of the people shall be considered equal. The British Government in India has been enforcing this principle for well over a century. On every occasion when the principle has been applied to a new sphere by the Government, loud outcries have been raised against it by the conservative section of the population; but nowadays there is no thinking man in India who would raise his voice against the equality which all classes of the people enjoy in the law-courts, in schools and colleges, in Government service, on trains and trams and such like. In certain parts of the country Government has not yet ventured to apply the principle in all its fullness to the Outcastes. But in Bombay advanced opinion has begun to beg the Government to apply the principle in their case in schools. The attempt made by Europeans to treat Indians in South Africa as an inferior caste has raised vehement protests in India, protests which are absolutely justified from the Western standpoint, but very strange indeed when raised by men who defend and practise the caste system.

Lastly, the desire for equality shows itself in the matter of social intercourse. The finest example yet given is that of Japan. Forty years ago all the old caste distinctions were abolished, and the people became socially one. Much of the solid progress which the country has achieved since then is traceable to that remarkable revolution. Within the pale of Hinduism it is only the Social Reform party that call for equality between the castes; but, with a blind yet healthy inconsistency, the high-caste Hindu who will not eat with his low-caste brother Hindu demands, in some degree, social recognition from Europeans. This, too, is to be welcomed. In every Oriental land the educated man wishes to dine with the cultured European.

The second direction in which this movement tends is towards *complete social freedom.* In Egypt and Turkey educated Muḥammadans are now demanding much more freedom in diet and other matters than their ancient laws and customs allow. Many wish to give up the Fast; multitudes of women wish to lay aside the veil; and the most advanced men are eager to have their women appear in public and even take part in social or political events. Far away in China the same spirit is working on other elements of daily life. The cruel system of foot-binding has been an almost universal custom throughout China for many generations. To-day, wherever the spirit of the West has gone, there is a passionate agitation for freedom in this matter. The desire for social freedom has perhaps made more progress in India than in any other Eastern country outside Japan; for Western influence has had a long and powerful reign here. We have seen above how many changes are arising in caste practice, and all towards freedom; and Chapter II showed how much is happening in family matters. The practice of interdining is spreading steadily. The writer had one day the pleasure of travelling in a second-class compartment in Western India along with a party of three business men, a Jew, a Parsee, and a Hindu. Towards evening, the Jew called his servant and got him to lay out the evening meal. All ate together, and at their invitation the writer joined the party. They were intelligent men. Each acknowledged that he was acting in direct infringement of the laws of his religion. No scene could have been more typical of our time or more prophetic of the future.

In the third place, modern social agitation seeks complete *social justice.* The Hindu condemns as unjust the attempt to treat Indians in South Africa as pestilent aliens, and holds that indentured labour, whether in Assam or in the West Indies, is immoral. The extreme rudeness of certain Europeans to Indians on railways and elsewhere is rightly condemned as an offence against social morality. The same spirit is working in the West. The progressive organization of the working classes of Europe and America, the menacing strikes of the last few years, and the rise of militant socialism, all spring from a conviction on the part of the artisans and labourers that they are not receiving social justice. Much of the military activity of the British Empire consists of the police work of compelling semi-savage tribes on our frontiers to adopt a higher moral code in their relations with their neighbours. One of the reasons why Japan was forced open by Commodore Perry sixty years ago was this, that the Japanese were accustomed to murder foreign sailors shipwrecked on their coast. All over the world the establishment of fair and just relations between men is being more and more demanded.

Thus, social evolution is working in these lands towards a form of society in which new principles must rule. The equality of men must be recognized; all non-moral restrictions upon social life must be removed; and our social relations must be regulated by strict justice.

There can be no doubt that all these symptoms of social unrest, appearing in so many far-sundered lands, spring from a single cause, viz. the spread of Western ideas. The influences which are creating the upheaval in India are active wherever the modern spirit has gone. They will inevitably find wider extension and win still greater victories, unless some stronger force is ready to counteract them. But of that there is no sign. Everywhere the methods and the principles of modern life are winning their way with increasing momentum. Many Hindus believe that there is still sufficient resisting power left in caste to carry them through the present distress. If the situation consisted merely in the struggle of one national method of social life against another, there would be considerable reason for hoping that caste would be victorious; but, when we realize that the very men who uphold caste do not believe the religious principles on which it rests, and when we perceive that, whether in Turkey or Egypt, Persia or China, Japan or India, the modern atmosphere renders the old beliefs utterly incredible, then the ultimate result seems scarcely doubtful.

IX. If, then, the religious basis of caste is fading out of men's minds, we are driven to ask what is to take its place. It is clear that a strong, lasting, social order can be built only on a religious foundation. The whole marvellous history of Hinduism bears this upon its forehead. Apart from the religious character of caste, the Indo-Aryans could never have gathered the races of India into a great religious empire nor could the people have held together through all the storms and changes of three thousand years. The study of religions is steadily revealing the same truth in other spheres. For the purpose of creating a living social order, a living religion is needed. It alone provides moral conceptions of strength and reach sufficient to lay hold of man's conscience and intellect and to compel him to live in society in accordance with them. No lasting society has ever yet been formed on a secular basis. Above all things, nothing but religion will ever provide a force of strength and binding power sufficient to control the turbulent primary passions which in every race and country produce narrow social cliques and vehemently oppose every movement towards equality, freedom, and justice.

The truth of this great principle of social growth stands out more clearly so soon as we realize that each social organism corresponds in character to the leading conceptions of the religion that gave it birth. Caste is the natural outcome of the doctrine of karma and transmigration. The disappearance of all race differences in Islam is the necessary result of the conception of the infinite exaltation of Allah and of the littleness and weakness of man. The dogma, that believers are the objects of Allah's high favour and unbelievers of His utter displeasure, expresses itself socially in the enslavement of unbelievers captured in war; and the polygamy, free divorce, and concubinism of Muḥammadan lands are easily intelligible in view of the Muslim doctrine that women are far inferior to men. The same stringent logical connexion between belief and social organization is visible in all religions.

Where, then, shall we find a religion whose governing conceptions, when they take organized form in society, will incarnate the great principles of the essential equality of all men, the rectitude and high value of complete social freedom, and the obligation of moralizing all social relations, which, we have found, characterize the social agitations of India, Turkey, China, and the other lands at present?

It is a very remarkable fact that these three social principles spring directly from the central doctrine of Christianity; so that, the more seriously Christianity is held, the more fully must society incarnate these ideals.

But a consideration may be urged at this point that would render any appeal to Christ worthless; so we had better deal with it at once. Hindus frequently argue that there is as much caste in England as in India, and therefore that Christianity is no cure for Hindu social evils. Our analysis has shown that the doctrine, that each man is born in that caste for which his past lives have fitted him, gives caste the strongest possible religious sanction and renders Hindu social organization altogether unique. Thus to call the social life of England caste is simply to talk nonsense. On the other hand, every Christian acknowledges with shame and distress that, despite the teaching and example of Christ, in certain sections of Western society there are men and women who show a very large amount of the class and race feeling which lie behind caste, and who practise an exclusiveness that is most offensive and unchristian. But the crucial point is that they are guilty of all this in defiance of their religion, while Hinduism commands the exclusive life which Hindus now recognize to be so antisocial. Thus, as in the chapter on the family, we must again point out that Christianity, like Hinduism, must not be judged by those who refuse to obey it. What we have to inquire is whether Christ taught the principles which underlie healthy social life. We therefore turn now to His teaching.

A. We have already seen that the central thought in the mind of Jesus is the Fatherhood of God, and that in that great doctrine there is contained also Christ's anthropology, the conviction that man, in his spiritual nature, is a finite child made in the image of his infinite Father, and is therefore priceless in worth and deeply loved by God. Since, then, all men have one common origin, Christ can recognize no such thing as caste divisions among them. Being a child of God, every human being has a patent of nobility. There is no such thing as a low-caste man. All are of one caste; for they belong to the family of the ever-blessed Father. Since God is our Father, all men are necessarily brothers. If the Fatherhood is real, the brotherhood is real also. If the very essence of humanity be kinship to God, then men are essentially brothers. All differences are trivial; this is the only thing that matters. That which makes me a man makes every man my brother.

1. Jesus taught this rich truth and the deep obligations it brings in the most moving way. In His great picture of the day of judgement[1] all the nations are gathered before Him, and He separates them into two companies, placing on His right those who have served their fellow men, and on His left those who have failed in the great duty. In this wonderful passage He brings home to us the worth of the most despised men by speaking of them as 'the least of these my brethren'.

2. Holding that all men are children of the Father, Jesus necessarily held that they ought all to be taught about the Father. His message is to be proclaimed to all men:

> Go ye into all the world, and preach the gospel to the whole creation.[2]

He could have no doctrine of a special revelation, reserved for a few, as śruti is restricted to the three twice-born castes:[3]

[1] Matt. 25, 31–46, quoted below, p. 286. [2] Mark 16, 15.
[3] Above, p. 164.

No one lighteth a lamp and covereth it with a vessel or putteth it under a bed, but placeth it upon a lamp-stand, that they who come in may see the light.[1]

What I tell you in the darkness, speak ye in the light: and what ye hear in the ear, proclaim upon the housetops.[2]

3. Again, since all men are children of God, there can be no men who are essentially impure and unfit for intercourse. The Jew classed all non-Jews together as Gentiles, and declared them sinners and unclean. No Jew would eat with them. The same rule applied to the Samaritans. There was also a considerable section of the Jewish people in the time of Jesus who did not pretend to keep the Jewish religious law strictly. In consequence, the leaders declared them to be sinners, and forbade orthodox Jews to eat with them. Finally, leprosy was believed to be a disease inflicted by God as a punishment for sin. Hence the Jews not only adopted the wise precaution of avoiding close intercourse with the leper for fear of contagion, but drove him out of society and pronounced him religiously unclean, and therefore untouchable.

Jesus taught, on the contrary, that there are no walls of division between the races of mankind. On one occasion, in answer to a teacher of the Jewish law, he gave as a compendium of duty the twin precepts, 'Love God supremely,' 'Love your neighbour as yourself.' The teacher at once asked, 'Who is my neighbour?' and Jesus replied with the following story:

A certain man was going down from Jerusalem to Jericho; and he fell among robbers, which both stripped him and beat him, and departed, leaving him half dead. And by chance a certain priest was going down that way: and when he saw him, he passed by on the other side. And in like manner a Levite also, when he came to the place, and saw him, passed by on the other side. But a certain Samaritan, as he journeyed, came where he was: and when he saw him, he was moved with compassion, and came to him, and bound up his wounds, pouring on them oil and wine; and he set him on his own beast, and brought him to an inn, and took care of him. And on the morrow he

[1] Luke 8, 16. [2] Matt. 10, 27.

> took out two pence, and gave them to the host, and said, Take care of him; and whatsoever thou spendest more, I, when I come back again, will repay thee. Which of these three, thinkest thou, proved neighbour unto him that fell among the robbers? And he said, He that shewed mercy on him. And Jesus said unto him, Go, and do thou likewise.[1]

Thus Jesus teaches, in full accordance with the truth of the Fatherhood of God, that the man who needs your help is your neighbour, no matter what race he may belong to.

But Jesus felt that these superstitious rules could not be broken down by mere words, but only by revolutionary practice. Hence He habitually ate with the 'sinners' whom no Jew would have anything to do with, to the great scandal of the leaders and the orthodox:

> And it came to pass, as he sat at meat in the house, behold, many publicans and sinners came and sat down with Jesus and his disciples. And when the Pharisees saw it, they said unto his disciples, Why eateth your Master with the publicans and sinners?[2]

> Now all the publicans and sinners were drawing near unto him for to hear him. And both the Pharisees and the scribes murmured, saying, This man receiveth sinners, and eateth with them.[3]

> And he entered and was passing through Jericho. And behold, a man called by name Zacchaeus; and he was a chief publican, and he was rich. And he sought to see Jesus who he was; and could not for the crowd, because he was little of stature. And he ran on before, and climbed up into a sycomore tree to see him: for he was to pass that way. And when Jesus came to the place, he looked up, and said unto him, Zacchaeus, make haste, and come down; for to-day I must abide at thy house. And he made haste, and came down, and received him joyfully. And when they saw it, they all murmured, saying, He is gone in to lodge with a man that is a sinner.[4]

His practice in this matter was so well known that His enemies used it to make biting sarcasms about Him:

> A glutton and a winebibber, a friend of publicans and sinners.[5]

The answers of Christ to their reproaches are full of instruction. On one occasion He said,

[1] Luke 10, 30–37. See below, vii. 45.
[2] Matt. 9, 10–11.
[3] Luke 15, 1–2.
[4] Luke 19, 1–7.
[5] Matt. 11, 19.

> They that are whole have no need of a physician, but they that are sick. But go ye and learn what this meaneth, 'I desire mercy, and not sacrifice': for I came not to call the righteous, but sinners.[1]

On another, He gave utterance to the parables of the Lost Sheep, the Lost Piece of Money, and the Prodigal Son.[2] The great principles expressed in these replies are (*a*) that these people are very dear to God; (*b*) that they are at present 'lost', 'sick', far away from their Father; (*c*) that it is possible to save them; (*d*) that, in order to save them, it is necessary to seek their society. These rich religious truths, which have proved so mightily living and effective in many lands since the time of Christ, and are now proving of transcendent value to the Outcastes of India, provide an immovable ethical foundation for treating the most degraded peoples of the earth as human brothers. So soon as a man is grasped by these truths, it becomes impossible for him to believe in the Hindu laws against interdining. Christ dining with publicans and sinners has once for all rendered these customs irrational, obsolete in the modern world. He sets the Hindu free in the matter of eating with men of other castes, religions, and races.

4. But Christ's principles do not merely make it possible for us to eat with men of any race: they make it a duty for the religious man. Brotherly social intercourse is one means whereby our brothers may be raised. He who knows and enjoys in his own life the love of the Heavenly Father, cannot but wish to use this means to save His lost sheep.

5. There is another incident in the life of Jesus which is full of significance for India:

> So he cometh to a city of Samaria, called Sychar, near to the parcel of ground that Jacob gave to his son Joseph: and Jacob's well was there. Jesus therefore, being wearied with his journey, sat thus by the well. It was about the sixth hour. There cometh a woman of Samaria to draw water: Jesus saith unto her, Give me to drink. For his disciples were gone away into the city to buy food. The Samaritan woman therefore saith unto him, How is it that thou, being a Jew, askest drink

[1] Matt. 9, 12-13. [2] Luke 15, 4-32.

> of me, which am a Samaritan woman? (For Jews have no dealings with Samaritans.) Jesus answered and said unto her, If thou knewest the gift of God, and who it is that saith to thee, Give me to drink; thou wouldest have asked of him, and he would have given thee living water.[1]

Thus, as Jesus was ready to eat with any child of His Father, He was ready to take water from any human hand. The love of the Heavenly Father will open Hindu eyes to the truth that no man is unclean, that water, that great gift of the Father, is not polluted by coming from the hand of the humblest of His children, but comes none the less filled with His love and blessing.

6. But the most moving of all incidents in this connexion is Christ's meeting with the 'Outcaste', 'Unclean', 'Untouchable' leper:

> And there cometh to him a leper, beseeching him, and kneeling down to him, and saying unto him, If thou wilt, thou canst make me clean. And being moved with compassion, he stretched forth his hand, and touched him, and saith unto him, I will; be thou made clean. And straightway the leprosy departed from him, and he was made clean.[2]

Jesus usually healed with a word, and He felt as we do the repulsiveness of leprosy; but He knew that the leper had been excommunicated, that he had to call out 'Unclean' as he walked along the road, and that no kindly human hand had been laid on his shoulder for years; so He not only cleansed but touched him. The problem of the Untouchables of India was solved that day. What sort of men would Christians be, if, having such a Master, they did not go to seek the Outcaste?

The Fatherhood of God as taught by Jesus thus forms precisely the religious foundation that is wanted for the social law of the equality of all men. No man can hold the Fatherhood as taught by Jesus and believe that men are of different species. If all men are not recognized as social equals, then the brotherhood of men, even if it be nominally accepted, is

[1] John 4, 5–10. [2] Mark 1, 40–42.

not made the essence of humanity, but is pushed aside by some other consideration.

Hindus recognize that man is related to God, and they are learning to speak of the brotherhood of men ; but, according to all Hindu teaching, man is related to God in precisely the same way as every other form of life, whether vegetable or animal, is ; so that to the Hindu it is not the divine relationship that is significant, but the stage of progress which the soul, whether in plant, animal, or man, has reached. That is of infinite importance, and in the case of man is registered in caste ; and a man's place in caste is not only the reward of past achievement but also the starting-point of all his future progress in the things of the spirit. Thus the inevitable social outcome of Hindu theology is caste ; just as the inevitable social outcome of the teaching of Christ is equality.

It is of the utmost importance to recognize frankly that, if we consider men from the point of view of physique, mental capacity, education, efficiency, culture, attainments, character, they are very far from equal. So long as we take any one or all of these things as the essentials of humanity, to speak of equality is sheer nonsense. There are two articles side by side in the *Hindustan Review* for August, 1912, in which equality is ridiculed ; and rightly so, from the standpoint of the writers. It is only on the basis of the serious faith that each man is a child of God, spiritual, priceless, dearly beloved, that one can look the whole world in the face and say with reason and conviction, All men are equal. That is the sole justification possible of the political equality of European and Indian, of the uplifting of the Outcaste, of social equality, of democracy.

B. One of Christ's leading thoughts about those who have recognized the Fatherhood of God is their freedom. Perhaps the most vivid piece of teaching is found in the passage quoted above,[1] in which the idea is that the sons of God are free from the Temple tax. But their freedom has many forms. The

[1] P. 125.

most noteworthy proof of the stress which Jesus laid on the principle is the fact, which we have already dealt with,[1] that He laid down no detailed law for His followers, but left them to form systems of conduct for themselves, bidding them only remain loyal to the spiritual principles which He taught.

1. We have already seen that the universality of the doctrine of the Fatherhood of God necessarily sets the Christian free in all his intercourse with men, and that Christ has taught us by His example also that we may eat with any one, receive water from any one, and touch any human being. We next notice that He has also given us freedom in the matter of food:

> And he called to him the multitude again, and said unto them, Hear me all of you, and understand: there is nothing from without the man, that going into him can defile him: but the things which proceed out of the man are those that defile the man. And when he was entered into the house from the multitude, his disciples asked of him the parable. And he saith unto them, Are ye so without understanding also? Perceive ye not, that whatsoever from without goeth into the man, it cannot defile him; because it goeth not into his heart, but into his belly, and goeth out into the draught? This he said, making all meats clean. And he said, That which proceedeth out of the man, that defileth the man. For from within, out of the heart of men, evil thoughts proceed, fornications, thefts, murders, adulteries, covetings, wickednesses, deceit, lasciviousness, an evil eye, railing, pride, foolishness: all these evil things proceed from within, and defile the man.[2]

There is thus no food that is unclean in itself.

2. In the matter of occupation also, we have freedom. Since the human race is the family of God, every piece of work that is necessary for our welfare is worth doing and bears no stigma. The toil of the artisan, the ploughman, the cooly, the shopkeeper, aye the scavenger, is worthy of all honour. This ennobling truth Jesus taught by His example; for He toiled for some eighteen years as a carpenter. Thus only in Christ are our Brāhmans justified who sell hides, or make soap, or struggle to start some other industry to-day. Christ has taught us the nobility of the service of humanity.

[1] P. 58. [2] Mark 7, 14-23.

In the teaching and life of Jesus, then, we have the religious foundation for a society characterized by freedom.

Does it not seem as if in all these acts and words He must have been thinking of India?

C. But these two principles—equality and freedom—standing by themselves would create social chaos. They generate life and health only when they are fully controlled by the righteous will of the Heavenly Father. They must be completely moralized. But here again the central conception suffices: since we are brothers, we must act as true brothers in all things. In Christ's moralization of our social relations two distinct ideas rule.

1. First, in all our relations with our fellow men we must be just. Our Father in heaven can be satisfied with nothing less than *equal justice between man and man*, whatever their race, creed, or social position may be, the very reverse of the Hindu law, that each man must be dealt with according to caste.[1] It prohibits everything in the nature of aggression or unfairness. Brotherhood makes lies, slander, oppression, theft, adultery, murder impossible: a true man can do a brother no wrong. Christ's loftiest indignation is roused by men who profess to lead a religious life and yet are guilty of unrighteousness in their social relations. To Him they are hypocrites of the coarsest fibre:

> And Peter said, Lord, speakest thou this parable unto us, or even unto all? And the Lord said, Who then is the faithful and wise steward, whom his lord shall set over his household, to give them their portion of food in due season? Blessed is that servant, whom his lord when he cometh shall find so doing. Of a truth I say unto you, that he will set him over all that he hath. But if that servant shall say in his heart, My lord delayeth his coming; and shall begin to beat the menservants and the maidservants, and to eat and drink, and to be drunken; the lord of that servant shall come in a day when he expecteth not, and in an hour when he knoweth not, and shall cut him asunder, and appoint his portion with the unfaithful.[2]

> Beware of the scribes, which desire to walk in long robes, and love

[1] *Supra*, p. 164. [2] Luke 12, 41-46.

> salutations in the marketplaces, and chief seats in the synagogues, and chief places at feasts; which devour widows' houses, and for a pretence make long prayers: these shall receive greater condemnation.[1]

> Woe unto you, scribes and Pharisees, hypocrites! for ye tithe mint and anise and cummin, and have left undone the weightier matters of the law, judgement, and mercy and faith: but these ye ought to have done, and not to have left the other undone. Ye blind guides, which strain out the gnat, and swallow the camel.[2]

Christ's teaching that men are brothers and must deal with each other in strict justice is the only possible dynamic of reform in the modern world. To that we owe the prohibition of the slave-trade, the abolition of slavery, the cleansing of prisons, the amelioration of the conditions of labour, the temperance movement, the acknowledgement that Britain is responsible for the welfare and the progress of the people of India. Hence has Britain put down corruption among her Indian civilians and enforced equality in the law-courts. Hence also the abolition of satī and of cruel religious rites, and the prohibition of gross obscenity. As we have already seen, it is from the spirit of Christ that the whole reform movement in India has arisen.

Without this universal ethical postulate, that equal justice shall be done between man and man, whatever their race, religion, wealth, or position, healthy modern life is utterly impossible; and, so long as the caste system stands, such equality is altogether unattainable.

2. Secondly, to a brother I owe, not only strict justice, but all the help that he needs and that I can give. *Service according to need* is Christ's second moral principle for the social life. If every human being is of priceless value to my Father, as priceless as I am myself, then I must do all in my power to uplift those around me from suffering and degradation. Philanthropy is not an extra, to be taken up or laid aside according to whim, but a duty of the utmost obligation.

[1] Luke 20, 46–47.
[2] Matt. 23, 23–24.

This principle is dealt with below,[1] so that we need not spend time over it now.

Christ thus provides the necessary religious foundations for a society characterized by equality, freedom, and strict justice. Social evolution all over the world is steadily tending in the direction of these Christian ideals,[2] and the needs of modern men will inevitably increase the rate of the movement. Universal intercourse necessarily demands a universal society, complete social liberty, and a social morality of depth and strength sufficient to bear the unparalleled strain of the new state of affairs. Nothing but a conception of human brotherhood which contains within itself these liberties and obligations is equal to the creative task. Thus Christian society is the evolutionary goal of all living forms of society and of all the social unrest and agitation of our day.

But there is another important observation to make. These three outstanding features of the modern social movement—the demands for complete social equality, for full social freedom, and for real justice in our social relationships—are simply the culmination of what we found to be the characteristics of all social progress in the ancient world, viz. a wider society, greater freedom and fuller moralization.[3] Society, made as wide as the race, would give the social equality which the modern man wants; and the removal of the last barrier to freedom and the bringing of every social relationship under moral categories would secure the complete liberty and the social justice which all now desiderate. The evolution of society will thus reach its highest possible form under the guidance of Christian principles.

In so far, then, as India shows to-day social phenomena analogous to those found in Egypt, Turkey, Persia, China, and Japan, it is clear that the goal in view is a society inspired by the truths of the Fatherhood of God and the brotherhood of men. Only a society built on these heavenly

[1] P. 285 ff.
[2] *Supra*, pp. 187–190.
[3] *Supra*, pp. 156–7.

principles can meet the needs of modern India. Only by such breadth of law can the Indian nation come into being.

X. But there is a further question which we may well raise, whether the specific ideals to which the caste system has given such emphatic expression are likely to be lost in the vast social upheaval on the verge of which we stand, or will find clear re-expression in the new world-society; whether aspects of social life which were neglected even in Greece and Rome, but have been seriously insisted on in India, will blossom and bear fruit in the new society or are doomed to extinction. Hindu convictions on the subject of caste may be summed up under four heads:

A. The working principle of the caste system is *the dependence of duty and privilege on birth*, in fact *naissance oblige*, if we may remould the fine old watchword. The Brāhman alone may undertake priestly duties. Only the twice-born may hear the words of revelation and press on to release. Only the four groups of castes are fit for ordinary intercourse: all others are unclean.

But there have been many notable strainings of the Hindu spirit towards wider things.

The *Gītā* opened the doors of spiritual religion to women and to Śūdras;[1] and the bhakti sects opened them to Outcastes.[2] But, while it was acknowledged that women, Śūdras, and even Outcastes were spiritual enough to win emancipation, nay, to become teachers of spiritual things and to be worshipped as saviours, yet the doors were shut in their faces for everything else.[3] The Outcaste is still untouchable, a thing of horror to the Brāhman. Experience has shown that they can grasp spiritual things; but their birth remains; and over that impassable barrier no true Hindu dare step.

The Vīra Śaiva sect was founded in opposition to Brāhman privilege and caste distinctions; when the Sikhs became

[1] See below, p. 371. [2] See below, pp. 387, 399.
[3] See below, pp. 399–400.

a military order, they gave up caste; and the founder of the Ārya Samāj condemned caste with unsparing voice; yet all these bodies are in chains to-day, fast bound by that which they originally repudiated.

Some far-sighted Hindus have started the Depressed Classes Mission, and many would like to give help, but they are restrained by the suspicion, which is in truth well founded, that all such work undermines Hinduism.

The caste belief is that a Brāhman who eats with a Śūdra, an Outcaste, or a Mleccha suffers serious spiritual pollution. But the modern educated Hindu knows from experience that he is helped instead of injured by dining with the right type of Śūdra, Outcaste, Christian, Parsee, or Muḥammadan.

Caste belief as taught in the *Gītā* runs that it is better for a Brāhman to do bad work as a priest than to do excellent work as a doctor, a manufacturer, an engineer, or a business man;[1] while the modern Hindu sees plainly that India is dying from the work of its bad priests and being rejuvenated by its Brāhman manufacturers and its Outcaste educationalists.

Many a Hindu to-day sees that the restrictions of caste are very bad for Hindu society; but, still dominated by the religious belief that it is wrong to neglect the ancient laws founded on birth, he chooses to suffer loss in this world rather than risk a frightful punishment in the next.[2]

How is Hinduism to be set free from this haunting influence, which, despite the highest yearnings of her thinkers and leaders, steals over every community within the fold and binds it in chains, which paralyses the educated man in spite of both conscience and experience, which keeps the simple-minded Hindu from doing what he sees to be for the good of his people?

Christ is the Liberator; for by means of the truth about human birth he will set the Hindu free from caste. He does

[1] See above, p. 160. [2] See what Ranade says, above, pp. 117-8.

not degrade the Brāhman to the level of the Outcaste, but reveals the high truth that the savage, the cannibal, and the Outcaste are all Brāhmans and more. Every human unit has the supreme dignity and capacity of a child of the Most High. When this ennobling truth breaks in upon the sensitive Hindu spirit there will be no more terror and paralysis of soul at the thought of intercourse with others.[1] It will then become clear that there is no reason why people of different castes should not marry, provided they are really well matched in other respects; for they are all of the highest birth. Hindus will then gladly dine with Outcastes, as Jesus did. They will rejoice to recognize in every man a Brāhman; for, as children of God, we are all fit for the priestly work of offering spiritual sacrifices.

Thus, under Christ, birth is still the key to life; the high rule, *naissance oblige*, remains: the health of society and the progress of mankind depend upon our living up to our lofty duties and privileges as children of God.

B. The Hindu is profoundly impressed with *the sacredness of the social order*. Our study has made it abundantly clear to us that every element of caste has a religious basis and bears a religious significance. This is the secret of the invincible pervasive power it has shown throughout India, and also of its unparalleled grip on the Hindu spirit. Hence, to the Hindu, every rule and custom of caste is inviolably sacred. Indeed, nothing is more remarkable in this remarkable religion than the lofty conception the people have of the divine social order and the boundless reverence with which they regard it. As the thoughtful Hindu contemplates the stately social edifice, planned by divine wisdom from all eternity and linked adown the centuries by unerring righteousness with the spiritual progress of millions of transmigrating souls, he cannot but believe that its scrupulous preservation

[1] *I. S. R.*, April 20, 1913, p. 397, shows how even educated and progressive Hindus who believe in equality shrink from intercourse with Outcastes.

from wrong is the highest of all duties. By virtue of their place in the social order and of their faithful performance of all the details of the traditional law of the order, the Hindu people regard themselves as holy and as vowed to the faithful upbuilding of the divine society to which they belong. The maintenance of the divine society is called *dharma*, the Hindu ideal of social order and righteousness.

Since, to the Hindu, caste is a divine institution which he is bound to revere and maintain, he regards the Christian missionary as a coarse, irreverent, social iconoclast, laying impious hands on that which he can neither appreciate nor understand, and as altogether incapable himself of building anything in place of the thrice-noble edifice which he seeks to pull down. To Hindus Christian society seems at first utter chaos—race confusion in conspiracy with wild licence. Such thoughts are quite natural when men do not understand. This chapter, however, will have made it clear that the social order is as truly divine to the Christian as it is to the Hindu. Every detail of it is a reflex from the Fatherhood of God. Every social duty is transfigured in the light of His love for man. The sacramental note is everywhere ; for in doing the humblest duty to my brother I touch my Father's hand.

Nay, the truth is that society is more sacred to the Christian than to the Hindu. It is possible for the Hindu householder to cast aside all the duties and obligations of the family and society. By becoming a sannyāsī he rises to a plane of life where social obligations no longer hold.[1] Within the bounds of human life there is a sphere in which the divine society does not exist. No such idea is possible to the Christian. The married man can never, while he lives, lay aside his duty to his wife. The father never ceases to be responsible for his children. Nothing on earth or in heaven can ever absolve me from my common duty to my brother men. The closer I cling to Christ, the more seriously do my social

[1] See below, pp. 262–3.

duties rise upon my heart and conscience; for His example and His teaching equally stir us to a faithful social life. The deeper my faith is that God is my Father, the more conscious I am that the human race is His family, and that He is toiling and suffering to create the Kingdom of Heaven on earth. Thus, the Hindu consciousness of the sacredness of society will find a higher and wider sphere under Christ than in caste.

C. Hindu social life aims above all things at the *preservation of solidarity and of purity.*

The Hindu is most sensitively conscious of the need of a settled, well-balanced, self-sufficient community, and he believes it cannot be maintained apart from caste. How could men get work, prices and wages be regulated, skill and learning be preserved from generation to generation? The poor must be helped, the sinful restrained, enemies kept at a distance. How, without caste, would true mutual responsibility be maintained? Thus, on the faithful performance of all that the ancient rules enjoin depend the health and stability of the whole community.

In Christ we have not the narrow caste-group within which solidarity is comparatively easy to achieve, but we have the wider society which modern India needs, and ethical teaching of the greatest depth and power to make solidarity real. Towards the working out of the new national solidarity every patriotic Hindu now strains. But how is it to be accomplished? Only through Christ's conceptions of brotherhood, social justice, and social service. The bringing in of the Outcastes, the gathering in of the wild tribes, and the building, out of all the races of India, of a united and holy nation is a task that may well stir the noblest heart. Can Hindus stand by and see the alien missionary achieve this glorious enterprise? From the unexampled variety of Indian race and life, in the new rich conditions of the twentieth century, and with Christ's thought of the Kingdom as guide and plan, what manner of work may Indians not accomplish? Here is a sphere in which Christ gives an ideal of solidarity far beyond the dreams of caste.

To the Hindu, caste is the stronghold of purity, manners, culture, and of the whole religious heritage of the race. The high-caste man thinks of himself as one of a small number of pure-blooded, cultured, religious men amidst such vast numbers of unclean, vulgar, vicious people that the light is in grave danger of extinction. Aeneas-like, he bears through seething crowds of foes his ancestral heritage, bound by every duty to pass it on intact to those who follow him. Only in caste can he preserve from wrong the sacred trust of his fathers, that deposit of custom, practice, and law which regulates his religion, morals, and habits. It is this heritage which has made him what he is. In every act he does and every thought he thinks he is conscious of its influence. Each caste has its own distinct tradition. Amongst Brāhmans to this day the standard of cleanliness, speech, and behaviour is far higher than in other castes. It is impossible to simulate the Brāhman. A hundred trifles would betray the pretender. Feeling runs still deeper with regard to the rites of religion, the great doctrines of the faith, and the Vedānta. How can these survive if caste be tampered with? To allow these to be shared by low-born, ignorant men would be to court not only contamination but destruction.

Christ is as eager for purity, manners, culture, and spiritual religion as the holiest Hindu ever was; but He has another method for their preservation. The whole of the old world believed that truth and wisdom were so precious that they ought to be restricted to the few. But Christ holds that the only way to preserve truth is to spread it broadcast, that the only way to secure the triumph of wisdom and righteousness is to speak them out to all men and to trust to their own vitality for their survival. So with culture and manners. To tolerate multitudes of ignorant and vulgar men is to prepare an avalanche to overwhelm culture. The wider culture and good breeding are spread, the more secure they are. Hence Christ's words:

What I tell you in the darkness, speak ye in the light: and what ye hear in the ear, proclaim upon the housetops.[1]

Will not Hindus make it their ideal to bring the gentle manners, the cleanliness, and the pleasing speech of the Brāhman to the humblest Indian? Would such a consummation be dishonouring to the Hindu community? So with all truth. Every Indian, since he is a man, is heir to all the spiritual truth which the human race holds. We only bring him into his own estate when we tell him of his heavenly Father. Can we think of a more ennobling piece of work than the task of teaching every Indian the highest religious truth? The new social life in Christ is the real stronghold of culture and truth.

D. In Christ even the more detailed ideals of caste find fulfilment. The Brāhman is the man of prayer and sacrifice, the man who has direct access to God: in Christ Jesus this is every man's birthright. Every man and every woman is fit to be a priest of God, to offer spiritual sacrifice, to have unceasing, personal intercourse with the heavenly Father. The Śūdra was bid serve the three castes: Christ, who came not to be served but to be a servant,[2] shows us that the true man is a servant of his fellow men. The Śūdra ideal, as well as the Brāhman ideal, is universalized in Him.

The Hindu holds that even the men who are by birth spiritually fit for the highest privileges, viz. the Brāhman, the Kshatriya, and the Vaiśya, cannot enter upon these privileges until they have passed through a second birth. Originally, this sacred birth consisted in a long course of religious training and discipline; and an infinitesimal minority still take the course; but for the vast majority it has shrunk to the ceremony of initiation.[3] That which was originally so great has become an empty bubble shaming its high name.

But turn to Christ. Here the second birth is conversion, a revolution within the soul, a spiritual transformation of the

[1] Matt. 10, 27. [2] Matt. 20, 28. [3] See above, pp. 86 and 163.

man. Only he who undergoes the overturning change of repentance, forgiveness and union with Christ, enters upon the privileges of the kingdom of heaven. But the change is open to every one. Any child of God may yield to the influences of the Holy Spirit, repent of his past life, surrender to Christ, and through Him enter by the portal of the second birth into the new life. That which in Hinduism has become a formal ceremony is in Christ a spiritual reality.

CHAPTER V

THE ESSENTIALS OF HINDUISM

I. WHEN the invading Aryans entered India they merely sought lands on which to settle and live. For a considerable length of time they were content with small things. But gradually there arose among them the imperial instinct, and as a result they became masters, politically and religiously, of the whole of North India, and, at a later date, of the South also.

In the course of their gradual conquest of the North the simple religion of the *Ṛigveda* was transformed into Hinduism. The thought and culture of the invaders were spontaneously advancing; the impact of the innumerable tribes of aborigines with their varied religions and modes of life necessarily brought them much fresh material and vital quickening; while their new imperial position demanded a practical system applicable to their subjects as well as to themselves. In these circumstances a new set of beliefs arose and a new social and religious organization took form. Hinduism, the religion of India, was born. Innumerable changes have taken place since then; but they have all been within the lines of the original plan; they have all been branches of the primeval tree.

Our study of the life of the early Indo-Aryans left us with several ideas clearly defined before our minds. Their religion was a polytheistic worship of the powers of nature by means of prayer, hymn, and sacrifice, but without temples or images. We also found a few traces of a more spiritual faith and of philosophic speculation. The worship of ancestors held a large place in their minds and in their social organization. To this simple people the world was real and life was good. Men prayed to live a hundred years. Asceticism was unknown. The family was still in a healthy condition. There was no caste. There was no doctrine of transmigration. Man lived and died once, and after death was led by Yama to heaven, where he enjoyed an immortality of bliss with the 'fathers' and the gods. From this simple system was developed the elaborate theology and highly organized community of Hinduism.

It was the doctrine of karma and rebirth that gave character and form to the new system. While on the surface it is but a theory of birth and death, it is essentially the Hindu moral theory; and, as we have already seen, it enters as an element into every part of the religion.

There was another doctrine which proved of importance in the creation of the new thought, but it did not exercise such an influence as the transmigration theory did. The idea is that there exists one supreme divine Being, eternal and unknowable, who is manifested in all the gods and all the religions of men. He is spiritual and real; he is in nature and in man; he is the cause of all things, the Veda and caste included; in a sense, he *is* all things; and yet he is free from karma, which controls all things. Since he stands apart from karma, he is actionless. Being unknowable, he cannot be worshipped; but, since he is manifested in all the gods, the worship of any god is quite legitimate. The Brāhmans thus developed a simple philosophy of religion which they used to explain matters to themselves and to all eager inquirers, as they proceeded with their work of bringing the peoples of India under their influence. They must have met with many forms of religion, some of them very strange indeed, as they extended their sway over the land; yet every form of belief and every cult could be brought under this simple formula. It is this idea of the one God behind all the gods which the

Hindu villager uses to-day when any one asks him why he acknowledges many gods.

But the more clearly they envisaged the Supreme as real, the more worthless the world became to them. Thus, ever since these ideas took form, the Hindu has held that all worldly things are vain, valueless, empty, as compared with God. The doctrine that all material things are illusion is a much later development, and is not a necessary part of essential Hinduism ; but the worthlessness of the world is one of the central ideas of the religion.

But while in comparison with God the world was seen to be paltry, in the light of the doctrine of karma and rebirth, it was held to be eternal, coeval with God. It was a transitory, phenomenal system, completely controlled by karma, yet without beginning and without end. The course of the world's history is a continuous process of degeneration from the Golden down to the Iron age. Progress is impossible. But when things reach their worst, the whole world passes into invisibility and lies in peace and silence for countless ages; and, when it is re-manifested, things are once more at their best.

All souls, whether living as gods, demons, men, animals, or plants, are afloat on the stream of transmigration (*saṁsāra*). Their life is at once retribution for the past and opportunity for the future. But, though a man may rise by persistent good conduct, by sacrifice and austerity, to the highest position among men or even to the station of a god, release from the ever-whirling wheel of birth and death is not to be won by an ordinary life, but only by stepping out of the common course of existence into the life of world-renunciation.

The gods may be worshipped, in accordance with the old cult, by means of sacrifice, prayer, and hymn, conducted in the open air, or by means of temple and image; but, whether the old or the new method is followed, only a Brāhman is allowed to officiate as priest; and the Vedas must be acknowledged as the one Revelation. It must be noticed, however, that the old cult is open only to the three twice-born castes, and no woman can sacrifice without her husband; while all Hindu temples are open to the four castes and to women as well as men.[1]

Caste is the Hindu form of social organization. No man can be a Hindu who is not in caste; and if a group of outsiders is admitted into the community, they must organize themselves as a caste.

In the times of the *Ṛigveda* there were schools for young priests. These grew in importance with the growth of the ritual and of the power of the priests. More and more literature had to be mastered by the priestly student. Only the Brāhman could teach, and only men of the three highest castes were admitted to the schools. All women were excluded. During this period of reconstruction it became the custom to send every boy of the Brāhman, Kshatriya, and Vaiśya castes to school to receive the sacred education. Each boy underwent initiation before beginning his course. Nowadays very few indeed receive the old education.

This radical system was held by the Brāhmans and taught by them, in whole or in part, according to circumstances, as they pursued their work of subjugating the races of India to their authority. The ignorant were taught only as much as was necessary to enable them to take their place in the great organization; but, when thinking men asked questions, an answer was ready for them. This system of thought and life will not be found in this cut-and-dried form, separated from all else, in any Hindu manual; yet it lies behind every form of Indian religion and philosophy which appears on the stage of history throughout the centuries. In Buddhism, Jainism, the Sāṅkhya philosophy and the great sects, one or other element has been somewhat modified; yet the forms of these systems would scarcely be comprehensible to us, did we not know the great ancestor from which they sprang.

II. The leading constituents of this system will be found to

[1] See above, p. 164.

fit very well together. If we hold that the invisible God behind all things takes no part in the activity of the phenomenal universe, then we can readily believe that the whole world is destitute of worth and substance. Again, if the world is so distinctly a vain show, it is not unnatural to think that souls, once caught in its meshes, may live beclouded and dazzled for ages, finding no way back to the divine Source, until their blind eyes are opened to see through the shows of Time to the one Reality. In these circumstances caste appears at once reasonable and right, as marking stages of the soul's progress towards enlightenment. The advance of the soul is of so much moment that the social system may well be made stern and unyielding, in order to conserve gains as they are made; and the spiritual advancement which is believed to lie behind the birth of every Brāhman is quite a reasonable basis for the religious authority which is demanded for him. Similarly, the conception that the Veda is the eternal utterance of the divine Mind, revealed anew in divers portions to the Ṛishis at the opening of every world-era, is a reasonable ground for the practical authority claimed for it.

Perhaps the most noticeable thing about the system is the way in which it fits practically into the circumstances of the time. It is, first of all, the old system to which the people were accustomed; for it is the religion of the *Ṛigveda*; yet it is so transformed as to satisfy the intellect of the most advanced Aryans of the day. It is, on the other hand, a philosophy of religion, which enables the grossest of the pagan cults of the aborigines to be included in the same imperial system with the highest speculations of philosophy and with the elaborate sacrificial performances of the Brāhmans. Had there been no caste to bind the people together, the speculative religious ideas would have been ineffectual; while, without the doctrine of transmigration, caste would have had no intellectual or moral justification and could have never laid hold of the popular conscience.

The strength and greatness of the whole group of ideas will be at once apparent. The thought of the worthlessness of the world in contrast with the glory and spirituality of Brahman is one that lays hold of the intellect and has many interests for philosophy. The emptiness of the world is a powerful moral conception, and has been one of the chief sources of all the forms of spiritual religions which India has exhibited during the centuries. Every religion has found it necessary to persuade man to seek emancipation from the power of the sense-world. Hinduism has no need to search for reasons to support this teaching: it springs inevitably from the Hindu conception of things. Then, on the other hand, if the system deprives the world of all claim to final reality, the doctrine of transmigration and karma expresses in the most powerful way possible its actuality and its grip over the human spirit. The unbending, remorseless law of karma has a cosmic grandeur and a kind of scientific completeness about it which at first sight are very captivating. Given these conceptions, the elaborate organization and the strict rules of caste appeal to the thinking mind as an orderly and reasonable system.

Here, then, we have the Hindu world-theory in all its permanent essentials: God real, the world worthless; the one God unknowable, the other gods not to be despised; the Brāhmans with their Vedas the sole religious authority; caste a divine institution, serving as the chief instrument of reward and punishment; man doomed to repeated birth and death, because all action leads to rebirth; world-flight the only noble course for the awakened man and the one hope of escape from the entanglements of sense and transmigration.

III. We have been accustomed to think of Hinduism as an unchanging system, the home of all the conservatisms. Now, it is very true that the Hindu seeks to live in most things precisely as his ancestors lived centuries ago; yet conservatism and stagnation are not the whole story. In Hinduism there are certain large freedoms. To the European these liberties are at first sight worthless: the Hindu seems to be free where he ought to be bound and bound where he ought to be free. Yet, rightly or wrongly, there are these freedoms; and, in order to understand Hinduism and its working, it is most necessary to realize what parts of Hindu life are free and what parts are under stern regulation. In this chapter we isolate the things which are regarded by the Hindu as eternal, and therefore as allowing of no liberty.

The ordinances to which a Hindu must conform fall into three groups: the family, caste, and religion.

A. An orthodox Hindu must have been born in a Hindu family, must have undergone all the necessary ceremonies as a child and young man, and must continue to live as a member of his family, obeying all the regulations and fulfilling all the duties of a householder. These duties include the family rites mentioned in our second chapter, viz. the sacraments, the worship of ancestors, the worship of the family gods, and the observance of the annual feasts and seasons of worship. If he is a twice-born Hindu, he ought also to observe daily, morning and evening, the prescribed ablutions, prayers and offerings.

B. An orthodox Hindu must have been born in a Hindu caste, must have undergone initiation if he is a Brāhman, Kshatriya, or Vaiśya, or some other equivalent ceremony if he belongs to a lower caste; and he must continue to observe all the rules and regulations which are traditional in his own caste, as was set forth in Chapter IV.

C. An orthodox Hindu must worship the gods either in the old Vedic fashion or in the temples. He must acknowledge the Vedas as the one revelation, and he must employ Brāhmans for all priestly duties, whether in his home or elsewhere. No one but a Brāhman can sacrifice, conduct religious ceremonies, act as a religious teacher, or proclaim the law.

All this, then, is obligatory on the Hindu. In these matters he is bound. The observance of these laws and customs is called *dharma*, i.e. right conduct. *Dharma* is explained and discussed in detail in the books known as *Dharmaśāstras*, the greatest of which is the *Mānava Dharmaśāstra* or code of Manu. Here is what is laid down on this point by the highest authorities. We quote the *Gītā* first:

> Therefore, realizing the *śāstra* to be the standard for determining right and wrong, thou should'st do here the works specified in the ordinances of the *śāstra*.[1]

Then Śaṅkara:

> The knowledge of one action being right and another wrong is based on scripture only.[2]

The liberties of the Hindu are outside the circle of *dharma*. A man may remain an orthodox Hindu without believing in any god or any theology, and without knowing or reading any sacred book. He may be a Christian, a Muḥammadan, an agnostic, or an atheist in his convictions. No question is raised so long as he conforms to usage.

[1] xvi. 24. [2] *S.B.E.*, xxxviii. 131.

CHAPTER VI

THE SUMMIT OF INDIAN THOUGHT

If a cultured Hindu were asked to select the loftiest aspect of his religion, there can be little doubt that he would name the Vedānta philosophy. To that, therefore, this chapter will be given. In order to understand it, we shall have to trace its history in outline.

I. There are a number of philosophic hymns in the *Ṛigveda* and also in the *Atharvaveda*, and some of the ideas suggested in them reappear in later philosophy; but, for the purpose we have in view here, it will suffice if we begin our survey with the conceptions expressed in the Brāhmaṇas. Amid the innumerable speculations and guesses scattered through these priestly works two are worthy of all attention.

The first conception is Brahman, which by derivation is connected with the idea of sacred utterances, whether hymn or prayer, but which in the Brāhmaṇas is thought of as the one source of the visible universe. Brahman was called the source of all things, the Creator and the Ruler of the universe.

The other concept is Ātman, which means self. At first the word was used in various senses; but gradually it came to stand more distinctly for the conscious thinking power, whether in man or in the universe. There was no sharp distinction between the self in man and the Self of the universe. The idea seems to have been that of an all-pervading consciousness, which appears in each man as a speck of light, the thought-power within him, while remaining the Self of the universe. This concept, like Brahman, the reality of the universe, was used to explain the world. The Ātman was spoken of as the Creator and the Controller of the world.

There were thus the two outstanding conceptions, Brahman and the Ātman, each of which had been declared the source of all things. Brahman, however, had been reached objectively, by considering the world as a system of nature subject to religious influences, while it was the inner psychical world which had given birth to the conception of the universal Ātman.

Next came the moment when some thinker combined them, saying, 'Brahman is the Ātman.' The source of all things thus came to be definitely recognized as intelligent, psychical. The Brahman-Ātman was regarded as the secret of the universe, and as present in every man. The identification of the two would greatly stimulate thought; and the consciousness, unity, universality, and divine character of Brahman-Ātman would gradually rise in men's minds and receive clearer definition.

The Ātman was further defined in contrast with the gods. These early thinkers watched the religious life around them and saw that each god was conceived as eager to receive the homage and the sacrifices of men, and in order to receive them was ready to give men gifts in return. Each god was thus an individual spirit, having his own selfish interests, and was subject to motives similar to those that rule men. Hence the Ātman was conceived as free from desire, and, therefore, not liable to be tempted by the sacrifices of men. He was desireless, actionless, at peace.

There is no doubt that these thinkers had lighted on a most difficult problem. Turn to the religions of Egypt, Babylonia, Greece, or Rome, and you will find that the above description is true of their gods. They listen to praise and prayer, and are responsive to human need, but they quarrel about the things of earth, intrigue to get the support of men, and show the vilest passions. This is true even of the mighty Zeus of Greek poetry, who is conceived as the Supreme and so named.

The formation of this developed conception of the spiritual Reality behind the world necessarily modified thought in other directions. The world began to appear changeful and ordinary in the light of the thought of the spiritual, invisible, unchangeable Ātman. The gods also took a subordinate position when contrasted with this omnipresent, omnipotent, omniscient Divinity. Necessarily, a desire arose to attain union with the Ātman; and there are certain passages in the Brāhmaṇas which teach that men may rise to him by knowledge and find immortality and release from desire and action.[1] Once or twice we receive intimations of the coming of the great doctrine of the identity of the human soul and Brahman;[2] but as yet the idea is not seriously taken up.

Up to this point Indian thought contained innumerable speculations, some of them barren, others full of promise. But we must draw a broad line between these early flashes of speculative genius and the rise of the earliest Indian philosophy. It was the coming of a new element into Hindu belief and thought that finally led to the production of something like a speculative system. It was the rise of the doctrine of transmigration and karma that proved the occasion at least, if not the cause, of that splendid excitement of the Indian mind which created Hindu philosophy. This fact must never be lost sight of in our study of the evolution of Hindu thought. Clearly, belief in transmigration and karma was taken very seriously by the men of those days. The soul, as they conceived it, was a prisoner fast bound in the system of rebirth, inevitably performing actions which would in turn bind it as fast in another life.

The doctrine of karma fitted in very well with the conception of Brahman-Ātman also. He had been conceived as unborn, immortal, ever free, and also as desireless and actionless. Hence, when the theory of karma and rebirth appeared,

[1] *Taittirīya B.*, iii. 12. 9, 8; *Śatapatha B.*, x. 5. 4, 15; x. 6. 3; Deussen, 343.

[2] *Śatapatha B.*, x. 6. 3, 2.

he was the only being in the universe that was not under the sway of karma. Being desireless and actionless, karma could not lay hold of him. Had he been conceived as acting, he would necessarily have been thought of as bound by karma and liable to birth.

From this time, then, forward we recognize three strands of thought in the idea of the Supreme. As Brahman, he is most closely connected with the material world; as the Ātman, he is intelligent, self-conscious spirit; as free from desire and karma, he is actionless.

As a result of the appearance of the doctrine of rebirth and karma we also note a deepening of the contrast between the Ātman and the world. The whole universe is subject to karma, but the Ātman is free. The world is full of sorrow and everywhere in bonds: no spirit is exempt; every man and every animal is suffering or enjoying the inevitable requital of former deeds. Plants also are regarded as under transmigration. The whole creation is held in the hard grip of this remorseless force. Even the gods are recognized as being temporary beings, enjoying for a time in heaven the glorious reward of noble conduct in other lives, but destined each in turn to rebirth and possibly to a return to a far lowlier condition. They belong to the phenomenal universe as truly as man and the animals. Men could not fail to realize much more clearly than before the pitiful contrast between the world, on the one hand, with its pain and sorrow, its trouble and strife, its petty gods and sacrifices, its transmigration and karma, and the Ātman, on the other, in all its spirituality, power, and freedom. The Ātman was altogether free from the world. It had no share in its action, no relation to its religion or its morality, was undisturbed by its sorrow, unchained by its karma.

Thus thoughtful men began to feel most keenly their position in the world, subject to karma and rebirth, to suffering and repeated death. They were filled with a great loathing for these repeated births and deaths. It seemed to them a miserable thing to be whirled round for ever on this wheel of existence. They longed for something imperishable.[1] They could not acquiesce in continuous reincarnation. Was there no possibility of finding release from this galling necessity? Philosophy sprang into existence in response to that urgent question.

It was with the Ātman that the process began. At first the Ātman or Self seems to have been thought of as a sort of conscious essence diffused throughout the universe, present in all things, only showing itself most distinctly in man's conscious life, the human self. But as thinkers brooded over these ideas, the truth about spirit as such became clearer to their minds. They thought of the Self as pervading all things and appearing everywhere, yet beyond both space and time, and in, above, and beneath all things, yet truly one. In this way it became impossible to think of the Self as a subtle *physical* essence diffused throughout the universe: that idea was too materialistic and mathematical. Nor could they think of the Self as appearing *in part* in each man; for that was to divide the unity of the divine Spirit. Yet they found within themselves the basis of all their thought about the Self. In their own souls they found the unity, the intelligence, the unlimited thought which they predicated of the Divine. Hence some one was bold enough to say, 'The self in man is not merely the divine Self showing itself at one point; the human self *is* the divine Self, the divine Self whole and complete.' 'I am Brahman.' It was but a natural inference from foregoing thought, yet it was the boldest, the greatest venture ever made by the Indian mind.

Now, note carefully the inevitable result. When this mighty thought came home to a man as true, when he realized that he was the eternal Brahman, he felt instantly transported from his old worldly life to the changeless freedom of Brahman. Being the eternal Ātman, he was *not* bound by

[1] Aśvaghosha, *Buddhacharita*, v. 26.

transmigration and karma. In his new knowledge he stood emancipated for ever. Brahman is altogether free: I am Brahman; therefore I am free.

By this experience the man was completely transformed. He had hitherto regarded himself as an individual living being in the multitudinous kingdom of nature, not so very different from the animals, dependent altogether on the things of time and of the senses, hopelessly entangled in karma and rebirth. He now realizes that that is all a dream; that he is a spiritual being to whom all nature is but an empty show;[1] an immortal being to whom fear, sorrow, and death are meaningless;[2] an eternal being for whom the changes of time are less than nothing;[3] a self-sufficing spirit, requiring nothing and therefore desiring nothing; a universal being to whom individuality is but a speck; a free spirit, far beyond the reach of the fetters of karma, whether of past or of future actions. The experience has brought him such a joyous elevation of spirit that he can never fall to the old levels again. He knows himself the eternal God, present in all the universe, the sum and substance of all reality. He stands immortal, fearless, desireless, beyond the reach of pain, or sorrow, or doubt, his experience all ended, his soul filled with the blessedness of a great peace.

The necessary result of this condition of mind was that the man at once gave up all his connexion with the world. He did not belong to the fleeting world, but to the world of Brahman. What had the eternal Brahman to do with worship, children, comfort, pleasure, business, property, or government? Brahman had nothing to do with action, 'that evil thing.'[4] Now that the man had realized his own true being, he could never return to his old life of vanity, folly, and sorrow. For Brahman alone is peace: 'all else is full of sorrow.'[5] 'What shall we do with offspring, we who have

[1] *Kāṭhaka U.*, iv. 2; *Māṇḍūkya Kārikā*, i. 16.
[2] *Bṛihadāraṇyaka U.*, iv. 4, 15; *Chhāndogya U.*, vii. 26, 2.
[3] *Kaivalya U.*, 19. [4] *Taittirīya B.*, III. xii. 9, 8. Deussen, 343, 361.
[5] *Bṛihadāraṇyaka U.*, iii. 4, 2.

this Self and this world?'[1] 'Those worlds are in truth joyless.'[2] 'Sunless are those worlds, covered with blinding darkness.'[3] How could the man who, through his enlightenment, 'overcomes hunger, and thirst, sorrow, passion, old age and death,'[4] return to the life that is filled full of all these evils?

So the result of the transforming experience was that the man abandoned home, marriage, family, property, business, caste, his sacred thread, the worship of the gods, the worship of ancestors, and wandered about homeless, seeking solitude, sleeping at the foot of a tree or in a cave, and getting his food by begging. He was therefore called a Renouncer, *sannyāsī*, a Wanderer, *parivrājaka*, a Beggar, *bhikshu*. The word *sannyāsī*, Renouncer, is the most significant. The idea is that the man surrenders the world. They gave up all amusements, laid aside all jewellery and ornaments, shaved their heads, and wore only a minimum of clothing, or even went stark naked. Each carried a rod and a bowl in which he received the food he begged. It is most remarkable that these men not only gave up everything that makes life comfortable and attractive, but gave up caste also, thus stepping outside Hindu society altogether.[5] The thoroughness of the process is explainable only by reference to the conception of Brahman, who, conceived as the Absolute, was believed to be altogether untouched by any of the activities of phenomenal existence.

II. The deep sincerity and seriousness of the movement stand out perfectly plain in the extraordinary features of the life which we have just described. No thinking man can forbear to admire with the utmost heartiness the boldness of the thought and the supreme strenuousness of the discipline to which these men submitted themselves. We do not wonder

[1] *Bṛihadāraṇyaka U.*, iv. 4, 22. [2] Ib., iv. 4, 11.
[3] *Īśā U.*, 3. [4] *Bṛihadāraṇyaka U.*, iii. 5, 1.
[5] For further details see below, pp. 254, 262–263.

that they made a tremendous impression upon the people of their time and gained influence by their life.

All scholars recognize at once the great insight revealed and the essential truth attained in the conceptions of Brahman as the spiritual Self of the universe and of the identity of Brahman and the individual self. These ideas form the fountain-head of all the greatest thinking that has been done in India.

The conception of the Ātman is clearly and vividly spiritual. While conceived as immanent in all things and transcending all things, as truly omnipresent and universal, yet the Self is described as invisible, impalpable, timeless, spaceless, a perfect unity. Consciousness and omniscience are the very nature and being of the Self; and the perfect unity of the eternal mind is beyond the reach of sorrow, change, or death. So far as it is positive, the conception of the infinite Spirit is true and rational.

The doctrine of the identity of man with God suggests a great many valuable thoughts. No modern thinker is likely to accept the dogma as it stands; but all will agree that it comes so near to being the right expression of a group of priceless truths that it is no wonder that early India hailed it as a revelation. Every one will recognize how close the relationship is between the doctrine and the following ideas: man's dignity and spiritual grandeur; the immensity of his intellectual faculty; the boundlessness of his desires; his passion for immortality; his nearness, likeness, and kinship to God; the immediacy of the intercourse which he may have with God; God's actual presence in every human heart and conscience; and lastly, the spontaneous desire of the soul for union with God. The doctrine is thus of very great value as a testimony to the divine side of human nature.

But we may go one step farther. These men had not merely thought out a conception of God and of man. Their new belief touched them in the depths of their spiritual nature, and overflowed in religious experience. The exalted language of the best passages[1] of the earliest literature is sufficient to attest the reality of their intercourse with God. In these passages several distinct elements of their experience are frequently described, which further strengthen our inference.

(*a*) The Ātman has become inexpressibly dear to them :

Were a man to offer this earth surrounded by water and filled with wealth, yet is this more than that, more than that.[2]

He who sees, perceives and understands this loves the Self, delights in the Self, revels in the Self, rejoices in the Self.[3]

This, which is nearer to us than anything, this Self, is dearer than a son, dearer than wealth, dearer than all else.[4]

(*b*) The world has lost all its power over them :

Wishing for that world only, mendicants leave their homes. Knowing this, the people of old did not wish for offspring. 'What shall we do with offspring,' they said, 'we who have this Self and this world?' And they, having risen above the desire for sons, wealth and new worlds, wander about as mendicants.[5]

They're simpletons who follow outward pleasures!
They fall into the snare of widespread Death.
But wise men, understanding immortality,
Seek not th' Unchangeable 'mid things that change.[6]

He who beholds that Loftiest and Deepest,
For him the fetters of the heart break asunder.[7]

What can he desire who has all?[8]

(*c*) In their conscious knowledge of God they feel they have reached immortality:

On whom the fivefold host of living beings,
Together with space depend,
Him know I as my soul,
Immortal the Immortal.[9]

[1] *Chhāndogya U.*, vii. 11; viii. 4; *Bṛihadāraṇyaka U.*, i. 4, 8; ii. 4, 5; iv. 4, 12-25; *Kāṭhaka U.*, v. 9-15; vi. 2-3, 9, 14-15.
[2] *Sāṅkhāyana Ā.*, xiii.
[3] *Chhāndogya U.*, vii. 25, 2.
[4] *Bṛihadāraṇyaka U.*, i. 4, 8.
[5] Ib., iv. 4, 22.
[6] *Kāṭhaka U.*, iv. 2.
[7] *Muṇḍaka U.*, ii. 2, 8.
[8] *Māṇḍūkya Kārikā*, i. 16.
[9] *Bṛihadāraṇyaka U.*, iv. 4, 17.

All this existing universe
Moves in the Life from which it sprang.
A mighty terror 'tis, a thunderbolt upraised!
The men who know It, they become immortal.[1]

When man forgoes all those desires
That lie within his heart,
The mortal then becomes immortal,
And here and now gains Brahman.[2]

III. The relation of the Ātman to the universe is of so much importance that we must attempt to make the connecting ideas as clear as possible. The human soul was held to be identical with God, as we have seen. We have now to realize that the world also was in a way identified with God. The great phrase in which this idea was expressed is *Ekam eva aditīyam*, 'One there is, without a second.' Frequently the world is simply said to be God. This idea comes, clearly, from the original conception of Brahman as the invisible source and support of all that is. In the earliest literature the phrases are still fluid and living, not carefully defined. Hence thinkers developed the idea in different directions. One would construe the one Existence as physical, absolutely identifying Brahman with the universe, losing the spiritual in the material. Another would strain towards an idealistic interpretation, making the spiritual Brahman the sole existence and almost depriving the physical world of reality. A third would think the monistic thought fully satisfied if he spoke of the world as a product of Brahman and everywhere interpenetrated by him. This last comes nearest the original idea; and, in whatever direction thinkers may have leaned, they never forgot that God was all-pervading.

But, as we have seen, the Ātman, being completely free from desire, was actionless. Thus God pervades the universe in every part, but he does not act upon it. The idea is rather difficult to hold, but it must be grasped if we are to understand the system. God is immanent in the universe, all-pervasive,

[1] *Kāṭhaka U.*, vi. 2.   [2] *Kāṭhaka U.*, vi. 14.

yet he does not act. To conceive the Ātman as acting would be to subject him to karma and therefore to birth, sorrow, and death. Hence these thinkers declared that he was altogether untouched by what happens in the world. Here is one of the passages where this conviction is vigorously expressed:

> He, however, the Ātman, is not so, not so (*neti, neti*). He is incomprehensible, for he is not comprehended; indestructible, for he is not destroyed; unaffected, for nothing affects him; he is not fettered, he is not disturbed, he suffers no harm.[1]

Śaṅkara constantly emphasizes the actionlessness of Brahman.[2] From this absolute severance of the all-pervading Ātman from the work and experience of the world several results of the utmost importance followed.

A. The first result of declaring Brahman to be apart from all action is that he is conceived as being above morality. He is quite apart from the petty distinctions of right and wrong. Moral rules belong to human life, not to the transcendent life of the Source of the universe. Brahman is declared to be reality, consciousness, bliss, but he is never said to be righteousness. He is fully recognized as the intelligence behind the universe, but he is never spoken of as having a character, or as being the source and centre of the moral order. Indeed, we are carefully taught that, as the Absolute, he is separate from all action, whether good or bad, just as he is above time and change:

> The Self is a bank, a boundary, so that these worlds may not be confounded. Day and night do not pass that bank, nor old age, death and grief; neither good nor evil deeds.[3]

> Distinct from right, distinct from wrong,
> Distinct from causes and effects,
> Distinct from past and future too,—
> What seems to thee like that, declare.[4]

[1] *Brihadāraṇyaka U.*, iv. 2, 4; Deussen, 147.
[2] *S.B.E.*, xxxiv. 33, 62; xxxviii. 355.
[3] *Chhāndogya U.*, viii. 4, 1; *S.B.E.*, i. 130.
[4] *Kāṭhaka U.*, ii. 14. Cf. *Brihadāraṇyaka U.*, iv. 4, 5.

Hence emancipation is not conceived as being dependent on morality in any way. It arises altogether from knowledge. Realization of one's unity with Brahman is itself release from rebirth and from the world. This clear and comprehensible doctrine is taught without any ambiguity in the early literature and is expounded and defended by the greatest authorities.[1] Brahman not being conceived as the source of morality, the method whereby a man realizes his identity with Brahman is not a moral process. Only enlightenment could give the end aimed at, namely complete emancipation from transmigration and karma.

Even when a man has found emancipation, he does not necessarily become moral. Even if he be guilty of vicious actions, his actions do not stain him. Indeed, for the man who has realized his identity with Brahman, all moral distinctions have lost their meaning. Morality is only one element of the phenomenal life, and the difference between right and wrong disappears like all other differences in the blaze of the light of the Absolute. Morality belongs to the unreal world, which the released man sloughs off in completeness on finding release. It belongs to the sphere of 'change' and 'becoming' with which he has nothing more to do. Hence the life of the monk was originally under no moral law:

> Then (i. e. when he has realized his identity with the Ātman) he is unaffected by good, unaffected by evil.[2]
>
> He is not exalted by good works, he is not degraded by evil works.[3]
>
> He who has found it is no longer sullied by any evil deed.[4]
>
> As water does not cling to a lotus leaf, so no evil deed clings to one who knows it.[5]
>
> He does not distress himself with the thought, 'What good have I left undone, what evil done?'[6]

[1] For Śaṅkara, see *S.B.E.*, xxxiv. 29, 63, &c.; for Rāmānuja, *S.B.E.*, xlviii. 9, &c.

[2] *Bṛihadāraṇyaka U.*, iv. 3, 22.

[3] Ib., iv. 4, 22.

[4] Ib., iv. 4, 23.

[5] *Chhāndogya U.*, iv. 14, 3.

[6] *Taittirīya U.*, ii. 9.

> As the water-bird is not defiled by moving in the water, so a liberated yogī is not polluted by merit or by demerit.[1]

> Evil adheres not to an enlightened man any more than water clings to a leaf; but much sin sticks to the unenlightened man, just as lac to wood.[2]

> Abandoning truth and falsehood, pleasure and pain, the Vedas, this world and the next, he shall seek the Ātman.[3]

> And no sin can touch them, though they behave and conduct themselves in any way that pleases them.[4]

Even the *Gītā* contains this doctrine :

> He who neither loveth nor hateth, nor grieveth, nor desireth, renouncing good and evil, full of devotion, he is dear to me.[5]

Thus, in the earliest days, the search for the Ātman was not conditioned by morality. But soon many men who did not know Brahman but were eager to come to a realization of their identity with him became monks. Thus the monastic life came to be thought of as a discipline leading to knowledge of Brahman. Consequently, three forms of discipline from the life of the hermit (which we deal with in our next chapter)[6] were adopted. First, the practice of austerities, *tapas*, was accepted by many monks as a means of complete conquest over their own souls. The systematic exercises for the regulation of breathing and the control of the intellectual processes called *yoga* were also adopted by many sannyāsīs. Lastly, the law of *ahiṁsā*, harmlessness, was imposed on all, that is, the law against killing any animal or breaking a twig from any living plant. The conception of Brahman as unaffected by any passion gave the rule for their conduct to outsiders, viz. *Indifference*:[7] love and hate, gratitude and resentment, envy and pride are to be all crushed. Hence, also, complete chastity, truthfulness and honesty were demanded. As time went on, the moral side of monastic life produced a beautiful ideal of the passive virtues.

[1] *Mahābhārata*, xii. 247, 17.
[2] Ib., xii. 299, 7.
[3] *Āpastamba*, ii. 9, 21, 13.
[4] *Mahānirvāṇa T.*, viii. 268.
[5] xii. 17.
[6] p. 249 f.
[7] *Gītā*, v. 19; ix. 29.

B. The second result of depriving Brahman of action was that men tended to conceive him as impersonal. He was self-conscious thought, but not will. Hence it did not seem natural to credit him with personality. The earliest texts are by no means consistent in this matter, for many passages are distinctly theistic in tone;[1] but there can be no doubt that the farther reflection went the stronger became the drift towards an impersonal Supreme.

C. The third result was this, that Brahman was necessarily conceived as not communicating with man. One of the great statements which they made about him is that he is 'beyond the reach of thought and voice'. This phrase is repeated thousands of times in the later literature. Hence, though Brahman pervades the whole universe, and is close by us all the time, it is quite impossible to worship him, or even to utter prayer to him. He can neither hear prayer nor receive worship. We have already seen that sannyāsīs gave up ordinary Hindu worship. We now see that Brahman could not be worshipped. The monk worshipped no one. His time was spent in realizing his identity with Brahman.

D. The fourth result was that he could not be thought of as creating the universe. Such an act would have involved him in karma. In the earliest literature phrases may be found which come very near representing him as Creator, but the more careful thinkers avoid such statements; and the farther down the stream we go the more clearly do we find the point realized.

These four points will come up again later.[2]

IV. The relation of these thinkers to popular Hinduism must also be made clear. We have already seen that they gave up completely the worship of the Hindu gods. We must now note that in the earliest texts we find these gods, the priests who worship them, their sacrifices, their liturgy, and the books in which these are enshrined all spoken of

[1] Deussen, 175 ff.; see also p. 352, below.

[2] See below, pp. 244–246, 392–407.

most contemptuously,[1] as worthless to the man who knows Brahman. They seem to have shaken themselves free from popular religion as completely as from ordinary society. The Vedas and the Vedic School were now useless. What need had they to sacrifice to the gods? They no longer desired those things which Hindus expected to receive from the gods in return for their sacrifices.

But, although it is perfectly plain that they stood apart in supreme contempt from the whole Hindu system at first, yet they raised no protest against either the religion, or the life, or the literature. They were simply altogether indifferent to it. Another thing which strikes one as very strange is this, that they did not declare all the old gods fictions of the imagination. We should be inclined to think that any mind virile enough to think its way through so many obstacles to the splendid conception of the one God, spiritual, absolute, supreme, would have had vigour and sense enough to see that the whole mythology of Hinduism was a web of baseless imaginations. But that was not so. All the philosophers up and down the centuries, even the founder of Buddhism himself, believed in the existence of all the Hindu gods. They regarded themselves as superior to these gods, and neither worshipped nor honoured them any longer; but there was not in their thought sufficient real insight to expel the vast noxious growth of the pantheon and the mythology from their beliefs. The gods are transmigrating souls, just like men, only through their conduct in past lives they have risen to the position of divine beings. When their merit is consumed, they will be born again, and may possibly be in very low positions. It is of the utmost consequence that we should remember this in all our study of Indian philosophy; for without it the course of the history is unintelligible.

The discussions which created this system of philosophy did not take place in the Brāhmanic schools, but in the streets,

[1] See below, pp. 260-261.

in the forest and at sacrifices; and men of any caste, and women also, took part in them. It was at first a most democratic movement. Yet, though the movement was powerful enough to send many men out into the forests as monks, it might soon have withered and have produced no very permanent result.

But in this matter the genius of the Brāhman showed its masterly power once more. Though the new thought was so revolutionary as to drive men away from ordinary Hindu worship and to make them despise the Veda, yet the Brāhmans saw how it could be tamed. They introduced it into their schools and taught it as the last and highest subject of the course. Students studied the sacrificial system first, and then the philosophy. They called it the Vedānta, i.e. Veda + end, the final aim of the Veda. Gradually the oral instruction, in which the philosophy was taught, took definite shape and was handed down from teacher to pupil in fixed language, each school having its own sacred deposit. Thus were formed those wonderful treatises which we know as the Upanishads. To this period belong only the *Bṛihadāraṇyaka*, *Chhāndogya*, *Taittirīya*, *Aitareya*, *Kaushītaki*, and *Kena* Upanishads. They are in simple discursive prose, and show clearly the process of transition from the old sacrificial teaching of the Brāhmaṇas to philosophy. We must remember that only boys of the three highest castes were admitted to the Brāhmanical schools, that no girl was admitted, and that only Brāhmans were allowed to teach. Hence, from this time onward, the Vedānta was taught only to men of the three highest castes, and only Brāhmans were allowed to teach it.

Note how it was possible to introduce the new philosophy into the schools. It could not have happened if the new thought had led the monks to a serious protest against the whole practice of Hinduism as dishonouring to God; but as their attitude to the gods was a good-humoured if superior contempt, there was no inseparable barrier between them and the old religion; and thus the philosophy could be drawn into the schools and shut up under the stern caste rules of the Brāhmans.

V. We now pass on to the second period of the history of Indian philosophy. The chronology here becomes a little clearer. We may date this period as beginning about 550 B.C. or soon after. The chief mark of the new period is this, that there are now many competing systems of philosophy. The almost complete monopoly enjoyed at first by the thinkers of the Upanishads has passed away. Everywhere one meets a philosopher with a system of his own and with his following of monks. It would be impossible, even if it were advisable, to give anything like a complete catalogue of the extraordinary variety of belief professed in North India at this time. Three things, however, are well worth notice. The first of these is this, that the one aim of all the systems is to win release from transmigration. Each is a philosophy of emancipation. The second point is this, that all these philosophers practised the monastic life, giving up the world and wandering about in beggary. Though their theories of the world varied very greatly, they all agreed that in the ordinary life of man it was impossible, or next to impossible, to win release. The third point is the most interesting of all. Of the many varied schools of thought then existing only three found their way to fame and survived, and these three have one great characteristic in common: they all deny the existence of Brahman, the Absolute. It is surely a matter of the very deepest interest that this, the foundation of a philosophy so striking and so profound, should have already been so seriously discredited that the greatest of the new thinkers of the time should have turned away from it altogether. But the reason is not far to seek. The Brāhman of the Upanishads is so exceedingly abstract and tenuous that for the ordinary man it is very hard to grasp the conception and feel its utility. This clearly had become evident to many; so that the acutest thinkers of the period actually formed their systems without using God. It is of the utmost importance to realize that, though these system-builders denied the existence of a supreme Spirit, they, like the rest, continued to believe in the existence of the Hindu gods.

The three schools which have survived are the Jains, the Sāṅkhyas, and the Buddhists. The three seem to form a sort of progressive series, when taken in the order in which we have named them; and tradition suggests that this is also the order of their appearance.

Jainism in its ideas of the world stands very near essential Hinduism. The world and souls and the gods are all real. It does not accept the doctrine of the supreme Ātman. In this matter we may either regard it as representing the old unconscious thought of the people before the emergence of the belief in Brāhman, or as maintaining a sceptical attitude to that philosophic conception. The former is probably the best way to look at the matter; for early Jainism is more closely connected with animism than with philosophy. There is very little speculation in it. Indeed, we shall understand the system best if we think of it as merely a specialization and intensification of the old hermit[1] discipline under the influence of an extreme reverence for life and of a dogmatic belief that not only men, animals, and plants, but the smallest particles of earth, fire, water, and wind are endowed with living souls. Consequently, a very large part of the Jain monk's attention was directed to using the extremest care not to injure any living thing.[2] So eager were the Jains to part with the world to the uttermost that many of their monks wore not a scrap of clothing. Twelve years of most severe asceticism were necessary for emancipation. After that, if a monk did not wish to live longer, he was recommended to starve himself to death.

The Sāṅkhya system also holds that the world and souls and the gods are real, but a large sceptical element comes in;

[1] See below, pp. 249–253. [2] See below, p. 258.

for Sāṅkhyas say that the soul is not the organ of the intellectual or volitional life of man.

Philosophically, the system is a dualism. It denies the existence of the Supreme, and teaches the existence of *prakṛiti*, an eternal fundamental substance from which all phenomenal nature arises, and of innumerable individual souls, existing as gods, demons, men, animals, and plants. Every soul is an eternal self-conscious spirit, but without desire, or object, or power to act. It is light, but no more than light. The soul is eternally free, but, through its association with matter, the man believes himself to be bound. Every man who will accept the Sāṅkhya philosophy and lead a life of world-renunciation as a sannyāsī will in time awake to the knowledge of the true relation between the soul and matter, and will thus reach emancipation. His soul will be set free from matter, and thereafter will live for ever in that isolation (*kaivalya*) which is its native right and joy.

It is most striking that the individual soul is conceived in this system precisely as Brahman is conceived in the Upanishads. Intelligence, self-consciousness, freedom from desire, from action, from karma, and from suffering, and isolation from phenomenal existence, are the marks of spirit and the spiritual life to early Indian thinkers.

The Sāṅkhya has not had any great influence as a religious system. But the character of its principles compelled those who held it to think out the way in which the things of the universe come into existence and also the relation of the soul to matter. The metaphysical and psychological doctrines which they reached in this process were found to be acceptable in the main to Indian thinkers, and they were therefore adopted at a later date, with or without modification, by all the schools. It would take far too long to expound these ideas fully, but it is important that we should grasp the two most salient features of this part of the system.

We take first the process whereby the things of nature come to be. During a pralaya, or period between the dissolution and the reappearance of the world, matter is in its quiescent, invisible, impalpable state: it is *prakṛiti.* When the moment for a new creation comes, there is evolved from this primordial stuff a subtle cosmic substance called *buddhi* (intelligence). From *buddhi* is evolved a second subtle cosmic substance called *ahaṁkāra* (egoism). From *ahaṁkāra* are evolved five subtle cosmic elements, earth, air, water, fire, ether. Finally, from these five subtle elements are evolved the actual constituents of matter, earth, air, water, fire, ether. This series of emanations from beginning to end is material.

Next comes the psychological problem. The two subtle cosmic substances, *buddhi* (intelligence) and *ahaṁkāra* (egoism), reappear in the individual. Here *ahaṁkāra* evolves another subtle substance called *manas* (mind), and with it the five senses, each corresponding to one of the constituents of matter, and with them the five organs of action. Once more the whole series of emanations is purely physical. Now, the significant point to be grasped is that the whole of our inner life, intellectual and volitional, is held by Sāṅkhyas to be conducted by these physical substances. Man has no real personal life: the belief that we think and will is a pure hallucination. All that happens within us is the work of these physical powers. The senses, straining outward, obtain impressions of physical things, because they correspond to them. The *manas* receives these impressions from the senses and conveys them to *ahaṁkāra* and *buddhi.* This latter power discriminates the impressions of the senses and acts upon them. Thus all our inner life is physical and there is no personal activity in it.

What, then, does the soul do? The self-conscious soul, enmeshed in the body, sheds the light of its self-consciousness upon these inner organs; and the man, confusing this self-conscious light with the automatic physical work of the inner organs, forms the foolish fancy, 'I personally do all this,' stamps each sense-impression as it passes through *ahaṁkāra* as 'mine', and calls the discrimination and determination of the *buddhi* 'mine' also. The soul has thus nothing to do with intellectual or moral life: that is all carried on outside the soul. The process may be graphically represented thus:

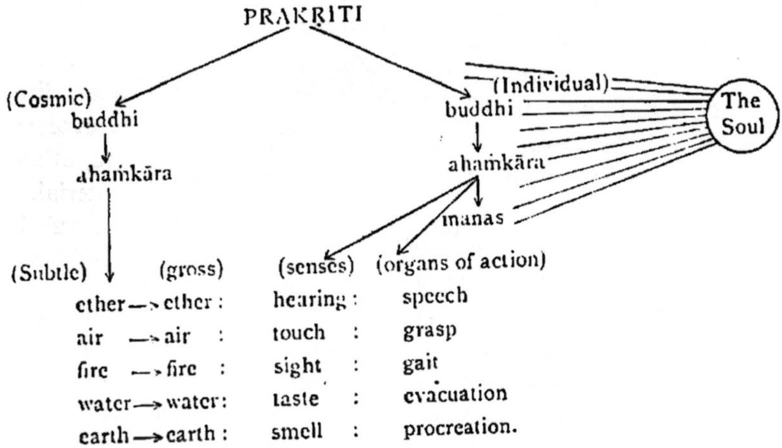

Gautama, the Buddha, like the Jain and the Sāṅkhya leaders, denied the existence of the Supreme; but he went still further. The Sāṅkhyas had deprived the soul of all real share in life. Buddha took the next step: he denied the existence of the soul altogether.

In contrast with Jainism, Buddhism recommended a mild asceticism, but condemned self-torture, and sought emancipation by *knowledge* and *right living*. Hence the Buddhist monk pressed on beyond the Hindu monk in the matter of morality, and Buddhist ethics exercised a precious influence later on in Hinduism. The knowledge which Buddha taught was summed up in three propositions, known as 'the three characteristics of being', namely,

All its constituents are transitory;
All its constituents are misery;
All its constituents are lacking in an ego.

This last proposition is the most important. If nothing has an ego, then the world has no God, man has no soul, and all things are phenomenal. Man consists of five groups of phenomenal elements. Desire is the power that leads to the formation and the preservation of the individual. Buddha's method of life[1] leads to the elimination of desire, and hence to the dissolution of the individual. This insistence on desire produced large results later on.

The Buddhist word for emancipation is *nirvāṇa*, the etymological meaning of which is extinction, i. e. of a light. It is used in two senses. A man who lives faithfully as a Buddhist monk will experience the *nirvāṇa* of lust, hatred, and ignorance. At death he will pass into final *nirvāṇa*: he will not be born again. No one knows whether Buddha believed final *nirvāṇa* to be annihilation or not. He refused to discuss that question. But what is absolutely clear is that the characteristics of final *nirvāṇa* are identical with the negative characteristics of the philosophic Brahman and of the individual soul in the Sāṅkhya system, viz. isolation from phenomenal life, from desire and from action, freedom from transmigration and karma, from pain and from suffering. Nirvāṇa in Jainism is conceived in precisely the same way.

The Sāṅkhya, Buddhist, and Jain systems had one point in common with the Vedānta: the monks of all four systems practised no worship. The three had also one point of order in common which distinguished them from the Vedānta: only men of the three twice-born classes could study the Upanishads and the system of the Vedānta; while the monastic orders of the other three systems were open to all men. Buddhists and Jains had each an order of nuns also. The Sāṅkhyas remained in Hinduism, while the other two philosophies went out and finally became distinct religions. The reason for this breach did not lie in their doctrines. These could have easily been accommodated within Hinduism. The reason is that they would not submit to being included in the Brāhmanic schools and brought under the authority of

[1] See below, pp. 258–259.

Brāhmans, while the Sāṅkhyas agreed. Hence the Sāṅkhya system is to this day acknowledged to be one of the orthodox philosophic systems of the country. Their denial of the existence of God did not stand in the way at all. From this point, then, Buddhism and Jainism drop out of Hinduism, though they continue to influence the religion of the country very seriously for more than fifteen hundred years.

VI. We know very little about what happened in the school of the Vedānta during the five centuries preceding our era. Doubtless an unending succession of twice-born students learned the Upanishads from the lips of their gurus; and at some time during those centuries the first attempt to systematize the doctrines of the Vedānta in a set of *sūtras* occurred. These are aphorisms of the briefest and most pregnant description, requiring a commentary to make their meaning clear. But of all this we have no record. The one thing that stands out in full certainty is that towards the Christian era the school rose to extraordinary influence among thinking men; for, as we shall see, its leading doctrines won their way in whole or in part into all the leading sects.

But, though we cannot trace the history of the school during those centuries, a little of its literature has survived. The best part of it is the little group of verse Upanishads, the *Kāṭhaka*, *Īśā*, *Śvetāśvatara*, *Muṇḍaka* and *Mahānārāyaṇa*. The pithy aphoristic character of these poems shows that they were written to be committed to memory. In the main they teach what was taught in the earliest Upanishads, but there are also several new points to notice. There is first the appearance, especially in the *Kāṭhaka*, of a number of Sāṅkhya ideas and phrases, which show that the two schools were drawing nearer to one another. Along with these are a number of references to Yoga methods; but, as yoga exercises were probably introduced among the monks at a very early period, these need occasion no surprise. The most noteworthy fact, however, is that a new theistic strain of thought makes its appearance in these poems, especially in the first three. It is very slight in the *Kāṭhaka*, more marked in the *Īśā*, but very prominent indeed in the *Śvetāśvatara.* Clearly there was a group of men in the school of the Vedānta who believed that Brahman was personal. In the *Śvetāśvatara* he is identified with the ancient Vedic god Rudra. The grace of God is here spoken of in connexion with Brahman, and the *bhakti*, or loving faith of the devotee of a personal god, is once referred to.

After the Christian era we get a little more light on the history of the Vedānta. By this time the six orthodox schools of philosophy[1] were all in existence, and each was taught by means of a sūtra-manual elucidated with a commentary. From time to time a new set of Sūtras, or an amended edition of an old set, might force its way to the front and become the recognized manual of a school. In other cases a sūtra-work might remain the standard work for centuries. That is what happened in the school of the Vedānta. For many centuries Bādarāyaṇa's *Vedānta-sūtras* have stood supreme. At quite an early date it was recognized as inspired; and ever since has been a part of the canon of the Vedānta. No one knows when it was written. Various dates from the Christian era down to the fourth century have been suggested for it. The tendency at present is towards an early date. It is quite clear that it is founded on earlier manuals.

The theistic tendencies of the verse Upanishads culminate in the *Bhagavadgītā*, a remarkable poem which occurs as an episode in the *Mahābhārata*, and which is one of the fundamental scriptures of the Vishṇuite sect. Scholars are not all agreed as to how the *Gītā* came to be what it is, but probably all would acknowledge that, in its present form at least, it is post-Christian. We deal with it at greater length in Chapter IX. Here we merely want to realize its relationship to the school of the Vedānta. The following is the *Prasthāna-traya* or triple canon of the school:

[1] These fall into three pairs, the *Karma Mīmāṁsā* and the *Vedānta*, the *Sāṅkhya* and the *Yoga*, the *Vaiśeshika* and the *Nyāya*.

(*a*) The *Upanishads.*
(*b*) The *Bhagavadgītā.*
(*c*) The *Vedānta-sūtras.*

How a sectarian work such as the *Gītā* is ever came to occupy this position is a most difficult question. It teaches that Brahman is personal, that he is identical with Vishṇu, and that he became incarnate in Kṛishṇa. This is all very strange in the school which sprang from the teaching of the *Brihadāraṇyaka* and *Chhāndogya Upanishads* and which accepts Bādarāyaṇa's *Vedānta-sūtras* as an inspired expression of its teaching. Bādarāyaṇa's work does not acknowledge the doctrine of incarnations and is in no sense sectarian. Some scholars suppose there was a long-continued struggle between the Vishṇuite Church and the Vedānta school and that the *Gītā* marks a stage of compromise in that war. To the present writer it seems more likely that from the very beginning there were Vedāntists who tended to think of Brahman as personal, that they leaned on the theistic expressions of the earliest Upanishads for support, that the theistic elements of the verse Upanishads are evidence of their presence in the school, and that the *Gītā* marks rather the moment when the leaders of the Vishṇuite sect, feeling the need of the support of the Vedānta, joined forces with the theists within the school. The discussion in Chapter IX will make this theory much more comprehensible.[1]

VII. Were this a work on the philosophy of the Vedānta, it would be necessary to discuss the work of Śaṅkara at considerable length; but, as our purpose is to understand Hinduism as a religion, we need only draw out the significant points in his historical position. He is said to have been born in South India in the year 788 A.D., and scholars believe he lived

[1] The question is often asked whether the *Gītā* or the *Vedānta-sūtras* is the earlier work. The truth probably is that each work is the result of growth and progressive editing, and that they were thus parallel rather than successive in origin. If this is so, we can believe that the *Vedānta-sūtras* refer to the *Gītā*, as all early commentators say, and that the *Gītā* refers to the *Vedānta-sūtras* in the phrase *Brahma-sūtra-padais*, xiii, 4.

until about 850 A. D. He was a sannyāsī of the school of the Vedānta; and his fame rests on his commentaries on the Upanishads, the *Bhagavadgītā* and the *Vedānta-sūtras*, his greatest work being his *bhāshya* on the *Vedānta-sūtras*.

He was a man of great learning and of high philosophic ability. He worked out the Vedānta philosophy so as to make it a more self-consistent system than it ever was before. Necessarily, in the process certain points became elaborated which give form and character to his interpretation. Of these the most important are the emphatic declaration that Brahman is impersonal, the equally express declaration that the world is not only worthless as compared with Brahman but is in very truth illusion, *māyā*, and the positing of an illusory personal god, the lower Brahman, Brahmā, as the ruler of the world of māyā and the object of theistic worship.

For our purpose the points that are most significant are those we discussed above[1] in seeking to understand what is meant by the doctrine that Brahman is actionless.

A. Since Brahman is actionless, he is non-moral.[2] We saw how clearly this is recognized in the early literature. We saw also that, according to the Vedānta, nothing but knowledge can obtain emancipation, and nothing else is needed. Morality is without significance in this matter. This point is dealt with by Śaṅkara at the beginning of his great commentary, and is most clearly set forth.

B. Since Brahman was conceived as actionless, the early thinkers tended towards an impersonal theology. Śaṅkara's systematic thinking led him to the definite result that Brahman is impersonal. Here theistic thinkers differed seriously from him, as we shall see. But Śaṅkara in the severe consistency of his thought made the human spirit impersonal also. In the full Vedāntic account of man as given by him the soul is encased in several physical sheaths, and in these physical

[1] See above, pp. 228–232.

[2] In Śaṅkara he is ever pure, but he has no character, and no moral act is attributed to him.

sheaths are all the personal and moral faculties. Thus Śaṅkara frankly makes the divine-human spirit impersonal and unmoral. This doctrine of sheaths is clearly derived, primarily, from the well-known passage in the ānandavalli of the *Taittirīya Upanishad*; but it seems to have arisen under the influence of the Sāṅkhya doctrine set forth above,[1] as the following diagram suggests:

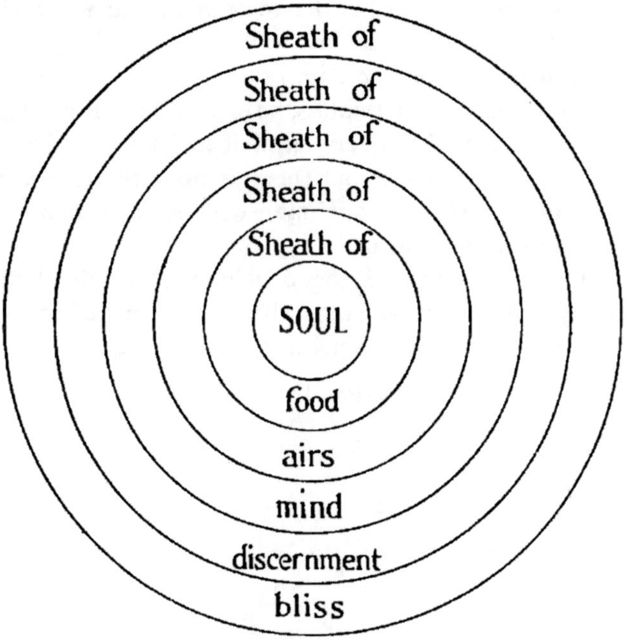

VEDĀNTA	SĀṄKHYA
mind, *manas*	= *manas*
discernment, *vijnāna*	= *buddhi*
bliss, *ānanda*, *ahaṁkāra*	= *ahaṁkāra*.

C. Since Brahman is cut off from all communication with man, he cannot be worshipped. The early sannyāsīs, in consequence, worshipped no one. But in Śaṅkara we have some-

[1] pp. 237–239.

thing very different. The early thinkers acknowledged the existence of all the gods; but they disdained to worship these temporary, transmigrating beings. Śaṅkara, on the other hand, worshipped them and taught their worship. He says they do not eat the sacrifices, but he acknowledges that they enjoy them, and he explains how a god can be present at a number of different places at the same moment to receive and enjoy the sacrifices. Further, he recognized the use of idols, and is himself represented by idols and worshipped as a divinity in many temples to-day.

D. Since Brahman is actionless, he cannot be conceived as the Creator. This thought is very explicit in Śaṅkara. Brahman is the source of the world, but there is no action involved in its production. All that Brahman does is mere sport, *līlā*,[1] and thus involves no karma.

The full significance of the development of the Vedānta philosophy will be considered when we have before us the history of the sects which worship Vishṇu and Śiva.

[1] See below, IX. 403–407.

CHAPTER VII

THE YELLOW ROBE

I. It is most necessary at the outset to distinguish between the practice of austerity and asceticism. Austerity is the endurance of pain in order to gain pleasure, power, or some other material end. Asceticism, on the other hand, is the endurance of pain or the giving-up of comforts in order to gain moral or spiritual ends. Austerity is secular, materialistic; asceticism is moral and religious.[1]

Among most primitive peoples we find the practice of various forms of abstinence and self-torture, which may be summed up under the word austerities. At certain significant periods in the life of both men and women these have to be undergone as tests of endurance and forms of discipline. In the case of drought or famine or any other serious trouble, attempts are made by means of self-denial or self-inflicted pain to persuade the gods to remove the calamity. All these practices rest on the idea that pains bring gains, and that it is worth while enduring a certain amount of suffering to obtain a greater boon. Sometimes the belief takes the definite form that the gods delight in seeing men under pain, or that by suffering demons may be circumvented, or that 'pain is the root of merit'.[2]

We find phenomena of the same general character, but much more developed, among the Indo-Aryans, towards the end of the period of the *Ṛigveda*, and onwards into the time

[1] See art. *Austerities* in *E. R. E.*
[2] Aśvaghosha, *Buddhacharita*, vii. 18.

of the Brāhmaṇas. The word for austerities is *tapas*. It is conceived as a mighty power. The Creator underwent *tapas* before He created the world.[1] Truth and Right are born of *tapas*.[2] In the great hymn of Creation in the *Ṛigveda* the one Reality is born from *tapas*.[3] Manyu, the personification of Wrath, is a mighty warrior through *tapas*.[4] The 'fathers', pitṛis, practised *tapas*, when they were on the earth;[5] so also the seven Ṛishis.[6] The purpose they had in view was the winning of bliss.[7] Through their *tapas* they became invincible; they won heaven.[8] Through *tapas* the worlds can be conquered.[9] The sacrificers speak of themselves as practising *tapas*,[10] and the austerity of the students of the Brāhmanical schools is alluded to in another hymn.[11] There is no mention of men living a life of austerity as such, unless scholars be right in thinking that the *Muni* of the following verses is a man who has won his extraordinary powers by *tapas*. As several features of the practice of later days appear in the lines, it is probable that the conjecture is right:

> The Munis, girdled with the wind, wear dirty robes of saffron hue.
> They, following the wind's swift course, go where the gods have gone before.
>
> The Muni, made associate in the holy work of every god,
> Looking upon all varied forms, flies through the region of the air.[12]

Here we have the yellow robe, which through all the centuries has been the commonest symbol of the austere life in India, and also the miraculous power which enables the devotee to fly through the air and to mingle with the gods.

The ends aimed at, then, by these practices at this time were invincibility, warlike prowess, miraculous powers, heaven.

[1] *Śatapatha B.*, XI. v. 8, 1.
[2] *Ṛigveda*, x. 190; *Atharvaveda*, xv. 1, 3.
[3] *Ṛigveda*, x. 129, 3.
[4] *Ṛigveda*, x. 83, 2–3; *Atharvaveda*, iv. 32, 2–3.
[5] *Ṛigveda*, x. 154, 2; 4.
[6] *Ṛigveda*, x. 109, 4.
[7] *Atharvaveda*, xix. 41.
[8] *Ṛigveda*, x. 154, 2.
[9] *Bṛihadāraṇyaka U.*, vi. 2, 16.
[10] *Atharvaveda*, iv. 11, 6.
[11] *Atharvaveda*, xi. 5.
[12] *Ṛigveda*, x. 136, 2, 4.

Those who practised tapas did so with a view to personal gain. It was not yet asceticism, but austerity.

II. The second stage is very similar to the first. Here, too, the main aim seems to be materialistic, the endurance of bodily torture, or abstinence from what is pleasant, in order to win magic powers and such like. But ascetic motives now begin to mingle with the old ideas so distinctly, that we are justified in distinguishing this period from the preceding. We have here reached a real asceticism.

The men who show these characteristics lived in the forest and built themselves huts of wood or leaves in some pleasant spot near a stream.[1] The order seems to have come into existence in the period of the Brāhmaṇas, perhaps about 700 B.C. They were called *vānaprasthas*, forest-dwellers. We shall call them hermits. The name for a collection of their huts is *āśrama*. This word means literally, 'a place for self-mortification', but in ordinary usage the idea of a residence came to the front. It is therefore translated 'hermitage'. They wore coats of bark or skin,[2] dressed their hair in matted braids,[3] and lived largely on woodland fare. But they kept stores of grain and were allowed a fire to cook their food, if they wished it.

But they did no work of any kind. Their life had but one interest: they gave their undivided time and attention to religious exercises. They kept up the traditional worship of the gods by prayer, hymn, and sacrifice with great care,[4] although unable to perform the greater sacrifices. They subjected themselves to rather severe discipline. Three points must be noted.

They practised various methods of austerity, *tapas*, enduring extreme cold and heat, strange food, most painful postures, and such like. They believed that by subjecting themselves

[1] *Rāmāyaṇa*, II. lvi.

[2] *Gautama*, iii. 34; *Vasishṭha*, ix. 1; *Baudhāyana*, iii. 3, 19; *Āpastamba* ii. 9, 22, 1; *Rāmāyaṇa*, II. xxxvii.

[3] *Gautama*, iii. 34; *Vasishṭha*, ix. 1; *Rāmāyaṇa*, II. lii.

[4] *Rāmāyaṇa*, III. i.

to torture they could acquire miraculous powers, for example, the power of flying through the air, of rendering themselves invisible, or of making the gods do whatever they liked. Self-torture was also believed to purify the man's moral nature and to bring him near the gods.

Amongst these men there also gradually grew up a series of physical and intellectual exercises, meant to train the body and the mind. They began in bodily postures and breathing exercises which were intended to subdue the senses and quiet the body, and passed on to intellectual exercises intended to control the attention, to still the mind, and to lead up to ecstatic trances. This discipline was regarded as a bringing of both body and mind under the yoke, and was finally called *yoga*, i. e. 'yoking'.[1]

The idea that life is sacred was very strong in hermitages, so that it became the rule that a hermit must not kill any animal.[2] At first there seems to have been no rule restricting the hermit to vegetarian diet. In several law-books he is allowed to eat the flesh of animals if killed by other animals[3] or given him by a householder. The idea was that the man who wanted to live the holy life must avoid taking life. This law was called harmlessness, *ahiṁsā*. Hence in the *Rāmāyaṇa* one of the most beautiful features of the hermitage is the countless thousands of birds and beasts that live there in perfect peace.[4]

But, although these hermits gave up the life of the city and the quest of gain, they did not cut themselves adrift from society. As we have already seen, they continued the sacrificial worship. The worship of ancestors[5] was also retained, and distinctions of caste were not lost sight of. The hermit was allowed to have his wife with him in the forest, if he so desired; and children were frequently born in the hermitages. When *Rāma* was sent into banishment, Sītā decided to go

[1] Deussen, 384 ff. [2] *Baudhāyana*, iii. 19; *Manu*, vi. 8.
[3] *Baudhāyana*, iii. 6; *Gautama*, iii. 31. [4] III. i.
[5] *Vasishṭha*, ix. 12; *Rāmāyaṇa*, II. ciii.

with him; and they became hermits, wearing coats of bark, living in a forest-hut, and eating woodland fare. Similarly, when the five Pāṇḍavas went into exile, Draupadī accompanied them, and shared their hermit-life in the Kāmyaka forest. In the case, however, of warrior-hermits such as they were the rule against killing animals was not enforced. They hunted the deer of the forest. Many hermits, on the other hand, lived in celibacy, and even gave up the use of a hut. As time went on, the rule tended to become stricter.[1]

It is not possible to form an exhaustive catalogue of the practices of these austere ascetics. No man will ever be able to tell the self-inflicted horrors which the forests and mountains of India have witnessed. Fasting carried to the point of extreme emaciation is one of the commonest methods. Silence frequently continued for very long periods is another. Among the more usual forms are the endurance of frightful heat or excessive cold; the use of unnatural food; the tolerance of unspeakable dirt; the maintenance of a fixed position for weeks, while unimaginable vermin creep over the body and feed upon it; and painful postures maintained for many months or even years, until the limbs become useless.[2]

Men believed that by self-torture almost anything could be accomplished. They thought that by torture they could get whatever they longed for, whether wealth, strength, valour, kingship, high position, children, or good fortune. The best illustration of this is perhaps the case of Viśvamitra, who, though a Kshatriya by birth, is said to have attained Brāhmanhood after thousands of years of superhuman austerities. But magical powers seem to have been more desired than anything else. Men sought power over their enemies, over their friends, over nature, over the three worlds, even over the gods. They sought freedom from mortal wounds,[3] power to fly through the air, power to procure whatever they wanted. The curse

[1] *Baudhāyana*, iii. 3. 9–14; *Rāmāyaṇa*, III. vi.
[2] *Rāmāyaṇa*, I. lxiii, lxiv; III. vi. [3] Ib. III. iii.

of a hermit was a thing of utmost dread, as may be seen in the plot of the famous Indian drama, *Śakuntalā*.[1] His prayer was equally powerful. The gods and demigods came down at Bharadvāja's request, and prepared a heavenly banquet for Rāma, Sītā, and their train.[2] The Vindhyas bowed their wooded tops that Agastya might pass,[3] and Jahnu drank up the Ganges at one draught.[4] Through their austerities many hermits are believed to have lived for centuries or even millenniums, and to have lived without food.[5] Hermits might even become gods through long-continued austerities. The gods were often afraid that they would be dethroned by some persistent hermit with his unbounded austerities;[6] and the way in which they usually sought to meet the danger was to send down a heavenly nymph to draw the ascetic away from his self-torture.[7]

A special form of teaching, called *āraṇyaka*, i.e. belonging to the forest, seems to have been given to young men who were about to enter upon the hermit life. The essential element in this forest teaching was an attempt to spiritualize the sacrifice by means of allegory. This instruction would then form the basis of the hermit's meditation in the forest.

The formation of this hermit practice seems to antedate the appearance of the doctrine of transmigration. In none of the elements of the discipline is the influence of karma visible. Even as early as the *Chhāndogya Upanishad*[8] this life is mentioned as a distinct religious vocation alongside the life of the student and the life of the householder. In Gautama's *Dharmasūtra*,[9] which dates from about 500 B.C., detailed regulations are laid down for the hermit life; and we find numerous descriptions of these anchorites and their hermitages in the earliest parts of the *Rāmāyaṇa* and of the *Mahābhārata*.

What was it that led to the formation of this peculiar

[1] Cf. also *Rāmāyaṇa*, I. xlviii. [2] Ib., II. xci. [3] Ib., III. xi.
[4] Ib., I. xliv.
[5] *Māṇḍakarṇi* lived ten thousand years on air. *Rāmāyaṇa*, III. xi. The Sampraksālas lived on light. Ib., III. vi. [6] Ib., III. xi.
[7] See below, p. 298. [8] II. xxiii. 2. [9] III. 26–35.

discipline? Probably in casting about for a mode of life less luxurious and more holy than the ordinary life of cities in North India then, it occurred to them that the simple life led by the far-away ancestors of the race, while they lived in the forest and had learnt neither to till the soil nor weave garments, would be pleasing to the gods and likely to lead to holiness. This would account for the forest life, the hut of leaves, the tangled hair, the coat of bark or skin, and the simple woodland fare. In the earliest surviving set of rules for the life of the hermit it is laid down that he must not enter a village, nor step on ploughed land.[1] This regulation also fits in well with the idea that this form of asceticism was a reversion to primitive life, like the case of the Rechabites in the Old Testament and other instances elsewhere. In one of the Dharmasūtras[2] the value of the hermit life is put down to its being like the life of birds and beasts.

III. As we have seen above,[3] the new doctrine of transmigration and karma broke in upon the old life and the old thought with elemental force, transforming many things, altering relationships and upsetting the balance of the old theology. The more reflective men, stirred to the very depths by their loathing for the repeated births and deaths and the never-ending sorrow of ordinary existence, were eagerly looking for a means of release.

A. Many suggestions were made; but it was the doctrine of Brahman and of man's identity with God that laid hold of the best men with most force. Realizing the freedom, the spirituality, and the peace of Brahman in contrast with the sorrow and bondage of the world, and believing the startling doctrine of their own identity with Brahman, they felt it impossible to live the ordinary life of men any longer. Emancipated from the fruits of action by their new knowledge, they could not again subject themselves to the enchaining life of action. They must live a life more worthy of

[1] *Gautama*, iii. 32–33. Cf. *Manu*, vi. 16.

[2] *Baudhāyana*, III. iii. 21, 22.

[3] See pp. 134, 138, 221.

Brahman. They no longer desired wealth, position, success, children, pleasure. Human life and all earthly things were not only empty and worthless but evil powers, clouding the soul with ignorance, and entangling it more and more in the net of birth and death. The whole world of phenomena was inherently antagonistic to the spiritual life. They therefore decided to divest themselves of every element of the common life of man.[1] They renounced the worship of the gods, the worship of their ancestors, caste, home, the use of fire,[2] marriage, family, money, property, amusements, work of every kind, and ordinary food and dress, and lived a wandering life, getting their food by begging. Their aim was to lay aside everything that belonged to the sphere of karma, i.e. the whole world. Thus the word *sannyāsa*, which may be translated 'renunciation', 'world-surrender', was used to designate their practice as a whole. They were therefore called *sannyāsīs*, Renouncers. Since they wandered about and begged their bread, they were called *parivrājakas*, Wanderers, *bhikshus*, Beggars. All this is true of each of the great schools of the time, of Buddhists and Jains as well as of Hindus. We shall use the word 'Monk' as the best word for covering all schools and all disciplines.

Thus, when a man decided to adopt this life, he gave up his work, turned away from the worship of the gods, abandoned his property, parents, wife, children, home, and, with them, the worship of his ancestors, shaved his head and laid aside his sacred thread,[3] his clothes and ornaments. He then put on either a yellow robe, like the Munis of the *Ṛigveda*, or a mere rag round his loins, or went stark naked. He carried a staff (*daṇḍa*) and a beggar's bowl, and daily begged the food he needed. He spent his time largely in silent meditation,

[1] See above, pp. 224–225.
[2] Hence the sannyāsī is buried, not burnt.
[3] At a later date it became customary to perform the funeral service over the man who was becoming a sannyāsī, to indicate that he was altogether cut off from society. *Mahānirvāṇa T.*, viii. 239.

seeking solitude, avoiding villages, except when the hour for begging his food came round. He slept in a cave or at the root of a tree.

Many of the monks, in their anxiety to win release, adopted, in addition to all their renunciations, the old forms of self-mortification, tapas,[1] in the belief that by these potent self-inflicted tortures they would the sooner conquer the stubborn sensual tendencies of the body and the dense ignorance of the soul, which were the chief hindrances to true knowledge and final release. It is most curious that these practices, which were originally resorted to in order to secure material blessings, should now be used to crush out the desire for these things.

The monk usually also adopted the bodily and mental exercises which had been formed in the hermitages for the progressive restraint of body and mind, and were called yoga, which means 'yoking', 'means of restraint'.[2] The physical side of yoga was in two parts. The yogī practised postures and breathing exercises. He learned to sit absolutely motionless in certain postures which were believed to be favourable to peace of mind and to meditation, thus learning to restrain and control his limbs and his senses. Breathing exercises were believed to purify the man and to enable him to control his inward organs. But both postures and breathing exercises were merely the physical preliminaries and foundations of the intellectual exercises. These began in simple meditation on symbolic words or on religious ideas; but they culminated in an attempt to exclude the phenomenal world from the mind altogether, the idea being that in this way the human spirit would come nearer the Divine. The concentration of the whole intellectual faculty on a single point to the exclusion of all phenomena, the merging of one's consciousness of plurality in an ecstatic vision of unity, was conceived to be the best way of approaching God. To think nothingness was believed to be the path which led to the apprehension of the Absolute.

[1] See above, pp. 248–249. [2] See above, p. 250.

At quite an early date the law of ahiṁsā,[1] which had grown up in the hermitages, was imposed on the monk, forbidding him to kill an animal;[2] or even to break a living twig from a tree or to destroy seeds.[3] All action would produce karma, but the act of taking life would produce very bad karma indeed.

As we saw above,[4] the monk was at first subjected to no moral rules. Morality being no mark of Brahman, it was not demanded of the man who was identical with Brahman. But as the monk begged his food from householders day by day, and had frequent intercourse with other monks and the general public, a simple code of conduct became necessary. Here too the conception of Brahman gave the main principle, namely, *Indifference*:[5] as Brahman lived in perfect peace, untroubled by love, hatred, desire, envy, gratitude, ambition, or resentment, the monk was taught to conquer and crush out all his passions. He must neither love nor hate any one, must show neither gratitude for favours nor resentment at cruelty. He must be indifferent to all men, feeling neither attachment for the good nor repulsion for the evil:

> The learned look with indifference alike upon a wise and courteous Brāhman, a cow, an elephant, a god, or an Outcaste.[6]

This rule was quite in keeping with the monastic ideal of complete control over both body and mind. Unless a man's mind was at peace with itself, with others, and with the outside world, it was impossible to induce that motionlessness of the body and that stillness of the soul which were sought so eagerly. Hence the monk was bid to be gentle in speech and behaviour to all, never resenting an injury nor answering insult with hard words, but ever preserving a peaceful and humble demeanour.[7] The perfect detachment of Brahman also necessitated complete chastity on the part of the monk.

[1] See above, p. 250. [2] *Baudhāyana*, ii. 10, 18, 2; *Vasishṭha*, x. 3.
[3] *Gautama*, iii. 20; 23. [4] See p. 230. [5] See p. 231.
[6] *Gītā*, v. 18; cf. v. 19; ix. 29.
[7] *Vasishṭha*, x. 29-30; Deussen, 72, 382.

There thus grew up a code of behaviour, expressed in five vows, which every novice had to take: (1) ahiṁsā, (2) truthfulness, (3) no stealing, (4) chastity, (5) liberality.[1] Gradually the value of character for the development of the monk made itself more distinctly felt; and so, here and there, in the verse Upanishads and later literature, moral conditions for the attainment of Brahman appear:

> Who has not ceased from wickedness,
> Who is not tranquil and concentrated,
> Whose heart is not at peace,
> Cannot attain him even by knowledge.[2]

B. As time went on, the number of schools that sought to win emancipation became exceedingly numerous. The variety of philosophic conception of God, man, and the world taught at the beginning of the fifth century B.C. in northern India from Taxila to Rājagṛiha is perfectly wonderful. In an old Buddhist book sixty-two distinct heresies are briefly characterized.[3] They differed in their monastic rules to some extent also. Most of these schools soon passed out of existence, and so need not detain us; but a number of those that existed then have had a very great history, and their beginnings are full of instruction for us.

Each was a sort of spiritual brotherhood; for the monks of each school were closely bound together in a religious order. Its disciplinary rules were never divulged;[4] and its meetings were held in secret. Some schools had orders of nuns as well as of monks.

The school of Mahāvīra, which is to-day Jainism,[5] holds a most interesting position among the orders of the sixth century before Christ. The school has no doctrine of God at all, and must therefore be classed as atheistic. Indeed, their main ideas are animistic: not only men, animals, and plants, but also the smallest particles of earth, fire, water, and wind are held

[1] *Baudhāyana*, ii. 10, 18, 2.
[2] *Kāṭhaka U.*, ii. 24.
[3] See Rhys Davids, *American Lectures*, 31 ff.
[4] *S.B.E.*, xxxv. 264–266.
[5] See above, p. 236.

to contain souls. This doctrine led to their giving extreme emphasis to the doctrine of ahiṁsā.[1] The practice of a Jain monk was most carefully regulated, in order that he might avoid doing the slightest injury to any living thing. Hence his broom to sweep insects from his path, the prohibition of the use of cold water, and other regulations. But, apart from that, they were amongst the most extreme of the Renouncers. They gave up all care for their bodies; plucked out their hair by the roots; wore only a rag of clothing, or else lived stark naked; ate no savoury food; drank no cold water; and never bathed. They also carried the practice of self-torture to great extremes. Meekness and uncomplaining endurance were amongst their highest virtues. Twelve years of severe ascetic practice were necessary to win release. After that a Jain monk was allowed to starve himself to death, if he chose to do so. At a later date monasteries were introduced into Jainism.

Gautama, the Sākya saint, is the founder of Buddhism.[2] He was a junior contemporary of Mahāvīra. He left home, when he was a young man, determined to find release. After following two masters for some time, he resolved to be his own master, and began a course of excessively severe torture, consisting of self-inflicted pain and extreme fasting. But, when he was emaciated to the last degree and his life was on the point of flickering out, he came to the conclusion that such practices were useless as means towards emancipation, and gave them up once and for all. Hence the old tapas,[3] self-torture, has no place in Buddhism. Its original aim was material benefit, and its adoption at a later date as a means of winning release was very curious. Gautama's strong good sense enabled him to see its valuelessness and to reject it. But he practised and also imposed on his followers the abandonment of all the ordinary forms of human life. He also practised and taught the law of ahiṁsā. His conception

[1] See p. 250. [2] See above, p. 239. [3] See pp. 248–249.

of release—his name for it was *nirvāṇa*—was largely moral, and he saw that it could only be reached under certain moral conditions. Consequently, his rule had a great deal more of humanity and consideration in it than other disciplines. He bade his monks and nuns wear decent if simple clothing, allowed them a sufficiency of plain food, permitted the erection of monasteries for them and consented to many small comforts. Indeed, although he demanded the complete renunciation of home life, business, and ordinary society, a new, happy, quiet, social life sprang up in the monasteries; and thus the most noticeable evils of monasticism were softened. Buddhist monks and nuns wore clothing of a dull saffron tint; and thus, through the spread of Buddhism far and wide, the yellow robe became the chief symbol of asceticism all over Asia.

The other schools of the period do not stand out with sufficient clearness to make it worth our while to attempt to describe them; and during the next thousand years all the innumerable varieties of ascetics were included either in orthodox Hinduism, in Buddhism, or in Jainism. Further, while ascetic practice varied greatly in details and in rigour, the three great spheres of aim and effort which we have described, austerity, asceticism, and world-surrender, cover all that monasticism stood for.

C. Early asceticism imposed its ideals in part on Hindu society. From a very early date the students of the Brāhmanical schools had to practise asceticism, living in complete chastity, eating simple food, and enduring light austerities. The householder was also taught to practise austerities throughout his life.

At a later date a new ideal was set before the Brāhman. He was advised to spend twelve years at school, to pass his prime as a householder, and, when he had reared a family, to retire as a hermit to the forest. All three stages were then called *āśramas*, i.e. stages in self-mortification, the life of the student and of the householder obtaining recognition as ascetic as well as the hermit life. Later still, probably after the Christian era, the life of the monk was added as a fourth *āśrama*. At the end of his days the Brāhman was to give up even the hermit life and become a wandering mendicant.[1]

We have already seen how the widow came under ascetic discipline.[2]

D. There are certain large controlling ideas which were common to all the ancient ascetic schools, whether Hindu, Buddhist, or Jain. The fundamental convictions which underlie the whole movement, namely, that the true life of the soul is actionless, and that the ordinary life of man exercises a very evil influence upon religion and spirituality, have been already noticed. But besides these foundations, so to speak, part of the superstructure in each case was common to all the schools.

1. One of the curiosities of the thought of the period is this, that, although the Sāṅkhyas, as well as the Buddhists and the Jains, absolutely denied the existence of the Supreme, they continued, along with the Vedāntists and all other thinkers, to acknowledge the existence of the personal gods and all the heavenly host of Hinduism. It is most curious to find these divine and semi-divine beings reappearing in Buddhist and Jain teaching, and bringing with them large pieces of the old mythology.

2. But, although the Hindu, Buddhist, and Jain monks took all the gods, demi-gods, angels, and other orders of the Hindu pantheon for real beings, they gave them a very humble place; and they held the whole sacrificial system by which they were worshipped in profound contempt.[3] In consequence, they also regarded the whole of the ritualistic literature of the Brāhmans as absolutely worthless. No proof need be given of this with regard to Buddhists and Jains; for they rejected the Brāhmanical literature absolutely. But the same contempt is found clearly expressed in the sayings of those who held the Ātman philosophy:

[1] *E. R. E.*, art. Āśrama.
[2] Above, pp. 100-101.
[3] Deussen, 61-62.

> So then, after that the Brāhman has rejected learning (*pāṇḍityam nirvidya*), he abides in childhood.[1]

Very soon, however, the Brāhmans effected a reconciliation with the philosophers by the introduction of their system into the Vedic schools; so that in some of the later Upanishads sacrifices are recognized as of real value. For example, in the *Maitrāyaṇīya* we are told that the fire-laying for the ancestors is a sacrifice to Brahman;[2] and later works are still more definite. Finally, the Upanishads took their place as part of that very Brāhmanical literature which the early thinkers had completely rejected.

3. The ascetic thought of India, Hindu, Buddhist, and Jain, held the human body in serious contempt and even loathing, as the following quotations show:

> In this evil-smelling, substantial body, shuffled together out of bones, skin, sinews, marrow, flesh, seed, blood, mucus, tears, eye-gum, dung, urine, gall, and phlegm, how can we enjoy pleasure?[3]

> This monstrous wound hath outlets nine;
> A damp, wet skin doth clothe it o'er;
> At every point this unclean thing
> Exudeth nasty, stinking smells.[4]

4. All schools also agree that the senses and the intellectual faculties must be severely restrained. In one of the earliest Upanishads the monk is urged to 'bring all his organs to rest in the Ātman',[5] and the demand is constantly repeated later. All schools of thought refer the intellectual, emotional, and active life, not to the soul, but to certain subtle physical organs, called *manas*, mind, *ahaṁkāra*, egoism, *buddhi*, understanding, by the Sāṅkhyas.[6] Monks were urged to reduce these organs to passivity. Here is a stanza from the *Kāṭhaka Upanishad*:

[1] *Brihadāraṇyaka U.*, 3. 5. 1; Deussen, 58.
[2] Deussen, 64.
[3] Quoted in Deussen, 284, from *Maitrāyaṇa U.*, i. 3.
[4] Warren, 423.
[5] *Chhāndogya U.*, viii. 15.
[6] See p. 239.

When the five tools of knowledge
Stand, with the Manas, absolutely still,
And the understanding makes no move,
Then that is called the highest state.[1]

The following is from a Buddhist sutta:

> Perceiving this, O priests, the learned and noble disciple conceives an aversion for contact, conceives an aversion for sensation, conceives an aversion for perception, conceives an aversion for the predispositions, conceives an aversion for consciousness. And in conceiving this aversion he becomes divested of passion; and by the absence of passion he becomes free; and when he is free he becomes aware that he is free; and he knows that rebirth is exhausted, that he has lived the holy life, that he has done what it behoved him to do, and that he is no more for this world.[2]

This whole process was believed by all schools to culminate in the highest form of meditation and contemplation called *samādhi*, wherein

> subject and object, the soul and God, are so completely blended into one that the consciousness of the separate subject altogether disappears, and there succeeds that which is described as *nirātmakatvam*, i.e. selflessness.[3]

5. There is one point in the practice of sannyāsīs of all schools which shows very clearly how completely they had broken with the Brāhmanical system. When a man decided to become a monk, he repudiated his father and mother, his wife and his children, and declared they had no further claim upon him. He simply left them, adopted the houseless life, and allowed them to get their living as they might. There were many heartrending scenes in consequence. The case of the Buddha is well known. Another famous case is that of Rāja Gopī Chandra. The pathetic but fruitless appeal made to him before his departure by his beautiful young queen has found a place in Bengali literature.[4] The idea was that the monk, through his abandonment of ordinary society,

[1] *Kāṭhaka U.*, vi. 10; cf. iii. 13; *Śvetāśvatara U.*, ii. 9.
[2] Warren, 152. [3] Deussen, 392.
[4] Dinesh Ch. Sen, *Bengali Language and Literature*, 58 ff.

was cut away completely from it, had risen to a higher sphere, and could not in any sense be held responsible for those still living in the system which he had repudiated. To this day the old ideas remain unchanged: if a man wishes to become a sannyāsī, he may simply leave his wife without making any provision for her. The wife may go to her husband and beg him to return; but she has no claim upon him, and he feels no obligation, nay, rather perhaps resents her interference.[1]

6. It has often been asserted that early Buddhist and Hindu monks were vegetarians. This seems to be a mistake. In those early days people did not condemn the eating of flesh: it was the killing of the animal that was wrong. The Buddha transgressed no Buddhist law when he ate the pork which gave him dysentery and killed him. The idea at the basis of ahiṁsā is that all life is sacred, and that no holy man can take life. Hence the monk, whether Hindu, Buddhist, or Jain, was forbidden to kill any animal, or to take the life of a twig by breaking it from the stem, or even to crush a living seed. The reaping of a field of wheat or rice would have been quite as heinous a sin as killing a deer or an ox. This is one of the reasons why it was a rule for monks of all orders to beg their food: they could never do any of the cruel work of killing plants or animals, but received their food already cooked from the hands of householders. The taking of life was not so serious for the householder, as he did not profess to be a saint. The same explanation is required with regard to the hot water which was the only drink of the Jain monk. Cold water has so many lives in it that he must not drink it on any account; but if a householder kills all the animalculae by boiling the water, he may then use it.

The rule of ahiṁsā was binding only on the hermit and the monk; but it was recognized in Buddhism that the layman

[1] Oman mentions a case, 48.

could win merit by doing all in his power to save animal life. Hence Aśoka, the Buddhist emperor of the third century B.C., used his imperial position for this purpose, issuing several edicts to restrict the slaughter of animals in various ways.[1] As animal sacrifice was still one of the most prominent features of Hinduism, these laws must have been unpopular in Brāhman circles. It is noteworthy that it is only animal life that Aśoka legislates for. From this time forward we hear far less of the law against destroying vegetable life.

It was only when the original reverence for all life, vegetable as well as animal, began to fall into the background and the idea of the merit of saving animal life became prominent that the conception arose that the monk ought to restrict himself to a vegetarian diet. How this idea passed from the monk to the layman we shall see in a later chapter.[2]

IV. When we turn to our own times we find that the hermits have disappeared, and also all the ancient orders of monks except the Jains. Modern Jains are divided into three sects: Digambaras, Śvetāmbaras, and Sthānakavāsīs. Each sect has its own order of monks, and the two latter have nuns also.

Śaṅkara, at once great Vedantist and great champion of Hinduism against the Buddhists, reorganized the ascetic orders in his day. Among the changes introduced by him was the adoption of the use of monasteries from Buddhism. The modern word is *maṭha*. The leading monasteries which he founded became centres of sacred learning which were of inestimable service in the long-continued struggle with the rival faith. Four of these monasteries are still in existence, the head of each bearing during his term of office the master's name, Śaṅkarāchārya.

Rāmānuja, the great Vishṇuite leader of the twelfth century, is said to have founded a very large number of monasteries; and their use has passed into all the modern bhakti[3] sects.

[1] Vincent Smith's *Asoka*, 56–57.

[2] See pp. 381–382.

[3] See pp. 380, 386.

Each religious leader—Madhva, Rāmānanda, Kabīr, Gorakhnāth, Nānak, Dādū, Vallabha, Chaitanya—not only gathered the laity round him but formed his own order of ascetics.

Of all these orders two are much nearer the ancient sannyāsī in practice than the others, viz. those that have held by Śaṅkara's rules, and those that follow Rāmānuja. In the life of these strict sannyāsīs there are four stages. Each is called a *Kuṭīchara* sannyāsī to begin with. In the later stages of their progress they are called successively *Bahūdaka*, *Haṁsa*, *Paramahaṁsa*.[1]

Śaṅkara's immediate followers were called *daṇḍīs*, because they carried the daṇḍa,[2] or rod, which the original sannyāsī usually carried. Since they were divided into ten groups, each ruled by one of Śaṅkara's disciples, they were called *daśnāmīs*, ten-name sannyāsīs. Four only of these ten groups retain their original purity, the names being *Tīrtha*, *Āśrama*, *Sarasvatī*, and *Bhāratī*. These still refuse to receive as members any others than Hindus of the three twice-born castes; and, as Kshatriyas and Vaiśyas are so few, they are practically restricted to Brāhmans. These men are usually called *Ekadaṇḍīs*, i.e. single-rod men, to distinguish them from the followers of Rāmānuja. They carry a rod with a little red pocket attached, like a flag, to its upper part. The sacred thread which the man discarded when he became a sannyāsī is contained in the pocket.

Rāmānuja's followers are called *Tridaṇḍīs*, three-rod men, because instead of the single daṇḍa they carry three rods fastened together. Another difference between them and the *Ekadaṇḍīs* is that they retain their caste and the sacred thread.[3] The triple rod also has a little red flag, but it contains the cloth for straining water, which the man carries as a sannyāsī. Only Brāhmans are admitted to this order.

Like all other modern ascetics these strict sannyāsīs worship some god or gods belonging to the Hindu pantheon. That is

[1] Deussen, 379. [2] See p. 254.
[3] Rāmānuja, 70, 72, 113.

a point in which they are like the hermit and unlike the ancient sannyāsī. All modern ascetics are sectarian. Ekadaṇḍīs are Śivaite, while Tridaṇḍīs are Vishṇuite. Both these orders contain a considerable number of learned men.

The remaining six groups of Daśnāmīs are open to Hindus of all castes, and in many other points they have departed from the ancient discipline. In fact, they are on the same level as the other modern ascetic orders. We shall call all these ordinary ascetics *sādhus* to distinguish them from strict sannyāsīs of the Ekadaṇḍī and Tridaṇḍī orders.

The practice of the sādhu is a hybrid, a combination of the life of the ancient hermit and the ancient sannyāsī. In general, the discipline is of the latter type, but the rules have been relaxed in several particulars. Many of the orders admit men of any caste.[1] Discipline is rather lax in most cases. All the orders are sectarian, practise sectarian worship, and read sectarian literature. Sādhus believe that the pilgrimage is a valuable religious exercise. They spend their time in long leisurely journeys to the great places of pilgrimage, visiting all the fairs and festivals on the way, and halting now and then at a monastery or, it may be, all alone at some pleasant spot. The sādhu has a few more belongings than the ancient monk had. The rosary was first used in the worship of Śiva, but it is now found in the service of all the gods, the sects varying in the material and in the number of the beads. The old staff and bowl are almost universal. The pipe has been added, and hemp and other drugs are often smoked. The yellow robe is still common, but nakedness, a scanty loin-cloth, or an outfit of rags are almost as frequently encountered.

The sādhu usually wears a sect-mark on his forehead and frequently carries some sect-symbol. If he recognizes Śiva, he will carry a trident or wear a miniature *liṅga*[2]; and in his hut will be found a human skull, a tiger skin, or a *damaru*

[1] *Mahānirvāna T.*, viii. 224.

[2] See below, p. 310.

drum. He will probably have his whole body smeared with white ashes. This is in imitation of Śiva, the Destroyer, who is fond of the burning-ghat, and is believed to smear himself in this way.[1] When he settles in a place, he will set up a *liṅga* for worship. If he recognizes Vishṇu, he may possess a discus, a *śālagrāma* stone, a conch shell[2] or a *tulsī* plant. Wherever he settles, he will set up an image of Rāma, or Kṛishṇa, or whatever form of Vishṇu he adores.

The old rule that a monk may not adorn himself is relaxed in many orders, and the result is often very picturesque. The hair is dressed in some most unusual fashion or is allowed to grow wild and matted. The body is marked, or the dress is arranged, so as to recall the god whom the sādhu worships. Showy badges are worn indicating the places of pilgrimage he has visited.

A number of new forms of tapas are found among sādhus. One frequently sees the bed of spikes, meant to represent Bhīshma's arrowy bed described in the *Mahābhārata*. Shoes filled with spikes are not uncommon. Now and then an ascetic will hang head downwards from a tree above a smoky fire, or wear an enormous weight of chains, or use mechanical means to keep down his passions, or measure his length along the road for hundreds of miles. Most of the old forms of austerity are also in use. Yoga practice is still common, but the mental exercises are usually sectarian.

Asceticism has greatly deteriorated in modern times. There is no serious thought-movement in it; a large proportion of sādhus are ignorant men; many are grossly immoral; some of the orders are coarse and indecent; and Hindus acknowledge that there are but few sincere and earnest men amongst them. Yet here and there one meets a man of character and learning.[3]

There are certain other phenomena connected with asceticism which are well worth our notice.

[1] Pope, 159. [2] See pp. 314, 362, 392.
[3] For modern sādhus see Oman.

V. It was universally believed in ancient India that, if a hermit lived a life of purity and austerity, or if a monk achieved release and lived the life of world-abandonment faithfully, his body would gradually become spiritualized, so that it would be very different in appearance from the bodies of ordinary men. Not only would all signs of passion disappear from the features and frame; the anatomy and the material elements of the body would actually change until, refined and etherealized, it became a fit expression of the exalted spirit within. The muscular system would become less prominent; the trunk would become smooth and delicately shaped; the man would glow with beauty and supernatural light; and the physical nature of the frame would be so transformed as to be no longer subject to gravitation and other ordinary restrictions.

The earliest references to these results of asceticism occur in the original *Rāmāyaṇa* of Vālmīki. We read of a hermitage where

> Dwelt many an old and reverent sire
> Bright as the sun or Lord of Fire,
> All with each earthly sense subdued
> A pure and saintly multitude.[1]

Of Śarabhaṅga we are told that his

> lustre vied
> With gods, by penance purified;[2]

Agastya is said to be

> Through fierce devotion bright as flame;[3]

and Bharadvāja is described as

> Calm saint, whose vows had well been wrought,
> Whose fervent rites keen sight had bought.[4]

We do not meet with the idea in the earliest Upanishads, but in the *Śvetāśvatara*

[1] III. i.
[2] III. v.
[3] III. xii.
[4] II. liv.

> Activity, health, freedom from desire,
> A fair countenance, beauty of voice,
> A pleasant odour,[1]

are stated to be among the first results of yoga. The *Yoga-sūtra*[2] does not mention beauty and spiritualization as a result of yoga, but makes much of etherealization.

Buddhism followed Hinduism in this matter. Of a monk who has attained wisdom it is said in the Pāli books, 'Placid, brother, are all your organs of sense; clear and bright is the colour of your skin.'[3] Gautama is said to have radiated a golden sheen,[4] and his body is spoken of as being like the trunk of a lion,[5] that is, smooth, lithe, slender-waisted. In the later *Questions of King Milinda* we are told of Buddha that 'he was golden in colour with a skin like gold, and there spread around him a glorious halo of a fathom's length'.[6]

Of Mahāvīra, the Jina, it is said, that he was 'refulgent like the sun, pure like excellent gold', that 'like a well-kindled fire he shone in his splendour'.[7] He was very beautiful.[8] His body emitted an exquisite perfume.

When, at a later date, Buddhists began to use images, this belief produced some of their noblest qualities. The images of the Buddha owe their suggestion of deep spirituality partly to the meditative pose of the body and the calm of the features, but largely also to a peculiar treatment of the trunk whereby everything speaking of activity, effort, and sense pleasure is excluded, and 'an extreme simplicity of form and contour' gives a powerful impression of religious exaltation and balanced peace. The Buddhist sculptor actually succeeded in creating a style which gives expression in stone to a lofty spirituality. The same type of religious art is found also in Jainism and Hinduism. Indeed, all the best image-sculpture of India owes its power to this mighty mode of artistic speech. Thus the

[1] ii. 13. Deussen, 395. Cf. *Maitrāyaṇa U.*, i. 2.
[2] Book III. [3] Warren, 88. [4] Warren, 71, 73.
[5] Grünwedel, *Buddhist Art in India*, 161.
[6] *S.B.E.*, xxxv. 116. [7] *S.B.E.*, xxii. 261.
[8] *S.B.E.*, xxii. 256, 258.

loftiest Indian conception of divinity, whether among Hindus, Jains, or Buddhists, is an idealization of the wandering ascetic. This aspect of Indian art is most convincingly expounded by Mr. E. B. Havell in his *Indian Sculpture and Painting*; and the dignity and beauty of the finest examples of Indian plastic art are brought out with surpassing strength in the plates in the same volume.

The shining radiance of the ascetic's body referred to above reappears in the halo which in Buddhist sculpture so often encircles the head or even the whole body of the Buddha. This, too, was copied on occasion by Jain and Hindu artists. The golden hue of Buddha's body has found further expression in the custom of gilding Buddhist images prevalent in all Buddhist lands.[1]

VI. We have seen that the Muni in the *Ṛigveda* flies through the air and that the hermit of a later date acquires magic powers and wins all his desires, even to the dethronement of the gods, by means of his austerities. It is a most curious fact that these miraculous results of the endurance of pain were finally attributed to the houseless monks, who were believed to have emptied themselves of all desires, and who despised heaven and all the gods. In all the schools these powers are regarded as a natural outcome of sainthood,[2] although they are often closely associated with the practice of yoga, especially with its more advanced forms.

In the earliest Upanishads they do not occur, but, when we reach the *Śvetāśvatara*,[3] we read

> He knows nothing further of sickness, old age, or suffering,
> Who gains a body out of the fire of yoga;

the *Maitrāyaṇa*[4] has a similar passage; and, later, the *Amṛitabindu*[5] declares that the yogī after three months attains to knowledge, after four to the vision of the gods,

[1] *J. R. A. S.*, 1911, p. 715.
[2] *Āpastamba*, ii. 9, 23, 7–8.
[3] ii. 12. Deussen, 395. Cf. vi. 13.
[4] vi. 28.
[5] 28 ff. Deussen, 395.

after five to their strength, and after six to their absolute nature.

In the *Yogasūtra* of Patañjali, which dates from the middle of the second century B.C., these powers are described, classified, and explained as arising from yoga exercises.

What Gautama, the Buddha, may have believed on this subject we do not know; but in the books of the Pāli canon he and his followers are credited with the most extraordinary powers. Perhaps the following paragraph will give most succinctly the early Buddhist belief:

> If a Bhikkhu should desire, Brethren, to exercise one by one each of the different Iddhis, being one to become multiform, being multiform to become one; to become visible, or to become invisible; to go without being stopped to the further side of a wall, or a fence, or a mountain, as if through air; to penetrate up and down through solid ground, as if through water; to walk on the water without dividing it, as if on solid ground; to travel cross-legged through the sky, like the birds on wing; to touch and feel with the hand even the sun and the moon, mighty and powerful though they be; and to reach in the body even up to the heaven of Brahma; let him then fulfil all righteousness, let him be devoted to that quietude of heart which springs from within, let him not drive back the ecstacy of contemplation, let him look through things, let him be much alone![1]

All this is continued in Buddhist *Mahāyāna* literature and exaggerated beyond all bounds.

A cursory glance through the life of Mahāvīra in the *Kalpa Sūtra* of the Jains will show that they attributed the same powers to their Jinas, Kevalins, and holy men of other degrees. Of Mahāvīra it is said, 'like the firmament he wanted no support; like the wind he knew no obstacles.'[2]

These beliefs were accepted by Śaṅkara[3] and Rāmānuja,[4] and can be traced in all the bhakti[5] sects of the last thousand

[1] *Akankheya Sutta*, 14; *S.B.E.*, xi. 214 ff.
[2] *S.B.E.*, xxii. 260.
[3] *S.B.E.*, xxxiv. 200, where we are told a yogī may assume many forms.
[4] *S.B.E.*, xlviii. 331. Cf. *Rāmānuja*, 182, where the philosopher is said to have become a thousand-headed serpent, and to have argued with the Jains with each head.
[5] See below, p. 386.

years. Many of the old marvels are repeated, and new stories, often grotesque in form, appear. Madhvāchārya, for example, was able at any time to eat a meal fit for an ox.[1] Chaitanya is credited with the same power.[2]

In the last few centuries hypnotism, mesmerism, jugglery, spiritualism, and quackery in general have been used by yogīs to win the reputation of supernatural power. The production of a state of coma or trance was carefully practised, until adepts could actually allow themselves to be buried for a lengthened period and come out from their entombment alive. Until recently, yogīs now and then pretended to possess the power of levitation and such-like. We need scarcely say that they were more indebted to fraud than to miracle. Madame Blavatsky's escapade settled the general question for all thinking men.

This belief, that the saint possesses supernatural power, is the source of one of the most notable elements of the Buddhist cult, namely, relic-worship. The power is a sort of holy contagion which inheres in the saint's body and in everything he has used.

The same reasoning lies behind a practice which is found in all the Hindu sects. When a disciple meets his religious teacher, *guru*,[3] he prostrates himself before him, and takes some of the dust from his guru's feet and places it on his head. In many of the sects it is considered a high spiritual privilege to be allowed to drink the water in which the guru has washed his feet. Holiness is held to be physically communicable.

VII. When the monastic movement first appeared in India, it was the greatest intellectual and religious force of the time. It laid hold of all the noblest minds and ruled them; and for many centuries thereafter the highest spiritual life of the country found for itself in its discipline a sufficient, a satisfying expression. Nor need we wonder. Surely no one can study this great old history without being struck with the splendid

[1] *Madhva*, 36, 97, 124, 176, 177.

[2] S. K. Ghose, *Lord Gauranga*, vol. ii.

[3] See below, p. 402.

height and dignity of the aims of the movement and the seriousness of the men who took part in it. Only high ideals most earnestly pursued could have produced the lofty literature of monasticism, the Upanishads and the Buddhist Suttas. But if the principles were high and noble, they were applied with a fearlessness, a devotion, a courage, and a constancy to which there are very few parallels. As long as the world lasts, men will look back with wonder upon the ascetics of India. Their quiet surrender of every earthly privilege and pleasure, and their strong endurance of many forms of suffering will be an inspiration to all generations of thinking Indians. For nearly three thousand years the ascetics of India have stood forth, a speaking testimony to the supremacy of the spiritual. Whether men were willing to learn the truth or not, no one could shut his eyes to the object-lesson held up before India. The very fact of the existence of the order of sannyāsīs set material splendour and worldly pleasures in their proper place of complete subordination to the spiritual. Further, the life of the sannyāsī has dignified poverty in India. Amidst its rising prosperity may India never lose the conviction, which has been worked into the common mind of the country, that a poor man is worthy of as much honour as a rich man.

Yet the whole monastic movement of modern India is already in full decay. Sādhus stand nearer the popular faith than the ancient orders did, but they cannot be said to wield great influence. Comparatively few men of culture and intellectual power enter the orders; and, while here and there men of real spirituality and beautiful character are found among them, and now and then a man of education and distinction becomes a sannyāsī, Hindus are forward to confess that most of the ascetics of to-day are of little worth. The man who is too lazy to work finds the holy life a paradise. The yellow robe is only too often used to hide the criminal. There is no living thought-movement among them. Most of them are ignorant men. Many use the *Gītā*, the Hindi work, *Vichāra-sāgara*, or some other philosophical manual; but more are content with the *mantra*[1] and the symbols of their order. As the deeper ideas of the movement have gradually been lost sight of, the spirit of pagan polytheism has re-asserted itself; and the ascetic life is more and more conceived as a sort of meritorious discipline which makes the man religiously holy, but has no connexion with morality. The following is from Pandit S. N. Śāstrī's recent work, *The Mission of the Brahmo Samaj*:[2]

> Even the ordinary householder looks upon the sannyasi or mendicant as an ideal of perfection. The conviction is so ingrained in the Hindu mind, that let a man but wear the mendicant's garb and profess contempt for the world, he is at once installed as a spiritual guide and worshipped as such. And the beauty of the thing lies here, that this *guruism* will continue undisturbed in spite of many secret and open irregularities in such a guide's life. I have seen with my own eyes a man in a mendicant's dress drinking wine in a public street, singing indecent songs and taking indecent liberties with a woman, yet all the time worshipped and helped with pecuniary contributions by a number of common people as their guru or spiritual preceptor.

The sādhu is outside the modern movement altogether, a boulder left in our fertile valley by a moving glacier which has long ago spent itself. He is altogether out of touch and sympathy with the large questions and mighty activities which are agitating India to-day: Education, Social Reform, Religious Reform, Politics, Economic Progress. He knows nothing of them, or is opposed to them, like the temple Brāhmans all over the land. He is quite unfit to lay his hand on any of the interests of our time. The men who really lead India to-day are in law, medicine, education, government service, journalism, business. The ideas which interest these men, the ideas which are creating the new India, are not the fundamental ideas of Hindu asceticism, and thus the sādhu knows nothing about them.

Here is a quotation from a Hindu paper which will show how the educated Hindu regards the modern sādhu:

[1] See below, pp. 392, 449.

[2] pp. 58 and 59.

In this utilitarian age, the general tendency is to utilize everybody and everything. It is a noble ideal, the pursuit of which certainly deserves appreciation and encouragement. In India the *Sadhus* or professional ascetics, who live upon mendicancy, form a pretty numerous band, and though a few of them may be men of genuine piety and spirituality, it goes without saying that the majority of them are little better than beggars and vagabonds. Well, it has occurred to Mr. Tahl Ram Gangaram that instead of allowing thousands of able-bodied men to grow up and die in mendicancy, an effort should be made to give them some kind of education so as to make them useful members of society. Being unmarried and utterly free from all cares and anxieties, they may, for instance, be usefully employed as itinerant preachers of religion and morality or as medical missionaries whose services will be available whenever and wherever there may be a serious outbreak of epidemics.[1]

The following sentences are from a brief report of a speech delivered by Mrs. Besant in Benares, and shows the attitude of the Theosophical Society to modern ascetics:

They did not want thousands of idle beggars in the garb of Sannyāsīs, but a large number of Brahmachārīs who would sacrifice five or six years of their life and wander from village to village educating every child, sacrificing themselves for people instead of going to jungles or caves, seeking liberation for themselves.[2]

Compare also what Prof. Har Dyal says in the passage quoted above in the Introduction.[3] These quotations are quite sufficient to show that Hindu asceticism is dying, and that the modern sādhu is altogether out of touch with the modern movement.

These sentences also enable us to see what is wrong with asceticism and what is wanted in its place: the sādhu is *inactive*, while *self-sacrificing service* is what India needs to-day. The difficulty could not be more explicitly stated than in these brief quotations.

It is of the utmost importance to notice that the sādhu in being inactive is absolutely true to the movement which has

[1] *The Bengalee*, Oct. 13, 1904.
[2] Cut from *The Statesman*.
[3] p. 36 f.

created him. Here is what the great German scholar, Deussen, who calls himself a Vedāntist, says on the point:

> Eternal philosophical truth has seldom found more decisive and striking expression than in the doctrine of the emancipating knowledge of the Ātman. And yet this knowledge may be compared to that icy-cold breath which checks every development and benumbs all life. He who knows himself as the Ātman is, it is true, for ever beyond the reach of all desire, and therefore beyond the possibility of immoral conduct, but at the same time he is deprived of every incitement to action or initiation of any kind; he is lifted out of the whole circle of illusory individual existence, his body is no longer his, his works no longer his, everything which he may henceforth do or leave undone belongs to the sphere of the great illusion which he has penetrated, and is therefore of no account. . . . When the knowledge of the Ātman has been gained, every action, and therefore every moral action also, has been deprived of meaning.[1]

Thus the reason why the educated Hindu criticizes the ascetic is that his own mind is filled with new ideas, while the ascetic is still true to the principles of Hinduism. The spirit of the West has come in and revolutionized the mind and the environment of the educated man. In consequence, the more faithful the ascetic is to the ancient ideal, the more hopeless and useless he appears to the modern man.

Thus the ancient asceticism is doomed. Nothing can save it. The modern spirit demands something else, and the educated Hindu is the man through whom the new spirit is being disseminated in India.

VIII. But the acknowledgement of this fact leaves us face to face with a gigantic problem. Hinduism has produced for quite two thousand five hundred years an unending procession of men and women ready to devote themselves, body and soul, to the highest; but, when they are produced, they are comparatively useless; for the mighty religion which inspires them to enter the ascetic life sets before them as their ideal the life of the actionless Brahman. But what India needs to-day is a great army of self-sacrificing men, ready to toil for the

[1] p. 361.

uplifting of the poor and the downtrodden,[1] and for the advancement of education, agriculture, industry, art, morality, religion. What is needed is the man inspired to living service, not the yogī rapt in oblivious meditation. The Hon. Mr. Gokhale remarked in one of his speeches:[2]

> Full-time workers renouncing everything for the sake of the country are what are urgently needed in India.

Thus the problem is, How are Hindus to be inspired to unselfish service? Clearly, it cannot be by any form of Hindu philosophy; for that leads to inaction. Nor can there be any doubt that such inspiration can come only from religion. Where can we find a motive sufficient for the purpose?

Whatever Hindus may think of Christianity, every one acknowledges that it stirs men and women to unselfish service. It can and does produce men and women who toil for others. That Christ has been a ministering angel to India, no honest son of India will deny. Who will ever be able to measure the amount of service done to India by Christians along the following lines?—education for boys, primary, secondary, university, and industrial; education for girls in school, college, and zenāna; orphanages, widows' homes, education for the blind; medical relief by means of doctors (both men and women), nurses, dispensaries, hospitals; leper asylums; rescue homes for fallen women; famine relief; and, last of all, the uplifting of the depressed classes.

Most thoughtful Hindus are ready to acknowledge the very great service missions have done to India. Here is a general testimony from a Hindu paper, called out by the fact that $30,000 had been sent from America 'in the name of Christ' to the starving people of India:

> The Christian religion is truly fruitful in practical philanthropy to an extent unparalleled in the case of any other religion. Whatever may

[1] Compare the passage quoted from Pandit Śiva Nāth Śāstrī, above, pp. 142–143.

[2] Briefly reported in *I. S. R.*, Dec. 26, 1909.

> be its theoretical faults and philosophical incompleteness (we can afford to let that pass), here it stands head and shoulders over every other religion. By its side, the most ancient religions and grandest philosophical systems of the world sink into insignificance, as a motive for philanthropic action.[1]

We give next a very emphatic statement which occurs in a letter by Mr. K. Śrīnivāsa Rao, Sub-Judge, Tuticorin, to *The Indian Social Reformer*:[2]

> The feeling of prejudice against Christian Missions and Missionaries is an old feeling based on the apprehension that they are engaged in the work of proselytism, pure and simple. As a matter of fact, however, in the first place, they are engaged in the work largely of educating the country. The educational institutions bear witness to it. Secondly, they are engaged in relieving the sick, and, for instance, the hospital of Jammalmadugu is resorted by all classes for treatment of some of the most difficult cases of diseases of women and diseases of the eye. Brāhman ladies of position have been availing themselves of this splendid institution. Thirdly, they are engaged in raising the status of the depressed classes and educating their boys and girls, in a manner that must fill us all with gratitude, that but for them these poor children and these despised classes will both continue to be in the same degraded condition in which they have been born for ages.

Our next quotation is from a Parsee paper[3] and deals with missionary education:

> The aid of Missionary enterprise may be enlisted with enduring benefit to teachers and scholars in India. Christian Missionaries as school-masters have done lasting and material good to the cause of moral education in Indian schools and colleges. Order, method, and discipline are nowhere observed and enforced at school with greater sternness as they are done here. The personal influence of these missionary teachers is in itself a great asset. Drawn from a class of men of high character and moral worth who have taken to teaching as a labour of love and a life-long profession, they have left a permanent mark on the educational work in India. Their educational activity has furnished Indian towns and cities with some very ably conducted schools and colleges. The selfless nature of their work and the high

[1] Quoted by T. E. Slater in *Missions and Sociology*, p. 55.
[2] March 13, 1910, p. 328.
[3] From the *Rast Goftar*, a Bombay paper. Quoted in the *Bombay Guardian*, April 30, 1910.

moral tone of individual workers among them have invariably impressed students who have received education under them with that esteem and reverence which we would wish to see established in youngsters towards their betters in age and wisdom. The relation between the teacher and his pupil in their schools has always been one of perfect cordiality, and when the student enters life the memory of the gratitude he owed to his school in his young days never forsakes him. The missionary in India acts as a connecting link between its rising generation and his own race in the same sense that he ties together Christian and non-Christian races in this country by his philanthropic social work.

The following, a brief leader from the Calcutta Hindu daily, *The Bengalee*,[1] deals chiefly with mission work for the depressed classes:

There are missionaries and missionaries. The type of the Christian missionary, who delights in reviling the religions of Hindus and Mohammedans, is familiar to every one of us and it is a type which does little credit to Christianity. But there is another, if rarer, type. Go to Sonthal Parganas and the Central Provinces and you will find Christian missionaries literally sacrificing their lives for the amelioration of the condition of the aboriginal population in whose midst they work and live. Go to Southern India and you will see what missionary effort has achieved in the way of the regeneration of the despised Pariahs. These missionaries do not dwell in palaces nor enjoy the income of a petty principality. Luxury's contagion, weak and vile, has not enervated them nor has physical discomfort and privation damped their ardour in the furtherance of their self-imposed task. They left their native country as young men. They have grown grey in their noble ministry. Some of them have not revisited their native land even once in twenty or thirty years, and not a few of them are destined to lay their bones under the sod in some remote, obscure and out-of-the-way hamlet in India, which has been the centre of their life's work. They are not necessarily Englishmen. Germans and Frenchmen, Belgians, and even the Swiss from his mountain home are found among these toilers in the Indian vineyard. Talk to them and you would be surprised at the utter absence of that arrogance and racial pride which are seldom inseparable from even the mildest of the European laymen. It is they who exalt their nations and their religion. They give to their work their very life; they collect funds from their countrymen to enable them to carry on their work; they appeal to and work among the

[1] March 17, 1903.

millions whom Hindu Society has cast out of its pale and looks down upon with contempt. They are teaching the pariah to consider himself, not an outcaste, but a member of the great human family. They are teaching him to reclaim jungles and establish prosperous settlements. They are giving him food when he is in want and medicine when he is attacked with disease. The world knows them not, cares not for them and would not miss them were they to withdraw in a body from India. But to the pariah in his hovel, to the Ko in the forest glades, the difference would be immeasurable—the loss would be irreparable. Nor must it be forgotten that in the days when the schoolmaster had not been abroad, the Christian missionary was the pioneer of education in this country.

The last extract we shall quote speaks of the value of the work of missionaries in the matter of social reform, and as a humanizing and elevating influence:

We hold that most of the good influence at work in India is to be traced, not to the fantastic and obscure teaching of theosophists, but to the devoted efforts of the noble band of foreign missionaries who have ever been foremost in every effort for the good of the country. Whether as philanthropists, as social regenerators, industrial benefactors, or workers on behalf of the depressed classes the Christian Missionaries have been pioneers in every good cause and it is doubtful if the country would have progressed in the marvellous manner it has done if no Christian Missionary had ever set his foot in India. We do not here refer to the spiritual side of the missionary's labour although even here his influence has been exerted to the dispelling of ignorance and grovelling superstitions among the lower orders. We would rather dwell on the humanizing and beneficent work of the missionary for the social, mental and moral upliftment of India. Judged by any standard the influence of the missionary has always been exerted on behalf of all that is good and noble and of good report. Modern India owes a debt of gratitude which it will be difficult to acknowledge adequately.[1]

There can, therefore, be no doubt that Jesus Christ has raised up a great company of men and women in India, both Indian and foreign, who have shown the spirit of self-renunciation in priceless practical service to this country.

[1] From *United India.* Quoted in the *Madras Christian College Magazine*, Feb. 1910.

Hindus now and then go so far as frankly to recognize the contrast between Christianity and Hinduism in this regard :

> One of the foremost causes of success of the missionary is his burning zeal for his religion. He believes in his message. He has left his parents, his friends, and his native land to spread his Gospel. He has crossed the seas to attack us. He belongs to a cold country, but he chooses to live under the scorching Indian sun, in order to save us from going to a hotter place after death. Young men belonging to the richest families, have sacrificed their all in order to fight our civilization. I know persons of the most brilliant parts at Oxford—first-class scholars who have won any number of prizes and degrees—who throw up their whole career and come out as missionaries.
>
> Our young men can have no idea of the sacrifice these people undergo ; they accept exile for the sake of their religion ; they work day and night, like coolies, in a country thousands of miles from their home. Many of them are quite young. They have not tasted any of the sweet things of life. They are determined, earnest men, who are devoid of avarice, who know no rest in pursuit of their aim, who never lose heart amid difficulties, and who realize that life is given to man to be spent for some great and good cause. Such tremendous enthusiasm can overcome many obstacles. Endowed with such enormous moral capital, a movement can go a long way, even against heavy odds. . . . Give me such workers and I will Hinduise the world in a decade.[1]

It is from this point of view that we shall best understand Vivekānanda's scheme of what he calls 'Practical Vedānta'. He expects Vedāntists to be stimulated by their faith to practical service for India. Prof. Deussen's words quoted above[2] show that one might as well attempt to warm the house with ice. The Roman Empire offers an interesting parallel to Vivekānanda's exhortations: Julian the Apostate 'urged benevolence on his fellow-pagans, if they wished to compete with the Christians'.[3]

IX. It will therefore be well worth while to inquire how it is that Christ succeeds so much better than any other leader in turning his followers into servants of humanity. Can we see what the Christian process is?

A. If a man wishes to become a Christian, *complete self-*

[1] From *The Vedic Magazine*. [2] p. 276. [3] Glover, 162.

surrender to Christ is the primal law of discipleship laid down for him. This is stated quite clearly by Jesus Himself:

> If any man wishes to come after me, let him renounce himself and take up his cross and follow me.[1]

Paul understood the law perfectly, and gave it classic expression:

> And Christ died for all, that they which live might no longer live unto themselves, but unto him who for their sakes died and rose again.[2]

What is called for in these words is an act of will in which the man surrenders himself completely, gives up the citadel of his being to Christ, so that henceforward he may obey Christ in all things.

This is the significance of the fact that everywhere throughout the New Testament Jesus is called the Christian's Lord. The word is no otiose or ornamental epithet, but vividly expresses the fact that the Christian is a man wholly surrendered to Christ, that he is bound to obey his Master in all things. Christ Himself says,

> And why call ye me, 'Lord, Lord,' and do not the things which I say?[3]

This yielding up of the whole inner nature to Christ is a spiritual act, an inner change, a change from self to God, from sin to righteousness. Such an act is impossible so long as Christ is regarded as an ordinary man. It is possible only when one realizes the absolute supremacy of Jesus, when one realizes that He has the right to demand complete allegiance, that He is the Lord of the soul and of righteousness. When one realizes that, and surrenders to Him, then a mighty spiritual change passes over the soul.

This change also contains within itself, implicitly, the surrender of all things. Christ demands the perfect yielding of the self, including the heart and the will. If I have actually

[1] Matt. 16, 24. [2] II Cor. 5, 15. [3] Luke 6, 46.

given myself up in completeness to Christ, there is nothing else that I can wish to hold back. The self is the citadel of the man, and things are of value only as they are related to the self. Hence the surrender of the self contains within itself the surrender of all things. If there is anything I am unwilling to give up for Christ's sake, clearly I have not given myself up to Him. Hence Jesus declares that we cannot be His disciples, unless we let go everything else:

> So then whosoever he be of you that does not give up in his heart *all that he hath*, he cannot be my disciple.[1]

This act of letting everything go appears in different forms in His teaching:

> The kingdom of heaven is like treasure hid in the field, which when a man found he hid and from the joy thereof goeth and selleth *all that he hath* and buyeth that field.[2]
>
> Again, the kingdom of heaven is like unto a man that is a merchant seeking goodly pearls; and having found one pearl of great price, he went and sold *all that he had*, and bought it.[3]
>
> He that loveth father or mother more than me is not worthy of me, and he that loveth son or daughter more than me is not worthy of me.[4]
>
> If any man cometh unto me and hateth not his father and his mother and his wife and his children and his brothers and his sisters, yea and his own life also, he cannot be my disciple.[5]
>
> Whoever wishes to save his life shall lose it, but whoever will lose his life for my sake shall find it.[6]

But, mark, while Jesus demands that we shall make an inner surrender of everything, He does not demand that we shall actually abandon everything. What He wants is to have the heart so closely bound to Himself that all earthly ties shall become loose. He wishes us to remain in the world, but to hold its goods, its pleasures, and its relationships, our very lives, so lightly that at any moment we may be ready to give them up for the sake of the Kingdom. Self-surrender puts the whole world in subjection to Jesus. Only in complete

[1] Luke 14, 33. [2] Matt. 13, 44. [3] Matt. 13, 45–46.
[4] Matt. 10, 37. [5] Luke 14, 26. [6] Matt. 16, 25.

obedience to Him can I enjoy the purest and simplest pleasures of the world; and if He desires me to give up any or all of them, I must yield at once.

Jesus knows that it is quite possible for a man to give up property or any other thing, if he thinks he shall thereby be the gainer religiously, and yet to love the world all the time. It is far easier to give up all worldly things than to give up the heart wholly to Jesus. Therefore He demands the deeper, the far more difficult, renunciation, the surrender of the heart. The heart surrendered to Jesus is necessarily severed from the world. Here, as elsewhere, Jesus holds the spiritual position, and takes external actions and external things at their true value.

Christ's way actually enables a man to conquer the stubborn hold which earthly things have upon him. Attachment to Christ brings detachment from the world. Love for Jesus necessarily leads to a transference of interest from earthly to spiritual things, a changed estimate of the value of property, place, and pleasure, a splendid slackening of the hold which the world has on the affections; and the full surrender of the will cuts these things adrift. Complete surrender to Christ brings complete emancipation from the world.

Nature and all its gifts to man are thus put in their true place. They are good, but not the best. We ought to use them and enjoy them, but in completest subordination to spiritual ends. Since the Son of God took to Himself a human body, we cannot despise, or condemn, or destroy our physical nature; but, since He yielded His body to be crucified for the sake of higher things, we, too, must be ready to lay aside all earthly things for the sake of the Kingdom.

B. The principle which Jesus gives His disciple for his intercourse with men in the world is *love*:

> Thou shalt love thy neighbour as thyself.[1]
>
> Love your enemies.[2]

[1] Matt. 22, 39. [2] Matt. 5, 44.

This law is no mere pretty saying, no mere call to sentiment, but the Christian law of conduct. It rests on the solid foundation of the truths, that God is our common Father, that all men are therefore full brothers, and that, in consequence, love is the only rational rule possible for their mutual intercourse. Christ points out that love to God and love to man sum up our whole human duty:

> On these two commandments hangeth the whole law, and the prophets.[1]

They are thus not mere exhortations to good feeling, but supreme principles of conduct. From them every other duty can be deduced. Paul saw this clearly:

> Love worketh no ill to his neighbour: love therefore is the fulfilment of the law.[2]

Christians have learned how to use love as the supreme moral principle from the example of Christ. His every action was ruled by love. The man who takes Christ as his Lord has abundance of guidance in this matter. This law works by way of restraint. As Paul says, 'Love works no ill to his neighbour.' The man who loves will be kept from anger, revenge, selfishness, adultery, theft, lying, abuse, slander, cruelty, injustice, envy. Each of these is the negation of love. But love is also the mightiest stimulus in all the world. It has inspired the most heroic and the most unselfish actions. It is the secret of the possibility of forgiveness, that most difficult act. But the active side of love brings us to the next law of the Christian life. It is but one application of the supreme law of love; but it is so important that we must set it down by itself.

C. The most important clause in the all-inclusive law of love is, *Serve every man according to his needs*. How strongly Christ felt on this point is evident from two great passages in the Gospels. In the first we have, to begin with, the state-

[1] Matt. 22, 40. [2] Romans 13, 10.

ment of the supreme principles, 'Love God with the utmost intensity,' and 'Love thy neighbour as thyself'; and then in answer to a question as to the meaning of the latter law, Jesus tells the parable of the Good Samaritan, which we have already quoted.[1] The other passage is, if possible, charged with deeper feeling:

> But when the Son of man shall come in his glory, and all the angels with him, then shall he sit on the throne of his glory: and before him shall be gathered all the nations: and he shall separate them one from another, as the shepherd separateth the sheep from the goats; and he shall set the sheep on his right hand, but the goats on the left. Then shall the King say unto them on his right hand, Come, ye blessed of my Father, inherit the kingdom prepared for you from the foundation of the world: for I was an hungred, and ye gave me meat: I was thirsty, and ye gave me drink: I was a stranger, and ye took me in; naked, and ye clothed me: I was sick, and ye visited me: I was in prison, and ye came unto me. Then shall the righteous answer him, saying, Lord, when saw we thee an hungred, and fed thee? or athirst, and gave thee drink? And when saw we thee a stranger, and took thee in? or naked, and clothed thee? And when saw we thee sick, or in prison, and came unto thee? And the King shall answer and say unto them, Verily I say unto you, Inasmuch as ye did it unto one of these my brethren, even these least, ye did it unto me. Then shall he say also unto them on the left hand, Depart from me, ye cursed, into the eternal fire which is prepared for the devil and his angels: for I was an hungred, and ye gave me no meat: I was thirsty, and ye gave me no drink: I was a stranger, and ye took me not in; naked, and ye clothed me not; sick, and in prison, and ye visited me not. Then shall they also answer, saying, Lord, when saw we thee an hungred, or athirst, or a stranger, or naked, or sick, or in prison, and did not minister unto thee? Then shall he answer them, saying, Verily I say unto you, Inasmuch as ye did it not unto one of these least, ye did it not unto me.[2]

Here Christ tells us that our final relationship to Him will be determined by the question whether we have served our brothers and sisters or not. Six forms of help only are mentioned; feeding the hungry, giving drink to the thirsty, clothing the naked, visiting the sick, giving hospitality to strangers, visiting those in prison; but no one can mistake

[1] Above, pp. 194–195.

[2] Matt. 25, 31–45.

what Christ means to teach: the principle clearly is 'Serve your fellow men according to their needs'. Thus every one who has surrendered to Christ is bound to serve those round him, ministering to all their needs as far as lies in his power.

These passages show with the utmost clearness how practical Christ's understanding of the law of love is. To Him the humblest human being is a child of His heavenly Father; and therefore no service that any man can do can be too great. What is the limit of the honour, the kindness, the help due to my own brother, when we are both children of the Lord of all things?

The example of Christ has been of priceless value in the matter of service. His words, 'The Son of Man came not to be served but to be a servant,'[1] are but a simple statement of fact. He went about doing good. Every miracle was an act of service. He cured fever,[2] atrophy,[3] paralysis,[4] lunacy,[5] epilepsy,[6] leprosy;[7] He made the blind see,[8] the deaf hear, the dumb speak,[9] the lame walk;[10] He raised the dead;[11] He fed the hungry crowds;[12] He made water wine at the marriage feast;[13] and He stilled the tempest;[14] in each case serving some man, woman, or child in need. But, apart from miracle altogether, Jesus constantly found opportunity to serve those round about Him. He waited on His own disciples;[15] on one occasion at least He washed their feet;[16] He took the little children in His arms and blessed them, at the request of their mothers;[17] He thrilled the leper with His touch, because no kindly hand had been laid on his unclean shoulder for years;[18] He sat at the tables of rich and poor alike, to give them the help of His presence and of His words, in order that social intercourse might become a hallowed thing.

[1] Matt. 20, 28. [2] Mark 1, 29-31. [3] Mark 3, 1-5.
[4] Matt. 8, 5-13. [5] Mark 5, 1-20. [6] Matt. 17, 14-20.
[7] Mark 1, 40-42. [8] Luke 18, 35-43. [9] Matt. 9, 32-33.
[10] Matt. 11, 5. [11] Matt. 9, 23-26. [12] Mark 6, 35-44.
[13] John 2, 1-10. [14] Matt. 8, 23-27. [15] Luke 22, 26-27.
[16] John 13, 1-12. [17] Mark 10, 13-16. [18] Mark 1, 41.

No less significant are those bold acts of public service by which He protested in the most effective way possible against certain moral and religious abuses which marked orthodox Jewish life in His day, and thereby became the pioneer and the example of moral and religious reform to the nations. He exposed the social exclusiveness of the Pharisees by dining with 'publicans and sinners', i. e. the social Outcastes of the day;[1] He ate food without washing His hands ceremonially in advance, to teach the Jews that spiritual purity is not a matter of a clean skin;[2] He did not keep the stated fasts, that men might learn that the mere abstinence from food is in itself of no religious value;[3] He persisted in healing on the Jewish Sabbath, in order to rouse men to observe the day in the spirit and not in the mere letter;[4] He drove the buyers and sellers out of the Temple, publicly showing that one man at least would not tolerate the use of God's house for money-making.[5]

D. The last point to be noticed is one that is involved in the first law. We saw that to every disciple Jesus says,

> If any man wishes to come after me, let him renounce himself and take up his cross and follow me,[6]

and we recognized that it was a summons to full self-surrender to Christ as the Lord of the human spirit. We have now to notice another element contained in it, namely the implication that a man cannot follow Christ without carrying a cross. Christ went out through the streets of Jerusalem carrying His cross on His shoulders; and He here warns every would-be follower that to follow Him is to be a cross-bearer. The meaning is plain: the faithful follower of Christ will have to endure *suffering* as a result of his faithfulness as Christ did. The same warning is given over and over again with the utmost explicitness by Jesus in His teaching:

> In the world ye have tribulation.[7]

[1] Matt. 9, 9–13.
[2] Matt. 15, 1–20.
[3] Mark 2, 18–22.
[4] Mark 2, 23–28; John 9.
[5] Mark 11, 15–18.
[6] Matt. 16, 24.
[7] John 16, 33.

> Behold I send you forth as sheep in the midst of wolves.[1]
>
> But take heed to yourselves: they shall hand you over to councils; and in synagogues you shall be scourged; and before governors and kings you shall stand for my sake; . . . and brother shall betray brother to death, and father child; and children shall rise against parents and have them put to death; and ye shall be hated by all men for my name's sake.[2]

Suffering comes in two ways. There is first the simple truth that every act of service involves self-sacrifice. It is done for others, not for self. At the very least it costs a little time, money, or effort that might have been expended on oneself. Even the work of establishing and conducting a little school for poor children will cost much effort and the patient expenditure of hours of time. When the service one attempts to do is something new, such as Howard's crusade for the betterment of European prisons, it will demand the sacrifice of almost everything, time, money, comfort, and home-life, and will bring scorn and misrepresentation, and probably severe suffering besides.

Whoever wishes to serve his fellow men in non-Christian lands must make great sacrifices. He may have to give away his property, like Robert Haldane, in order to provide funds for the work. He may have to give up the society of his loved ones, and live with coarse savages, with no friend, no congenial society, like James Gilmour in Mongolia. He may have to live in some lonely spot in New Guinea all alone, or, if married, must risk the health and life of wife and little ones. The scholar gives up all chance of a life of study and preferment to live a teacher's life in China or Japan. Or, if he is a business man, and God calls him to preach, he must lay aside his business and its success. Or he takes his life in his hand and lives with lepers on their island. All this comes, even if no one oppose.

But, besides that, the faithful servant of humanity must expect opposition and persecution. Vidyāsāgara's memory is

[1] Luke 10, 3. [2] Mark 13, 9, 12–13.

now honoured for his noble struggle on behalf of Hindu widows, but during his lifetime the reward he received was persecution and social ostracism. So, wherever the faithful Christian goes with the message of Christ, he must be ready for opposition and unpleasantness. It may be only the cold shoulder, the scornful answer, the biting phrase; or it may be petty persecution at home; or forcible separation from one's own flesh and blood; or opposition in society; or disturbances and assaults in the streets and squares of the city; or coarse slander; or sudden violence; or secret murder; or imprisonment, condemnation, and death.

This is all very strange at first sight. People are inclined to say, 'These Christians must be very fanatical, or at least very unwise in their methods, else they would not suffer so much.' The reasoning seems good until we think of Christ Himself. He was 'meek and lowly in heart';[1] He 'went about doing good';[2] He was the greatest teacher the world ever saw; yet He was crucified. What can the faithful Christian expect?[3]

The experience of the first generation of Christians in all lands has fully agreed with Christ's warnings. The mere public confession of Christ by word and deed in a non-Christian country usually entails suffering. It was so during the lifetime of Jesus Himself:

> For the Jews had already agreed among themselves that, if any one should confess him to be Christ, he should be put out of the synagogue.[4]

Here is what Paul says in this connexion with reference to himself and the other apostles:

> For I think God has made a display of us apostles last of all as men condemned to death; for we are become a spectacle to the world and to angels, and to men. . . . To this present hour we suffer hunger and thirst and nakedness and blows and homelessness, and we toil, working with our hands. . . . We are made as it were the scum of the world, the offscouring of all things, even to this moment.[5]

[1] Matt. 11, 29. [2] Acts 10, 38. [3] Matt. 10, 24-25.
[4] John 9, 22. [5] 1 Cor. 4, 9, 11-12, 13.

Again he speaks of himself as preaching the Kingdom,

> . . . in afflictions, in necessities, in straits, in scourgings, in imprisonments, in houselessness, in toils, in watchings, in fastings.[1]

The persecutions of the Roman Empire are the next chapter in the long story. For three centuries there was no continuous peace. Men, women, and children suffered equally. At any moment the Christian was liable to prison, torture, fire, sword, the cross, the lions. And everything turned on this single principle, the duty of frank confession of Christ and fearless loyalty to Him in all circumstances. If the Christians had been willing to palter, and to yield here and there to pagan practice, there would have been no martyrs.

The same has been true of every land where the faith has laid hold. Christianity made great headway in Japan in the sixteenth century; but in the seventeenth the Government rose in opposition and stamped it out in such a carnival of cruelty as has seldom been seen in the world.

> We read of Christians being executed in a barbarous manner in sight of each other, of their being hurled from the tops of precipices, of their being buried alive, of their being torn asunder by oxen, of their being tied up in rice-bags, which were heaped up together, and of the pile thus formed being set on fire. Others were tortured before death by the insertion of sharp spikes under the nails of their hands and feet, while some poor wretches by a refinement of horrid cruelty were shut up in cages and there left to starve with food before their eyes.[2]

Again, in the South Seas, where, after incredible sufferings on the part of the missionaries of the London Mission, the people of several islands were won for Christ, thousands of these Polynesians, once savages, now Christians, have from time to time gone out to other islands to preach the Gospel, and many of them have suffered death at the hands of the ignorant barbarians whom they sought to help. In the four months of the Boxer rising in China (only thirteen years ago), many missionaries were killed, and thousands of Chinese Christians

[1] 2 Cor. 6, 5-6.
[2] Quoted from *Asiatic Society's Transactions* in Murray's *Japan*, 249.

joyfully met scourging, burning, anguish, and death for the love of Jesus. In England, in the autumn of 1899, the writer stood on the same platform with a young man who thereafter left home with a high heart, looking forward to a life of great usefulness in New Guinea. Within eighteen months he was killed and eaten, along with the heroic Chalmers, by one of the wilder tribes of the country.

In India such things do not happen; yet what terrible agony many a high-caste convert has had to go through in order to be faithful to his Lord! Driven from his home, forcibly separated from father, mother, wife, child, brother and sister, deprived of his property, and persecuted socially in every possible way, he has had to endure a fiery ordeal indeed.

But now let us realize the most startling fact with regard to cross-bearing: suffering, patiently endured according to the command of Jesus, produces extraordinary spiritual results. Who can measure the influence which has been exercised by Christ's death? Millions of men and women have thereby been turned from sin to God. So in the Roman Empire, when Christians were thrown to the lions or burnt in the fire, the usual result was a great accession of new converts; so that the saying of Tertullian, 'The blood of Christians is the seed of the Church,' became proverbial. The same is true of modern times. During the persecution in Madagascar, which lasted twenty-six years, thousands of Christians were sold as slaves, hunted like wild beasts, imprisoned, tortured, flung over precipices, burnt to death; and yet, at the end of the persecution, the Christians were far more numerous than they were at the beginning.[1] More Chinese became Christians in the eight years that followed the Boxer persecution than in the eighty that preceded it. In every case the sufferings of Christians have been greatly fruitful for the Kingdom. A Bengali student, who was mad against Christianity, flung a stone one day at a missionary who was preaching in the street, and

[1] Horne, *Story of the L. M. S.*, 356–357.

wounded him in the forehead. The man held his handkerchief up to the wound to stanch the blood, and, without an angry word, went on with his address. His behaviour so struck home upon his assailant that he became a Christian, and is to-day a preacher of Christ.

Such, then, is Christ's method of training men to be servants of humanity. Such is the secret of His unparalleled success in turning ordinary men into self-sacrificing servants.

It will be recollected that the Sanskrit word for the monastic life is sannyāsa, *world-surrender*. The essential characteristic of the Indian monk is his complete surrender of the world, all the comforts and interests of life, everything that could please or attract the human heart. He was then trained to complete *indifference*, to feel neither love nor hatred, neither gratitude nor resentment, neither ambition nor disgust: the ideal was, not that he should train, but that he should check, every active emotion. Thirdly, he was bid cultivate *actionlessness*. He was taught to restrain his senses, his intellect, and all his impulses to action, and to give up all the work of the world. He could take no part in government, agriculture, industry, art, literature, education, except in so far as he trained disciples in the Vedānta. Lastly, he was bid practice *self-torture*, subject himself to severe discomfort and long-continued pain, in order that he might subdue the stubborn strainings of our common human nature towards the joys and pleasures and amenities of life, and that he might win for himself 'the overlordship of nature and the eightfold divine faculty'.

Now Christ's method of training His men bears a very startling relationship to this stern discipline.

Instead of *world-surrender* Christ demands *self-surrender*. On the surface they seem to be opposed to each other; but self-surrender contains within itself world-surrender, as we have seen.[1] Christ's demand is infinitely the deeper of the two;

[1] See pp. 282–283 above.

for it is inner, spiritual, real; and while it brings all that detachment from the world which is necessary for the moral and spiritual discipline of the soul, it leaves the man in the world to do his work there. Hindu world-surrender thus finds its spiritual consummation in self-surrender to Christ.

Instead of *indifference* Christ's law is *love.* Are these not diametrically opposed? Let us see. Christian love leads to the giving up of anger, hatred, envy, greed, ambition, revenge, and lust, and the cultivation of meekness, gentleness, compassion, and mercy; is not that precisely what is meant by indifference? But Christ goes a long step farther; for these are all passive virtues, which could be safely cultivated by the monk, because they would not rouse him to action. The monk was told to suppress love, while Christ does all He can to stir up love; and love cannot but express itself in action. Thus the love which Christ commands is the next step after the restrained character of the meek and compassionate monk; but that single step makes all the difference.

Instead of the *inaction* which comes from indifference, Christ commands the *service* which springs from love. But the two are by no means so hopelessly opposed as one might suppose from a quick glance at the words, or from contrasting the sannyāsī in the depths of meditation with the busy missionary. Christ does not command action in general, but service. How much restraint and inaction are implied in that large word as well as active work! Further, the Indian monk has never been able to be truly inactive: the *Gītā* tells us frankly that complete inaction is impossible;[1] and all the best men have unconsciously found their way past the rule of inaction into acts of service. The followers of Gautama had many pleasant memories of their master, but none sweeter than his loving attendance on the sick. All the greatest sannyāsīs were teachers, writers, and preachers. Their own hearts and the needs of men were too strong for the rule under

[1] iii. 5.

which they lived. Thus the inaction of the monk finds its true climax in the service which Christ commands.

Lastly, instead of *self-torture* Christ leads us to *self-sacrifice.* There is as much suffering in Christianity as in Hindu asceticism, only it is not self-inflicted; and it is not endured for one's own advantage, but in loyalty to Christ and for the sake of others. The old monks were on the verge of a great discovery: they saw how noble it is to bear pain, and they had a hazy idea of something redemptive in it, but they just missed the divine truth. They expected to win miraculous results for themselves by their endurance of self-torture. The truth which they were seeking to reach appears in Christ. Suffering patiently borne does produce marvellous results, but not of the type they thought of. Its fruits are souls won from sin to God, men lifted out of selfishness into the spiritual life.

The convert from Hinduism to Christianity is the true modern sannyāsī. For the sake of the spiritual religion which he recognizes to be the truth he renounces the whole Brāhmanical system, precisely as the ancient monk did, giving up home, property, father, mother, sister, brother, and often wife and child as well! The act of world-surrender is appallingly real. It springs from self-surrender to Christ. An educated young Brāhman on the verge of baptism was offered Rs. 50,000 by his relatives, if he would remain a Hindu; but he chose the eternal riches. If the convert is a man of high caste, the funeral ceremony is performed over him in accordance with ancient law,[1] precisely as was the rule for the ancient sannyāsī.[2] He usually passes through bitter persecution; and, like the ancient monk, he is required by his religion to bear every insult and injury with patient meekness. The writer knows a Brāhman convert who one day, some time after his baptism, was going through the bazaar of his native town. His father met him and spat in his face. The Christian son walked on without a word. Thus the correspondence is most remarkable;

[1] *Gautama*, xx. 1-6. [2] See above, p. 254, note 3.

indeed, the chief difference between the ancient monk and the convert is this, that the latter is bound by his religion to become a servant of India. Is not that precisely the kind of sannyāsī India needs?

Christ Jesus makes His followers servants of humanity, and in so doing He completes and consummates the ideal of the Hindu monk.

CHAPTER VIII

THE WORK OF MEN'S HANDS

WHAT are we to say about the Hindu use of images in worship? Is it a valuable help to a monotheistic and spiritual faith, as the Neo-Hindu declares, or a coarse and degrading idolatry, as the missionary says, or does the truth lie somewhere between them? Here, as elsewhere, we shall seek to reach a just judgement through a careful survey of the facts from the point of view of history.

I. We begin with a brief statement of how the Hindus thought about their gods before the use of idols arose. The gods of Hinduism are the gods which the invading Aryans worshipped when they entered India, and many more introduced from various sources since then. We take our description of them chiefly from the original *Rāmāyaṇa*, a poem in which their nature and their worship stand out in pictorial vividness. The use of idols is already coming in, but the conceptions of the gods are still ancient; and the whole of this early picture remains true of the Hindu gods throughout their history. Later developments are mostly of the nature of additions, and are dealt with below.

In the *Rāmāyaṇa* the gods live a more or less happy family in the heavenly country, which is above the earth and yet near enough to allow a good deal that goes on here below to be seen and heard. They are conceived as being like men and women. They have physical bodies[1] which require food and which may be hurt. They are married and many of them

[1] See what Rāmānuja says, *S. B. E.*, xlviii. 328–331.

have children.[1] They are so like mortals that they now and then have sexual intercourse with men and women.[2] The great royal families of India are believed to be of divine origin.

Indeed, it is clear that to the ancient Hindus the gods were like Hindu kings, only they possessed supernatural powers. As there were many kings in North India in early times, each with his palace, his consorts and his train, so in heaven there are many gods; and each has appropriated a mountain of the heavenly country and has decked it out to be his residence. Here he dwells with his wife or wives and children in splendour and luxury. A Hindu king had his courtiers, his companies of musicians, his dancing and singing women of very easy virtue,[3] his hundreds of slaves and servants, his clowns, and his horses and carriages. The gods are pictured in precisely the same way. Round each great god are troops of minor divinities and sprites, heavenly musicians called Gandharvas, heavenly nymphs of most yielding disposition called Apsarases, who are often sent to earth by the gods to beguile ascetics when their austerities become too serious,[4] and mixed human-animal creatures of wondrous forms. Each god has his heavenly car, which runs on the ground or sails through the air according to his pleasure, and also his favourite mount, whether elephant, bull, eagle, lion, or tiger.[5]

But, though they are like men and women, they are above man. They have large freedom and larger power. They are not bound by morality: the petty distinctions between right and wrong actions are necessary for human life, but the gods

[1] Kālidāsa's famous heroic poem, *Kumāra Sambhava*, is an account of the marriage of Śiva to Parvatī and of the birth of their son, the god of war. The marriage of Śiva and Parvatī occurs among the sculptures of the cave of Elephanta. Brahmā and Vishṇu have each three consorts.

[2] Indra seduced Ahalyā, a Brāhman's wife. *Rāmāyaṇa*, I. xlviii.

[3] This custom survives in modern India. See Vincent Smith's *Asoka*, 89.

[4] So the Apsaras Menaka, sent by the gods to disturb the austerities of the royal sage Viśvamitra, became by him the mother of the famous Śakuntalā.

[5] For this whole paragraph see *The Light of the School of Śrī Rāmānuja*, 133–135, where the heaven of Vishṇu is described. This authoritative work shows what the modern Vishṇuite theist holds.

are free. 'The mighty can do no wrong.' They have many superhuman powers. They can fly through the air at pleasure, render themselves invisible, and assume any form they please. Each can animate a number of bodies at the same time. But, though very powerful, they are by no means omniscient or omnipotent. They require to be told about things just like men. They are often in great danger. Extreme austerities on the part of human ascetics may lead to any result, even the conquest of heaven itself. Hence any man or demon who persists in long-continued self-torture causes the gods the utmost terror.[1] They are usually called immortal; yet they are thought of as having been born or created, early ideas about the gods not being a consistent or unified body of beliefs. The introduction of the doctrine of transmigration and of the one God behind the gods reduced them, in the eyes of thinking men, to transmigrating beings, who had risen to the power and position of gods by intense austerities or lavish sacrifices;[2] but popular belief inclined to think of them as immortal.

They often visit the earth. They come sailing in their cars or flying through the air. They may be invisible, or they may be seen by human eyes;[3] and at first sight it may be hard to tell them from men and women. But if you look carefully, you will see that their feet do not rest on the ground, that their bodies cast no shadow, that their eyes are unwinking, and that no dust lies on the garlands of flowers they wear.[4]

The worship of the gods by means of sacrifices in the open air, as we meet it in the *Ṛigveda*,[5] has through all the centuries been recognized as the normal worship; yet it fell almost altogether into disuse many centuries ago; and only occasionally has a sacrifice been offered in Vedic fashion in modern

[1] It was the terror of the gods over the austerities of Rāvaṇa that led to the incarnation of Rāma. See below, pp. 362–336.

[2] See above, p. 222.

[3] See an instructive theophany in *Rāmāyaṇa*, III. v.

[4] *Rāmāyaṇa*, III. lvii.

[5] See above, p. 73.

times. During the period when the other constituents of Hinduism arose, worship by means of temple and image came into use; and it is almost the only mode employed to-day.

The gods need nourishment. They live on the sacrifices and offerings made by men. Hence their interest in human worship and their favour for those who worship them. Food offered to them, according to the ancient ritual, is either laid out so that they may come and take it, or wafted to them on the flames and smoke of the altar. In temples it is presented to the idol, as we shall see. When men offer sacrifices, they ask and receive gifts from the gods. Indeed the doctrine tends to be this, that the sacrifice compels the gift. Any earthly blessing, such as pleasure, love, children, success, wealth, kingship, or power, may be got by sacrifice; and if men are able to make a sufficient offering, supernatural power may be acquired. At death the faithful worshipper is received by his god to his own particular paradise.[1]

II. We next give a brief sketch of the way in which idolatry is believed by students of religion to have arisen.

Most primitive men do not use images at all. Their beliefs and practices are such that they do not feel the need of anything of the kind. It is most difficult to make sure that one understands the mind of early peoples, yet one can probably see sufficient to distinguish between this period and the next, when images make their appearance. In the earliest forms of religion known to us men revere either an invisible life substance, the source of all life and power, portions of which they believe can be obtained by various means, or else visible things, whether certain classes of animals, plants, stones, or other objects, or the greater aspects of nature, such as sun, moon, sky, thunder, rain, wind, fire. In the former case an image is impossible. In the latter, while men usually think of the god as a living being, he is still so closely identified

[1] *Rāmāyaṇa*, III. v.

with that which is his manifestation that there is no need of an image: the god is present and visible when he is worshipped.

A time comes, however, when the personality of the gods becomes clearer, and they are habitually thought of as beings having a life of their own, apart from any natural objects with which they may have been associated. They are believed to have homes of their own, whether in heaven, the air, on earth, in the sea, or under the earth; and, while they are believed to appear to men frequently, their visits are irregular and unexpected.

(*a*) Hence, if there is a spot where a god appears from time to time, or, if he has done any noteworthy thing at some particular place, the spot becomes sacred, and is marked by *a stone or post.* People visit the place; a local worship arises; the blood of the sacrificial victim is splashed upon the stone or post; or offerings are placed beside it.

(*b*) As time goes on, the personality and the character of the god become much more clearly defined to his worshippers; he receives a personal name; and they form a definite picture of his form and appearance. He is thought of as being like a man or an animal. When this idea has been reached, it is quite natural to paint a face or carve a head on the top of the sacred stone or post. The second stage is thus *a pillar with a carved head.*

(*c*) Once this is done, the gradual evolution of a complete image is only a question of time. The rude block is carved into a form corresponding as closely as it is possible for the artist to make it to the popular belief about the appearance of the god. It is always possible, however, that the process may be arrested midway. At any particular moment the belief, that the existing form is a true image of the god and in accordance with his will, may fix the form irrevocably. But in most cases change does not cease until *a complete image, either human or animal*, is produced.

(*d*) Even then development does not cease. As thought

and civilization advance, a tribe whose god is an animal gradually forms a higher idea of his personality and powers, until it is impossible to think of him in purely animal form. Then appears *the half-animal image*, an animal with a human head, or a human body with an animal head.

(*e*) Later still, when the conception of the god has become still nobler, the mixed image cannot satisfy the worshipper, and the god is represented as completely human, while the animal becomes sacred to him and is recognized as his companion. Here then we have *a human god with an animal.*

(*f*) A further stage is also found in some lands. The gods are thought of as so great that it is felt that a merely human form is not a sufficient expression of their powers. Hence wings are added, or they are represented with several heads, or with many arms or eyes. The sacred animals share the same tendency, and mixed and monstrous forms are invented. Thus *human or animal forms with extra limbs* are evolved.

(*g*) The power of reproduction strikes the primitive mind as peculiarly god-like. Hence sex seems divine and worthy of worship. From this and other roots have come the phallic worship which usually accompanies idolatry. The emblem is usually a pillar, as the Hindu *liṅga* is.

(*h*) Sometimes a tribe continues to worship its own god by itself, but usually a number of tribes unite, thereby forming a nation, and then the united people acknowledge all the gods of the tribes. In some such way as this all the great national, polytheistic religions were formed. Hence we have *the group of gods of many various forms.*

Great advances may follow these changes. Unless religious progress is arrested, the gods are conceived more nobly. Their personality stands out more clear. Each is an individual with a character of his own. They are thought of as like men in their passions, thoughts, and purposes, only more powerful than men. As they are believed to be bound to the nation by ties of interest, they are thought of as watching over the welfare of the people, as sympathizing with them and helping them in difficulty and distress. The morals of the nation are usually, but not always, supposed to be under their care. If the nation prosper, they praise their gods for their kindness, and make their worship more dignified and more costly.

Civilization reaps a great harvest from these new developments in the religion. The interest of the people in their gods creates a mythology, which is handed down from generation to generation and held sacred. From the mythology there springs a literature, it may be epic, dramatic, or lyrical. When the moral customs of the people are believed to be in the care of the gods, they become more sacred than ever; and in any case they take shape in a code of laws. The priesthood rises in influence, and their training may create a national system of education, as happened in ancient India. The elaboration of the worship of the gods demands the most beautiful images possible, and worthy temples to receive them. To these creative needs we owe the appearance of sculpture and architecture. If the ritual is carried far, painting, music, and other arts may also arise. From speculations about the nature of the gods comes philosophy.

The history of the greatest nations of antiquity falls within this period of human life, Babylonia, Egypt, Assyria, Persia, Phoenicia, Greece, Rome, and likewise India.

III. We turn now to the rise of image-worship in India. Most of the gods worshipped in the Ṛigvedic age were natural forces—sun and wind, bright sky and thunder-cloud, fire and rain—powers which helped or hindered men and were therefore honoured with song and sacrifice. These gods were, however, conceived as personal, as possessing mind and will, and as having a life of their own; yet, being revealed to men in these visible natural phenomena, idols were never thought of and temples were unknown.

At some point late in the age of the *Ṛigveda*, however, idols began to find their way into the community. Some of the old gods (e.g. Indra) had by a gradual process become so anthropomorphic in character that it was no longer unnatural to represent them in human form. But in the whole *Ṛigveda* there are only a couple of references to images of the gods:[1] clearly the practice had only just begun to creep in before the final redaction of the *Ṛik.*

By 500 B.C., however, they were not only quite common, but had received some sort of sanction from the priests. They are frankly recognized in the earliest legal sūtras[2] that have come down to us; and thereafter Hindu literature is full of them.

Several Hindu gods are represented in the earliest surviving Buddhist sculptures, dating from about 200 to 100 B.C.; and it is evident that a long history lies behind them, for a number of the traditional types are already fixed. Amongst them are Śrī, i. e. Lakshmī, the wife of Vishṇu, Sūrya, the sun god, Kuvera, the god of riches, Nāgas, Yakshas, &c. Temples are also represented.[3]

Hindu coins of the first and second century A.D. give us representations of several gods, notably Śiva and his bull. A little later Hindu sculpture begins; and thereafter the whole history can be traced, at least in outline, in surviving specimens.

Although Buddhism and Jainism started as philosophies, protesting against all the follies of the Brāhmanic system, yet, before the Christian era, both had succumbed to the overpowering attraction of idols; and images of the Buddha and his followers, the mythical Buddhas of previous ages, and Maitreya the coming Buddha, on the one hand, and of the various Tīrthakaras, on the other, filled the Buddhist and Jain temples.

It is quite clear that in the early Christian centuries Hindu idols felt very deeply the influence of Buddhist and Jain image types. At a later date the same artistic forms were used in all the three religions; and, in consequence, Hindu, Buddhist,

[1] iv. 24, 9; viii. 1, 5. Kaegi, 119.
[2] *Gautama*, ix. 12; *Āpastamba*, i. 11, 30, 20, 22; *Vasishṭha*, xi, 41.
[3] See Cunningham, *Stupa of Bharhut*, and Maisey's *Sanchi Stupa.*

and Jain idols are, in numerous instances, scarcely distinguishable the one from the other.

Buddhism carried Indian image types into Ceylon and Tibet, and into every part of Eastern Asia; so that the whole history of idolatry in these lands is, in the main at least, dependent on India.

IV. If we compare the images of Hinduism with those of other lands, it will appear that parallels to almost every type of Indian image or symbol are to be found in the remains of the worship of Assyria, Babylonia, Syria, Egypt, Greece, and Rome; and, if some of the cruder and grosser idols of the ignorant classes are hard to match in classical archaeology, forms similar down almost to the last detail may be found to-day among the peoples of Polynesia and of Africa.

(*a*) The use of the stone or post to represent a divinity is very common in the ruder village worships of India to-day. The stone may be daubed with vermilion, or may have a simple pattern cut in it or painted on it, or it may be quite bare. It may stand alone, or in a little square outlined with rough stones, or in a very low simple shrine lighted only from the door. From time to time one may see a fowl or some other animal sacrificed there and its blood sprinkled on the sacred object.

(*b*) The earliest approach to an idol, the post or pillar with its top carved to some semblance of a human head, may be frequently seen in village shrines in India. The half-formed image is even more common. It may be seen even in some of the great Hindu temples. The image of Jagannāth at Puri is a rude unfinished figure; and Kālī is frequently but a head and shoulders.

(*c*) The animal god and the human god are both common in the shrines of Hinduism. The purely human image is quite frequent. Vishṇu, Kṛishṇa, Rāma, and their consorts are usually so represented.[1] This type of idol is found in many

[1] Most of the gods of Hinduism are pictured in Moor's *Hindu Pantheon*.

lands; but it reaches its summit in the images of ancient Greece,[1] where the greatest sculpture the world has ever seen produced the most exquisite idealizations of the human form.

The most notable of the animal gods that are worshipped in India are Hanumān, the monkey, Nāga, the hooded snake, and the ever-sacred cow. These are worshipped by themselves, not merely as companions of gods. Images of the baboon were common in Egypt,[2] also of the snake, the cow, and the bull. More than once Indian troops in Egypt have seen the cow upon the monuments and worshipped her. Nuit, the Egyptian goddess of the sky, with all the gods around her, is exactly like a Hindu picture of the sacred cow accompanied by her adorers.

(*d*) Next comes the half-evolved divinity, part man, part animal. In India we have the human body mingled with the fish, the tortoise, the boar, the lion, the horse, the elephant, the goat, and the snake: the animal-avatāras of Vishṇu are man-fish, man-tortoise, man-boar, man-lion, and man-horse; while Ganeśa has the head of an elephant, Daksha the head of a goat, and the Nāgas are half-man, half-snake. The adversaries of the gods, known as *Asuras*, are also represented with animal heads. In Egypt there is a similar catalogue of semi-animal forms. There man is compounded with the bull, cow, ram, lion, jackal, dog, cat, frog, snake, crocodile, ibis, hawk, and fish. In Assyria, the man-lion, the man-bird, and the man-fish forms are common; only the man-lion is always winged. Some of the parallels are so close as to be well worth notice. For example, the representations of the fish-avatāra of Vishṇu are practically identical with divine forms found in Assyria, and with all we know about Dagon, the Philistine god. The Greek Triton, a sea-divinity, is often sculptured in very similar fashion. The man-lion of Assyria, and Kronos, the man-lion of Mith-

[1] Classical divinities may be found in a Classical Dictionary, or in Gardiner's *Grammar of Greek Art*.

[2] The Egyptian deities mentioned in this chapter will be found in Wilkinson's *Egyptians*.

raism, are exceedingly like Narasiṁha, the man-lion avatāra of Vishṇu, except that they are winged. The wives of Kāliya, the great snake slain by Kṛishṇa, are pictured like Nereids. The sculptured boar-man incarnation of Vishṇu at Mahāvellipore is very like an Egyptian deity. The Nāga is represented in several ways in Hindu sculpture, each of which may be paralleled elsewhere. The human head and body with a serpent tail may be compared with the Greek giants; while the human body surmounted by the snake hood and head is found in Egypt. Daksha with his goat-head in Hindu sculpture is often scarcely distinguishable from the Egyptian Khnumu; and the Hindu Asuras at the churning of the ocean look like many of the images of the ram-headed Amen-ra of Thebes. The Hindu Kinnarīs, heavenly musicians, half-woman, half-bird, are precisely like the Greek Sirens, beautiful bird-women who beguiled sailors with their song. Vishṇu's vehicle, the man-eagle Garuḍa, is in many points as dignified as the eagle of Zeus, but in form, and also in his feud with snakes, he recalls the Greek harpy. Other Greek conceptions of similar character are the Centaurs, half-man, half-horse; the Sphinx, a winged man-lion; and Pan, the god of the woods, who has a man's head and body but the legs and tail of a goat.

(*e*) Sacred animals attached to individual gods are very common in India; and the parallels with other lands are very numerous. The bull is the companion of Śiva, as it was the representative of the Egyptian Osiris. So the Persian Mithra has a great bull on which he rides and which he slays. The mouse accompanies Apollo in Greece, as it does Ganeśa in India. The dogs of Yama, the god of death, have their parallel in the Egyptian Amt, a great dog guarding the gate of the lower world, and Cerberus, the dog of hell, among the Greeks. The monkey goes with Rāma in India and with Thoth, the god of letters, in Egypt. In the great gold and ivory image of Athene in Athens her snake appeared on the ground between her left foot and her shield; and a snake appears in Mithraic sculptures representing Mithra killing the bull. So Śiva frequently has a snake with him, and other Hindu gods also. The lion accompanies Durgā in India, as it did Cybele in Asia Minor. In a piece of ancient sculpture at Olympia, Artemis holds a lion in each hand. Seb in Egypt and Sarasvatī in India are accompanied by the goose. The ram is sacred to Agni in India, as it was to Amon in Egypt. The god of the sun rides in a horse-drawn chariot in both India and Greece, while in India the moon rides in a car drawn by an antelope. The elephant is sacred to Indra and the peacock to Kārttikeya. The remarkable Hindu conception of Vishṇu reclining on Śesha, the thousand-headed snake representing eternity,[1] finds a striking parallel in the Mithraic image of Kronos, infinite time, a winged figure encircled by the coils of a great snake.[2] Lakshmī, the wife of Vishṇu, is often represented seated on a lotus between two elephants pouring water over her. In Egypt, the following additional animals are sacred each to a divinity: cat, dog, jackal, wolf, fox, owl, hawk, eagle, crocodile, hippopotamus.

Frequently in India as elsewhere the divinity rides upon his sacred animal. This is true of Indra and the elephant, Kārttikeya and the peacock, Parvatī and the tiger, Durgā and the lion, Agni and the ram, Sarasvatī and the goose, Yama and the buffalo. Poseidon, the Greek god of the sea, rides on a dolphin precisely like Varuṇa, the Hindu god of the waters. Trivenī also, the mythical representative of the rivers Ganges, Jumna, and Sarasvatī, sometimes rides a dolphin. The Persian Mithra rides on his bull as Śiva rides on Nandī. Sometimes in India and in Egypt the god stands on his animal. As the youthful Kṛishṇa is represented standing on a snake, so the child Horus stands on two crocodiles. As Durgā stands on a lion, so does Ket, the Egyptian mistress of heaven, and Ishtar, the Babylonian Venus.

(*f*) The remains of classical antiquity do not give us many parallels to the very numerous class of Hindu images which

[1] See below, p. 404. [2] Cumont, *The Mysteries of Mithra*, 105–108.

are of human form but have extra limbs. Śiva, his wife Kālī, and his sons Ganeśa and Kārttikeya, are represented with a third eye set vertically in the middle of the forehead. Agni has two faces, three legs, and seven arms. The Trimūrti, representing Brahmā, Vishṇu, and Śiva as one, is really a three-headed figure. Brahmā, the Creator, has very frequently four heads; and one of the forms of Śiva has five faces. His consort in her various forms, Kālī, Durgā, Umā, &c., has four, eight, ten, or even eighteen arms; and the god himself has often four arms. Yama is said to have thirty-two arms. Vishṇu has often four arms also. All these monstrous additions to the human form were copied in Tāntric Buddhism, and are found to this day in Tibet. The nearest classic parallels are the Ephesian Diana with her many breasts, the Roman Janus with his two faces, the Greek Hecate, who is represented as a triple figure consisting of three women grouped back to back, and similar quadruple forms in Egypt.[1]

Animal forms with extra limbs are common in Hinduism. The five-headed snake, called Nāga, is well known, and Śesha, the thousand-headed snake, typifying eternity. The horse which draws the chariot of Sūrya, the sun, has seven heads. Indra's elephant, Airāvaṇa, has three trunks, while in Buddhism and in the paintings at Ajanta we meet an elephant with six tusks, Chhaddanta. There are classical parallels for some of these. Cerberus, the dog of hell, is represented as having three heads. Winged lions are common in Babylonian and Indian sculpture.

There are, then, mythical forms made up of parts of different animals. In India the best known of these are the *makara* and the *virātarūpa*, the former composed of an elephant and a dolphin, the latter as hard to describe as the chimera of Greece or the fanciful creatures with which the ancient Egyptians peopled the lone desert. Winged snakes are common in Egypt. Various forms of sphinx—a lion's body

[1] An example may be seen in the British Museum.

with the head of a ram, an eagle, or some other beast—received very skilful treatment at the hands of Egyptian sculptors.

(*g*) The great god Śiva is seldom represented by an image. His worship centres in the *liṅga*, the phallic symbol of India.[1] Hinduism in possessing a phallic worship is strictly parallel with the polytheisms of the ancient world[2] and of Japan. In India, the symbol is less suggestive than it was in many lands.

In the earliest times the liṅga was not associated with Śiva. He was represented by images, as may be seen from Kushān coins, before he was represented by the liṅga. There is no mention of the liṅga in the Vedic literature or in the *Rāmāyaṇa*. It is in the later parts of the *Mahābhārata* that we find the earliest references to the practice. Here is one of the significant passages:

> Is Īśā (i.e. Śiva) the Cause of causes for any other reasons? We have not heard that the liṅga of any other person is worshipped by the gods. Declare, if thou hast heard, what other being's liṅga except that of Maheśvara (i.e. the great god, Śiva) is now worshipped, or has formerly been worshipped, by the gods? He whose liṅga Brahmā and Vishṇu and thou (Indra) with the deities continually worship, is therefore the most eminent. Since children bear neither the mark of the lotus (Brahmā's), nor of the discus (Vishnu's), nor of the thunderbolt (Indra's), but are marked with the male and female organs—therefore offspring is derived from Maheśvara.[3]

(*h*) The vast collection of gods, human, semi-animal and animal, adored in India is parallel, in general, with the groups of divinities revered by nearly all the great nations of antiquity; but, in number, variety, and peculiarity of forms, the Egyptian pantheon comes nearest to the Hindu.

It will be well, also, to note the symbols which usually accompany images. Most gods are represented as wearing a head-dress or crown of some sort. Both in India and Egypt, these are often very high and very elaborate in structure. In Egypt the head-dress is filled with symbolism, while in India

[1] See below, pp. 314, 316, 361, 380. [2] Havell, *Benares*, 68.

[3] From the Anuśāsana Parvan of the *Mahābhārata*. The passage is translated by Muir in his *Sanskrit Texts*, iv. 161.

more attention is paid to artistic grace. Yet, even in India, numerous symbols occur on the head. There is usually a snake on the head of Śiva and of Ganeśa; and it frequently occurs in the case of other Hindu divinities: in Egypt, the sacred snake called *uraeus* occurs in the same way in a very large number of cases. The crescent moon was worn on her head by Astarte, the Syrian queen of love, and by the Egyptian gods Thoth and Khonsu, as it is frequently worn by Śiva and by Ganeśa. Śiva usually wears a symbol on his head to show that the river Ganges sprang from him, it may be the head of the goddess Gaṅga or the sacred stream itself. The consort of Śiva frequently wears his symbol, the liṅga, as an ornament on her head.

It is still more common for the god to carry a symbol in his hand. Indra, the greatest god of the time of the *Ṛigveda*, carries a thunderbolt, and so does Ramman, the Assyrian god of storms and thunder, Bel-Merodach of Babylon, and Zeus, the king of gods in Greece. Śiva holds a trident precisely like Poseidon, the Greek god of the sea. It is almost as common for an Egyptian divinity to carry a lotus in the hand as it is for an Indian god. Durgā frequently holds a snake in her hand, and the Egyptian Osiris is similarly represented. The gods of writing and learning in Egypt frequently hold a book, as Brahmā and Sarasvatī do. Osiris in Egypt and Śiva in India frequently hold an antelope by the hind legs; and weapons of war are constantly carried.

Symbols occur also beside the image of the god. Shamash, the sun-god of Babylonia, is represented with a great wheel, just like Vishṇu with his *chakra*. Beside the god of the Nile we find fishes and lotuses. In Egypt, as in India, standards and banners are common.

The attitudes of the gods also correspond in certain cases. The head of the goddess Kālī with her long protruding tongue is precisely parallel with the Egyptian god Bes, and with Medusa as represented in early Greek sculpture. All these are of Gorgon origin, i.e. each is a fierce countenance meant to frighten evil spirits.[1] The corpulent dwarfish body of Ganeśa is paralleled in many lands, for example in Egypt, in one of the forms of Osiris and in Bes, and in the god of good luck in China and Japan. When the Egyptian Thoth is represented with the head of an ape, the resemblance to the figure of Ganeśa is extraordinarily close. The child Hercules, like the youthful Kṛishṇa, is represented as killing a snake. The Hindu triad, Brahmā, Vishṇu, and Śiva, which gave birth to similar triads in Mahāyāna Buddhism in India, China, and Japan, has many parallels in Egypt, where nearly every district had its triad of gods, and in Babylonia, where we meet at least two triads, the first Anu, Bel, and Ea, the second Sin, Shamash and Ramman. Finally, in Egypt the sun-god springs from a lotus, just as Brahmā is represented in the great scene where he rises from the lotus which springs from Vishṇu's navel.

Thus Hindu images, from the crudest blocks and pillars up to the most beautiful forms and the most elaborate groups, are in all respects parallel to the idols of other lands, whether of ancient or of modern times.

V. We turn now to the temple and the cult. We have already seen[2] that, in the earliest literature, the great gods are conceived like Hindu kings. They live in their palaces in heaven, precisely like earthly kings, with their families, courtiers, and servants, in shining splendour and high luxury. They have physical bodies which need nourishment; so they come from heaven to enjoy the sacrifices offered by men.

But the temple and the image change things somewhat. Each divinity's temple is an earthly replica of his heavenly palace.[3] The beautifully sculptured tower of the temple represents the high architecture of heaven. Here the god lives with spouse and family. His subordinate sprites are also with him, sculptured in bronze or stone. Whatever the god's mount (*vāhana*) may be, bull, elephant, lion, or peacock, there it is ready for his use. The temple-musicians take the

[1] The writer owes this point to Prof. Rudolf Otto of Göttingen.
[2] Above, p. 298. [3] See *The Light of the School of Rāmānuja*, 96, 133.

place of the Gandharvas, who play before him in heaven. The nymphs of easy virtue called Apsarases, who dance and sing before him in heaven, are represented by the Devadāsīs of the temple, who sing and dance before him in the ritual and are most complaisant to worshippers.[1] The priests of the temple are the servants of the god. As in heaven he goes for an outing in his car, so in the temple there is the car for the use of the idol, when he goes round the town to be seen by his people, or when he pays his annual visit to his summer residence.

The cult is the personal service of the god by his servants, the priests. They wake him in the morning, give him a bath, offer him perfume and flowers, burn incense before him, and give him food and drink. They give him other meals at different times during the day. When an offering is made to him, a bell is rung to call his attention to it. At night he is put to bed,[2] and the shrine is closed.

Here are the sixteen operations of morning worship as set forth in the Vaishṇava manual, the *Nārada Pañcharātra*:

1. *pādya*: the priest brings water and washes the feet;
2. *āchamanīya*: gives water to rinse the mouth;
3. *arghya*: pours out a libation of water with several ingredients;
4. *madhuparka*: gives a mouthful of a honey-mixture;
5. *punarāchamanīya*: gives water to rinse the mouth again;
6. *snānīya*: bathes the idol;
7. *vastra*: puts on the under garment;
8. *uttarīya*: puts on the upper garment;
9. *yajnopavīta*: puts on the sacred thread;
10. *bhūshaṇa*: puts on all the ornaments;
11. *jala*: gives drinking-water;
12. *gandha*: gives perfumes;

[1] See below, pp. 314 and 315.

[2] The ritual and liturgy with which the idol is put to bed are described in *Agni Purāṇa*, lviii. 28–34.

13. *pushpa:*	gives flowers;
14. *dhūpa:*	burns incense;
15. *dīpa:*	swings a light before the idol;
16. *naivedya:*	gives the morning meal.

Readers may compare the account of the worship of Kṛishṇa given by Professor Monier-Williams.[1] In the case of a goddess number 9 is omitted, as no woman wears the sacred thread. In the *Mahānirvāṇa Tantra*[2] the worship of Kālī is described. There is some variation in the order and in the offerings, but most points are the same, and the operations are again sixteen. We are told how Mādhvas (a sub-sect of Vishṇuites) worship in their homes:

> Śālagrāma-stones, metallic or wood images, are set up on a throne, and homage rendered thereto as at the throne of an Emperor. The details comprise a long and elaborate programme. The stone and images are bathed with reverence, rubbed dry with cloth, ornamented with flowers, and prayed to with devotion. Bells, flowers, sandal, incense, and lights are used abundantly in the act of worship.[3]

In the temples of Śiva the service is practically the same; for the liṅga is treated precisely like an image. This may be clearly seen from Dr. Rājendralāla Mitra's description of the worship of the liṅga in the great temple of Bhuvaneśvara.[4] The Vallabhāchāryas worship the child Kṛishṇa eight times a day. A vivid description is given by Dr. Murdoch.[5]

A liturgy in Sanskrit accompanies the rites of the cult, and in the greater temples, especially in South India, hymns are sung, both in Sanskrit and the vernacular. The Tamil hymns of the Aḍiyārs[6] are sung with great feeling in Śaiva[7] temples, while in Vaishṇava[7] shrines the hymns of the Āḻvārs[6] stir quite as deep emotions. Bells are rung and drums are beaten at various points in the service. On special occasions the Devadāsīs and

[1] *Brāhmanism and Hinduism*, 144. [2] vi. 77–95.
[3] *Madhva*, 400. [4] *Brāhmanism and Hinduism*, 93–94.
[5] *Religious Sects*, 63. [6] See below, p. 384.
[7] Śaiva and Vaishṇava are very convenient Sanskrit adjectives for Śivaite and Vishṇuite.

the temple-band take part in the liturgy with instrumental music, dance, and song.

In most of the great temples the offerings are vegetarian;[1] yet in the temples of Kālī, and in vast numbers of village temples, animal sacrifice is still in use. It is not the ancient Vedic animal sacrifice, however. That has almost disappeared under the pressure of the doctrine of ahiṁsā. Where animals are now slain, it is clear that the custom has come from some aboriginal tribe.[2]

The ritual is all performed by the priests, and they also repeat the liturgy. But the worshipper is by no means left out of count. Though he can only watch the ceremonial and join in the hymns of praise, yet he is the guest of the god, and receives all the honours of the temple. He enjoys the greatest of all privileges, which is to 'see the face' of the god himself and to pour his prayer directly into the divine ear. He shares the god's banquet, receiving water (*tīrtha*) and food (*prasāda*) from his table. He is shown all the great sights of the temple, gazes at the sculptured record of the god's famous deeds, and hears some of the marvellous things which he does for his worshippers. If he visits the Devadāsīs,[3] he does no more than he expects to do when he reaches the heaven of his gracious god; for that is the meaning of the obscene sculptures on the gate and the idol-car, and of the lascivious paintings on the ceilings.[4]

How vividly real and right Indians have felt this cult to be

[1] See below, pp. 380–382.

[2] With regard to sacrifice the temple of Kālī at Kālīghāt, Calcutta, is very instructive. Within the temple itself only vegetarian offerings are made, in accordance with the rules of the Tantras, and only Brāhman priests officiate. But in front of the shrine and in full view of the goddess, there is a large porch whereon learned Brāhmans read sacred books and make offerings of ghī and rice in fire according to Vedic ritual. Beyond that again is the place where kids and buffaloes are beheaded by a man of the blacksmith caste. The body belongs to the worshipper, the head to the sacrificer, while the blood is Kālī's portion. Here human sacrifice used to be carried on. The worship of this temple is thus an epitome of the history of Hinduism.

[3] See p. 397.

[4] See below, pp. 397–398.

may be seen from the fact that Jain and Buddhist worship is in essentials the same. Though Tīrthakaras and Buddhas are believed to have entered nirvāṇa and thus can neither receive praise nor food, yet the main operations of the Hindu cult are carried out in their case also. Mrs. Sinclair Stevenson[1] has described Jain worship for us in detail. In the worship of the Śvetāmbara sect of Jains the image is bathed and dressed. Sacred marks are put on it with coloured paste. Then flowers are offered, incense is burned, a light is waved in front of it, and thereafter rice, sweetmeats, and fruit are offered. Any one who will watch a Buddhist layman at worship in Burma or Ceylon will see a number of the old Hindu rites carried out before the image of Gautama himself.

The worship of idols in other lands was of the same character, and the ritual startlingly similar. Let any one read pp. 71–72 of Flinders Petrie's little book, *The Religion of Ancient Egypt*, and note how amazingly like the above description of Hindu ritual his account of Egyptian worship is. In Babylonia, in Greece, and in Syria we find the same general features. The priests wait upon the idols like servants, attending to all their personal wants, offering them incense, flowers, and food; and in many places the worship is deeply stained with phallicism and immorality.

In certain temples of Śiva, especially in Northern India, another form of worship is found. Near the great temple of Kālī at Kālīghāt, Calcutta, there is a small temple of Śiva. It is square, and the upper part of the wall on all sides is open, so that an outsider can watch the cult. In the centre of the temple there is a circular tank, and in the centre of the tank a stone liṅga. The worshipper kneels on the outer edge of the tank, and, stretching over to the liṅga, places a few *bael* leaves and pours a little Ganges water on it, muttering a prayer the while. In certain temples there is an arrangement whereby water constantly falls in a trickling stream on

[1] *Modern Jainism*, 92 ff.

the liṅga from above. The idea is that the phallus is always in a state of heat.

VI. We are now in a position to realize how Hindus think and feel about the images of the gods.

The one great broad fact to be clearly grasped is that to the Hindu each idol is a living personal god. The image has been made by human hands, but the god lives in it, using the stone or metal body as the human soul uses the human body. He lives in the temple among his people, receives from their hands the food by which he subsists, welcomes them to his presence and makes them his guests. He listens to their prayers and answers them. He hears and speaks, eats and sleeps, moves and acts.

The whole of the temple-worship depends on this belief. What is the use of honey-mixture, perfumes, incense, waving lights, and food, if the image is not a living god? The villager goes to the temple 'to see Kālī's face'. He believes he looks into her own great divine eyes. He prays his fervent prayer, and hears the goddess answer him with her own lips. Nor the villager only. In the lives of all the saints we meet the same beliefs.

In the official life of Rāmānuja, written in Tamil in the thirteenth century by Pinbaḷagīa-Perumāl-Jīyar, we are told that there was a dispute in Rāmānuja's day as to whether the image in the great temple of Tirupati was Vishṇu or Śiva. Rāmānuja proposed that both sets of emblems—Śiva's trident and drum, Vishṇu's discus and shell—should be laid in front of the image, every person carefully excluded from the shrine, and the doors locked, so that the god himself might decide the dispute. The narrative proceeds:

> This test was gladly agreed to by all. The emblems were accordingly prepared and placed before the Image. Next day both the parties came in a body with eager expectations of their own opinion being realized. But when the doors were thrown open in full daylight and in the presence of the whole assembly, it was found that the Lord had assumed the Vaishṇava emblems, with the Śaiva emblems lying unused on the floor. Rāmānuja's joy knew no bounds. He sang and danced, eyes

streaming with tears of delight at the miraculous event and the Beatific Vision presented to his view.[1]

Here is another story from Rāmānuja's life. After completing his famous commentary on the *Vedānta-sūtras*, we are told that he took a long journey, visiting many sacred places, and finally reaching the temple of Sarasvatī in Kashmīr. The goddess asked Rāmānuja to explain a passage in the *Chhāndogya Upanishad*, the meaning of which has caused endless discussion among pandits. Rāmānuja embodied his explanation in a couplet of verse, and the narrative proceeds:

> On hearing this, Sarasvatī said: 'Rāmānuja! Śaṅkara had ere this unhappily interpreted this as "monkey's posteriors", and I was much grieved at his perverse understanding and warped heart. Thou hast now wiped my tears.' So saying she placed Rāmānuja's commentary, the *Śrī-bhāshya*, upon her head, drew Rāmānuja to her breast, gave him the title Bhāshyakāra, and handed him the image of Hayagrīva (i. e. Horse-mane, one of Vishṇu's incarnations) for worship.[2]

At a later date Rāmānuja was driven by persecution to take refuge in Mysore. There he found an image of Vishṇu and had a temple erected for it. But he had no processional image. In a vision he was told that the image he wanted was named Rāmapriya and was in the possession of the Muḥammadan king in Delhi. The saint journeyed to the capital, and there a second vision informed him that the king's daughter had the image in her rooms. We give the rest of the story from the text:

> The king took the Sannyāsin Rāmānuja into the seraglio, where no other man dared enter; and wonderful to relate, Rāmapriya was there found, fondled by the Sultāni, his daughter, to whom He played the husband. Rāmānuja, entering, called Him by His name, and lo, the image jumped down from the couch on which the Sultāni had placed Him, and walked to where Rāmānuja stood, in all the glory and grace of an incarnated deity.[3]

In the life of Tiru-maṅgai, one of the Vaishṇava poet-saints

[1] *Rāmānuja*, 143. [2] *Rāmānuja*, 140.
[3] *Rāmānuja*, 188.

known as Āḷvārs,[1] we are told that he went one day with two companions, Parakālar and Yatirāśan, to steal a golden image of Buddha from a disused Buddhist shrine. The only way in which they could manage the holy burglary was to get up on the tower and lower one of their number through an opening. We quote the rest of the story:

> Parakālar then let down his brother-in-law Yatirāśan into the aperture. When Yatirāśan laid his hands on the idol, it escaped; and he ran, and it ran, round and round the apartment. Parakālar suggested Yatirāśan's spitting on it. He did so, and the mantra-power which gave the idol motion vanished by this act of pollution. He then clutched the idol and hoisted it up to the aperture and Parakālar lifted it out.[2]

Mīrā Bāī was the wife of one of the Rājput kings of Udaipur, but she was driven from his bed and palace on account of her devotion to Kṛishṇa and her refusal to worship Devī, the wife of Śiva. She lived a wandering life for some time. Then Brāhmans were sent to Dvārikā to bring her home. Before departing she went to the temple of Kṛishṇa to take leave of him. Tradition says that, when she had completed her adoration, the image opened, and the princess leaped into the fissure, and was never seen again.[3]

Here is a story of an image of Devī, i.e. Umā, or Kālī, the wife of Śiva. Haryānand, a Vishṇuite saint,

> being one day in want of fuel to dress his meat, he directed one of his pupils to proceed to a neighbouring temple of Devī, and bring away from it any portion of the timber he could conveniently remove. This was done, to the great alarm, but utter helplessness, of the goddess, who could not dispute the authority of a mortal of Haryānand's sanctity. A neighbour who had observed this transaction laboured under a like want of wood: at the instigation of his wife, he repaired also to the temple and attempted to remove one of the beams, when the goddess, indignant at his presumption, hurled him down and broke his neck. The widow, hearing of her husband's fate, immediately hastened to the temple and liberally abused the vindictive deity. Devī took advantage of the business to make a bargain for her temple, and restored the

[1] See below, p. 384. [2] *Holy Lives*, 177. [3] *Religious Sects*, 71.

man to life, on condition that he would ever afterwards buy fuel for Haryānand.[1]

Innumerable passages in the same strain occur in the most reliable literature.[2]

The truth shines out from these narratives, but we may add a few clear statements from the most authoritative books. Here is how a modern Vishṇuite, a follower of Rāmānuja, puts the matter:

> The Manifestation worshipable is that form of the Lord, in which the Lord is pleased without any kind of limitation as to times, places, or persons, to be present and manifest Himself to all, in temples and homes, to wink at faults, and to be, for every movement or business, dependent on the worshipper.[3]

The following is a sentence from the paper by Mr. V. Śrīnivāsa Rao quoted above:[4]

> Whatever the apologists . . . may say, as for instance that . . . Idolatry is only keeping in view a concrete thing for concentration in worshipping the One True Spiritual God; the stern and incontrovertible fact remains . . . that the idolater *does* believe that some of the idols are the actual incarnations of God, called *Ārchavatāras* (incarnations for worship[5]), and not mere symbols, that there is not one God but many, quite independent of each other, one at Tirupati, the other at Chidambaram, and so on; that one should be worshipped on a certain day with different leaves; that the marriage and consummation ceremonies of one God should be celebrated on a particular day, and those of the other on another day, and so on.

Our next quotations are from a modern defence of the Mādhva sub-sect of Vaishṇavas:

> In daily service, we worship God dwelling in a metallic image, after invoking God's presence therein. The invocation is the most important part of the function, to make sure of God's special presence in the idol.[6]
>
> Every honour and every homage that the mind of man can conceive of, to glorify an Emperor of Emperors, if present in flesh and blood, is

[1] *Religious Sects*, 33.
[2] *Rāmānuja*, 5, 78, 125, 126, 140, 146, 149, 152, 155, 180, 202, 203, 217; *Holy Lives*, 108, 112, 114, 177; *Divine Wisdom*, 40; *Madhva*, 114, 254, 714; *Indian Interpreter*, April, 1913, p. 17.
[3] *Divine Wisdom*, 138–139.
[4] See pp. 111–112.
[5] This is the special teaching of the Mādhva sect, *Madhva*, 269.

paid with tireless patience and obeisance, day after day, in total forgetfulness of the fact that it is after all an image that stands before them.[1]

The following is from Max Müller's biography of Rāmakṛishṇa Paramahaṁsa, and refers to the time when he was priest of the temple of Kālī at Dakshineśvara near Calcutta:

He now began to look upon the image of the goddess Kālī as his mother and the mother of the universe. He believed it to be living and breathing and taking food out of his hand. After the regular forms of worship he would sit there for hours and hours, singing hymns and talking and praying to her as a child to his mother, till he lost all consciousness of the outward world.[2]

One of his own disciples reports[3] that he said,

We should believe in the Divine Presence infilling the Images of the Deity.

Mr. Havell[4] speaks of the image undergoing the *prāṇapratishṭhā* ceremony,[5] and adds,

Thereafter it is regarded as a being endowed with life and feeling.

It is because the god lives in the temple that it is sacred, and must be kept from all pollution. That is the reason why all Hindu sects believe that the shrines and the idols, and also the flowers, ashes, water, and food that have been presented to idols, all transmit spiritual efficacy.

The Hindu belief is that the gods live in heaven, but frequently visit earth. Thus, they have been often seen,[6] and the appearance of each is perfectly well known.[7] Hence it is quite possible for the Hindu artist to make a statue which is a true likeness of Vishṇu or Lakshmī, of Śiva or Brahmā, or of any other god that is wanted. The liṅga is not an image of Śiva, but it is believed that he himself took the form

[1] *Madhva*, 254. [2] *Rāmakṛishṇa*, p. 36.
[3] *Gospel of Sri Rāmakṛishṇa*, i. 187. [4] *Benares*, 161. [5] See p. 322.
[6] Śaṅkara confesses that the gods were never seen in his day, but says, 'What is not accessible to our perception may have been within the sphere of perception of people in ancient times. Smṛiti also declares that Vyāsa and others conversed with the gods face to face.' *S. B. E.*, xxxiv. 222.
[7] Śaṅkara writes, 'The Vedic injunctions . . . presuppose certain characteristic shapes of the individual deities.' *S. B. E.*, xxxiv. 221.

of a liṅga of light in heaven, in order to manifest his greatness, and that he created the earliest liṅgas on earth. Consequently, it is easy to cut a stone in accordance with his will.

The next step is to transform the mere statue or carved stone into a sacred image or symbol by inducing the god to come and live in it. The priest performs a ceremony over it, using holy *mantras*, i.e. sacred formulae instinct with magic power, and thereby brings the god into the statue. This ceremony is called *āvāhana*, a bringing in [*sc.* of the god into the image], or more often *prāṇapratishṭhā*, the establishment of life, the installing of vital breath [*sc.* in the image]. The ceremony of bringing Kālī into an image is thus described in the *Mahānirvāṇa Tantra*:[1]

> Having thus welcomed the goddess, one should install vital breath into her. Having first recited *Am*, *Hrim*, *Krim*, *Shrim*, and *Swāhā*, he should exclaim 'Life unto all the gods; life unto this god'. Next he should recite the five mantras. Then he should exclaim 'May Jiva (individual soul) be in this god and may the deity have all the senses'. Again reciting the five mantras, he should say, 'Speech, mind, eyes, nose, ears, speech be unto her.' Afterwards he should recite twice the mantras, 'May Prānas (vital breaths) come here and live happily for ever, Swāhā.' Having thus written thrice on the Yantra, with the help of Lilihān Mudrā, the mantra of inspiring vital breath, he should with folded hands exclaim, 'Welcome unto thee, O Prime Kālī. Auspicious is thy coming here, O great goddess.' Thereupon reciting the principal mantra for purifying the image of the goddess, he should sprinkle her thrice with the water of special *arghya*. Then, consecrating all the limbs of the goddess with six sorts of *nyāsa*, he should worship her with sixteen ingredients.

The translator's note on the first sentence of the above account is,

> The word in the text is *Prāṇa Pratishṭhā*. We have given the literal rendering, besides which the phrase has a theological significance. The practice among the Hindus is that they first make an image of the deity they worship either with clay or stone. This image is not considered sacred till this ceremony is performed. It thus goes to prove that they do not worship the image but the spirit indwelling it.

[1] vi. 70–77. Dutt's translation, 88.

On the word *nyāsa* in the last sentence his note is,

> The assignment of the limbs of the body [*sc.* of the goddess] to the corresponding parts of the image.

Vishṇuites say that Vishṇu exists in five modes, as the Absolute in heaven, in his emanations, in his incarnations, in his saints, and in images. Pope describes Śaiva practice and belief: 'Each image by a peculiar service which is called *Āvāganam* (Sans. Āvāhanam, "bringing unto") becomes the permanent abode of an indwelling deity, and is itself divine.'[1] In the *Agni Purāṇa*[2] there occurs a description of a ceremony performed to open the eyes of the image and endow it with sight.

Buddhists and Jains seem to have taken to the use of images for reasons similar to those that move Roman Catholic Christians, viz. to stimulate feeling and meditation. But how dangerous it is to play with fire in this way is plain from the history of the practice both in Jainism and Buddhism. Despite the fact that the Tīrthakaras and the Buddhas have entered nirvāṇa, and therefore can neither listen to praise and prayer nor receive gifts, in both religions food,[3] flowers, and incense are offered and many a prayer is uttered. Nor is that all. In Ceylon the last act in the making of an image is the painting of the eyes, a magical ceremony, clearly copied from the Hindu rite for the opening of the eyes. In Burmah the image is dedicated in a ceremony called 'the giving of life', which thus corresponds precisely with the Hindu *prāṇapratishṭhā*. Here is what we are told about Buddhist images in China:

> The images of the gods are usually made from wood or clay, gilded or painted; specially costly ones are bronze or marble. When the craftsmen have finished their work, the image is vivified by a special

[1] *Tiruvāśagam*, xxxv. [2] lviii. 7–10.

[3] The writer had the privilege recently of travelling in the same railway carriage with an intelligent Jain lady, who is an eager promoter of education in her own community. Her theory is that Jains offer food to the images in order to learn self-denial.

> rite, and is raised to the actual godship. As a rule there is a small hole in the back of the image, through which some animal—a snake, a cat, a frog, or a centipede—is inserted into the hollows inside, and the opening is closed. The soul of the creature gives the impetus of life to the dead image. Afterwards the pupil of the eye is painted in, and thereby the deity has taken full possession of the image. This act is called *K'ai kuang*, the opening of eyelight.[1]

Let any one look through Hiouen Tsang's travels, and it will become plain that the greatest Buddhist teacher which China ever bred believed implicitly that the images of the Buddhas and Bodhisattvas were alive and could walk about, speak, and act.

There are innumerable images of each of the great gods in India, and each is regarded as a living god. But this creates no difficulty to the Hindu mind; for one of the many supernatural powers which the gods are said to possess is the capacity of assuming many bodies at the same moment. Śaṅkarāchārya and Rāmānuja both tell us this quite plainly in their commentaries.[2]

Further, it is of great importance to realize that it is not the connexion of the idols with their original in heaven, but their local personality and power that makes them of value to the Hindu. The living beliefs of the people, which make their religion a helpful reality to them, and the whole practice of the temple, depend upon the conviction that each idol is a distinct and independent divine personality. Each idol has his own personal name, suggested by some episode in his history or by the particular blessing which he is believed to bestow. Each idol has usually his own local form. Each idol has his own biography recorded in the legend of his temple, the *Sthala-purāṇa*. It is on the idol that the saint lavishes his love.[3] It is in looking in the eyes of his beloved local lord that he kindles his emotion to rapture and breaks

[1] Hackmann, *Buddhism as a Religion*, 214. [2] *Infra*, p. 331.

[3] A saint now and then gets the malady known as 'sunset and sunrise', i.e. he falls ill because he cannot see his favourite god, the doors of the shrine being closed by night to allow the god to sleep.

into a song of *bhakti.* So the villager trusts the power of each separate idol. A Hindu wife goes to one divinity if she wants to get a son, to another to pray for her husband's recovery from a serious illness, to a third to ask for the removal of cholera from the village.

Here is a very significant passage from the life of Rāmānuja. While still young, and living in Kāñchī, i.e. Conjeeveram, in the service of the temple of Vishṇu there, he became a sannyāsī, and took up a course of philosophic study. But his help was greatly needed in the metropolitan shrine of Trichinopoly. The Vishṇu of Conjeeveram is known as Lord Varada, the Boon-giver, while the Vishṇu of Trichinopoly is called Lord Raṅga, Lord of the World-stage, and his temple is called Śrīraṅgam. The narrative proceeds:

> While such studies were being prosecuted, the tidings travelled to Śrīraṅgam of the assumption by Rāmānuja of the sannyāsī order, and other events rapidly succeeding it. Mahāpūrṇa and other disciples of Yāmunāchārya received the tidings with joy, and longed for Rāmānuja's coming to Śrīraṅgam, making it his permanent quarters. But they were helpless; and Rāmānuja too had once before in grief and despair returned from the place without even visiting Lord Raṅga, being disappointed at the sudden death of Yāmunā. So they went in a body to Lord Raṅga and petitioned to Him to prevail upon His Type at Kānchī —the Lord Varada—to spare Rāmānuja for them. So a message from Lord Raṅga was sent to Lord Varada. But a reply came to the effect: 'If it is possible for one to forego his love, I too can part with my Rāmānuja.' On hearing this, Mahāpūrṇa and other worthies were much disconcerted, but after some deliberation, determined to depute an elder in person to approach Lord Varada and persuade Him by hymns to *grant* them Rāmānuja, inasmuch as the Lord's very name Varada meant: 'Grantor.' They besought accordingly Tiruvaraṅgap-perumāl Aṛaiyar, the Venerable Elder of the place, to march to Kāñchī on their behalf, and so extol Lord Varada as to make him condescend to grant them Rāmānuja. Aṛaiyar immediately left Śrīraṅgam on this holy errand, after obtaining leave to do so from Lord Raṅga. On his nearing Kāñchī, his relative there, by name Varantaram Perumāḷ Aṛaiyar, met him and escorted him to the Holy City, and tended him under his roof as befitted a distinguished visitor. The next morning, in due fashion, Aṛaiyar proceeded to the Temple.

Lord Varada had that day taken His august seat in the pavilion called *Kacchikkuvāyttān*, surrounded by the Holy Assembly; Kāñchī-pūrṇa, stationed before the Lord, reverently doing his allotted service of fanning. Rāmānuja stood by his side devoutly uttering the *Devarāja-Ashtaka* hymn sung by Pūrṇa. Rāmānuja saw Aṛaiyar, went forward and received him most cordially. 'May I be allowed to pay my obeisance to Lord Varada?' inquired Aṛaiyar. Pūrṇa led him to His august presence, in full Holy Council seated, and Aṛaiyar fell prostrate before Him, repeating Yāmuna's verse: 'Oh, when, O Strider of the Three Spheres, will Thy Lotus-Feet, decked with all the signs such as the discus, bedeck my head?' Rising, he was honoured with *tīrtha*, *prasāda*[1] and Śrī Śaṭhakopa.[2] Aṛaiyar then chanted a select number of the Lyrical Psalter of the Aḻvārs, set to celestial music; and as he sang, danced and went into raptures.

'When His faithful sing and dance for joy, God Himself keeps time,' it is said. So, Lord Varada was pleased with the devotion of Gāyaka, i.e. Aṛaiyar, and vouchsafed to Him all the honours belonging to His Shrine. 'Why do I want these?' said Gāyaka, 'my wish is not for these. Pray grant me a boon, as Thou art, O God, famous as the Boon-Giver.' And so saying, he continued his song and dance with more fervour. Pleased, Lord Varada spoke thus: 'Ask, my beloved, anything, except Me and My Consorts.' 'Him, pray grant,' readily replied Gāyaka, pointing to Rāmānuja, who was close by. 'Oh lost,' exclaimed the Lord, 'I wish I had had the forethought to include Rāmānuja on the side of exceptions. However, son, except Rāmānuja, ask for any other boon.' 'But', remonstrated Gāyaka, 'dost Thou retract also like mortals? Are not Thy own words these: "Rāma hath no two tongues"?' On hearing this, Lord Varada had no alternative but to reluctantly say: 'Well, we grant you Rāmānuja; take him. And we bestow on him the title, Yatirāja.' No sooner was this said, than almost convulsively Gāyaka grasped Rāmānuja by the hand and said: 'Proceed, Sire.' Rāmānuja said not a word. He fell prostrate before Lord Varada and saying: 'Thy will be done,' he immediately started, not even caring to enter his cloister.[3]

This narrative is quite sufficient by itself to prove that even to the most cultured Hindus two images of the same god are distinct persons, who may disagree the one with the other.

[1] See above, p. 315.
[2] Śaṭhakopa is the greatest of the Āḻvārs. See below, p. 384. His sandals are presented to specially honoured guests.
[3] *Rāmānuja*, 74–76.

Hinduism has proved itself a most powerful system both in organizing the people and in stimulating them religiously; and no part of the religion has been more living and effective than the worship of the temple. But the grip of that worship on the heart of India depends altogether on this cardinal belief, that each idol is a living god. The temple is a constant joy to the Hindu, because he can go and actually look on the face of the god whom he loves, express his affection by giving him a gift of food, pour into his ear all his sorrows and all his desires, hear the god's reply from his own lips, and go home fortified against evil spirits and ill-luck through eating a portion of the food that has been offered to the divinity. The *bhakti* of the Hindu, whether villager or saintly poet, is usually a passionate devotion to a single idol. He dances with rapture, or falls in a swoon from sudden emotion, when he sees the glory of the divine eyes.

No one who knows what polytheism has been in other lands will have any doubt as to the truth of this account of Hindu image-worship. The ritual is everywhere of the same general type; and, though the beliefs vary in particulars, the groundwork is the same in every case: the image is a living god; the temple is his house; he receives his worshippers in audience, listens to all their requests, makes them his guests, treats them royally, and gives them his personal blessing.

VII. Now that we have got a firm hold of the facts of image-worship among Hindus, we are in a position to trace the history that lies behind.

A. The use of the temple and the image is one of the elements of the fresh fabric of Hinduism which took shape while the invading Aryans were bringing North India under their sway. It arose rather later than the doctrine of transmigration and the philosophy of Brahman; yet it came from the same general period of the history and from the same conditions.

The next point to notice is that, from the beginning down to our own days, all temples have been open on the same terms to Hindus of all the four great castes,[1] both men and women. This proves incontestably that temple-worship had a different origin from the regular sacrificial worship of the gods; for that has always been restricted to the three twice-born castes; and no woman can take any part in it except along with her husband. The temple, on the other hand, is open to the Śūdra on the same terms as to the Brāhman; and any woman, whether wife or widow, may worship there by herself, and will receive the same welcome as a man.

Thirdly, a vast number of divinities are found in the Hindu pantheon which do not occur in the Vedas. It is clear that, while some of these were created by priestly and philosophic reflection, the great majority of them passed into the religion and found recognition through temple-worship. It is also most noteworthy that goddesses play a very minor rôle in the Vedic religion, while in Hinduism they receive quite as much attention as gods.

Fourthly, a type of worship which has never received official sanction in Hinduism is found in every part of India, viz. the cult of the village gods. Most of these divinities are goddesses, and they are, therefore, frequently referred to as the Mothers. There are three points to be noted with regard to them. First, each is a local divinity distinct from every other and with a name of her own. Secondly, each has a holy place where she lives. Thirdly, she is represented at the holy place by an image, a stone, or some other symbol. There is thus a good deal of difference between one of these goddesses and one of the heavenly gods of the Indo-Aryans as described above.[2] The one is local, the other is heavenly. The one is a present divinity, the other only visits. The one is represented by a symbol, while the other has none.

Fifthly, from the beginning the priests in Hindu temples have been always and everywhere Brāhmans.

Sixthly, for centuries the ancient Vedic worship was regarded

[1] See above, p. 164. [2] pp. 297–300.

as the only perfect worship for twice-born men; but after the Christian era temple-worship gradually rose in favour; and in modern times the ancient sacrificial cult has fallen into almost complete disuse.

On the very surface these facts suggest that the temple and the idol came into Hinduism with the aborigines who became Śūdras, and that the new worship was admitted on condition that only Brāhmans should officiate as priests. If we suppose that the worship of the aborigines was in the main similar to the cult of the village divinities of to-day, then all the features of Hindu image-worship are easily comprehensible. Each local aboriginal god of note would be identified with one of the Vedic celestials, while each goddess would find recognition as the wife of one of those heavenly gods. Minor divinities became Hinduized through receiving recognition as children or dependents of the great gods. In this way we account, on the one hand, for the growth of the pantheon and the increased importance of goddesses, and on the other, for the fact that though there are thousands of images of such a god as Vishṇu, each idol is a living god, a distinct personality with his own name, character, and history, and yet is held to be, in a sense, the great heavenly god himself. One competent Hindu scholar, Mr. P. T. Śrīnivāsa Iyengar, has realized part of the truth. He writes that Hindu temple ritual

> was primarily based on the ceremonies of the fetish-worship of the Dravidian races, many of which are still observed in villages and under wayside trees in all their primitive barbarism.[1]

Necessarily, the temples were open to Śūdra men and women after they were Hinduized just as they were before; so that the ancient temple-rule causes no difficulty.

The gradual acceptance of temple-worship by the twice-born castes and the progressive decay of the ancient cult are accounted for by two facts. First, the presence of Brāhman priests in every temple made it possible for the twice-born to

[1] *Outlines*, 128.

use them. The women of these castes would be especially eager to go to temples, since they could worship there by themselves and when they pleased. Temple-priests, naturally, would do all they possibly could to induce high-caste people, both men and women, to visit the shrines. But the second fact is the real reason for the final predominance of idolatry over the old cult. In temples Hindus had their gods living with them and visible to their eyes. The present divinity grips the heart, creating keen religious feeling and fervent worship. The absent and invisible celestials were at a great disadvantage.

B. The rise of the early philosophy of India must next be noticed. The basis of the whole is the idea of Brahman, indissolubly one, spiritual, real, unknowable. In the light of this conception the old gods appeared transient, immersed in phenomenal things, able to give only phenomenal gifts. From them the philosopher turns away, renouncing, in sannyāsa, all phenomenal things. He seeks not the world, but release from transmigration, and he believes it can be won only by knowledge of Brahman.

But though the philosopher turned away from the popular faith, that faith went on unchanged and with as much vigour as ever.

We have seen how the Brāhmans introduced the philosophy of Brahman into their schools, how it there received the name Vedānta, and how the earliest records of the philosophy, the Upanishads, became integral parts of the Brāhmaṇas of the Vedas. This naturally led in the long run to a close alliance between the Vedānta philosophy and the sacrificial system which it had originally repudiated. How soon this was worked out we do not know, although traces of it appear in the later Upanishads; but the *Vedānta-sūtras* make it plain that the alliance was complete before the time of Bādarāyaṇa; so that we may use the *Sūtras* and Śaṅkara's *Bhāshya* freely as evidence. We note four significant points.

(i) It is acknowledged that the gods are transient beings, finite, mortal, transmigrating, spirits, with physical bodies, as the early Upanishads declare them to be; but it is contended that, *when one god dies, another exactly corresponding to him takes his place.*[1] There is thus a permanent succession, and the basis of the popular faith remains undisturbed.

(ii) It is clear that the idea that the gods feed on the sacrifices created a difficulty for the philosophic mind. Indeed, Śaṅkara says they do not eat them; yet he acknowledges that they do enjoy them. *The eating is thus volatilized, so as to satisfy philosophic scruple, but is retained as a reality* because of the popular faith.[2]

(iii) We are also told that there is no difficulty in believing that the gods are present at all sacrifices, though many may be offered to one god at the same moment; for, through his supernatural power, *a god can assume as many bodies as he pleases.*[3] Śaṅkara is here thinking primarily of Vedic sacrifice; yet his words justify idol-worship also.

(iv) The contention of the early philosophers, that the phenomenal gifts of the gods are worthless, Release being the only thing worth striving for, is acknowledged; yet it is argued that, though the gifts, which are the fruit of sacrifice, are of no value in themselves, *yet the worship of the gods is of service in ripening the man for final Release.*[4]

C. In this way philosophy held by the old teaching, yet found ways of justifying the whole of the popular religion. When the Vaishṇava and the Śaiva brought the Vedānta philosophy into the theology of the sects, they declared Vishṇu, in the one case, and Śiva, in the other, to be Brahman. That is, instead of saying with the strict Vedāntists, 'All the gods are created, mortal, transmigrating beings,' each sect said, 'All minus one.'[5] The theist accepted the Vedāntic statement that release is obtained by knowledge of Brahman only, but

[1] *S. B. E.*, xxxiv. 203. Compare *S. B. E.*, xlviii. 331.
[2] *S. B. E.*, xxxviii. 110–111; xxxiv. 201. Cf. *Six Systems*, 217.
[3] *S. B. E.*, xxxiv. 199–200. Compare *S. B. E.*, xlviii. 331.
[4] *S. B. E.*, xxxiv. 197 n.; xxxviii. 306–309; 313–315.
[5] See below, pp. 364–367.

he added the rider, that a man may rise to knowledge by means of *bhakti*, deep, strong devotion to the personal god.

With the exception of the results produced by the doctrine of ahiṁsā,[1] there is no thought of reform. Apart from that, the worship went on absolutely unchanged. The pantheon is not altered in a single particular. Vishṇu, though now equated with the incomprehensible Brahman, is worshipped just as he had been during the centuries when he was regarded as merely one of the celestials; and the same is true of Śiva. The whole of the mythology remains unchanged.

VIII. We have next to notice certain rather important movements arising from criticisms of idolatry.

A number of very outspoken criticisms occur in Tamil and Telugu literature, especially in the poems of Paṭṭaṇattu Piḷḷai, of 'Śivavākyar' and Vemana;[2] but, as we do not know the dates of these writers, it is impossible as yet to tell whence they received their inspiration. Nāmadeva, the Marātha saint who flourished about 1300 A.D., also condemns idolatry in his *abhaṅgs*.[3] But it seems clear that no religious sect rejecting idolatry sprang from these efforts; so that we need not linger over them.

We find ourselves in another atmosphere when we turn to the North in the time of Muḥammadan supremacy. During the conquest the Muḥammadans expressed their detestation of idols by the destruction of temples and images and the murder of their priests; but these violent methods do not appear to have produced any religious result. Peaceful teaching, however, did what the hammer and the sword failed to do. Through the instrumentality of Kabīr,[4] who seems to have been half a Muḥammadan, the stern monotheism of Islam and its hatred of idolatry passed into Hinduism and took organized form. The followers of Kabīr to this day are a separate Hindu sect who do not visit Hindu temples, but worship in their own buildings without images. Still more important than the sect

[1] *Infra*, pp. 380–382. [2] *Heart of India*, 88, 91, 110, 112.
[3] *Indian Interpreter*, April, 1913, p. 17. [4] See p. 387.

of Kabīr is the famous Sikh sect, founded by Nānak, a disciple of Kabīr.[1] A smaller body, the Dādūpanthīs, arose in Ahmadabad rather later. They also look back to Kabīr as the source of their ideas. Both groups condemn the use of idols. There is also a Jain sect, the Sthānakavāsīs,[2] who have renounced idolatry. They are a branch of the Śvetāmbara sect, and belong to Gujarat; so that it is probable that they sprang from the same movement as the Dādūpanthīs.

It is a very remarkable fact that these sects have failed to influence Hinduism in general. Outside the small groups of their own members they have had very little influence indeed. Even in their own midst they have found it difficult to maintain the pristine ideal. It is well known that certain groups of Sikhs were long addicted to idol-worship; and in the Golden Temple of Amṛitsār their sacred book, the *Granth*, is to this day treated like an image. It lies open in the centre of the temple. Priests fan it with chowries, while the people bow down before it and offer flowers to it. At night it is put to bed, and brought out for worship again next morning. It is significant, also, that groups of Sikhs go on pilgrimage to visit Hindu temples. When questioned on the subject, they say they go to look at the idols, not to worship them.

A new era begins with the opening of the nineteenth century. The bold teaching of the Serampore missionaries found its way into Hinduism; and Rāmmohan Rai founded the Brāhma Samāj, a theistic body which is vehemently opposed to idolatry. The Samāj has exercised a wide influence among educated men, especially in North India. Its greatest triumphs have been won in Bengal, but there are groups of men in other cities, notably in Bombay, Lahore, and Madras, who follow its teaching. For many years there were thousands of educated men within Hinduism, outside the Samāj, who refused to worship idols, and in consequence never visited temples nor took part in the daily worship of the family idols. The

[1] *Infra*, p. 388.

[2] *Modern Jainism*, 13-14.

Prārthanā Samāj in Bombay sprang from the Brāhma Samāj and testifies as frankly against idolatry.

During the last twenty-five years the Ārya Samāj has done a good deal to rouse opinion against idols in North India. This body was founded by Dayānanda Sarasvatī in 1875. Its influence is not very great outside the Punjab and the United Provinces; but within those limits its earnest crusade against image-worship has attained a measure of success.

IX. But a very great reaction has been in progress for some years. The movement is to be traced to two sources. The first of these is the teaching of Rāmakṛishṇa Paramahaṁsa, who has been already mentioned and quoted. The warm defence of everything Hindu, including idols, which he started, and which his disciples, and especially Vivekānanda, continued, has been caught up with the utmost eagerness by Hindus everywhere. The second source is the Theosophical Society, which unquestionably owes its great popularity in India to-day almost exclusively to its defence of caste and idols. These movements arose some thirty-five years ago; during the last ten years their influence has spread with great rapidity; and to-day it is felt in every part of India. In consequence, instead of the thousands of educated men who twenty years ago were ashamed of idolatry, there are tens of thousands who defend the practice. The movement for the removal of idols from Hinduism has been flung aside and forgotten. So that to the casual observer it might seem to-day as if the battle had been finally decided in favour of idolatry in every part of India, except in the two provinces where the Ārya Samāj is powerful.

Yet Hindu idolatry is dying. The educated Hindu who defends it does not believe in it. That is perfectly clear from the various arguments he uses in favour of it.

(*a*) The most common defence is that the image is a symbol of God, and that the ordinary man cannot worship God without having some sort of symbol on which to concentrate his attention. Those who follow this line of defence usually go on to urge that Protestant Christians use symbols also, and, therefore, are as idolatrous as Hindus are. It is almost unnecessary to point out how absurd the comparison is: Protestants do not *worship* these things, whether they think of them as in any sense symbols or not. To compare a Protestant's feeling for the Church or the Bible with the Hindu process of feeding an image and expecting it to speak is simply utter futility.

> Alas! the iconoclasts of this fashion miss the point or purposes of true idolatry altogether. They fail to realize what powerful aids images are for concentration. Human thoughts allowed to roam about to catch an abstraction seldom attain the object. We think in pictures and forms, and whenever the picture or the form is vague, the mental grasp is feeble. To conceive of the Formless and fix it in the mind is an impossibility.[1]

> Protestants hold that churches are more sacred than other places. This church, as it is, stands for a symbol. Or there is the Book. The idea of the Book, to them, is much holier than any other symbol. The image of the Cross with the Protestants takes the place of the image of the Saint with the Catholics. It is vain to preach against the use of symbols, and why should we preach against them? There is no reason under the sun why man should not use these symbols. They have them in order to represent the thing signified behind them. This universe is a symbol in and through which we are trying to grasp the thing signified, which is beyond and behind. This is the lower human constitution, and we are bound to have it so. Yet, at the same time, it is true that we are struggling to get to the thing signified, to get beyond the material, to the spiritual; the spirit is the goal, and not matter. Forms, images, bells, candles, books, churches, temples, and all holy symbols are very good, very helpful to the growing plant of spirituality, but thus far and no farther.[2]

Clearly this is no explanation of Hindu idolatry. If the image is merely a symbol, what is the use of the ceremony of *prāṇapratishṭhā*, the bringing of life into the image? It is quite true that many an educated Hindu, who, like Vivekānanda, has felt the force of Christian criticism of idolatry, no longer thinks of the image as a living god, but, in loyalty to Hinduism, attempts to use it as a symbol to lift his thought to the

[1] *Madhva*, 142. [2] Vivekānanda, 340.

Invisible. But that is not Hindu idolatry. That is not what the idol is to the Hindu villager.

(*b*) Mrs. Besant knows that. She, therefore, goes a step further, frankly acknowledging that the Hindu does not use an image until it has been consecrated by this ceremony, but attempting to justify the ceremony as a magnetizing of the idol:

> You know how, from time immemorial, pictures and images have been used for the purpose of worship among Hindus of all shades of thought. . . . Now, what is the connexion between the sacred image, the sacred picture, and the magnetic bodies I have been talking about? They have the same force. Only the force of a higher grade of fineness and complicacy. You don't, in Hinduism, take an ordinary image, an ordinary picture, and use it in worship straight away. On the contrary, you subject it to a divine ceremony. You recite over it certain Mantras, you use certain objects, you pour certain liquids, and it is only after all this ceremony has been performed that the image becomes sacred and fit to be used for purposes of worship. Now, what have you been doing by these ceremonies, by these Mantras, by the substances you used? To put it in ordinary scientific language, you have been magnetizing your image or picture. . . . And if a European doctor, a sceptic, or an unbeliever is able to magnetize a physical object for the curing of a physical disease, do you mean to tell me it is superstition to believe that a man or a Devata can magnetize another object for the curing of mental disease and helping a man to devotion?[1]

But, if the idol is merely a magnetized stone, or a piece of magnetized brass, able to cure a man of materialism and make him a spiritual man, what is the use of worshipping the image? What is the use of singing praises to it? Magnetism does not require to be worshipped before it will act. Clearly Mrs. Besant's defence does not explain image-worship at all.

(*c*) Others, realizing this, go a step further. To them it is perfectly evident that the Hindu believes that God is in the image. Unless that point is explained, the Hindu use of images is not explained at all. A famous Vaishṇava scholar, therefore, acknowledges the fact and undertakes to prove that it is quite rational to worship images on that understanding:

[1] *Speeches at Trivandrum*, 36–38.

> When we speak of 'an animated discourse', even the most ignorant among us do not mean that the discoursing person began to live, i.e. had his *Prāṇpratishṭhā* for the first time, at the moment of his making that discourse, but only that his animation or power of life was realized by his audience by attending to his discourse. So likewise, our greatest slanderer cannot ascribe to us the folly of believing that the Infinite Omnipresent Lord, Vāsudeva, began to penetrate any particular image, i.e. any particular part of His nature or universe, after a particular devotee's performance of the ceremony of *Prāṇpratishṭhā*, but that the worshipper, as a witness is by an oath, has, by the power of the consecrating ceremony, become self-recollected, and he so realizes the Divine Presence in (among the infinity of others) those particular images of the Lord and Lady of the Universe, that, henceforth, to use the calumniator's own language, they are esteemed the arbiters of his destiny, and continually receive his most ardent adoration.[1]

The defence here is that, since God is everywhere, He is in the image also. Thus there is nothing irrational in worshipping God as present in the image. The ceremony is merely to enable the worshipper to realize God's presence in the image. We need only refer readers to the quotation above,[2] in which the ceremony is described, to show that this is not the truth. The ceremony is undoubtedly performed in order to bring the god into the image. Before the ceremony, the image is a piece of inert matter. After the ceremony, it is a living god who speaks, moves, eats, and acts. Clearly the divine omnipresence is no explanation of idols. If God is in the image merely in the same way as He is in any ordinary stone, what is the reason for worshipping that particular stone more than any other? why is it carved into the shape of a man? and why, in the name of everything, is food offered to it?

(*d*) A few of the more sincere souls frankly acknowledge the truth, that Hindus believe that each image is a living god; but no attempt is made anywhere to show that it is reasonable to treat every image as a living being:

> And where worship is found enjoined in the case of *āveśa* Avatāras, and even Images of God, it means that God elects to be specially

[1] Pārthasārathi Aiyangar, *Holy Image Worship*, 31.
[2] p. 322.

present in such media—the *soul* in the former case, and *matter* in the latter case.[1]

> Image worship is not the worship of the mere symbol, but what it imparts. The visible symbol, to the knower of the secret thereof, becomes the very transcendental person of God.[2]

> The bare fact is that ninety-nine out of every hundred of image-worshippers believe that the images consecrated in temples are really the gods whose names they bear.[3]

Clearly, no one of all these writers really grapples with the problem. What they say throws no convincing light upon the Hindu use of images. The truth is that they have lost all genuine faith in idolatry themselves; yet they are dimly conscious of something noble and good in the practice; but, being unwilling to admit even to themselves that it is indefensible to modern thought, they fail to bring out in clear and convincing fashion the real religious elements which find expression in it.

That the average educated man no longer believes in idolatry is sometimes naïvely confessed. Oftener it shows itself in the writer's own tone:

> Image-worship is a large question. It has suffered deadly attack from iconoclasts both physical and theoretical from every quarter. The foreign missionary levels all his blows at it in the belief that it is the most vulnerable point of the Hindu system. The University man suppresses a sneer rising to his lips out of a conflict between patriotism on the one hand and intellectual honesty on the other. He wishes in his heart of hearts that this practice were swept away, and sees, with a sigh, no signs of the consummation.[4]

> Śālagrāms are worshipped in India as stones of peculiar merit, as the special abode of Vishṇu. The orthodox read the various configurations of circles in the gaping mouths or simple holes of the Śālagrām stones, and identify the tracings as representing some form of Vishṇu.[5]

With regard to the liṅga we have indisputable evidence that

[1] *Holy Lives*, xxviii–xxix. [2] *Holy Lives*, 216.

[3] From the article, parts of which are reproduced in the Introduction, pp. 40–42. [4] *Madhva*, 214.

[5] Ibid., 165. Cf. the passage quoted on pp. 320–321 above from p. 254 of the same volume.

men have lost faith in it. The pressure of Western thought and Christian criticism is so great that no modern educated Hindu can accept a phallic symbol as a worthy representation of the one living and true God; and consequently Vivekānanda, the great defender of the faith, gets out of the difficulty by declaring that the liṅga is not a phallic symbol at all, but that Hindus, in their most degraded days, mistook it for such.[1] It is a most remarkable fact that Dr. Coomaraswamy, the art critic, and Mr. Nallasvāmī Pillai, the most notable living writer among Śaiva Siddhāntists, endorse this judgement. The latter thinks that the liṅga may have originally been a model of a sacred hill.[2] But it is clear from the passage quoted above[3] from the *Mahābhārata* that from the very time when the liṅga was introduced into the worship of Śiva Hindus have recognized it to be a phallic symbol. Indeed nobody ever questioned the fact till our own days. Oddly enough, a fresh piece of archaeological evidence has recently turned up which proves the point conclusively. In a temple at Guḍimallam in North Arcot there stands a very ancient liṅga, dating clearly from one of the early Christian centuries, which is such a realistic representation of the *penis* that Mr. P. T. Śrīnivāsa Iyengar, to whom a photograph of it was sent, does not venture to publish it.[4]

Thus the various defences of idolatry by educated Hindus reveal nothing so clearly as their own want of faith in the practice.

X. But surely what the defenders of idolatry say is not all that can be said in rational exposition of the use of images in Hinduism. A method of worship which began among the lower classes and which yet finally won the allegiance not only of the upper castes but of such master-spirits as Śaṅkara, Māṇikka Vāchakar, Rāmānuja, Rāmānanda, Tulsī Dās, and Tukārām must have something of real power and value in it. No one who truly honours these great men can believe that the

[1] *Śaiva Siddhānta*, 294.
[2] Ibid., 295, 339.
[3] See above, p. 310.
[4] Iyengar's *Outlines*, 165-166.

peddling explanations quoted above really explain how image-worship was so much to them. The following thoughts are flung out tentatively, with the desire to reach the truth. Readers will judge for themselves whether they get at the real reasons for the popularity of idols in India or not.

(*a*) A temple with its image has usually been founded and dedicated because it was believed that a god had manifested himself or had done some noteworthy deed, and people wanted to do him honour for his grace and goodness. The temple usually marks the very spot where the theophany is believed to have taken place. It would be possible to compile an endless list of examples of such foundations. The legendary histories of the temples (*sthala purāṇa*) are filled with evidence of this kind. The human heart is deeply touched by the idea that God cares for us and has done something for us.

(*b*) The image is meant to be a faithful representation of the god. If he were to appear himself, he would be just like the image. This has been already brought out in our account of how Hindus think about their idols.[1] Thus the making of images is a response to the eager human desire to know God's nature and character. The idol seems to meet this need in the happiest way: there it stands, permanently showing what the revered Being is like. You can gaze on the great features, read the character, and carry away a picture in your heart. The ineffaceable impression produced on the Greek mind by the image of Zeus at Olympia may help us to understand how idols lay hold of the common heart of man. Under this spell many a man, who ordinarily is far enough removed from reverence, feels he can adore and pray. His god is now no mere thought or imagination to him, but a definite person whose character he is in touch with. Religion becomes at once a reality, a practical sort of intercourse which he can understand.

(*c*) But the lives of the great saints show us that the chief

[1] *Supra*, 321.

joy they received from idols was in seeing them daily, in asking for guidance from them, in hearing them speak, in rapturous dancing and singing before them, in receiving food and water from the god's table, and in the ecstasy of bhakti. The ordinary Hindu wants a temple near his home, that he may be able to see his god at any moment, to make him an offering of food, to ask for his help in distress or in danger, to pour out his heart in prayer or in praise. It is the living, present god that the human heart adores with rapture and gratitude. This is the reason for the limitless multiplication of temples, for the idols of the home and the little shrines by the roadside. The Hindu must have a living god to turn to wherever he is.

The use of idols is thus completely justified in the case of men who really believe in them. If each image is a living god, then every detail of the worship is not only natural but right; and we have no difficulty in understanding how men and women lavish their affection upon idols.

From the same point of view we can sympathize with the Hindu people in gradually adopting temple-worship in place of the ancient mode of sacrificing. In temple-worship the gods are so near to man and so accessible that the ancient cult is scarcely comparable with the new.

Idolatry brought to the Hindu people something which their philosophy never gave them, and never could give them, present and accessible gods. Brahman, being 'beyond thought and speech', can never be to any man what an idol is. It is the god to whom a man can turn in prayer at any moment and receive the help or the answer he wants that will finally hold the human heart.

It is thus evident that idolatry ministers to some of the most powerful and most valuable of our religious instincts. That is the reason why it has laid such a hold of the heart of the Hindu people. That is the reason why it has played such a great part in the religious history of our race. Every nation that rose to great power and influence in the ancient world bowed down to idols. We have only to think of Babylon and

Egypt, those mighty peoples whose science and art lie behind all the progress of the West, of Greece, the homeland of culture, and of Rome, the practical, sober-minded mistress of the world, to realize how completely the ancient world was under the sway of image-worship. Even Persia, for long content with fire as a symbol of the Divine, sent idols of Mithra throughout the length and breadth of the Roman Empire. If further proof is wanted of the part idolatry has played in human life, let us recollect that to it we are indebted for architecture, sculpture, and painting.

But idolatry is dying among educated Hindus; and the exigencies of the time will soon compel Indian leaders to seek to destroy the practice among the common people. For the belief that every image is a living god, who is able to bless or curse, and that food, water, flowers, and every other thing that comes in contact with the image is charged with supernatural power, is the chief source of the limitless mass of superstitions under which the Hindu people live enslaved. Two things at least are necessary if a vigorous modern people is to be built up in India: the villager must be set free from superstition, and he must be educated. Idolatry is thus one of the chief hindrances to the progress of India. The clear-sighted patriot will do his utmost to wean the simple Hindu villager from idols.

Therefore, educated men, who are themselves already emancipated from idols, ought at once to turn to the task of setting the people free from their superstitions. But how? Man has his clamant religious needs. History brings us face to face with this most solemn fact, that, if these needs are not fulfilled spiritually, they seek satisfaction in the grossness of idolatry. One writer proposes to cleanse the temples from idols and use them as schools for religious instruction. But that will not prevent the reappearance of idols. We must find a spiritual force as vivid and as real as idolatry, and as fully charged with religious emotion, a spiritual dynamic which will render idols obsolete by appealing as successfully as they do, and yet in healthy spiritual fashion, to the religious imagination and feeling.

XI. It is one of the marvels of Christ that He is able to make such an appeal and to make it effectively; so that the man who has been used to the accessibility of idols and the joy and passion of their worship finds in Him, in purest spiritual form, more than all the emotion and stimulus to reverent adoration which their vividness used to bring him.

There is the richest devotional life and the most living worship in Christianity without idols, because Christ takes their place. In Him the purest spiritual monotheism rises to the highest joy and adoring veneration; so that the full range of man's religious faculties find exercise and expression, but in noblest, truest forms, altogether apart from the degrading superstitions of idolatry.

Idolatry has proved its power not only by its mastery over the nations but by creating architecture and sculpture. One of the clearest proofs that Christ has completely taken the place of idols is this, that in Judaism and Muḥammadanism, the other two faiths which condemn idolatry, the consciousness of the danger and the fascination of idols is so great that the faithful are forbidden to make statues and other representations of men and animals, lest they should be drawn to worship them, while Christians, by their knowledge of God in Jesus Christ, are set completely free from this terror, and are therefore able to use sculpture and painting with perfect freedom. Christianity, so far from standing in the way of art, has stimulated architecture, sculpture, painting, and music to the utmost.

This is precisely what India needs, a pure spiritual worship, to set her free from the need of idols. We shall, therefore, do well to ask how Christ satisfies the instincts which in so many lands have found satisfaction in idolatry.

We do not here make any attempt to demonstrate the truth of the Christian system. We merely seek to show how, by means of the central beliefs of the system, the worship of God is secured in living power and spirituality, apart from the superstitions of idols.

A. The Christian conception of the coming of Christ is that God, our Father, who had revealed Himself partially to men in former ages, sent His Son into human life, to crown all former revelation, and to draw the whole human family back to Himself.

Jesus opened His public life with the declaration,

> The time is fulfilled, and the kingdom of God is at hand.[1]

He calls Himself the Messiah, as introducing the Kingdom, and allows Himself to be crucified rather than give up the claim. The central idea of His teaching is that God is the Father; and He regularly calls Himself the Son in relation to the Father. But He uses the name the Son of Man still oftener, indicating at once His real humanity and His headship of the whole human race. As the Son of Man, He must die for men, in accordance with the will of His Father:

> The Son of man must suffer many things . . . and be killed.[2]
>
> The Son of man came . . . to give his life a ransom for many.[3]
>
> My Father, if this cannot pass away, except I drink it, thy will be done.[4]

His life is thus the central event of the world's whole history; so that even His disciples are of infinite import to all men:

> Ye are the salt of the earth.[5]
>
> Ye are the light of the world.[6]

The truth must be told everywhere:

> Go ye into all the world, and preach the gospel to the whole creation.[7]

The whole significance of Christ's coming is summed up by Paul in one brief sentence:

> God was in Christ reconciling the world unto himself.[8]

[1] Mark 1, 15. [2] Mark 8, 31. [3] Matt. 20, 28.
[4] Matt. 26, 42. [5] Matt. 5, 13. [6] Matt. 5, 14.
[7] Mark 16, 15. [8] 2 Cor. 5, 19.

B. We notice next that Jesus was able to reveal the Father, because He is the Son. This Jesus states most explicitly Himself:

> No one knoweth the Son, save the Father; neither doth any know the Father, save the Son, and he to whomsoever the Son willeth to reveal him.[1]

It was His conviction also that the revelation was not a mere matter of teaching: in His own personality, character, life, death and resurrection, as well as in His teaching, the Father was revealed. He was the full representation of His Father:

> He that believeth on me believeth not on me but on him that sent me; and he that beholdeth me beholdeth him that sent me.[2]

His relation to the Father is intimate in the extreme:

> I am in the Father and the Father is in me.[3]

Hence He is the perfect revelation of the Father:

> He that hath seen me hath seen the Father.[4]

Paul gave another expression to this thought. He calls Christ

> The image of the invisible God.[5]

Another early Christian writer used rather different words, calling Him

> The outflashing of God's glory, the perfect expression of His personality.[6]

It is very important that we should realize in what sense these great statements are made. Clearly God's omniscience, omnipotence, and omnipresence could not be revealed in a man. But we need no revelation of these: the things of nature make plain to us that He who made the world is infinite in wisdom, knowledge, and power, that He works in all places at all times,

[1] Matt. 11, 27.
[2] John 12, 44–45.
[3] John 14, 10.
[4] John 14, 9.
[5] Col. 1 15. Cf. 2 Cor. 4, 4.
[6] Hebrews 1, 3.

and that He is a God of system and order. What we need to know is what God is to man, how He regards our life, and whether He is able and willing to listen to us and do anything for us. In fact, we need to know God's person and character, so far as these affect man. It is in this sane and practical sense that Jesus is held to be the image of God. His life, death, and resurrection give us a complete revelation of the character of God in relation to men and human life. The man who understands Jesus understands the Father in heaven. The Son is a perfect likeness of the Father's person.

Two points stand out in the picture prominent beyond all others. There is first God's holiness, which is moral perfection of such a real and practical character that He can never rest until men have become holy too. Man must live a really lofty moral life if he is to please God:

> Not every one that saith unto me, Lord, Lord, shall enter into the kingdom of heaven; but he that doeth the will of my Father which is in heaven.[1]
>
> Ye therefore shall be perfect, as your heavenly Father is perfect.[2]

The other point is God's love for men, which Jesus declares to be so true and deep that the Father will shrink from no self-sacrifice to bring His children to Himself:

> How think ye? if any man have a hundred sheep, and one of them be gone astray, doth he not leave the ninety and nine, and go unto the mountains, and seek that which goeth astray? And if so be that he find it, verily I say unto you, he rejoiceth over it more than over the ninety and nine which have not gone astray. Even so it is not the will of your Father which is in heaven, that one of these little ones should perish.[3]
>
> God so loved the world, that he gave his only begotten Son.[4]

But teaching is of little force by itself. Hence, in His own life and actions Jesus exhibited the very love and holiness which He said belonged to the Father; and they thus stood

[1] Matt. 7, 21.
[2] Matt. 5, 48.
[3] Matt. 18, 12-14.
[4] John 3, 16.

out before the disciples as not merely credible but as actual, visible to their human eyes. Jesus lived out in our common human life the righteousness and the love which He described as being the life of God.

His perfect holiness they realized best in their own experience. They were driven by His utter sincerity and purity to a new life such as they had never dreamt of. The only alternative was the hypocrisy and deceit of Judas. So with others: the poor unfortunate weeps out her repentance at His feet;[1] Zacchaeus feels he cannot receive Him as his guest until he has turned his life outside in;[2] the robber is driven to confess his evil life even on the cross.[3]

His love they knew in His personal friendship, but it was also written publicly in such actions as no human eyes have seen in any other man. They saw it when He took the children in His arms,[4] when He touched the leper,[5] when He forgave the paralytic,[6] when he dined with the Outcastes,[7] when He fed the hungry,[8] when He opened blind eyes,[9] when He healed the sick,[10] when He restored the lunatic.[11] They saw it in the tears He shed over Jerusalem,[12] in the cleansing of the Temple,[13] in the agony and bloody sweat in Gethsemane,[14] in His meekness when His judges spat in His face,[15] and when He was crowned with thorns and mocked by the soldiers,[16] in His prayer for those who nailed Him to the cross,[17] when He died, saving others, not Himself,[18] and when He rose from the dead to bring us life and immortality.[19]

Thus, to His disciples Jesus proved Himself the very image of the Father of whom He spoke.

C. Jesus, then, was the image of the Father to those who knew Him. How was this used to create a worship of God at

[1] Luke 7, 36–50. [2] Luke 19, 8. [3] Luke 23, 40–41.
[4] Mark 10, 13–16.
[5] Mark 1, 41. [6] Matt. 9, 2. [7] Matt. 9, 10–13.
[8] Matt. 14, 13–21. [9] Mark 10, 46–52. [10] Matt. 8, 16–17.
[11] Mark 5, 1–20. [12] Luke 19, 41–44. [13] Mark 11, 15–18.
[14] Luke 22, 39–44. [15] Matt. 26, 67. [16] Matt. 27, 27–31.
[17] Luke 23, 33–34. [18] Matt. 27, 39–42, 50. [19] 2 Tim. 1, 10.

once purely spiritual and yet vivid and full of emotion? The means employed were two: first, Christ's teaching on the subject of prayer and of our Father's response to our needs; secondly, His own resurrection and ascension.

(*a*) In His time no people worshipped the Father with complete directness. Greeks, Romans, Egyptians, Hindus all either worshipped idols or merely meditated on God as beyond thought and speech, unreachable by prayer or praise. Even the Jew still felt the need of temple and sacrifice in approaching Jahveh.

Jesus taught that all this was unnecessary. The Father is as accessible, as reasonable, as loving as an earthly father:

> Ask and it shall be given you.[1]
>
> If ye then, being evil, know how to give good gifts to your children, how much more shall your heavenly Father give good things to them that ask him?[2]

His personal attentiveness to man's needs is as infinite as His power:

> The hairs of your head are all numbered.[3]
>
> Your heavenly Father knoweth that ye have need of these things.[4]
>
> Be not anxious . . . what ye shall eat; nor yet . . . what ye shall put on. . . . Consider the ravens, that they sow not, neither reap; . . . yet God feedeth them: of how much more value are ye than the birds! . . . Consider the lilies: . . . they toil not, neither do they spin; yet even Solomon in all his glory was not arrayed like one of these. If God doth so clothe the grass in the field, . . . how much more shall he clothe you?[5]

But though this is very beautiful teaching, the ordinary human heart finds it infinitely difficult to believe it with such conviction as to be able to live by it. Hence Jesus sought to bring the truth home to His disciples by His own life. We shall probably understand best if we take His example in two parts.

There is first His own religious life. He lived in human dependence on His Father. His disciples, spending their days

[1] Matt. 7, 7. [2] Matt. 7, 11. [3] Matt. 10, 30.
[4] Matt. 6, 32. [5] Luke 12, 22, 24, 27–8.

with Him, saw how He trusted His Father for everything, turned to Him in prayer in any place and at any time, and had His prayers answered. He lived with His Father, never losing the consciousness of His presence, sometimes seeking eagerly to learn His will, never opposing that will, once He knew it, and always basking in His love.

There is, in the second place, the way Jesus dealt with His disciples and all other men. He showed a most perfect love for every human being, a love which expressed itself in a lively sympathy with every sorrow, every need, and every temptation, and in an eager will to help with every available resource. It was from this point of view that the miracles struck home upon the heart of these simple Galileans: the power displayed in them was as nothing compared with the love that inspired them. They learned to trust Jesus absolutely. They knew He would always be ready to listen to them, to feel for them, and to help them to the uttermost of His power.

(*b*) When Jesus, whom they had learned to think of as the Christ, the Son of God, was suddenly snatched away and crucified, the disciples were overwhelmed with despair. But His resurrection brought Him back to them; and the meaning of the Cross began to dawn upon them.

When He left them, their real Christian experience began. Knowing that Jesus had gone to the Father, they found they were able to live the life of prayer, complete trust, and filial dependence which He had lived. They no longer needed temple, priest, and sacrifice; they needed no ritual, no forms of prayer. Like children, they turned to their heavenly Father with their every want, in joy or sorrow, in prayer or praise, as readily as Jesus used to do. But they did not do it as Jesus did, from immediate knowledge of the Father. Their knowledge of Him was found in Jesus: He was to them the image of God. Through all that they had seen in Him and heard from Him they had been set free from symbol, shadow, and form, so that they approached the Father directly, at any moment, in any place, with the full confidence of sons; and what filled their hearts with the deepest humiliation and the sincerest love and thrilled their worship with the most passionate devotion was the death of the Son of God on the Cross for men. The joy and solemnity of their adoration reached its climax in the eating of the bread and the drinking of the wine that commemorate the broken body and shed blood of our Lord; for it was on the Cross that He proved Himself the perfect image of the ineffable God by revealing to the uttermost the self-sacrifice and love of the Father's heart.

To later generations came the same freedom and the same confidence, mediated also by Jesus. We have not seen nor heard Him; but we have four sketches of Him in the Gospels which enable us to catch His spirit and realize His love. Never did Hindu gaze on the features of the image that he worshipped with such devotion of spirit, with such inexpressible depth of feeling, as the Christian reads the lineaments of his Lord in the Gospels. Jesus actually takes in the Christian's life the place which is held by idols in idolatrous systems. He is effectively the image of God, expressing to us with perfect clearness and convincing power the heart and the will of the Father, and teaching us to live day by day as He lived, in direct personal intercourse with the invisible God, speaking to Him at any moment, and receiving from Him the help, the courage, the guidance, the strength we require for our life as His children on earth. And, as to the disciples, so to us, it is the Cross that fills our worship with passionate humility, reverence, and triumph; for there the Son of God died for us in accordance with the Father's will.

Thus there is a great truth behind all idolatry, the truth that at any moment, in any place, we may have access to the Father's heart, but it is pitiably distorted by idols and mixed up with the most degrading and polluting superstitions. Christ by His life and teaching reveals the Father in His holiness, His self-sacrificing love, and His readiness to answer prayer, thus making idolatry impossible, and enabling us to worship the Father in spirit and in truth.

CHAPTER IX

THE GREAT SECTS

I. A. In the time of the *Ṛigveda*, as we have seen above, the worship of the people was polytheistic. The gods were spoken of as being thirty-three in number; and sacrifices, offerings, and prayers were offered to each in varying circumstances, or to all of them together in one group. Each of the greater gods had his own functions which dictated the time and manner of his worship.

Amongst these Vedic gods we find Vishṇu, who is said to have measured the whole wide earth in three strides. He is a kindly and friendly god who gave the vast expanse of earth with its rich pastures to man for a sure dwelling-place.[1] Another of these gods is Rudra, the god of the destroying storm. He smites the evil-doer with his mighty spear or swift arrow. He is called the best of physicians. His sons and companions are the well-armed Maruts, the gods of the thunder-storm, the heavenly singers.[2]

Neither of these gods occupies a very prominent place in the pantheon of the Veda. Indra and Agni are the greatest gods.

B. During the period of the Brāhmaṇas both Rudra and Vishṇu came into greater prominence than before, especially Vishṇu; but they were still far from being the greatest gods. The highest place is held by a rather elusive figure who is thought of as the Creator and is called Prajāpati or Brahmā.

C. There then came the time when the new Hindu system

[1] Kaegi, 56. [2] Kaegi, 38-39.

of religion and society, as described above in Chapter V, took shape. Very soon thereafter there arose the first speculative philosophy of India, outlined in Chapter VI above. We need say nothing further on that matter here, except to note that, for the subject of this chapter, it is important to realize that there are numerous passages in the early Upanishads which have a distinctly theistic tone. They tend to speak of Brahman as personal, speak of him as the *antaryāmin* or inward ruler of the soul, and represent him as producing and governing the world.[1]

We ought also to notice that in the whole compass of Vedic literature there is no mention of Rāma or Kṛishṇa as divine beings. Indeed Rāma is never mentioned at all. Kṛishṇa occurs once, but only once, and then as a mere man, a Vedic student. The passage is in the *Chhāndogya Upanishad*,[2] and he is called Kṛishṇa Devakīputra. Doubtless this is one of several strands, both historical and imaginative, which were later spun together to make the god.

D. While the new Hindu system and the philosophy of the Ātman were taking shape in the minds of the leaders of the community, the common people continued their religious life and practice as before. The formal acknowledgement of the existence of the one Supreme made no practical difference to their belief in the gods and their worship. Yet other changes were in process. The people tended to divide into sects, each giving prominence to one god, instead of worshipping the whole group of divinities. Vishṇu and Rudra (who had received the more auspicious name Śiva) gradually rose to great favour among the common people, while the Creator remained the chief god of the Brāhmans. The ideas the people had of their gods had meantime become much more definite. They had become more anthropomorphically conceived, and the appearance of each god had been definitely realized, as we have shown above in Chapter VIII. The use

[1] Deussen, 175–176. [2] iii. 17. 6.

of images had also come in, largely as a result of the animistic beliefs and practices of the aboriginal Śūdras, and had coalesced with sectarian religion. It will be remembered that, from the very beginning, temple-worship, unlike the ancient Vedic sacrifices, was open to Śūdras and to women on the same terms as to twice-born men.[1]

E. From this time onward our subject is closely intertwined with the rise of the two epics, the *Mahābhārata* and the *Rāmāyaṇa*.

While the legends which form the basis of the Great Epic are clearly earlier than the story of Rāma, it seems certain that the original heroic poem, the *Rāmāyaṇa* of Vālmīki, is earlier than the *Mahābhārata*. Vālmīki's poem corresponds in general with Books II–VI of our present *Rāmāyaṇa*. The poem is a unity, the work of one hand, apart from interpolations; and we need not doubt that its author was Vālmīki. It is clearly of fairly early date; for it shows no sign whatsoever of the influence of Buddhism, and there is scarcely any trace of the philosophy of the Upanishads in it. Scholars believe that it may be dated about 500 B.C.[2]

The poem is an account of how Rāma, the eldest son of the king of Ayodhyā, came to be banished to the forest by his father, how his young wife Sītā voluntarily went with him, and how she was carried away by the giant Rāvaṇa and finally recovered by Rāma. The work is a heroic poem, and not in any sense a religious book, although the very human hero and his wife are pious and faithful Hindus.

Rāvaṇa, a great Rakshas or demon-giant, by means of his austerities had obtained from Brahmā the great boon that he could not be killed by any god or demon. Relying on this immunity, he behaved with unmeasured insolence and violence, actually going the length of carrying off Sītā, Rāma's wedded wife. But his overweening arrogance met its just punishment. It had never entered his head that a man could overcome him; but this the pious hero did with the blessing of the

[1] See p. 164. [2] Macdonell, 302–309.

gods. Thus, his great boon proved in Rāma's case no protection; for he and his ally Sugrīva were neither gods nor demons, as Hanumān pointed out to Rāvaṇa.

> Thy pride has led thy thoughts astray,
> That fancy not a hand may slay
> The monarch of the giants, screened
> From mortal blow of God and fiend.
> Sugrīva still thy death may be:
> No Yaksha, fiend, or God is he.
> And Rāma from a woman springs,
> The mortal seed of mortal kings.[1]

The plot of the story thus turns on the fact that Rāma is a man and only a man. He and Sītā are ordinary Hindus. There is not a hint that they are incarnate gods. Indeed, the doctrine of incarnations never occurs. Rāma is not even a religious leader. He is a great king, a heroic warrior, a just and pious man, but nothing more. Sītā is a brave and faithful wife, and, like her husband, is careful to fulfil every religious duty. They are as simple-hearted a pair of polytheists as one will meet anywhere. They fulfil their duties to each other, to the gods,[2] to their ancestors, to their family, and to the kingdom. They keep caste, follow the rules of the family, and perform the śrāddha rites.[3] Sītā prays to rivers and trees as they fare onward in their long forest journey.[4]

The poem gives us very vivid glimpses of the beliefs and practices of popular Hinduism before 500 B.C. Brahmā, the Creator, is the greatest of all the gods; next to him are Vishṇu and Śiva; but all the other Vedic divinities are also acknowledged. Brahmā, Vishṇu, and Śiva have now each a traditional form and appearance, and are provided each with his own characteristic weapons and symbols, while we can trace the growth of a good deal of mythology since the close of the *Ṛigveda*. Śiva and his wife Umā both occur frequently. Śiva's bull Nandi,[5] his son Kārttikeya,[6] and his

[1] V. li, Griffith, 422. [2] II. lvi. [3] II. ciii. See p. 84, above.
[4] II. lii, lv. [5] V. l. [6] III. xii.

attendant Nandīśvara [1] are all mentioned. The story of Daksha's sacrifice and Śiva's fierce wrath occurs; [2] and we are also told that the love-god Kāma was consumed by the fierce gleam of Śiva's eye.[3]

Vishṇu occurs still more frequently in the poem, and also his consort Lakshmī. He is occasionally called Nārāyaṇa.[4] He rides on the great man-bird Garuḍa.[5] We hear now and then of Vishṇu's weapons, especially the discus.[6] Śesha, the divine snake which has a thousand heads, is the supporter of the earth,[7] but he is not as yet connected with Vishṇu.[8] We are told that the car of Rāvaṇa, the arch-demon, the enemy of Rāma, was covered with beautiful sculpture, and amongst the carvings was the consort of Vishṇu:

> There Lakshmī, beauty's heavenly queen,
> Wrought by the artist's skill, was seen
> Beside a flower-clad pool to stand
> Holding a lotus in her hand.[9]

We are not astonished to meet with this image of Lakshmī in the original Epic; for it is evident from the early Dharmasūtras that idols were already common in India by 500 B.C. It is also noteworthy that of the earliest representations of Hindu idols in Buddhist sculpture of the second century B.C. the most frequent is Lakshmī.

It was probably during the first half of the fifth century B.C. that the *Mahābhārata* first took shape. Like the *Rāmāyaṇa*, it was a heroic poem with purely human heroes. Kṛishṇa is one of the most prominent characters, but he is in no sense divine. He is king of Dvārikā in Gujarāt and a great warrior, but he is no god. As in the *Rāmāyaṇa*, so here, Brahmā is the greatest god, but Vishṇu and Śiva stand very near him. There is no doctrine of incarnations.

F. Somewhere about 525 B.C. Gautama, the Buddha, began

[1] VI. lx. [2] III. xxiv. [3] III. lvi. [4] IV. lxvii.
[5] VI. lix. [6] III. xxiv. [7] IV. xl.
[8] See below, p. 404. [9] V. vii, Griffith, 400.

to teach. He died about 480 B.C., leaving behind him a body of monastic followers, and also a large company of lay adherents more or less loosely attached to the monastic order. There was no worship of any kind in his system. Indeed, one of the fundamental principles of his teaching is the doctrine of *anatta*, i. e. of the absence of the self or ātman. The idea is that everything is impermanent, that no person or thing has a spiritual self or lasting centre. There is no Ātman or world-soul; man has no soul; and things have no underlying persistent reality.[1] Early Buddhism is thus an atheistic philosophy attempting to supply the consolations of religion. Gautama regarded himself simply as a man who had seen to the centre of things. His teaching is the very antipodes of an incarnation faith. Man stands here in his own strength, declaring that he needs no divine help, that he has within him no instinct that compels him to worship. Buddha, when dying, said to his disciples,

> Be ye a refuge to yourselves. Betake yourselves to no external refuge. Hold fast to the truth as a lamp. Hold fast as a refuge to the truth. Look not for a refuge to any one besides yourselves.[2]

Can we get further away from revelation, incarnation, and worship than this? Yet the main interest of the history of his system during the following centuries is his progressive deification and the rise of his worship.

In one of the Pāli Buddhist Suttas we have an account of the death of the Buddha and the events that followed it.[3] Though it is clear that the narrative is considerably inflated, we need not doubt the main statements of the Sutta, that the body of the great teacher was burned with much pomp, and that portions of his relics were laid in funeral mounds called *stūpas*.

Naturally, his followers went in large numbers to visit these most interesting monuments, and manifested their reverence

[1] Warren, 113. [2] *S.B.E.*, xi. 38.
[3] *Mahāparinibbāna Sutta*, *S. B. E.*, xi.

for the great dead each in his own way. Monks and other well-educated Buddhists would be stirred to brood all the more over his teaching and to emulate his example; but the illiterate layman would express himself by bowing low as he approached, prostrating himself on the ground and circumambulating the stūpa. Places connected with the leading events of Buddha's life were very soon marked by stūpas also, and became places of pilgrimage. These are the beginnings of Buddhist worship.

In each monastery there was a hall where the monks met regularly for confession, and where, at stated times, the laity gathered to receive instruction. These meetings formed another starting-point for Buddhist worship. At a later date a sort of model stūpa was introduced into the hall to stimulate meditation;[1] or a *dharmachakra*,[2] i.e. a wheel representing Buddha's doctrine, or some other symbol of the faith, was set up, and served to move the simple-hearted layman to demonstrations of love and veneration. Doubtless the monks kept themselves in the main to their meditations, and merely smiled indulgently at the growing worship among the laity.

While worship was springing up at the stūpas and in the Buddhist halls, expressions of reverence for the Buddha and for his immediate disciples were coming more and more into use. The use of Bhagavān, Lord, did not suffice. Very soon Buddhists learned to call Buddha by the word used by Hindus for a god, i. e. *Deva*. Then, even that seemed too little, and he was called *Devātideva*, the god above all gods.

Buddhists also gradually came to believe that the truth had been taught by a succession of Buddhas before Gautama, and that in the next age another would arise. At first three Buddhas before Gautama were recognized, then six, then as many as twenty-two. Each of these Buddhas also became an object of fervent adoration.

At first each Buddha was simply a man who, by dint of

[1] e. g. at Kārli. [2] Cunningham, *Stupa of Bharhut*, Pl. XXXI.

perseverance in the right path through innumerable births, had at last come to clear knowledge of the truth, and had thereby risen to a place of spirituality far above all the gods of the Hindu pantheon. But the exaltation of a man to a station religiously far above the gods could not fail to issue in his being placed above the gods in other relations also. He necessarily assumed divine functions. It is thus clear that the lay Buddhist was on the logical path, after all, when he went beyond meditations and exercises and actually worshipped the Buddhas; and the divine titles mentioned above were not only justifiable but inevitable.

The conversion of Aśoka, the great Maurya emperor, to Buddhism about the middle of the third century B.C. was an event of very great importance. He not only helped the religion by his potent example and by his precepts graven on rocks and pillars in every part of his vast dominions; he also erected large numbers of buildings for the various uses of the Buddhist faith.[3] The whole religion must have felt the stimulus of his efforts; and the growth of worship must have been greatly accelerated.

We ought also to notice that at some time after Aśoka, and seemingly in the first century B.C., Buddhists began to use images. It is most remarkable that, in all the beautiful sculpture of the Sāñchī and Bharhut Stūpas, Gautama is never once represented. His footprints, or the wheel of the law, or some other symbol, may be present; or his presence may be merely understood; in any case there is no image. Doubtless the consciousness that he had gone to nirvāṇa was still too strong to permit of his being represented like other men. But, by the Christian era, Buddhists used images freely for Gautama and the other Buddhas. It is the Buddhism of this stage which remains for us practically unchanged in Burma and Ceylon. The evolution of Jain worship seems to have followed precisely the same course; but we need not attempt to trace it here.

[1] V. Smith's *Asoka*, 107.

G. The descendants of Aśoka did not possess his strength; and in 184 B.C. the Śuṅgas seized the throne. The importance of this revolution for our subject lies in this, that the Śuṅgas were Hindus and were as ready to work for Hinduism as Aśoka and his successors had been to help Buddhism. From this point onwards for some time the old religion had a far better chance, and its growth is very marked. Scholars are inclined to believe that Hindu literature was greatly stimulated by Śuṅga patronage.

It is probably to them that we owe the new vigorous religious movement which laid hold of the two heroic poems above described and transformed them into Vishṇuite works. While it is quite impossible as yet to say with certainty that the recasting of the two poems comes from the years immediately following 184 B.C., there can be no doubt that it was about that time that the process of redaction was carried out;[1] and it seems very unlikely that such work would have been done except under the patronage of Hindu kings. We may thus be certain that we are not far wrong when we say that the transformed poems come from the first half of the second century B.C. A new book was prefixed to the *Rāmāyaṇa*, and considerable additions were appended, while much larger additions were made to the *Mahābhārata*. Instead of a poem of eight thousand eight hundred couplets it became a work of twenty thousand couplets.

This fresh outburst of religious literary activity is of the highest interest for our subject. In these rewritten poems the doctrine of incarnations suddenly, and seemingly without the slightest warning, appears in the Hindu faith. In the *Rāmāyaṇa* Rāma is now a partial incarnation of Vishṇu, while in the *Mahābhārata* Kṛishṇa is a partial incarnation of the same god. It must be carefully noted that there is no suggestion in either poem at this time that Vishṇu is the supreme and only God. In both poems Brahmā, Vishṇu, and Śiva are now

[1] Macdonell, 286, 309; Hopkins, *Great Epic*, 399.

practically on a level, the greatest gods of the Hindu pantheon, but that is all.

We must here note carefully the difference between ordinary man-worship and the incarnation doctrine. When the Hindu sees something very extraordinary in a man or an animal, or even in a thing, he is inclined to worship. He bows down in reverence, or it may be in fear, before that which strikes him as beyond the ordinary. Thus far the tendency is on a level with what happens among simple people all over the world. But the man who first called Kṛishṇa an *avatāra* of Vishṇu meant to say that a portion of the energy of the great heavenly god Vishṇu had descended to earth and had been born as a man. The early Hindus believed, as we have seen, that Vishṇu was accustomed to come to earth to enjoy the sacrifices offered to him; but never before had any Hindu thought of a part of the energy of a celestial god being born as a man and living a human life.

Nor is that all. The belief is that Vishṇu has been twice incarnate, once as Rāma and once as Kṛishṇa. Rāma is held to have lived at a much earlier date than Kṛishṇa; so that Vishṇu is thought of as having become in part incarnate at two distinct times.

It is not yet possible to say what led to the appearance of this doctrine. There was nothing precisely like it in Buddhism at the time, so far as we know. The utmost that can be said is that Buddhism had already formed, as we have seen above, the idea of a succession of supreme teachers who were worshipped and credited with divine powers; and the rise of that worship was contemporaneous with the rise of the worship of Rāma and Kṛishṇa. But the recognition of two deified men as repeated incarnations of a heavenly god who had been adored for many centuries is a different idea, and was the creation of the Vishṇuite sect. The one point that is clear is this, that the Hindu doctrine is absolutely new and appears suddenly in the history. Indian writers frequently assert that incarnations are to be found in Vedic literature, but that is a complete mistake. There are stories in Vedic literature which were turned into incarnation stories in the early Christian centuries; but within the whole compass of Vedic literature there is no reference to the doctrine.

Megasthenes, the Seleucid ambassador at the Court of Chandragupta about 300 B.C., tells us that Hercules was worshipped at Methora and Kleisobora. This probably means that Kṛishṇa was already worshipped as a god at Mathurā and a town, now unknown, called then Kṛishṇapur. If that is so, we have probably in this fact an intermediate step between the human hero and the incarnation of Vishṇu; but we dare not build very much on such an uncertain foundation.

A sketch of the theology of these additions to the *Rāmāyaṇa* will be useful for our subject. Brahmā is still the Creator and the great Father. He constantly comes forward as the adviser and comforter of the gods. He has the epithet, the Self-existent;[1] and he is already called 'four-faced';[2] so that we may be certain his traditional image was already common.

Śiva and his consort Umā are recognized as very great. He is still now and then called Rudra,[3] but much more frequently he is called Śiva (the kindly one), Mahādeva (the great god), Paśupati (lord of flocks), Bhagavān (the blessed one), or Śaṅkara (the beneficent).[4] He is the three-eyed god.[5] We are told how he slew the giant Tripura.[6] The story of his drinking the poison at the churning of the ocean of milk is told in detail; and he is spoken of as the god whose neck is stained with blue as the result of that draught of venom.[7] The river Ganges is said to flow down from heaven upon his head and thence to fall down to earth.[8] He carries the trident,[9] and is accompanied by his bull, but there seems to be no mention as yet of the liṅga.[10]

Vishṇu and his consort Lakshmī are very prominent indeed in the first and last books of our Epic. He is called Vāsudeva,[11]

[1] I. xvi. [2] I. ii. [3] I. xlv. [4] I. xlv.
[5] I. lxxv. [6] I. lxxv. [7] I. lxxv. [8] I. xliv.
[9] I. xliii. [10] See p. 310. [11] I. xli.

Nārāyaṇa,[1] and Hrishikeśa (the real meaning of all three is uncertain), Bhagavān (blessed), Prabhu (lord), Jagatpati (lord of the world), Purushottama (best spirit), and Hari (saviour). He is frequently spoken of as having slain the demon Madhu;[2] his exploits at the churning of the ocean are described; and we are told how, in the form of Kapila, he killed the sixty thousand sons of Sagara.[3] He is vividly described as carrying the shell, mace, and discus, as having four arms, as brilliantly bright, and as wearing saffron robes.[4]

The theology here is still completely polytheistic. Vishṇu is not yet raised above all others as the one spiritual Reality. Brahmā, Vishṇu, and Śiva are practically on a level; and each is still materialistically conceived as in the earlier theology. Of one of the great sacrifices we are told

> Now all the gods had gathered there,
> Each one for his allotted share;[5]

In one very striking passage Vishṇu and Śiva are spoken of as the great rivals. They meet in battle; Śiva is overcome;

> And gods and heavenly sages thence
> To Vishṇu gave pre-eminence.[6]

In another passage Vishṇu, addressing Śiva, calls him 'the first-born of the gods'.[7]

Kṛishṇa does not occur at all in these additions. Rāma is an incarnation of half the energy of Vishṇu, the other half being subdivided and incarnated as his three brothers. The fractions are given as $\frac{1}{2}$, $\frac{1}{4}$, $\frac{1}{8}$, $\frac{1}{8}$.[8] The reason given for the incarnation of Vishṇu in Rāma and his three brothers is that the giant Rāvaṇa is behaving in such a way as to strike terror into the hearts of the gods. Vishṇu must become incarnate as a man in order to kill Rāvaṇa, who is invulnerable by god or demon. Here is the appeal of the gods to the Creator. Was ever anything more clearly polytheistic written?

[1] I. xiv.
[2] I. xli.
[3] I. xli.
[4] I. xiv, xlv.
[5] I. xiv, Griffith, 25.
[6] I. lxxv, Griffith, 86.
[7] I. xlv.
[8] I. xv, xix.

O Brahmā, mighty by thy grace,
Rāvan, who rules the giant race,
Torments us in his senseless pride,
And penance-loving saints beside.
That lord of giants fierce and fell
Scourges the earth and heaven and hell.
Mad with thy boon, his impious rage
Smites saint and bard and god and sage.
The sun himself withholds his glow,
The wind in fear forbears to blow;
The fire restrains his wonted heat
Where stand the dreaded Rāvan's feet;
And, necklaced with the wandering wave,
The sea before him fears to rave.
Kuvera's self in sad defeat
Is driven from his blissful seat.
We see, we feel the giant's might,
And woe comes o'er us and affright.
To thee, O Lord, thy suppliants pray
To find some cure this plague to stay.[1]

The theology of the second stage of the *Mahābhārata* is precisely similar. Brahmā, Śiva, and Vishṇu are on an equality, and Kṛishṇa is a partial incarnation of Vishṇu.[2]

Several other scraps of evidence which are available fall in perfectly with the facts revealed in the Epics. The statement of Megasthenes has been already quoted. Patañjali, about 150 B.C., refers to plays which were representations of the slaying of Kaṁsa and the binding of Bali, episodes in the Kṛishṇa myth.[3] It is probable that, like the Greek drama, the Hindu drama was at first a religious performance, in which case these plays are further evidence of the cult of Kṛishṇa. There are also inscriptions which show that Saṁkarshaṇa[4] and Vāsudeva were worshipped in the second and first centuries B.C., and that the latter was called Bhagavān, while his worshipper might call himself a Bhāgavata. All this fits in well with what we have learnt of the sectarian worships

[1] I. xiv, Griffith, 25.
[2] *Great Epic*, 397–398.
[3] *E. R. E.*, iv. 887.
[4] See pp. 378–379 below.

before the birth of Christ. Vāsudeva was a title of Vishṇu; and he, Śiva, Indra, Brahmā, and even Gautama the Buddha and Mahāvīra the Jina, were honoured with the title Bhagavān. Another inscription shows that the worshipper who addressed Śiva as Bhagavān was also accustomed to call himself a Bhāgavata.[1]

II. As we have seen above,[2] the chief evidence of the activity of the school of the Vedānta in the five centuries preceding the Christian era that has survived to our day is a small group of Upanishads in verse, the *Kāṭhaka*, *Īśā*, *Śvetāśvatara*, *Muṇḍaka*, and *Mahānārāyaṇa Upanishads*. These are of interest for this chapter because of the theistic tone of the theology of the first three. They show that there were thinkers in the Vedānta school during those centuries who held that Brahman was a personal God. They used the words Deva, Bhagavān, Īśa, Īśāna of him, and spoke of his grace. In *Śvetāśvatara*,[3] the bhakti or adoring devotion of the worshipper is mentioned. The same work identifies Brahman with Rudra, and applies to him the adjective *śiva*, gracious.[4] The word does not seem to be used as a proper name. Another characteristic of later Hinduism also appears here, the doctrine that the *guru*, the philosophic teacher, is to be worshipped as God.[5] It is most important to realize that these theistic Upanishads do not imply the existence of a theistic sect with a priesthood and a worship, but merely the presence of theistic thinkers within the schools of the Vedānta.

A. Towards the Christian era new movements of thought make their appearance among educated Indian laymen. They were attracted by the philosophies, both as systems of thought and as means of reaching emancipation. But as these philosophies all indicated the monastic life as the road to emancipation, the layman found himself in a grave difficulty as soon as he began to think of seeking release for himself.

[1] *Indian Antiquary*, Nov., 1912. For a Bhāgavata sect who revere both Śiva and Vishṇu, see *Madhva*, 12.
[2] Above, p. 241. [3] vi. 23. [4] iii. 2–11. [5] vi. 23.

B. A new type of teaching then arose, probably suggested by Buddhist thought. Gautama taught his monks that desire was the great enemy: desire leads to action and action to renewed existence. Thus Buddhist discipline was framed with the object of destroying desire. Now the Hindu monk, as we have seen, aimed at complete inaction; and, with that in view, laid aside, by a great act of surrender, every detail of Hindu life, and lived thereafter as a man whose work was done, outside Hindu society. But the new thought distinguished from all other actions the acts prescribed in Scripture for the Hindu householder; and distinguished also between these actions and the rewards connected with them. Every act prescribed in Hindu law brings its own proper reward,[1] like the fifth commandment of the Decalogue. The idea was that these actions, being ordained in Scripture, must be so pure in themselves that the mere doing of them would not form karma and lead to rebirth, but that the doing of them with a desire for the rewards which arise from them as fruit necessarily formed karma and led to rebirth. Hence the new precept was, Lay aside all desire for the fruits of prescribed actions, but do these actions themselves, merely because they are ordained. In this way, the teaching ran, the layman may remain a householder and do all his duties in the family, in caste and in religion, and may yet win emancipation as truly as the monk. The phrases in which this idea is expressed are, 'Do your prescribed duties without attachment to the fruits of action'; or, more briefly, 'Do your duties without attachment.' This type of action was called *nishkāma karma*, 'desireless action,' *nivṛitti karma*, 'restraint action,' *karma-yoga*, 'the yoking of action.' These ideas and phrases occur in the *Gītā*,[2] the Laws of Manu,[3] the *Mahābhārata*,[4] and later literature; and the same thought is expressed in the great Buddhist work, the *Mahāyāna Śraddhotpāda Śāstra* of Aśvaghosha by the phrase 'spontaneity of action'.[5]

[1] *S. B. E.*, xlviii. 330. [2] See below, p. 371. [3] xii. 89.
[4] xiii. 54. [5] Suzuki, 94.

C. But the effect produced on laymen by the theology of the Vedānta is of even greater importance. How that philosophy gained its influence we do not know. Perhaps the fact that it was taught in the Brāhmanical schools, through which the flower of the twice-born youth passed, gave it an advantage over other systems. Whatever may have been the cause, it is clear that during the first century A. D. the leading conceptions of the Vedānta about God, caught up by the time-spirit, pressed very seriously on the best minds. The conviction that behind the phenomena of the world there exists one great spiritual Reality, and the conclusion which necessarily follows therefrom, that the ordinary gods are phenomenal, mortal, and unreal, became accepted as axioms by thinking men. The identification of the human spirit with the divine did not grip men so strongly; yet it was not without influence.

For those laymen who were ready to accept all the gods as partial manifestations of the invisible and unknowable Reality, the Vedānta was a help to thought, and also to religion; but, in so far as the old Vedic pantheon had decayed, and men's faith tended to fasten with greater courage and vividness on Vishṇu or Śiva, a grave difficulty arose. A man whose living religion centred altogether, say, in Vishṇu, and who yet felt the force of the great ideas of the Vedānta, was pulled two ways at once. He could not lay aside the philosophy, for it appealed to him as reasonable. He could not give up Vishṇu, for apart from him he had no real religion for himself and his family.

The difficulty was felt in Buddhist as well as in Hindu circles, but in a different way. Gautama taught that there was no spiritual reality behind phenomena.[1] Hence the thoughtful Buddhist found his reverence for Gautama severely strained by the growing conviction that there is a spiritual Existence immanent in the universe.

[1] *Supra*, p. 356.

The result of the crisis was that the two great Hindu sects, viz. the Vishṇuite and the Śivaite, and two distinct groups of Buddhists drew in and amalgamated with their old doctrine the main ideas of the Vedānta philosophy with regard to God, and taught that the layman could reach emancipation without becoming a monk. The new Vishṇuite teaching appears first in the *Bhagavadgītā*, and the Śivaite in the *Mahābhārata*, while the two types of Neo-Buddhist doctrine are found in the *Saddharma Puṇḍarīka* and in Aśvaghosha's *Mahāyāna Śraddhotpāda Śāstra*.[1]

These new doctrines fall into two groups, according as they construe the Supreme as personal or impersonal. The system of Aśvaghosha is impersonal in its theology, while the other three are personal. Aśvaghosha, and Nāgārjuna after him, posit the existence of the Absolute, eternal, immutable, unknowable, impersonal; and they represent the Buddhas as its embodiments.

Vishṇuites, Śivaites, and the author of the *Saddharma Puṇḍarīka*, on the other hand, declare the Supreme to be personal. This common faith, however, did not unite them; for the Vishṇuites identified Brahman with Vishṇu; the Śivaites identified him with Śiva; while the Buddhist identified him with Gautama, the Buddha.

D. But we must here note another important development of doctrine. We have seen that in the second century B.C. Rāma and Kṛishṇa were declared to be each a fractional incarnation of Vishṇu. When Vishṇu was identified with Brahman, the incarnation doctrine was also altered. Kṛishṇa and Rāma were declared to be full incarnations of Vishṇu. We thus reach a pair of double equations:

Kṛishṇa = Vishṇu = Brahman
Rāma = Vishṇu = Brahman.

Śivaites did not accept the doctrine of incarnations. The theophanies of Śiva correspond in their system. Both groups

[1] The influence extended to other schools as well. Iyengar's *Outlines*, 248.

of Buddhists, however, adopted the Hindu doctrine of *avatāras,* Aśvaghosha teaching that Gautama and the other Buddhas are 'unfoldings'[1] of 'the real Reality',[2] the *Saddharma Puṇḍarīka* declaring that Gautama is the one God, spiritual, personal, supreme, and that he becomes incarnate from time to time. Thus the system of the *Saddharma Puṇḍarīka* is precisely parallel to Vishṇuite teaching as given in the *Bhagavadgītā.* Gautama takes the place of Vishṇu.

E. We had better now deal briefly with the new systems in order. Readers will note how distinctly the main lines of the theology of the Vedānta reappear. The Supreme is one, spiritual, real. He is also the source of all things, but he has no purpose in view, and does not act: his activity in the world is magic or play, *māyā* or *līlā.*[3] He is beyond the range of thought and speech, and thus cannot reveal himself to man nor receive prayer nor worship. He is therefore revealed either by way of manifestation (by the old gods), by personal theophany, or by incarnations.

1. We begin with Aśvaghosha, as his impersonal theology stands so near Śaṅkara's system. In order that readers may see how close the resemblance is, we quote a few sentences and phrases:

(The system for all.)

That all beings may rid themselves of doubt, become free from evil attachment, and, by the awakening of faith, inherit Buddha-seeds, I write this discourse.[4]

(The Absolute.)

The oneness of the totality of things.

The oneness of the universe that has no second.

Completely set apart from the attributes of all things unreal.

The real reality; self-existent.

[1] Suzuki, 70. [2] Ib., 59.
[3] See above, p. 246, and below, p. 406. [4] Suzuki, 47.

(Ignorance.)

All modes of consciousness and mentation are mere products of ignorance.

(Illusion.)

All things and conditions in the phenomenal world, hypostatized and established only through ignorance and subjectivity on the part of all beings, have no more reality than the images in a mirror.

(The Buddhas.)

It transforms and unfolds itself . . . in the form of a Tathāgata.

All Tathāgatas are the Dharmakāya (i. e. the Absolute) itself.[1]

What a very striking development of belief this is in the system of Gautama, who taught most distinctly that there is no inner essence or self of things.[2] Here, then, the Absolute is impersonal, and the Buddhas are his incarnations.

2. In the *Saddharma Puṇḍarīka* Buddha is the Supreme, but is personal, and he becomes incarnate from time to time. Here are some of the phrases: Buddha is the Self-existent,[3] the Supreme Spirit,[4] the Great Father,[5] the World-Father,[6] the Ruler of the triple world,[7] the Creator,[8] the Destroyer,[9] the Father and the Protector of all creatures,[10] the Great Physician.[11] He is Everlasting,[12] All-knowing,[13] All-seeing.[14] Like Kṛishṇa he is indifferent,[15] yet compassionate.[16]

The world is illusion (*māyā*):[17] for the Buddha has created it in sport (*līlā*),[18] by his magic power (*māyā*).[19] He is not at rest;[20] for he is ever active; yet he is always at rest,[21] for he rules himself,[22] and his activity is sport.

He did not reach enlightenment at Buddh-Gayā, but hundreds of millions of ages before then;[23] and the measure of his life will yet contain countless myriads of ages.[24] He is repeatedly born in the world of the living.[25] When men

[1] Suzuki, 55, 116, 59, 59, 67, 77, 70, 99. [2] See above, p. 356.
[3] *S. B. E.*, xxi. 46, 217, 309. [4] 44. [5] 76. [6] 309.
[7] 275. [8] 290, 300, 308. [9] 122. [10] 81, 310.
[11] 310. [12] 302, 309. [13] 120, 291. [14] 120.
[15] 124, 125, 128. [16] 54, 76. [17] 136. [18] 291. [19] 76.
[20] 310. [21] 120. [22] 307. [23] 299, 300, 307. [24] 302.
[25] 124, 308.

become unbelieving, unwise, ignorant, careless, fond of sensual pleasures, and from thoughtlessness run into misfortune, he appears in this world to save.[1] When he passes away, he does not become extinct, but only makes a show of extinction on behalf of those who need help and teaching.[2]

The essence of salvation is deliverance, absence of passion, knowledge of the All-knowing.[3] He proclaims the law to men of all castes without distinction.[4] All may reach enlightenment and final release through faith in the Buddha and devotion towards him.[5] Emancipation is thus brought within reach of the layman. Those who worship any Buddhist symbol or relic, were it but with a flower, will reap endless benefit.[6] A story is told of a Bodhisattva who burnt his own body out of devotion to the Buddha,[7] and young men and young women are recommended to burn a finger, a toe, or a whole limb at a Buddhist shrine, in order to win great merit.[8] This reversion to ancient *tapas* is very extraordinary in Buddhism.[9]

The Buddha does not show his proper being when he is in the world.[10] He reveals his true nature only to saintly souls.[11] So, in the course of the narrative of the *Saddharma Puṇḍarīka* he appears in indescribable glory to countless multitudes of his followers,[12] just as Kṛishṇa does in the *Gītā*.[13]

Thus we do not wonder that he is represented as saying, 'Being perfectly at rest, I lead others to rest. Come to me, ye gods and men!' nor do we wonder at the stately worship of the Mahāyāna temple.

3. We now come to Vaishṇava[14] theology as we find it in the *Bhagavadgītā*. The *Gītā* cannot be understood unless we realize that in it the Vedānta philosophy and emancipation

[1] 124, 310. [2] 302. [3] 121. [4] 124-125.
[5] 49-53, 99, 124-128, 158, 379, 385. [6] 50-51. [7] 379.
[8] 385. [9] See p. 258, above. [10] 308. [11] 223, 225, 307, 321.
[12] 236-237. [13] Book xi.
[14] Vaishṇava and Śaiva are very convenient Sanskrit adjectives for Vishṇuite and Sivaite.

are brought within reach of the ordinary Vaishṇava layman. From beginning to end the *Gītā* shows the keenest interest in the position, the life, the worship, and the salvation of the householder and his wife.[1] The interlocutor of the incarnate God is Arjuna, a Kshatriya layman. Kṛishṇa says that the teaching of the *Gītā* brings emancipation within the reach of women and Śūdras.[2] This is most significant; for the old Vedānta was open only to men, and only to men of the three twice-born castes;[3] while in Vaishṇava, as in other temples, Śūdras and women were as welcome as twice-born men.[4] Again, throughout the *Gītā*, inaction, which is the ideal of the monk of the Vedānta, is condemned; action, which is the only life possible to the layman, is praised;[5] and the new theory of emancipation through karma-yoga explained above is elaborately set forth.[6] Amongst the numerous passages which show a special interest in laymen we must reckon the very noteworthy verses in the third book,[7] where the enlightened man is urged not to disturb the minds of ordinary householders by speaking to them of the value of inaction. Not only is the incarnation doctrine used throughout the poem, but in several passages we are shown the value of the ordinary worship of the four-handed human form of Kṛishṇa in Vaishṇava temples.[8] The *Gītā* is the layman's Upanishad.

Kṛishṇa is very fully dealt with. He is Vishṇu[9] and Vāsudeva.[10] He is also *Brahman*,[11] *the Ātman*,[12] *Tat*[13] (that), *Purushottama*[14] (the supreme Spirit), and is unborn,[15] eternal,[16] without beginning,[17] without end,[18] imperishable,[19] unknowable,[20] omniscient,[21] and omnipotent.[22] He is Father of this universe, Mother, Ordainer, Grandsire,[23] the Way, the

[1] vi. 37–44; vii. 21; viii. 5; ix. 23–26.
[2] ix. 32.
[3] See above, p. 234.
[4] See above, pp. 164, 327–328.
[5] iii. 3–9, 19; xviii. 2–11, 56.
[6] Especially in Books iii and xviii.
[7] 26–29.
[8] xi. 46, 51; ix. 26.
[9] x. 21; xi. 24, 30.
[10] vii. 19; x. 37; xi. 50; xviii. 74.
[11] vii. 29; viii. 3–4; x. 12.
[12] x. 20; iv. 6.
[13] xi. 37.
[14] viii. 1; x. 15; xi. 3; xv. 18.
[15] iv. 6; vii. 25; x. 3, 12.
[16] x. 12.
[17] x. 3.
[18] xi. 37.
[19] xi. 18, 37.
[20] vii. 26; x. 2, 14.
[21] vii. 26.
[22] vii. 7; x. 40.
[23] ix. 17.

Supporter, the Lord, the Witness, the Dwelling-place, the Refuge, the Friend, the Origin, the Dissolution, the undecaying Seed.[1]

He is the source of the Universe.[2] He creates and causes all things to revolve as on a merry-go-round by means of his magic, i.e. *māyā*.[3] He creates the castes;[4] is the source of the Veda,[5] and the enjoyer of sacrifice.[6] But, while Kṛishṇa is thus the supreme power in the universe,[7] he is altogether without personal interest in the activity therein displayed;[8] he sits unconcerned,[9] always engaged in action,[10] yet controlling his own nature,[11] and therefore actionless and not bound by the results of his action.[12]

The doctrine of incarnations had better be given in the words of the text:

> Though birthless and unchanging of essence, and though lord of born beings, yet in My sway over the Nature that is Mine own I come into birth by my own Magic (*Māyā*).
>
> For whensoever the Law fails and lawlessness uprises, O thou of Bharata's race, then do I bring Myself to bodied birth.
>
> To guard the righteous, to destroy evil-doers, to establish the Law, I come into birth age after age.[13]

Since all the gods come from Kṛishṇa,[14] and since he is in the last resort the sole Reality,[15] worship offered to other gods is in a sense offered to him.[16] He accepts it and rewards it.[17] Yet the highest blessings fall only to those who recognize him directly.[18] Men may win release and immortality by Knowledge, by Action,[19] or by Devotion (*bhakti*) towards Kṛishṇa.[20] The value of personal trust in Kṛishṇa and fervent devotion (*bhakti*) towards him is strongly emphasized:

> If one of earnest spirit set before Me with devotion a leaf, a flower, fruit, or water, I enjoy this offering of devotion.[21]

[1] ix. 18. [2] vii. 6. [3] xviii. 61. [4] iv. 13.
[5] xv. 15. [6] ix. 24. [7] ix. 10, 17–18. [8] iv. 14. [9] ix. 9.
[10] iii. 22–24. [11] ix. 8. [12] iv. 14; ix. 9. [13] iv. 6–8.
[14] x. 2. [15] x. 1–3, 20. [16] ix. 23. [17] vii. 21–22.
[18] ix. 22; x. 7–11. [19] xii. 12.
[20] ix. 26–34; vi. 47; xi. 54; xii. 2. [21] ix. 26.

> Have thy mind on Me, thy devotion toward Me, thy sacrifice to Me, do homage to Me. Thus guiding thyself, given over to Me, so to Me shalt thou come.[1]

In the original Vedānta a man realizes his own identity with Brahman and thus reaches deathlessness and peace; but this identification leaves little room for personal feeling and life. But when the Supreme was recognized as personal, a personal immortality became possible. In the *Gītā* the soul is still too completely identified with God to allow the new and richer idea to arise in fullness, but there is an approach to it. The immortality which a man may win through karma-yoga and devotion to Kṛishṇa tends to be a personal immortality. The devotee goes to Kṛishṇa and abides in Kṛishṇa. Perhaps the most advanced expression is,

> On me then set thy mind, in me let thine understanding dwell; so shalt thou assuredly abide afterward in me.[2]

We have already pointed out that the teaching which encouraged the householder to seek emancipation by doing all his prescribed duties as a Hindu without any desire for the rewards connected therewith is adopted in the *Gītā*. We have now to note that the same poem carries this teaching one step farther, bidding the layman surrender all these actions to Kṛishṇa, i.e. do the actions and surrender the fruits to Kṛishṇa.[3] In other passages this type of desireless action is represented as a sacrifice to Kṛishṇa.[4] The original form of the doctrine and this form modified by a personal theology occur in the *Gītā* side by side.

It is of importance to note that the *Gītā* teaches in the clearest way possible that every Hindu should keep all the rules of Hinduism with the utmost strictness. Family duties, caste duties, and the laws of worship must all be kept with care.[5] No one must neglect ordained action. This is finally summed up in a verse in which the Dharmaśāstras are set up as the rule of conduct:

[1] ix. 34. Cf. xi. 54. [2] xii. 8. [3] iii. 30; xii. 16.
[4] ix. 27. [5] i. 40–44; iii. 8; v. 11; xviii. 5–7, 45, 47–48, 56.

> Therefore, realizing the *śāstra* to be the standard for determining right and wrong, thou should'st do here the works specified in the ordinances of the *śāstra*.[1]

The *Gītā* is in the form of a dialogue between Kṛishṇa and his warrior-friend Arjuna. When Arjuna has realized the idea that Kṛishṇa is not only divine but the absolute One, the Supporter of the world and all the gods, he asks Kṛishṇa to show him his supreme form. This Kṛishṇa does, manifesting himself as a glorious being of surpassing brilliancy, in which are contained all the worlds, all the gods, all beings of every name.[2] Arjuna worships him with lowly obeisance and faltering voice, and expresses his joy in having seen the indescribable glory,[3] but begs Kṛishṇa to return to his old four-armed shape, with diadem, discus, and mace.[4]

Rāma does not occur in the *Gītā* at all, but a passage interpolated into the sixth book of the *Rāmāyaṇa*[5] shows us that the theology which we find applied to Kṛishṇa in the *Gītā* was also applied to Rāma. He is equated with Vishṇu; and Vishṇu is called the true, eternal, undecaying Brahman. He is incomprehensible, beyond the reach of human sense, yet visible in all material things. We can, thus, trace within the *Rāmāyaṇa* itself the complete growth of the Rāma-myth. In the centre of the poem he is a man, and only a man. In the first book he is an incarnation of half the energy of Vishṇu. Here he is a full incarnation. But for a full delineation of Rāma as the incarnation of the Supreme we must turn to the Hindī poet Tulsī Dās.

4. The doctrine that Brahman is personal and identical with Śiva, the beginnings of which we found in the *Śvetāśvatara Upanishad*, first appears as the teaching of the Śaiva sect in the *Mahābhārata*; but, as there is no single document in the Epic that can be used for Śivaite theology as the *Gītā* can be used for Vishṇuite teaching, we may as well illustrate it from a work that is purely Śaiva, the *Tiru-vāchakam*

[1] xvi. 24. See above, p. 218. [2] xi. 1–13. [3] xi. 14–44.
[4] xi. 44–45. [5] Canto cxix.

of Māṇikka Vāchakar, a collection of Tamil hymns belonging to the tenth century. The following lines will show how completely the theology of the Vedānta has been absorbed. The italicized phrases are very noteworthy.

See Him the First! see Him the Whole!
See Him, the Infinite! See Him, the Ancient One!
See Him, the Great One Whom Brahmā and Vishṇu saw not!
See Him, the Wonderful! See, the Manifold!
See Him, the Ancient One, *transcending words!*
See, *He dwells afar where human thought goes not!*
See, He extends throughout the wide extended earth!
See Him, more subtile than an atom small!
See Him, the Lord Whom all may gain!
See, Śiva *Whom the gods know not!*[1]

The Śivaite denies that God is ever born of a woman,[2] but he believes that Śiva has manifested himself in human form innumerable times and still does so.[3] Here are a few lines from the same Tamil work:

Assuming diverse forms, and diverse habitudes,
As hundreds of hundreds of thousands of natures,
Īśan, Lord of the bull, that the world might be saved,—
He and the Lady, His partner,—came in grace.

. . . .

Becoming a Brāhman, graciously making me His own,
He showed a magic illusion.
Coming to Madura, the city great and fair,
He became a horse's groom.
And therein too, for the female devotee
He condescended to carry earth,
In Uttara-kōśa-maṅgai abiding,
He showed His special form.
In Pūvaṇam he vouchsafed to appear in beauty,
And showed His ancient spotless form.
In Vāthavūr he came sweetly gracious
And caused the sound of His tinkling anklets to be heard.[4]

F. 1. Probably about the very time when the sects, Buddhist and Hindu, adopted the theology of the Vedānta, Vedāntists

[1] Pope, 20–21. [2] *Śaiva Siddhānta*, 242, 299. [3] Ib. 299.
[4] Pope, 9–11.

began to combine the leading elements of the Sāṇkhya theory of the evolution of the universe with the Vedāntic conception of God and the soul. The Vishṇuite party were able to accept the whole almost without change;[1] Śivaites found a little modification necessary; while in the central school of the Vedānta a good deal of alteration was introduced.[2]

2. The theistic elements in the prose Upanishads and the more developed theism of the verse treatises show that the school has never been without theistic thinkers. When the great crisis occurred, the leaders of the Vaishṇava and Śaiva sects probably sought the help of theistic sympathizers within the school for the formulation of their new theology.

It seems most probable that the *Gītā* was produced within the school of the Vedānta. It appears to be an old verse Upanishad redacted and enlarged by some authoritative Vedāntī, in view of the needs of the times, to form a standard manual of Vaishṇava theology. This reading of the history seems to be the best way to account for all the facts. There is not merely the contemporaneous emergence of Vedāntic forms of theology in four sects. There is the strange fact that the *Bhagavadgītā*, which is a thoroughly sectarian work, recognizing Vishṇu as identical with Brahman and Kṛishṇa as his full avatāra, is not only accepted as a piece of orthodox Vedāntism, but is one of three books which form the canon of the school.[3] There is the other notable fact, that Śivaites and Vishṇuites regard themselves as Vedāntists as truly as the followers of Śaṅkara, and accept the whole canon as inspired. That is the reason why every Śivaite or Vishṇuite sect of importance has a commentary of its own upon the *Vedānta-sūtras*, expounding that old manual in accordance with its own views. It is of great interest to note that the *Gītā*, which makes Vishṇu the Supreme, and teaches the doctrine of incarnation, is accepted as an inspired work by Śivaites and is much used by them, though they refuse to recognize Vishṇu as Brahman and

[1] *Infra*, pp. 378–379. [2] *Supra*, p. 245. [3] *Supra*, pp. 242–243.

repudiate the doctrine of incarnation. But the most significant fact of all is this, that Śaṅkara, the greatest of all Vedāntists, is driven by the canonical authority of the *Gītā* to accept Kṛishṇa as an avatāra of Brahman.[1] How are we to account for these startling facts? If the *Gītā* was written within the school of the Vedānta, and accepted as authoritative in the school from the outset, then every other fact falls naturally into its place.

It is also noticeable that a work of such authority as the *Gītā* is—called 'the essence of all the Upanishads', and venerated almost as much as the greatest of them—should be called *smṛiti* and not *śruti*. The reason is that Śūdras and women were not allowed to hear *śruti*;[2] and the *Gītā* is the layman's Upanishad, intended for all caste Hindus.[3]

III. The history of later centuries must now be dealt with.

A. There is a passage in the *Mahābhārata* which requires special notice, because it gives us a glimpse of later Vishṇuite theology. It is the famous passage in the *Śānti Parvan* which contains the description of Nārada's visit to the White Island, where he saw the inhabitants worshipping Vishṇu, and had a vision of the god himself. Many have

[1] See below, pp. 389–390. [2] See p. 164.

[3] The writer regrets very much to be unable to follow Sir George Grierson, Sir R. G. Bhandarkar, and other honoured scholars in the theory that Bhāgavata theism had existed many centuries before the *Gītā* was written. It is only because the evidence in favour of the theory adopted in the text seems conclusive that it has been accepted. That there was theistic thought in the schools of the Vedānta in the centuries before our era is absolutely clear; but the theory, that in the early centuries the Vaishṇava sect held a theistic theology such as is found in the *Gītā* and in the *Śānti Parvan*, seems to rest on the assumption that the mere occurrence of the words Bhagavān, Bhāgavata, Vāsudeva in inscriptions proves that those who used them in the second, third, or fourth century before Christ held the beliefs which were associated with these names several centuries later. So far as existing records go, the right conclusion seems to be very different. Polytheistic Vaishṇavism we know from the *Rāmāyaṇa*; theistic Vaishṇavism filled with the Vedānta we know from the *Gītā*: where do we find a theistic Vaishṇavism that is not Vedāntic? We need not fix a definite date for the change: the crucial point which it seems necessary to grant is that it was the acceptance of the theology of the Vedānta that transformed polytheistic Vaishṇavism into a theism.

thought that the story contains reminiscences of Christian influence exerted on Vishṇuism. It would be most unwise to say that no such influence reached, or could have reached, Vishṇuites; for, from the first century onward, Christianity flowed, in varying channels and varying strength, into the lands adjoining India and into India itself; but, on the other hand, it is surely only candid to say that, if this passage is an echo of the acceptance of Christian ideas, then they must have been so modified as to make it impossible to put one's finger on a single thing that is clearly and decisively Christian in origin. So we need not discuss the question further here.

Vishṇuites are here called Bhāgavatas, i.e. worshippers of Bhagavān, the Lord, as they are in an early inscription. The system and the ritual are called *Pāñcharātra* and *Sātvata*, but the origin of these names has not yet been satisfactorily made out. We are told that the seven Ṛishis, who are known as the Chitraśikhandins, composed the supreme scripture, clearly a manual of Pāñcharatra theology, ritual, and law. This must refer to the original work on which the many existing Pāñcharatra Saṁhitās[1] depend. The chief advance in belief which the passage reveals is the appearance of the doctrine of *vyūha* or Expansion. We had better quote the most important lines. Vāsudeva, i.e. Vishṇu, is made to say,

> That which is my fourth form creates the indestructible Śesha. The Śesha is called by the name of Saṁkarshaṇa. Saṁkarshaṇa creates Pradyumna. I take birth myself as Aniruddha . . . From Aniruddha springs Brahmā. The latter takes birth from Aniruddha's navel. From Brahmā spring all creatures mobile and immobile. Know that Creation springs in this way repeatedly at the beginning of every Kalpa. Creation and destruction succeed each other even as sunrise and sunset in this world.[2]

Vāsudeva, Saṁkarshaṇa, Pradyumna, Aniruddha, Brahmā thus form a sort of family tree. A little earlier in the same section Saṁkarshaṇa is identified with *prakṛiti*, Pradyumna

[1] *Infra*, p. 383.

[2] *Śānti Parvan*, cccxli, 70–73 (12936).

with *manas*, and Aniruddha with *ahaṁkāra*; and here we are told that from Brahmā are produced the *bhutāni* or elements of matter. These are the series of cosmic existences posited by the Sāṅkhya philosophy for the explanation of the universe.[1] The system indicated may be graphically represented thus:

Vāsudeva = the supreme Reality.
↓
Saṁkarshaṇa = primeval matter, *prakṛiti*.
↓
Pradyumna = cosmic mind, *manas*.
↓
Aniruddha = cosmic self-consciousness, *ahaṁkāra*.
↓
Brahmā = Creator of the visible world, the *bhutāni*.

Clearly this genealogical series is meant to enable the untutored people to grasp the idea of the rather difficult emanation-series of the Sāṅkhya system.[2] The mythological character of the series, clear enough on the surface, becomes still clearer when we realize that Kṛishṇa was called Vāsudeva, that Balarāma, his brother, was called Saṁkarshaṇa, 'Drawn-out', because he was drawn out of his mother's womb and placed in Rohinī, while Pradyumna is Kṛishṇa's own son, and Aniruddha is one of his grandsons. We have evidence that Saṁkarshaṇa was worshipped before the Christian era.[3]

The doctrine of incarnations is also taught, the theory being that in each kalpa Vishṇu becomes incarnate ten times, as a swan, a tortoise, a fish, a man-horse, a boar, a man-lion, a dwarf, Paraśurāma, Kṛishṇa, and Kalki.[4]

B. Śiva is a very picturesque figure in the *Mahābhārata*. He has two aspects, one fierce and destructive, expressed in the names Rudra (roarer), Hara (he who sweeps all away), Kāla (Time), the other mild and beneficent, expressed in the

[1] *Supra*, pp. 237–239.
[2] See below, p. 405.
[3] *Supra*, p. 363.
[4] See below, p. 388.

names Śiva and Śaṅkara. In his fiercer aspect he has a revolting and terrifying appearance. He is death, pestilence, destruction. He is a mad ascetic, covered with ashes, carrying a skull, haunting the burning-ghāt. In his kindly aspect he is the dancer, fond of music and sport. But the most significant fact that meets us in the Epic is that Śiva's worship is now phallic.[1] His popularity rests on the liṅga, as Vishṇu's on his incarnations. The Śaiva theological system is called *Pāśupata*, from Paśupati, Lord of flocks, an old name of Śiva.

C. The introduction of the philosophical theology into the sects is the chief characteristic of their history in the later stages of the two epics. Along with the leading philosophical element, viz. the identification of Vishṇu and of Śiva with the supreme Brahman, came other philosophic and ascetic influences. The chief of these is this, that the aim of Hindu philosophy, namely, emancipation, is now brought into the sects and is sought by devotion, *bhakti*, to the sectarian god. Secondly, in order that the Vaishṇava or the Śaiva layman might learn a little philosophy, the institution of the *guru* or teacher was introduced from the philosophic schools. The devotee, whether man or woman, chooses a guru for himself or herself, and a permanent spiritual relation is supposed to be established between teacher and disciple. A concomitant idea, which came in at the same time, is that to the disciple the guru is God, and must be worshipped as such.[2] It was perhaps the coming of the guru that led also to the institution of the sectarian *dīkshā*, or ceremony of initiation. The name and the institution alike were already fully established in the philosophical schools.[3] Finally, it seems clear that it was the arrival of the philosophical element that brought the idea of ahiṁsā, or harmlessness, into the sects. It will be remembered that the law against the taking of animal life grew up among the vānaprasthas, hermits, in

[1] See p. 310. [2] See below, p. 399.
[3] Deussen, 377.

very early times,[1] and that it found its way much later into the discipline of the sannyāsīs, Hindu, Buddhist, and Jain.[2] In their case the prohibition usually extended to vegetable life as well. As we have already seen, the rule tended later to become restricted to the preservation of animal life, vegetable life being dropped out of consideration.[3] Since it was believed that the destruction of animal life made bad karma and hindered a man from ripening towards emancipation, it became necessary for the serious layman to keep the law of ahiṁsā. Care for animal life was certainly emphasized as a most serious duty in the two sects, for two far-reaching changes arose from it.

First, animal sacrifice was given up in all the temples of those sects who seriously claimed that they worshipped the Absolute.[4] To this day no animal sacrifice is tolerated in any Vishṇu temple, and in most temples of Śiva also it is prohibited. We can actually trace the working of the philosophic leaven in one case. When Madhva worked out his own philosophic theology, and founded his sect, animal sacrifice was forbidden in the temples of the sect, although his people had been used to it, and they were bid to offer instead images of animals made with rice-flour.[5] Animal sacrifice in Hindu temples may have been what it was in so many countries, a meal in which the god and his people ate together. In modern temples, the practice is to give every worshipper a portion of the food and of the water offered to the idol. The food is called *prasāda*, a grace-gift, and the water *tīrtha*, holy water.

Secondly, flesh-eating was condemned, and the exclusive use of vegetables gradually spread among the people. Vegetarianism is far from being universal among Hindus. There

[1] *Supra*, p. 250.
[2] *Supra*, pp. 256, 258.
[3] *Supra*, pp. 263–264.
[4] Yet both Śaṅkara and Rāmānuja declare that the killing of animals in sacrifice is not 'unholy': *S. B. E.*, xxxviii. 131; xlviii. 598–599. This was necessary in order to justify the Vedic sacrifices.
[5] *Madhva*, 147–148.

are groups of Brāhmans even who eat both fish and flesh. Wherever philosophic and ascetic ideas have been seriously pressed, however, vegetarianism has tended to increase.

D. There are three groups of books about which we had better say a word, the Purāṇas, the sectarian Upanishads, and the sectarian manuals, known as Saṁhitās, Āgamas, and Tantras. These all belong to the same general period. The leading books of each class fall between the close of the Epic period and the time of Śaṅkara, *c.* A.D. 800, but many are still later. The chief note of this literature is sectarianism: there is no longer any attempt at a national literature to which all might contribute, as was the case with the *Mahābhārata*.

1. The chief interest of the Purāṇas for our subject, apart from their violent sectarianism, is that they give us the whole cycle of the later myths about Kṛishṇa connected with Mathurā and Vṛindāvana. Here we find the story of his childhood in full detail, and all his pranks among the cowherds. The *Harivaṁsa*, the *Vishṇu Purāṇa*, and even the late *Bhāgavata Purāṇa* do not allude to Rādhā, Kṛishṇa's cowherd mistress, but the *Padma Purāṇa*, and the *Brahma-vaivarta Purāṇa* make a great deal of her.[1] This new element is the chief source of the immorality of certain Vaishṇava sects. There are a number of Purāṇas which favour the cult of Śiva: the *Skanda*, the *Śiva*, the *Liṅga*, and the *Bhavishya*.

2. Many Upanishads in prose and verse, of various doctrine and practice, were composed in the first millennium of the Christian era, and were loosely attached to the *Atharvaveda*. Among these are a number that teach the new philosophic theology of the Vaishṇava and Śaiva sects. Prof. Deussen in his *Sechzig Upanishad's des Veda* translates seven Vishṇu Upanishads and five Śiva Upanishads. In two of these treatises the object of meditation is the supreme Vishṇu incarnate as the man-lion, but usually it is Vishṇu himself,

[1] Macdonell, 301.

or else Rāma or Kṛishṇa, that is honoured. One of the Śiva Upanishads deals with the *tripuṇḍra*, the Śivaite sect mark, three horizontal lines drawn with ashes by the Śivaite across his brow.

3. There are then the sectarian manuals. Vishṇuites usually call their books *Pāñcharātra Saṁhitās*, while Śaivas call theirs *Śaiva Āgamas*. The Śāktas, who adore the wife of Śiva as his *śakti* or energy, call their manuals *Tantras*. All these poems, both in their form and in their teaching, are very like the Purāṇas; but they are of far greater importance, for they are the authoritative manuals for both the ritual and the theology of nearly all the Vaishṇava and Śaiva sects both in the North and in the South. In them we have the systems full grown. They give the laws for the construction of temples, lay down the rules for the temple ritual, and give instructions to the guru for initiating new members into the sect. They also contain sketches of the chief theological and philosophical doctrines of the sects. This is the literature which has guided the priests and the gurus in their labours up and down the centuries, while they have been regarded as inspired authorities by poets and thinkers, especially at times when the great books of the Vedānta have been little known. There are a few temples still to be found in which the ritual is controlled by the Kalpa-sūtras, but they are very few. They are known as smārta temples, because they are ruled by *smṛiti.* The Āgamas and Saṁhitās have been very little studied by Europeans as yet; so that it is impossible to speak definitely with regard to their dates. The utmost that can be said is that a few seem to be as old as the fifth century;[1] a larger number are known to have existed in the days of Rāmānuja; but many are still later.[2]

[1] Some scholars believe that there is evidence to prove that the earliest of these works is still older. See Schomerus, *Der Çaiva Siddhānta*, 10; Iyengar's *Outlines*, 173.

[2] For the Vishṅuite Saṁhitās see *J. R. A. S.*, October, 1911; for the Śaiva Āgamas see *Śaiva-Siddhānta*; and for the Tantras see Hopkins, *Religions of India*, 489–494.

E. In the seventh and following centuries Vaishṇavism and Śaivism in the South were greatly strengthened and inspired by two parallel lines of poet-saints, the Āḷvārs among Vishṇuites and the Aḍiyārs among Śivaites. These men drew their inspiration mainly from the Purāṇas, on the one hand, and from the Āgamas and Saṁhitās, on the other. They too identify Vishṇu and Śiva with the absolute Brahman. They gained their influence over the common people by their great enthusiasm and their fervid devotion to Vishṇu and to Śiva. They preached and spoke in Tamil, and their influence lives to-day in their Tamil hymns. These hymns are sung in the daily worship of most of the temples in the Tamil country, and even where the vernacular is Telugu or Canarese.

F. Both the great sects gave birth to erotic sub-sects with very immoral cults. The history of the rise of these movements has not yet been worked out. From Śaivism there sprang the two *Śākta* sects, that is those who worship the *śakti* of Śiva. Hindu sects recognize every goddess as the *śakti* or energy of her husband; but the sects called *Śākta* all worship Umā, Śiva's wife, as Durgā and Kālī, and are closely connected with Bengal. The right-hand Śāktas are respectable, but the left-hand Śāktas hold their worship in secret and are most immoral. Erotic Vaishṇavism seems to have arisen round Mathurā, where Kṛishṇa's childhood is fabled to have been led. Yet, like the Śāktas, these Vaishṇava sub-sects are found in many parts of India. These movements have produced very serious results in the Hindu community.

G. Early in the ninth century there appeared among the ascetic teachers of the ancient school of the Vedānta the famous Śaṅkara, a scholar of the highest capacity, who gave the philosophy its final and definite form. Partly through the splendour of his scholarship and his capacity, partly because he was head of the school to which all were proud to belong, Śaṅkara was able to carry almost the whole country with him in his monistic (*advaita*) exposition of the Vedānta.

H. But gradually the sects began to feel that his pantheistic doctrine of Brahman, his complete identification of the soul with God, and his theory that the world is altogether illusory, were scarcely compatible with the fundamental implications of their religion. If they were right in worshipping Vishṇu and Śiva as they did, clearly the Supreme must be personal, the soul must be in some sense distinct from God, and the world must have some reality. The first clear note of rebellion against Śaṅkara is found in Mānikka Vāchakar, the Tamil poet quoted above.[1] His date is perhaps a century after Śaṅkara. He expresses in his verse his detestation of the haughty creed of the Vedānta,[2] which must mean definitely, the system of Śaṅkara. The crusade was carried much further, early in the twelfth century, by Rāmānuja for the Vishṇuite Church. His commentary on the *Vedānta-sūtras*, known as the *Śrī-bhāshya*, is really a great piece of work, well worthy of a place beside Śaṅkara's masterpiece. The activity of Mey-kaṇḍa-devar, a Śaivite philosopher who wrote in Tamil in the thirteenth century, giving systematic expression in the vernacular to the philosophic theology of Śiva, may be taken as the next step. In the fourteenth century, Madhva founded his new Vishṇuite sect in the Canarese country and attacked Śaṅkara's system with great vehemence and success in a commentary on the *Vedānta-sūtras*, while Umāpati continued the fight for Śiva in the Tamil country. Later still came Vallabhāchārya and Chaitanya in the North, each a Vaishṇava leader, eager to hold his own as a theistic Vedāntist against Śaṅkara. The Śaiva commentary on the *Vedānta-sutras* is by Nīlakaṇṭha. His date is probably very early, but it is not yet known with certainty.

Rāmānuja's philosophic position is that there exists only the one Eternal Brahman, absolute, invisible, beyond the range of thought and speech. He is the god of the Vaishṇava

[1] See p. 375. [2] Pope, 33.

sect, known as Vishṇu and Vāsudeva. But, though he is absolute, he is personal and is not without qualities: he is separate from all evil and has innumerable excellent characteristics. He is a God of love and grace. While he is the one Absolute, he yet contains everything. Souls and the world are his body, each soul a portion (*aṁśa*) of God. Being the body of God, they have existed from all eternity and will never cease to exist. Both the world and souls are real. Souls and matter, however, exist at different times in two conditions, contracted and expanded, latent and causal. The body of God is in its contracted and latent condition during the *pralayas*, the periods between the destruction and the creation of the world, while it is in its causal and expanded state during the *kalpas*, the periods between the creation and the destruction, when the world is visible and active.

Souls live under the laws of transmigration and karma, undergoing an endless round of births and deaths. Release from this bondage can come only when the soul acquires knowledge of the eternal Brahman. This knowledge is possible through the grace of God to the soul and the response of the soul in *bhakti*, devotion. When the released man dies, his soul enters eternal bliss, retaining its individuality for ever. The emancipated soul is like Brahman in all particulars, except that it does not possess his power of creating, preserving, and destroying the world. This system is called *Viśishṭādvaita*, modified monism.

The philosophy of Śaivas is very little different from that of Rāmānuja, only they identify Brahman with Śiva, and they hold that the released soul at death actually merges in Brahman and loses all consciousness of individual existence. It is for this reason that Śaivas prefer to call their system *advaita*, monistic. When the released soul at death goes to Brahman, there is, according to them, no difference between it and Brahman.

Mādhvas also hold practically the same philosophy as

Rāmānuja, though they emphasize still more the distinction between the soul and God and therefore call their system *dvaita*, dualistic.

Thus, the philosophy of the theistic sects stands out as very distinct from Śaṅkara's, but the differences amongst themselves are of very little consequence, except in so far as the one group reverence Vishṇu and the other Śiva.

I. We now turn to the development of Vaishṇavism in North India, where certain features of the system receive fuller and clearer expression than elsewhere.

Rāmānanda, a follower of Rāmānuja, rebelled against the galling rules about food, dress, and the bath which characterize the sect, migrated to North India about A. D. 1400, and there preached to men of all castes, using the vernacular in everything. Yet even he did not propose to break down caste. He merely neglected it so far as preaching and worship were concerned. The sects that look back to him live in caste like other Hindus. He retained the old Vaishṇava theology and worship unchanged, except that he laid special stress on the worship of Rāma, while in the parent sect Rāma and Kṛishṇa are equally honoured. This feature marks all those who trace their spiritual lineage to him.

Kabīr was greatly influenced by Muḥammadanism as well as by the Vaishṇavism of his teacher Rāmānanda, and, in consequence, we find two very great departures from ordinary Hindu practice in his case. He took more seriously than the Vaishṇavas did the doctrine that the knowledge of God is not dependent on caste, and in consequence refused to submit to the rule of the Brāhman priest. Here, then, we have a definite break with caste. He also ridiculed the Hindu mythology, denied the doctrine of incarnations, affirmed that all the Hindu gods were dead, and forbade the worship of idols. His followers were thus not only cut off from Brāhman ministrations but from Hindu temple-worship also. They met for worship by themselves. Yet he retained many features of Vaishṇavism. He called God Rāma, gave the guru the same prominence which he has among Vaishṇavas, retained the *mantra*, the rosary of Tulsī beads, the vertical sect-mark in the forehead, and the sacred food known as *prasāda.*

Here are two quotations from him:

> The Hindus bathe in sacred streams, go on pilgrimage to sacred places, bow down to images of brass and stone, and think that in so doing they are honouring God. In this they are mistaken. What God desires is purity of heart; to rest in symbols that should lead men on to God is to be guilty of idolatry.[1]

> If by worshipping stones one can find God, I shall worship a mountain; better than these stones (idols) are the stones of the flour mill with which men grind their corn.[2]

Nānak, the founder of the Sikh sect, is said to have been a disciple of Kabīr, and it is clear that in certain large matters he followed his master. He would have nothing to do with idolatry; and thus the Sikhs cannot worship in ordinary Hindu temples, but have their own places of worship.[3] This meant a revolt from the Brāhmans in matters of worship, but it does not seem probable that Nānak condemned caste as such. That condemnation came under a later guru. Nānak was a theist, yet, like an ordinary Hindu, he retained the whole Hindu mythology. He did not go nearly so far in reform as Kabīr did. Caste has found its way back into the Sikh community.

IV. The influence of the doctrine of incarnation, especially as taught in the *Bhagavadgītā*, has been very great. Kṛishṇa and Rāma were the earliest incarnations; but very soon a number of old stories were taken from the Vedas and the Brāhmaṇas and turned into incarnations; and others were created; so that within the compass of the *Mahābhārata* itself we find a list of ten incarnations recognized. Some of these are of semi-animal form, the man-fish, man-boar, man-tortoise, man-horse, and man-lion incarnations.[4] Later still

[1] Westcott, 54.
[2] Westcott, 58.
[3] See above, pp. 332–333.
[4] See above, p. 379.

the number was raised to twenty-four, as we find it in the *Bhāgavata Purāṇa*. It seems certain that this long list is partly at least an imitation of the long list of Buddhas which we find in the Buddhist books at a much earlier date. The Jains have a long list of Tīrthakaras also.[1]

At a still later date every prominent Vaishṇava leader was declared to be an incarnation, not of Vishṇu himself, but of one of his attendant spirits or of one of his symbols. Thus Rāmānuja is usually said to have been an incarnation of the great snake Śesha. His predecessor in the metropolitan temple, Yamunāchārya, is held to have been an incarnation of Vishvaksena, Vishṇu's commander-in-chief. In two of his disciples, Dāśarathi and Kureśa, Vishṇu's shell and discus took human form. Earlier saints are said to have been incarnations of his necklace, mace, sword, bow, jewel, and eagle.[2]

Even sects whose chief principles are inconsistent with the doctrine of incarnations have later adopted it in one shape or another. Kabīr scoffs at the incarnations of Vishṇu; yet by his own followers he is praised as an incarnation of the Supreme.[3] His disciple Nānak, the founder of the Sikh religion, and all the nine gurus who followed him, are regarded as incarnations by the Sikhs.[4]

But it is still more remarkable to find the doctrine in the ancient Vedānta school. Since it is one of the chief doctrines of the Vedānta that the human spirit is God, it seems incredible that any strict Vedāntist should dream of accepting the doctrine of avatāras. There is no mention of such a thing in any of the early Upanishads; nor does it occur in the *Vedānta-sūtras*. Yet Śaṅkarāchārya accepts the *Bhagavad-gītā* as one of the authoritative books of the Vedānta, and calls Kṛishṇa an incarnation. But it is most noteworthy that he does not equate Kṛishṇa with Brahman: he makes him only

[1] See the author's *Primer of Hinduism*, 97.
[2] *Rāmānuja*, 91, 96, 104, 182, 231; *Holy Lives*, 1, 19, 41, 73, 74, 88, 117, 136, 145, 193.
[3] Westcott, 144.
[4] Trumpp, *Ādi Granth*, cxi. 34, 69, 73.

a partial incarnation.[1] The truth seems to be that he was conscious of the difficulty which the doctrine raises within the Vedānta system, and introduced this modification to lessen the pressure.

Stranger still is it to find the doctrine of incarnations among Śaivas; for it is one of the leading principles of Śaiva theology that God cannot be born of a woman. It is only among Śaivas of the last few centuries that we find the doctrine. Careful writers avoid it altogether. It seems certain that the idea crept in through the old doctrine that every Śaiva guru is to be received and worshipped as Śiva himself. From that it is but a step to the idea of incarnation. Hence, in later Śaiva literature, Śaṅkara and all the great āchāryas of the Śaiva sect are distinctly spoken of as incarnations of a portion of Śiva.[2]

V. We have now before us in outline the whole development of theology within Hinduism from the moment when, under the pressure of the karma theory, the doctrine of the Brahman-Ātman was produced down to the chief movements that occurred under Muḥammadan influence. The thought and the practice of the Vedānta remain the most notable achievement of the Indian religious genius from beginning to end; but the story which has unfolded itself before us in this chapter takes us nearer the heart of Hinduism than any other that can be told. To conceive the Supreme as truly absolute, on the one hand, and as personal and interested in man, on the other, is what the great central group of thinking Hindus have struggled to do since somewhere about the Christian era. The Sānkhya and the Vedānta have interested the intellectual man, and they have provided most of the metaphysical and psychological categories which have ruled the Hindu mind;

[1] See the introduction to his *Gītā-bhāshya*. The writer owes this reference to Pandit Sītānāth Tattvabhushaṇa. See *Śrī Śaṅkarāchārya*, 135.

[2] Appāyadīkshita's proem to his commentary on Nīlakaṇṭha's *Śaiva Bhāshya*.

but a worthy theism has been what the cultured Indian has longed for and worked for.

The introduction of Vedāntism into the worship of Vishṇu and Śiva greatly enlarged the spiritual outlook of the sects, and brought in its train important changes in ritual and in everyday life. It was an ennobling thing for the ordinary worshipper of Vishṇu or Śiva to be told that the God whom he revered is the Supreme, the inconceivable One, the object of the speculation of all the seers of India, and that he is a God of love and grace towards whom it is his duty to feel a passionate devotion. It was also stimulating to hear that each man is a portion of God. The new philosophic theology also brought near to him the idea that the real end of the religious life is not the petty things he asked from his god from day to day, but a complete release from the thraldom of sense and from the round of birth and death, a final escape from all that is transitory, unsatisfying, and sorrowful. The bringing of these ideas within the reach of the ordinary layman must have been a great uplift. Along with the idea of release came the thought that the destruction of animal life was one of the chief lines of action that would retard his progress towards the goal. Hence, he gladly acquiesced in the reform whereby offerings of grain, vegetables, fruit, and flowers were substituted for the animal sacrifices which his forefathers had offered so long. Still more striking is the fact that in large parts of South India, and also in certain parts of Central and Northern India, many groups of high-caste Hindus yielded to the pressure of this idea so far as to become complete vegetarians. As time went on, it was found that men of low caste were as able to grasp spiritual ideas as Brāhmans themselves; and henceforward we find the conviction in all the theistic churches that all men are capable of winning salvation.

Yet we must acknowledge that much superstition remained. Above all things idolatry was not laid aside. Animal sacrifice was given up, it is true; yet, though that is evidence of the existence of fine feeling, it was no gain to spiritual religion: the offering of fruits and vegetables to a stone is quite as superstitious as the offering of animal food. The shrine, the image, the food, and the water offered to the idol are all believed to be filled with divine power. We read of a dog that ate some of the food offered to an idol and straightway went to heaven.[1] Nay, Rāmānuja tells us that 'the killing of animals in sacrifice makes them to go up to the heavenly world'.[2] The belief in the magic potency of the mere utterance of the divine name and of the sectarian mantra continues in all its old strength. Indeed, it seems clear that the philosophy brought its own superstition with it: the guru is not only worshipped as God in both sects, but the dust of his feet conveys spirituality, and the water in which he has washed them is drunk by his disciples as nectar for the soul. The Vishṇuite declares that Vishṇu is present in great power in every *śālagrāma*, a black fossil found in the Gandak river,[3] while the Śivaite believes that Śiva resides in every round white pebble found in the Nerbudda. Hence, innumerable poisonous superstitions flourish in the unhealthy atmosphere, such as the value of spells, charms, and amulets, the divine nature and power of cows, bulls, monkeys, snakes, and of many trees and plants, the virtue of sacred rivers, springs, and ponds, and the efficacy of weird sacrifices and magic practices. Hinduism has never got beyond the superstition that holiness and divine power reside in things.

VI. We must now endeavour to understand what the great forces are which throughout the centuries have determined the main lines of the development of Indian theism and have given it its distinctive Hindu character. Our study has shown us that the interest of the history of the sects lies in the bold

[1] *Holy Lives*, 208.
[2] *S.B.E.*, xlviii. 599. Cf. *I.S.R.*, Feb. 13, 1910, p. 283.
[3] A Hindu scholar writes: 'The modern Vaishṇava sips the water in which the fossil ammonite is washed to the chanting of the *Purusha Sūkta*, for disinfecting his inside of the bacillus of sin.' Iyengar's *Outlines*, 191.

attempt they make to combine the loftiest features of the theology of the Vedānta with popular religion. We have here to consider how the two elements, the philosophy and the popular religion, have worked together, how the attempt to unite them has succeeded.

As in the original Vedānta, so here the doctrine of karma ruled the development. Brahman is still construed as actionless, in order that he may not fall under the sway of karma. The old phrase, 'Brahman is beyond thought and speech' is repeated thousands of times. Rāmānuja writes [1] that Vishṇu,

> after having created the universe from Brahmā down to stocks and stones, withdrew into his own nature, and thus became impervious to the meditations and worship [2] of the gods, from Brahmā downwards, and of mankind;

Māṇikka Vāchakar says:

> He dwells where human thought goes not; [3]

and Tulsī Dās writes,[4]

> Rāma is beyond the grasp of intellect, or soul, or speech.

Consequently we find the same results arising here as we met in the early Vedānta.

A. In the early period, before their alliance with the Vedānta, the sects never dreamed of subjecting Vishṇu and Śiva to moral restrictions. The gods are above moral law. We need not refer to the early mythology for proof. It is, however, of importance to remember the point, for the conception continued active throughout the subsequent history.

But the serious attempt to conceive the Supreme as personal necessarily led both sects towards moral ideas. Vishṇu and Śiva, like other Hindu gods, had been believed to be very gracious and kindly towards their own worshippers; and in the verse Upanishads we have the beginnings of the doctrine

[1] In the prelude to his commentary on the *Gītā*. *Heart of India*, 41.
[2] Compare what Śaṅkara says, *S.B.E.*, xxxiv. 31–32.
[3] Pope, 20. [4] Growse, 63. Also 97, 100.

that Brahman is personal and full of grace. Hence Vishṇu and Śiva, conceived as the Supreme, could not but be gracious. This finally led in each sect to the definite doctrine, that the Supreme is a God of love and grace. Besides that, the very attempt to make the personality of God real led to moral ideas. Hence to Rāmānuja Vishṇu is one

> whose essence is absolute negation of all evil, . . . who is an ocean of boundless and blest qualities of nature ;[1]

and, in the Śaiva Āgamas, Śiva is called *saguṇa* in the sense that he possesses all auspicious qualities. This is a most important fact. The theistic sects refused absolutely to receive the old Vedāntic idea, that God is non-moral.[2]

But mark the result. Brahman is personal and ethical, but he has 'retired into his own nature', as Rāmānuja says, and is absolutely actionless. Hence he cannot bring his moral nature to bear on the world or on men. It remains far withdrawn, in the unruffled peace of his transcendental life. He cannot be the source and centre of the moral order of the universe. He cannot rule over the nations as the righteous God. His ethical nature is thus altogether ineffective. He cannot be said to have a character. It is most necessary to realize this point; otherwise we are faced with an absolute contradiction. Except on the supposition that the moral nature of Brahman does not act effectively on the world and man, how can we reconcile his character with the following phenomena?

1. In the great books of the sects we still find the old conviction that the gods are above morality, and that they may do deeds which man must neither copy nor condemn. We begin with a quotation from the *Bhāgavata Purāṇa*,[3] one of the very greatest Vishṇuite authorities:

> The transgression of virtue and the daring acts which are witnessed in gods (*Īśvarāṇam*) must not be charged as faults to these glorious

[1] Prelude to commentary on the *Gītā*. [2] See above, p. 229.
[3] x. 33, 30–35. The passage occurs in Muir's *Sanskrit Texts*, iv. 50 f.

persons. . . . Let no one other than a god ever even in thought practise the same. . . . The word of gods is true, and so also their conduct is sometimes correct: let a wise man observe their command, which is right. . . . Since Munis are uncontrolled and act as they please, how can there be any restraint upon him (the supreme Deity), when he has voluntarily assumed a body?

We find the same thought in the biography of Rāmānuja. One day heavy rain came on while the image of Vishṇu was being carried in procession, Rāmānuja in its train. The image was carried into a Śaiva temple by the priests, but Rāmānuja refused to follow; for no serious Vaishṇava will enter a temple of Śiva. The story proceeds as follows:

'Sire! Thy Lord has taken shelter inside, why dost thou not do the same?'

'Fool thou art,' fulminated Rāmānuja, 'if the Emperor electeth to make love to a courtesan, doth it signify that his chaste Queen also should imitate her Lord by herself resorting to a courtier?'

We are like the chaste Queen and cannot do as the Lord doth.[1]

So Tulsī Dās, speaking of Śiva and other gods, writes:

The fool who in the pride of knowledge presumes to copy them, saying, 'It is the same for a man as for a god,' shall be cast into hell for as long as the world lasts.[2]

No argument is needed to show that we have in all these passages the pagan idea, that the gods are above morality, still unpurified.

2. Kṛishṇa is held to be a full incarnation of Vishṇu-Brahman, 'whose essence is absolute negation of all evil'; and yet, in the literature which is accepted by the sects as inspired, he is represented as having been guilty of lies, deceit, theft, murder, and limitless adultery. So Śiva is credited with acts during his theophanies which no self-respecting man would do. This extraordinary situation can be understood only when we take full account of the Vedāntic doctrine that the divine activity is sport, and recognize that it covers the old rule that

[1] *Divine Wisdom*, 198. [2] Growse, 38.

the gods are above morality. Indeed, it is only by the aid of these two ideas that we can realize how the sects retained the whole of the early mythology relating to the Hindu gods. Had there been one gust of pure moral air blown from Brahman, these unworthy stories about the gods, with their lusts and quarrels, their facile nymphs sent to draw ascetics into sin, their adultery and incest, their shameful fears and terrors, their spites and lies and revenges, would have been hurled into oblivion.

3. The stories about Kṛishṇa's amours among the milkmaids in Vṛindāvana, and, above all, his passion for Rādhā, gave birth to new sub-sects among the Vaishṇavas, some of them respectable in their worship, others very impure. The root-ideas which made the rise of these erotic sects possible within the great Vishṇuite community were clearly these, that, when a god appears in human life, his sports are unrestrained by moral law, and that, while in ordinary life man must not dream of imitating the divine sports, in worship such imitation leads to closest fellowship with the god. Further, while ordinary men who live in the world must submit to the moral laws of the community to which they belong, the priests of the god who became incarnate may be expected, as the representatives of the god, to copy in his worship his divine actions. From this point of view even the foulness of Vallabhāchārya practice is comprehensible.

As we have seen above, the Left-hand Śaktas are a branch of the Śaiva sect, and have most immoral practices. They worship the wife of Śiva, calling her Kālī and Durgā. It seems probable that this cult, which commands promiscuous sexual intercourse as part of its observances, is really an aboriginal worship, introduced, like many others, into Hinduism. The science of religion knows many examples of goddesses of fertility and reproduction in whose worship such practices are enjoined. For us the significant point is that this gross system was admitted by Brāhmans into Hinduism and placed under the aegis of the great god Śiva. The inevitable inference is that Śiva was not conceived as having a moral nature which would rise in righteous indignation against such a worship.

The great temple-gateways of South India known as *gopurams* and the temple-towers of Central India [1] are in many cases covered with sculpture of indescribable obscenity; while here and there, as in the metropolitan Vishṇuite shrine, Śrīraṅgam, at Trichinopoly, the internal walls and ceiling are, in Hopkins's phrase, 'frescoed with bestiality'—frescoes representing the pleasures of Vishṇu's heaven.[2] The car in which the god rides on great festival days is also frequently defiled with obscene carvings. To this day troops of dancing-girls, who are called *devadāsīs*, servants of the god, and who now and then do take part in the ritual, but whose real occupation is prostitution,[3] are connected with most of the great temples of the South and West,[4] and do immeasurable harm. Women scour the country, and adopt or buy little girls to bring them up for this infamous life.[5] In Śiva's temples in all parts of India one almost invariably finds his phallic symbol,[6] the *liṅga*, instead of an image. It seems clear that the symbol does not stir impure thoughts or feelings in the average Hindu; yet here we have a survival of coarse, indecent, barbaric religion tolerated for centuries under a theistic philosophy. The extraordinary thing is that the obscene sculptures, the foul frescoes, the dancing-girls, and the offensive symbols are found, not in private buildings, but in the temples, the high palaces made holy by the living presence of the gods. The inevitable conclusion is that neither Vishṇu nor Śiva has ever been regarded as having such a character as would be shocked by such things. Even the greatest philosophers failed to feel any incongruity

[1] It is to the devastation wrought by the Muḥammadans that we owe the fact that obscene sculptures are scarcely to be seen in North India.

[2] *Religions of India*, 456. [3] See above, pp. 314–315.

[4] In the North the dancing-girls are not permanently connected with the temples, but are hired for the great festivals. Havell, *Benares*, 87.

[5] See Amy Wilson Carmichael's *Lotus Buds*.

[6] See above, p. 310.

between these temples and the ethical Brahman of their theology. Śrīraṅgam is the temple in which Rāmānuja lived and ruled for many years as high-priest. There his great *Śrī-Bhāshya* was written. Māṇikka Vāchakar frequently bewails his own feebleness and folly in yielding to the attractions of the devadāsīs ; but he never demands that they should be driven from the temples as dishonouring to Śiva.

Animal sacrifice was given up in most temples, and multitudes of Hindus became vegetarians, because it was felt that the slaughter of animals would retard one's progress towards emancipation. Clearly, the sexual immorality of the Kṛishṇa myths, of the Kṛishṇaite sects, and of the temples was never seriously regarded by the sectarian leaders as an obstacle to release; else a resolute agitation would have been raised for their removal.

4. The greatest saints are guilty of most immoral acts in the service of their gods, and are held to be quite justified. Māṇikka Vāchakar, one of the greatest of Śivaite saints, who has been already referred to, was originally Prime Minister to the king of Madura. The king entrusted him with a large sum of money to go to a seaport and buy Arab horses. On his way he sees Śiva in the form of a guru surrounded by ninety-nine disciples, is converted and becomes a Śivaite ascetic. He then hands over the whole of the king's money to be distributed to the devotees of Śiva and the poor.[1] Tiru-Maṅgai-Āḻvār is one of the chief Vishṇuite saints of the South. Yet, in his official biography we have a narrative in which, in order to get money for the service of Vishṇu, he is guilty of lies, deception, burglary, murder, and sacrilegious theft: he breaks into a Buddhist shrine and steals a golden image of Buddha.[2] Numerous stories could be quoted in which devotees, both men and women, are guilty of gross immorality in order to serve the god or the guru.[3] Nay, the doctrine is frankly put into the mouth of Vishṇu in a Sanskrit couplet:

[1] Pope, xxi-xxiii. [2] *Holy Lives*, 173-179. [3] *Rāmānuja*, 117.

> If for my sake thou sinnest, it becometh merit;
> All merit without reference to me becometh sin.[1]

5. Had Brahman been effectively conceived as absolutely holy, it would have been impossible to think of the sectarian gurus and saints as his true manifestation. How are we to understand the following statements? *Unmai Viḷakkam*, one of the fourteen authoritative Tamil books of the Śaiva Siddhānta, says,

> They who regard and worship the Guru, the liṅga and God's devotees as the incomparable God will not suffer births and deaths.[2]

One of the Vishṇuite Saṁhitās reads,

> The guru is Parabrahman himself.[3]

These sayings and the worship of these men as saviours prove, at the very least, that in this connexion the perfect moral nature attributed to Brahman was neglected or forgotten; for men of most imperfect character are recognized as Brahman himself, and receive the worship which ought to be given to God alone.

6. One of the most precious doctrines held by Indian theists is this, that God is full of love and grace. Both Vishṇuite and Śivaite teach this faith most earnestly. It has inspired much beautiful literature and has touched the hearts of thousands of simple people. It is especially noticeable in the works of the great sectarian poets, Māṇikka Vāchakar, Tukārām, Tulsī Dās, and others.

Yet under this very faith there grew up both in the North and the South the practice of widow-burning. Under this very faith female infanticide was tolerated, and all the cruel inhumanities of caste. It is one of the principles of both these sects that the Outcaste is capable of bhakti and may attain emancipation as truly as the Brāhman; so that he too is an object of the love of God. Yet there has never been a movement within these great sects to set the Outcaste free from the

[1] *Rāmānuja*, 117. [2] *Śaiva Siddhānta*, 12.
[3] *Rāmānuja*, 105. *Parabrahman* means the transcendental Brahman.

intolerable position in which caste places him. Rāmānuja, clearly, was deeply impressed with the spiritual capacity of the Outcaste class. His biography contains many touching incidents to that effect. Yet he never proposed to change their social position.

Do we condemn Rāmānuja and the other leaders, both Śaiva and Vaishṇava? Nay, by no means. Who does not feel deeply the sincerity and nobility of those men, the high motives that inspired them, the heroic toils and sacrifices they endured for the faith they held? What is clear, however, is this, that the faith which they had received had not ethical force and warmth sufficient to condemn widow-burning, female infanticide, and the cruel tyranny under which the Outcaste lives.

The real explanation of the situation is this, that the Hindu system took shape, as we saw in Chapter V, while the religion was fully polytheistic, many centuries before the sects adopted the theology of the Vedānta and rose to the high faith that Brahman is a personal and ethical spirit; that the leaders of the sects as well as the common people held that the ancient system of religious, social, and family life was a divine creation, holy and unchangeable in every part, as it is represented in the *Bhagavadgītā*;[1] and that the ethical character ascribed to Brahman, being shut up in his transcendental nature, and never made manifest among men in action, was utterly impotent to stir even the best men to moral indignation against the immorality and social cruelty which the system inculcated. Whatever value the moral character of Brahman may have had, it never sufficed to rouse any theistic thinker to ethical criticism of the Hindu system. Brahman was never effectively moralized.

B. In Śaṅkara's Vedānta Brahman is held to be impersonal. To the theist, however, the main thought was that if Brahman was to be identified with Vishṇu (or with Śiva), he must

[1] *Supra*, pp. 218, 373–374.

be construed as a person. Both sects consistently taught that Brahman was personal. Here, then, we have a point on which the sects differed absolutely from the central school of the Vedānta.

C. All theistic thinkers accept fully the Upanishad doctrine that Brahman, being 'beyond thought and speech', can receive neither sacrifice nor prayer. The passages quoted above from Rāmānuja, Māṇikka Vāchakar, and Tulsī Dās show how these men felt,[1] and similar statements might be quoted from other theologians. Thus, it is one of the highest principles of Hindu theology that the Supreme receives no sacrifice and hears no prayer. Unless this principle be firmly grasped, the development of the theology will remain incomprehensible.

But if God receives no offering and answers no prayer, what is the use of religion, some one will ask, and how can there be theistic sects? Surely this cannot be a principle of Hinduism. The fact remains, however, that the absolute nature of God has been most strictly conceived by all serious thinkers of all sects. He is consistently regarded as deaf to prayer and unmoved by sacrifice.[2] What the sects worship are his representatives.

This is the reason why the worship of the two sects went on unchanged when the theology of the Vedānta was introduced. As Brahman could not be worshipped by the sannyāsī, so Vishṇu-Brahman could not be worshipped by the Vishṇuite. But, since Rāma and Kṛishṇa were already regarded as avatāras of Vishṇu, and since each image of Vishṇu was believed to be so instinct with his essence as to be a mighty living god, there was abundant opportunity and reason for worship. In precisely the same way, Śiva-Brahman was beyond the reach of the meditations, the prayers, or the sacrifices of the Śaivas; but he had poured his presence into every image of himself and into every liṅga all over the land, so that there was no difficulty about worship. All the old stories in the mythology

[1] Above, p. 393. [2] See above, p. 220.

about Śiva were also carefully treasured and interpreted as theophanies of the god for the benefit of his devotees. They thus took, in the Śaiva sect, the place occupied by incarnations among Vaishṇavas. And in both sects there was another object of worship.

In the schools of the early Vedānta the teacher was called *guru*, and the relation between the disciple and his teacher was very close and lasted throughout life. The disciple never wrote a book without expressing his reverence for his guru, whether the latter was alive or dead. No one would be recognized as a guru, unless he had already reached *jnāna*, i. e. the knowledge which is emancipation, viz. the clear realization that he is Brahman. Hence in the *Śvetāśvatara Upanishad* the wise Vedāntist feels the same devotion (*bhakti*) for his guru as for Brahman.[1] Now, when the sects adopted the theology of the Vedānta, they adopted this institution also. It became customary for the man who was a serious Vaishṇava or Śaiva to select a guru for himself, that he might receive instruction in theology. But along with the institution there came the doctrine, that the guru is Brahman. In both sects the disciple is taught to worship his guru as God. Thus Vishṇu in his own inner nature cannot be worshipped, but Vishṇu manifest in the guru can and ought to be worshipped. The Śaiva doctrine is the same. Then the rule was extended to saints as well as gurus. Nor is this a mere doing honour where honour is due. According to all the authorities, the worship paid to the guru is truly worship. Further, the guru is a Saviour, and emancipation may be achieved by devotion to him. The following sentences are from Rāmānuja's biography:

> When the gracious eyes of a good guru fall on a person, his salvation is sure, be he deaf or dumb, fool or wise, young or old.[2]
>
> Apart from Rāmānuja, no God exists for me.[3]
>
> The guru is even greater than God.[4]
>
> Nārāyaṇa . . . can both save and damn, but Rāmānuja . . . can only save.[5]

[1] vi. 23. [2] 170. [3] 197. [4] 117. [5] 249.

Hence it is that images of all the chief gurus are set up in the great temples, both Śaiva and Vaishṇava: they are placed there that people may get salvation by worshipping them.

The late Mr. Justice Ranade of Bombay, leader of the Prārthanā Samāj and also of the Social Reform movement, said in one of his addresses:[1]

> This contrast between the monotheistic spirit and the polytheistic observances strikes every student of our religious life as a puzzle which baffles the understanding. . . . I offer no solution of it myself to-day; because, though I have been thinking about it for a long time, I have not yet been able to find a rational and consistent solution of the difficulty.

The analysis of the history has now laid bare the cause. On account of the karma theory Brahman was conceived as actionless, 'beyond the range of thought and speech', altogether unmoved by prayer and sacrifice. Since, then, the Supreme could not be worshipped, there was no possibility that the characteristic rule of monotheism,

> The Lord thy God shalt thou worship, and Him only shalt thou serve,[2]

should ever grow up in the theistic sects. Both these sects call themselves *Ekāntins*, unitarians; but that word means 'Those who recognize one transcendental God alone': it has nothing to do with worship. Had that idea ever appeared among Vaishṇavas or Śaivas, it would have very quickly swept away the innumerable 'Lords',[3] who are worshipped each in his temple, and the gurus who are recognized as Saviours and receive fervent adoration.

D. Lastly, there is the conviction that Brahman, being actionless, cannot create the world. He is indisputably the source of the universe; but the mode of its production cannot be creation; for that would imply purposeful action, and

[1] *Essays*, 130–131.
[2] Deuteronomy, 6. 13; Matt. 4. 10.
[3] *Holy Lives*, 205.

would render him subject to karma. But Brahman has no desire, plan, or purpose that would lead him to creative action.[1] Yet, since the world proceeds from him, he is in some sense the subject of activity which is not truly action. The solution of this problem was suggested by the author of the *Śvetāśvatara Upanishad*. As the gods were believed to be able, through supernatural power, to conceal their identity under any form they pleased, so he conceived Brahman as a magician and the world as a sort of spectre conjured up by his magic.[2] This reappears in the *Gītā*:

> The Lord . . . by his magic makes all born beings whirl about as though set in a merry-go-round.[3]

Henceforward the activity of Brahman in the world is always construed as sport.[4] He is, therefore, constantly called juggler, magician, actor, by all the best writers.

In the original *Rāmāyaṇa*, as we saw above, Brahmā is the Creator and the greatest of all the gods, Vishṇu is one of the two that stand nearest him, and Śesha is a huge serpent with a thousand heads who supports the earth.[5] The three are in no way more closely connected with each other than any others of the denizens of heaven. But from the time when Vishṇu was identified with the transcendental Brahman a new piece of mythology makes its appearance. Śesha forms with his coils a couch for Vishṇu, from whose navel springs a lotus bearing upon it Brahmā the Creator. This remarkable conception brings before us the main elements of Vedāntic theology as held by Vishṇuites. It is meant to teach the people, in vivid pictorial fashion, that Vishṇu is the supreme Brahman, that Brahmā, Creator though he be, is but a

[1] So Bādarāyaṇa, Śaṅkara, and Rāmānuja, *S.B.E.*, xxxiv. 356–357 and xlviii. 477.

[2] iv. 9–10.

[3] xviii. 61.

[4] So Bādarāyaṇa, Śaṅkara, and Rāmānuja in the passages just referred to.

[5] *Supra*, p. 355.

temporary being, springing from the source of all life, and that Vishṇu, though the whole universe proceeds from him, is yet actionless and at rest, reclining as he does on the emblem of eternity. This pictorial myth is referred to in the interpolation in the sixth book of the *Rāmāyaṇa* referred to above,[1] and is given also by Rāmānuja.[2] It is this representation of Vishṇu that is worshipped in the metropolitan temple at Trichinopoly. In this form he is called Raṅganātha, i.e. lord of the stage, and the temple is called Śrīraṅgam. He is the lord who looks on while the drama of the world is played. It is his sport.

In the same way the identification of Śiva with Brahman led his worshippers to think of him as producing the world in sport. Hence his activity, whether in the world or in the soul, is symbolized in his dance. He is called Naṭeśa, the dancing lord, Naṭarāja, the dancing king, and in thousands of beautiful works of art is represented as dancing.

But a different way of looking at things was worked out from Sāṅkhya conceptions in some Kṛishṇaite centre in the later period of the Epic. According to the Sāṅkhya there is no supreme Spirit, and the world is evolved from a formless substance called *prakṛiti*. Every group of Vedāntists adopted the Sāṅkhya theory of the production of the visible world; and each, in its own way, fitted it into its main conceptions. Now to the Vishṇuite the world is real, as it is to the Sāṅkhya, only he believes it comes from Vishṇu-Brahman, who is personal but actionless. How is the connexion to be formed? The myth of Vishṇu, Śesha, and Brahmā given above is one way; and it has the merit of representing Brahmā in his ancient rôle of Creator, but it leaves no room for the Sāṅkhya evolutionary series. Such are the considerations that led to the creation of the emanation-series given above[3] from the Śānti Parvan of the *Mahābhārata*. As in the Gnostic systems the Supreme is several steps removed from the Demiurge. To

[1] See p. 374. [2] *S.B.E.*, xlviii. 334. [3] p. 379.

the Gnostic, however, the aim was to avoid bringing God into contact with matter, while the Hindu motive is to separate him from action.

Still another method was employed to connect the far-away, uncommunicating God with the world. The new idea was that the wife of the god is a much more approachable being than her husband, and stands nearer the world and men. She is usually thought of as his energy in action, while he remains absolute and at rest. Thus, among Vishṇuites, Lakshmī is said to be the *śakti* or energy of Vishṇu, while Śivaites say that Umā is the *śakti* of Śiva. How widespread and popular the idea must have been we can see from the fact that it actually found its way into Buddhism. In Tāntric Buddhism the great Buddhas and Bodhisattvas are each credited with having a *śakti* or wife.

But it was the conception of sport that was most widely used. Śaṅkara, Māṇikka Vāchakar, Rāmānuja, and all the other authorities use the word *līlā*, sport, to denote the activity of the Supreme in the production of the world. All the theophanies of Śiva to his worshippers are also spoken of as sport. Hence, they were expected to be whimsical, playful, wild, unaccountable. They show no settled purpose, and come under no law. In this way, all the early myths about Śiva, which took shape long before any one dreamed of calling him the Supreme, were retold as gracious theophanies of Śiva-Brahman; and all the early legends about Vishṇu, such as the salving of the earth, were transformed into incarnations of Vishṇu-Brahman.

This is the point of view from which we can understand Kṛishṇa's boyish knaveries and his immoralities among the milkmaids. He was an incarnate god, and therefore all his actions were bound to be *līlā*, sport. If they were full of fun and amusement, they were worthy of a divinity. You must not judge a god by the standard that obtains among men. To bind him down to moral action would be to deprive him of his divine freedom. Neo-Hindus who defend these immoralities by interpreting them as mere allegories are very wide of the mark. How broadly the writers of the *Padma* and *Bhāgavata Purāṇas* would smile, if they could hear them!

These considerations show how far Indian thought is from conceiving the Supreme as the Creator.

CHAPTER X

GOD WITH US

IN this chapter we endeavour to bring Christian teaching into faithful comparison with the karma doctrine, with the theology of the Vedānta and of the great sects, and with the Indian incarnation ideal. The connexion between these doctrines is so close that it will greatly conduce to clearness to deal with them as one body of thought.

I. We begin with the nature of God. The evidence is presented by means of direct quotation from the Old Testament [1] and from the Gospels, with an illustrative phrase here and there from the Epistles.

A. In Christianity God is conceived as perfectly spiritual and absolutely transcendent. He is the supreme Spirit:

> God is a Spirit.[2]

> The Lord is high above all nations,
> And his glory above the heavens;[3]

the only God of the whole universe,

> I am the first, and I am the last; and beside me there is no God;[4]

everlasting,

> From everlasting to everlasting thou art God;[5]

timeless,

> The high and lofty One that inhabiteth eternity;[6]

changeless,

> For I the Lord change not; therefore ye, O sons of Jacob, are not consumed;[7]

[1] For the Christian use of the Old Testament, see p. 52.
[2] John 4, 24. [3] Ps. 113, 4. [4] Isa. 44, 6.
[5] Ps. 90, 2. [6] Isa. 57, 15. [7] Mal. 3, 6.

invisible,

For he endured, as seeing him who is invisible;[1]

incomprehensible,

Canst thou by searching find out God?
Canst thou find out the Almighty unto perfection?[2]

of infinite understanding,

Great is our Lord, and mighty in power;
His understanding is infinite;[3]

omniscient,

All things are naked and laid open before the eyes of him with whom we have to do;[4]

omnipotent,

The Lord God omnipotent reigneth;[5]

omnipresent,

Do not I fill heaven and earth? saith the Lord;[6]

immanent in nature and in man,

One God and Father of all, who is over all, and through all, and in all;[7]

yet transcending all things,

Behold, heaven and the heaven of heavens cannot contain thee.[8]

The God of the Bible is thus as truly transcendent, spiritual, and absolute as Brahman in the Upanishads.

B. The next element to be realized is God's moral nature. He is perfectly righteous in Himself. No man's character may be compared with His: he is *morally* transcendent and absolute. He is

The high and lofty One that inhabiteth eternity, whose name is Holy.[9]

The Rock, his work is perfect;
For all his ways are judgement:

[1] Heb. 11, 27. [2] Job 11, 7. [3] Ps. 147, 5.
[4] Heb. 4, 13. [5] Rev. 19, 6. [6] Jer. 23, 24.
[7] Eph. 4, 6. [8] 1 Kings 8, 27. [9] Isa. 57, 15.

A God of faithfulness and without iniquity,
Just and right is he.[1]

The Lord is righteous; he loveth righteousness.[2]

The word of the Lord is right.[3]

God is light, and in him is no darkness at all.[4]

Thy lovingkindness, O Lord, is in the heavens;
Thy faithfulness reacheth unto the skies.
Thy righteousness is like the mountains of God;
Thy judgements are a great deep.[5]

Thy righteousness is an everlasting righteousness,
And thy law is truth.[6]

Lift up your eyes to the heavens, and look upon the earth beneath: for the heavens shall vanish away like smoke, and the earth shall wax old like a garment, and they that dwell therein shall die in like manner: but my salvation shall be for ever, and my righteousness shall not be abolished.[7]

He is the Centre and Source of the moral order of the universe, the Author of the moral law, the Creator of man's moral nature:

The Lord reigneth; let the earth rejoice;
Let the multitude of isles be glad.
Clouds and darkness are round about him:
Righteousness and judgement are the foundation of his throne.[8]

The earth is full of the lovingkindness of the Lord.[9]

The earth is the Lord's, and the fulness thereof;
The world, and they that dwell therein.
For he hath founded it upon the seas,
And established it upon the floods.
Who shall ascend into the hill of the Lord?
And who shall stand in his holy place?
He that hath clean hands, and a pure heart;
Who hath not lifted up his soul unto vanity,
And hath not sworn deceitfully.[10]

[1] Deut. 32, 4. [2] Ps. 11, 7. [3] Ps. 33, 4.
[4] I John 1, 5. [5] Ps. 36, 5. [6] Ps. 119. 142.
[7] Isa. 51, 6. [8] Ps. 97, 1–2. [9] Ps. 33, 5.
[10] Ps. 24, 1–4.

The law of the Lord is perfect, restoring the soul:
The testimony of the Lord is sure, making wise the simple.
The precepts of the Lord are right, rejoicing the heart:
The commandment of the Lord is pure, enlightening the eyes.[1]

And God said, Let us make man in our image, after our likeness.[2]

From the place of his habitation he looketh forth
Upon all the inhabitants of the earth;
He that fashioneth the hearts of them all.[3]

We saw in Chapter III that the source of nearly all the weakness of the doctrine of karma and transmigration arises from the fact that it is conceived as automatic, self-acting. The system and the laws of karma do not proceed from Brahman. The moral system is divorced from God.

This fatal error is avoided in Christianity. God is conceived as essentially ethical. His innermost being is moral. He is the God of righteousness as well as the God of intellect and power. He is transcendently, absolutely good. He is incapable of doing wrong, right in all His thoughts, right in all His emotions, and perfectly righteous in will. He is the source of all the morality inwoven into the constitution of the world and into the nature of man. Moral law is as truly an expression of His sovereign will as natural law is. There can never be any separation between God and the moral system of the universe.

C. God, then, is the moral Absolute; and, being perfect in moral character, He is able to act. In this way the problem which has vexed Hindu theology from beginning to end is solved once for all. There is no reason why the ethical Soul of the universe should be actionless.

Having only perfect ends in view, being guided by motives which are absolutely righteous, God is able to rule every detail of the physical world, to come into closest personal contact with the needs and the sorrows of man, to rule the nations, to listen to men's praise and prayer, to speak in each

[1] Ps. 19, 7–8. [2] Gen. 1, 26. [3] Ps. 33, 14–15.

man's conscience, condemning or approving his actions, to plague the criminal with remorse and to comfort the penitent with His presence, and yet to remain the universal, the perfect, the unchangeable God, glorious in action and full of all lovingkindness to men.

The wonder of this relationship of God to the world and man was very clearly before the Jewish mind. God is God alone, high above all height, dwelling in eternity, yet near the humble man, sublime in His exaltation, yet condescending to the lowliest things. The following sentences give expression to the wonderful contrast of His majesty with His active interest in the tiniest worm and in the sorrows of the poor:

Who is like unto the Lord our God,
That hath his seat on high,
That humbleth himself to behold
The things that are in heaven and in the earth?[1]

For thus saith the high and lofty One that inhabiteth eternity, whose name is Holy: I dwell in the high and holy place; with him also that is of a contrite and humble spirit, to revive the spirit of the humble, and to revive the heart of the contrite ones.[2]

The eternal God is thy dwelling place, and underneath are the everlasting arms.[3]

Trust ye in the Lord for ever; for in the Lord Jehovah is an everlasting rock.[4]

We shall consider singly the chief aspects of God's activity in the world.

1. Being perfect in righteousness, having filled the world with righteousness, and having created man a moral being, it is possible for God to influence the moral life of the world at every point. He controls the course of events, and rules among the nations. He watches what goes on in every human heart, speaking in each human conscience, stirring the sinner to remorse and repentance, and strengthening the man who does what is right. God is with us in our moral life:

[1] Ps. 113, 5-6. [2] Isa. 57, 15. [3] Deut. 33, 27. [4] Isa. 26, 4.

I am the Lord which exercise lovingkindness, judgement, and righteousness in the earth: for in these things I delight, saith the Lord.[1]

The Lord hath made known his salvation:
His righteousness hath he openly shewed in the sight of the nations.[2]

But God is the judge:
He putteth down one, and lifteth up another.[3]

The Lord executeth righteous acts,
And judgements for all that are oppressed.[4]

The Lord is in his holy temple,
The Lord, his throne is in heaven;
His eyes behold, his eyelids try, the children of men.[5]

He that planted the ear, shall he not hear?
He that formed the eye, shall he not see?[6]

The Lord is righteous in all his ways,
And gracious in all his works.[7]

Here are a few passages which tell of his dealings with individuals:

He hath shewed thee, O man, what is good; and what doth the Lord require of thee, but to do justly, and to love mercy, and to walk humbly with thy God.[8]

If I regard iniquity in my heart,
The Lord will not hear.[9]

Search me, O God, and know my heart:
Try me, and know my thoughts:
And see if there be any way of wickedness in me,
And lead me in the way everlasting.[10]

Create in me a clean heart, O God;
And renew a right spirit within me.
Cast me not away from thy presence;
And take not thy holy spirit from me.[11]

[1] Jer. 9, 24. [2] Ps. 98. 2. [3] Ps. 75, 7.
[4] Ps. 103, 6. [5] Ps. 11, 4. [6] Ps. 94, 9.
[7] Ps. 145, 17. [8] Mic. 6, 8. [9] Ps. 66, 18.
[10] Ps. 139, 23-24. [11] Ps. 51, 10-11.

If thou, Lord, shouldest mark iniquities,
O Lord, who shall stand?
But there is forgiveness with thee,
That thou mayest be feared.[1]

The Lord is full of compassion and gracious,
Slow to anger, and plenteous in mercy.[2]

Blessed is the man whom thou chastenest, O Lord,
And teachest out of thy law.[3]

2. Being the moral Absolute, God is construed not only as a person, but as the supreme Personality, the universal personal Spirit, on whom all spirits depend, and as sustaining relationships at once personal and perfectly moral with every human being. This last conception, so full of all spiritual riches, is expressed by Christ in the doctrine of the Fatherhood of God. God is with us personally:

The Father of spirits.[4]

In him we live, and move, and have our being.[5]

Thou hast beset me behind and before,
And laid thy hand upon me . . .
Whither shall I go from thy spirit?
Or whither shall I flee from thy presence?[6]

Our Father which art in heaven, hallowed be thy name. Thy kingdom come. Thy will be done, as in heaven, so on earth.[7]

God dealeth with you as with sons.[8]

If ye then, being evil, know how to give good gifts to your children, how much more shall your Father which is in heaven give good things to them that ask him?[9]

3. God bears the closest possible religious relation to every human being. This never-ceasing religious action, this unlimited participation in the spiritual life of men, is possible, because God is altogether independent of men, their praises and their sacrifices. He receives their worship and listens to their prayers for their good, not for His own sake. Christ put

[1] Ps. 130, 3-4.
[2] Ps. 103, 8.
[3] Ps. 94, 12.
[4] Heb. 12, 9.
[5] Acts 17, 28.
[6] Ps. 139, 5, 7.
[7] Matt. 6, 9-10.
[8] Heb. 12, 7.
[9] Matt. 7, 11.

the matter clearly: He is our Father and is guided by love. He can thus act from purpose, in the most serious way possible, without acting selfishly, or becoming dependent on the objects of His action. God is with us religiously.

He speaks to man, revealing Himself and His will:

He made known his way unto Moses,
His doings unto the children of Israel.[1]

God having of old time spoken unto the fathers in the prophets by divers portions and in divers manners, hath at the end of these days spoken unto us in his Son.[2]

Blessed art thou, Simon, son of John; for flesh and blood hath not revealed it unto thee, but my Father which is in heaven.[3]

He knows all about us, and sympathizes with us:

He knoweth our frame;
He remembereth that we are dust.[4]

Your heavenly Father knoweth that ye have need of all these things.[5]

He hears and answers prayers:

O thou that hearest prayer,
Unto thee shall all flesh come.[6]

Ask, and it shall be given you; seek, and ye shall find; knock, and it shall be opened unto you: for every one that asketh receiveth; and he that seeketh findeth; and to him that knocketh it shall be opened.[7]

He guards and helps the poor and the oppressed:

The Lord also will be a high tower for the oppressed,
A high tower in times of trouble;[8]

The poor and needy seek water and there is none, and their tongue faileth for thirst; I the Lord will answer them, I the God of Israel will not forsake them.[9]

He is our comforter:

As one whom his mother comforteth, so will I comfort you.[10]

He healeth the broken in heart,
And bindeth up their sorrows.[11]

God shall wipe away every tear from their eyes.[12]

[1] Ps. 103, 7. [2] Heb. 1, 1–2. [3] Matt. 16, 17. [4] Ps. 103, 14.
[5] Matt. 6, 32. [6] Ps. 65, 2. [7] Matt. 7, 7–8. [8] Ps. 9, 9.
[9] Isa. 41, 17. [10] Isa. 66. 13. [11] Ps. 147, 3. [12] Rev. 7, 17.

He does not depend upon man for anything:

> I know all the fowls of the mountains:
> And the wild beasts of the field are mine.
> If I were hungry, I would not tell thee:
> For the world is mine, and the fulness thereof.[1]

> The God that made the world and all things therein, he, being Lord of heaven and earth, dwelleth not in temples made with hands; neither is he served by men's hands, as though he needed anything, seeing he himself giveth to all life, and breath, and all things.[2]

Yet He asks for our love, worship, and service. It is the duty of every human being to love, worship, and obey God, and God alone:

> My son, give me thine heart.[3]

> The Lord thy God shalt thou worship and him only shalt thou serve.[4]

> Thou shalt love the Lord thy God with all thy heart, and with all thy soul, and with all thy mind.[5]

Every sin is thus an act of personal rebellion against God, deserving severest punishment:

> The soul that sinneth, it shall die.[6]

But God woos every soul to repentance, and offers forgiveness to the man who will give up sin:

> Come now, and let us reason together, saith the Lord: though your sins be as scarlet, they shall be as white as snow; though they be red like crimson, they shall be as wool.[7]

> John came, who baptized in the wilderness and preached the baptism of repentance unto remission of sins.[8]

He sent His Son into the world, and surrendered Him to shame, agony, and death, in order that His children might be drawn back to His love:

> For God so loved the world, that he gave his only begotten Son, that whosoever believeth on him should not perish, but have eternal life.[9]

[1] Ps. 50, 11–12.
[2] Acts 17, 24–25.
[3] Prov. 23, 26.
[4] Matt. 4, 10.
[5] Matt. 22, 37.
[6] Ezek. 18, 4.
[7] Isa. 1, 18.
[8] Mark 1, 4.
[9] John 3, 16.

4. He is clearly and definitely conceived as the Creator of the universe. This is possible, because He is so truly absolute morally. There is no danger of His being lost in His world, or conquered by it. His perfectly holy character enables Him to form the highest of all purposes, to create the world so that it may be the field for the execution of this purpose, and then to guide the course of events so as to help in the accomplishment of that which He has at heart. God is with us in our physical relations:

> In the beginning God created the heaven and the earth.[1]
>
> The God that made the world and all things therein . . . made of one blood every nation of men to dwell on all the face of the earth, . . . that they might seek God, if haply they might feel after him, and find him.[2]

He is not merely immanent in the world in the sense of being present everywhere: He maintains the closest practical relations with all nature, organic as well as inorganic, and with the spirit of man. His hand is first of all on every part of the material universe:

> One God and Father of all, who is over all, and through all, and in all.[3]
>
> He telleth the number of the stars;
> He giveth them all their names.[4]
>
> In his hand are the deep places of the earth;
> The heights of the mountains are his also.[5]
>
> Who maketh the clouds his chariot;
> Who walketh upon the wings of the wind;
> Who maketh winds his messengers;
> His ministers a flame of fire.[6]
>
> He sendeth forth springs into the valleys;
> They run among the mountains;
> They give drink to every beast of the field;
> The wild asses quench their thirst.[7]
>
> Who looketh on the earth, and it trembleth;
> He toucheth the mountains, and they smoke.[8]

[1] Gen. 1, 1. [2] Acts 17, 24, 26, 27. [3] Eph. 4, 6. [4] Ps. 147, 4.
[5] Ps. 95, 4. [6] Ps. 104, 3-4. [7] Ps. 104, 10-11. [8] Ps. 104, 32.

He causes plants and trees to grow:

He causeth the grass to grow for cattle,
And herb for the service of man.[1]

The trees of the Lord are satisfied;
The cedars of Lebanon, which he hath planted.[2]

He cares for all animals:

He giveth to the beast his food,
And to the young ravens which cry.[3]

Are not two sparrows sold for a farthing? and not one of them shall fall on the ground without your Father.[4]

He cares for man in the matter of all his needs, physical, mental, and spiritual:

The Lord is my shepherd; I shall not want.
He maketh me to lie down in green pastures:
He leadeth me beside the still waters.
He restoreth my soul:
He guideth me in the paths of righteousness for his name's sake.
Yea, though I walk through the valley of the shadow of death,
I will fear no evil; for thou art with me:
Thy rod and thy staff, they comfort me.
Thou preparest a table before me in the presence of mine enemies:
Thou hast anointed my head with oil; my cup runneth over.
Surely goodness and mercy shall follow me all the days of my life:
And I will dwell in the house of the Lord for ever.[5]

In particular, He cares for the bodies of men:

The very hairs of your head are all numbered.[6]

My God shall fulfil every need of yours.[7]

He protects man from danger:

God is our refuge and strength,
A very present help in trouble.[8]

As the mountains are round about Jerusalem,
So the Lord is round about his people,
From this time forth and for evermore.[9]

[1] Ps. 104, 14. [2] Ps. 104, 16. [3] Ps. 147, 9. [4] Matt. 10, 29.
[5] Ps. 23. [6] Matt. 10, 30. [7] Phil. 4, 19. [8] Ps. 46, 1.
[9] Ps. 125, 2.

Thou shalt not be afraid for the terror by night,
Nor for the arrow that flieth by day;
Nor the pestilence that walketh in darkness,
Nor for the destruction that wasteth at noonday.[1]

The great problem which has vexed Hindu philosophers and theologians from the very beginning; which deprived God of a living, active character; which made it impossible to conceive the supreme Person as in constant practical touch with every human spirit; which set an impassable barrier between the ardent worshipper and Brahman, 'beyond thought and speech'; and which gave birth to the idea that God's only action is sport, and thereby opened the door to so much unworthy mythology—that age-old Hindu problem is solved in Christianity. The righteous Father of Jesus Christ is the end of the long, noble, passionate quest of Indian philosophy.

II. The second great doctrine of the Vedānta is the identity of the soul and God. We have already thought of the value of the idea, and of the lofty testimony it bears to the divine side of human nature. Man's greatness cannot be assessed more highly, nor his kinship to God more emphatically expressed.

But Indian thinkers have felt very distinctly that it fails to deal seriously with man's moral nature. If man is identical with God, then man's vice must be a negligible element; for it is impossible to conceive that as belonging to the Absolute.

The doctrine also makes love for God and union with God impossible. These religious activities imply that man is distinct from God, and that the two can come into close spiritual intercourse, while remaining distinct.

Then, if the doctrine is to be held in its fullness, God must be construed impersonally. So soon as the divine personality is vividly conceived, it becomes impossible to equate man and God. The differences then become too glaring. Now, the

[1] Ps. 91, 5-6.

religious experience of India throughout the centuries has consistently demanded a personal God: that is the lesson of the whole history of the great sects, and of Buddhism and Jainism as well. Nay, even Śaṅkara's Vedānta is driven to bear the same testimony; for, in order to explain religion and to provide for the clamant needs of the human heart, there appears, in the strict Vedānta, beside the mighty Brahman, a pale spectre, the personal, but temporal and unreal Brahmā. The whole history of Hinduism thus proves that man cannot live without a personal God.

But, given the personal God, the identity of man and God disappears. So, in all the sects, man's spirit is no longer the supreme Spirit whole and undivided, but an *aṁśa* or portion of God. The Śaiva sect still call their system *advaita*, pure monism, and they say that, when the released man dies, he is absorbed in God and loses his individual consciousness. Yet a clear distinction is made between the human spirit and the divine, and the *aṁśa* idea is distinctly held.

The idea that man is but a portion of the divine Spirit escapes the difficulties which the identity doctrine brings to the theist, but it involves others scarcely less serious. It makes it possible to conceive God as a person, but it fails to explain man. How can a fragment of God be a person? Whence come man's personal will, his highly charged emotions, his vivid self-consciousness?

But turn to Christ's doctrine of man. Each human being is a child of God, made in the image of his Father, possessing a spiritual nature that is finite, yet parallel with the divine in its capacities. Man is so like God as to be fit for the immediate, personal, spiritual converse of a son with a father: yet, being a son, he does not lose his personality in God. Man is thus uplifted as high as he is in the old Vedānta: yet all the hallowed relationships of prayer, worship, and love of God are possible. Since he is a son of the personal and righteous God, his self-consciousness and his moral freedom occasion no surprise: while human frailty and sin, though clearly unnatural and unworthy of our high birth, are not altogether incomprehensible. Indian theists have felt very distinctly that God is a God of love and grace; and they have felt that it was both natural and right that man should feel bhakti —deep trust and warm affection—towards God. These high spiritual truths find their full justification only in the teaching of Jesus. If God is truly the Father of all men; and if every human being is a finite child, made in the image of the eternal Father, then God will undoubtedly shower His love and grace on us, and man's highest privilege and duty must be to trust, to love, and to obey his Father. Christ's doctrine of man is, thus, the final truth of which the strict Vedānta and Hindu theism offer each a partial adumbration.

III. The brief outline of the growth of the Indian belief in incarnations given in our last chapter brings us into close touch with one of the most powerful forces working in Hinduism. In these matters we do not deal merely with the ideas of individuals, or of isolated groups of individuals, but with those hidden powers which refuse to submit to the control of man, and work out, in the course of the centuries, vast historical results. That the doctrine of incarnation, which appeared originally in the ancient Vishṇuite sect, should have found its way into almost every division of the Hindu people, and into every corner of Eastern Asia, is the strongest possible testimony to the religious value it possesses for the Hindu and the Asiatic spirit. Nor can there be any doubt as to what element in the doctrine it is that has given the movement its power: it is the belief that God actually appeared as a man, was born, and lived and died among men. This fact comes out quite clearly in the literature; but it becomes still more manifest in intercourse with the people.

A. We must now note and seek to understand certain rather remarkable modifications which the incarnation doctrine has been undergoing in the minds of educated Hindus for some time. It has been both narrowed and widened.

It will be recollected that in both the great sects it has

been usual for centuries to call every outstanding leader an incarnation. Śaṭhakopa, Yamunāchārya, and Rāmānuja among Vishṇuites, Śaṅkara, Śvetāchārya, and Nīlakaṇṭha among Śivaites, and scores of minor saints and scholars of these and other sects, have been recognized as avatāras for several centuries. No thoughtful Hindu would press this seriously to-day. It is too big a stretch to ask any one to believe that Vishṇu's necklace or his discus took human birth. It is quite true that a few enthusiastic disciples have called Rāmakṛishṇa Paramahaṁsa and Mrs. Besant avatāras; but no thoughtful man takes such a proposal as a piece of theology: it is merely a way of testifying to their great services to Hinduism. Faith in the animal incarnations of Vishṇu has also disappeared. It is simply impossible for the modern man to believe that God appeared on earth in the form of a monster, half-man, half-lion. These things are too clearly mythology to be believed to-day.

The only incarnations which the modern Hindu attempts to hold by seriously are Rāma and Kṛishṇa. He may give some sort of acknowledgement to earlier stories, but he does not vouch for them. Rāma and Kṛishṇa, however, he does defend. Indeed, one of the most significant things in Neo-Hindu literature is this, that books have been written to attempt to prove that the accounts given in the Epics of Rāma and Kṛishṇa are historical.[1] Thinking men have realized that, unless these things can be shown to be really historical, the old incarnation faith cannot but disappear. These books make sorry reading; and no wonder; for they undertake an impossible task. During the last few years Hindus have usually contented themselves with bold assertions: so far as the writer knows, no serious treatise on the subject has been published recently.

On the other hand, there has been a very significant widening of the old idea, so as to cover Christ, Muḥammad, Confucius,

[1] For an account of some of this literature see the Appendix to the present writer's *Gītā and Gospel*.

and other religious leaders; and many a modern Hindu believes that he holds a philosophy of religion not only reasonable but liberal, because he acknowledges all the great teachers of mankind to have been incarnations. Such a theory draws out one's sympathy very deeply. The modern man cannot get on without a working theory of religion covering all the phenomena. But what a change this registers in Hindu belief! Buddha was long ago acknowledged to have been an incarnation of Vishṇu, but only in the sense that Vishṇu became embodied as Buddha to deceive men and seduce them into a false religion. Here we have all the great religions of the world acknowledged as good, and as having been founded by real incarnations. Do Hindus realize what a revolution in Hindu thought and practice the sincere acceptance of such a doctrine would involve?

B. We cannot wonder at this serious unsettlement of opinion; for our study of the history has made it absolutely plain that all Indian stories of incarnation are baseless. Rāma, Kṛishṇa, and Gautama the Buddha, as they appear in the earliest literature, are men, and men only, indeed, are as far from being incarnations as any men could possibly be. Rāma and Kṛishṇa are not even religious leaders in any sense: they are but kings and warriors; and it was only some three hundred years after their appearance in literature that the belief arose that they were incarnations. It was much later still before they were called full incarnations of the Supreme. In the case of Gautama, the Buddha, the history is rather different. He was one of the greatest religious leaders the world has ever seen. A large section of the human race still draw their religious inspiration from him. But his system was determinedly opposed to the ideas that lie behind incarnation. To have thought of himself as an incarnate god would have been revolting to him; and it was at least five hundred years after his death before his followers dared associate his name with the doctrine of the one living God. Only on the basis of such a doctrine was the idea of incarnation possible. Gautama had been five hundred years dead before he was called an avatāra. Thus every Indian incarnation story is a myth.

Philosophic Hinduism is independent of history: no matter when or by whom the ideas were first expressed, they retain their intrinsic value. Hindus are keenly conscious of this fact and often refer to it. But the principle does not apply to the belief in incarnations: the very pith of the doctrine is the appearance of God in human history. As we have seen, the power the doctrine wields over the Hindu heart springs from the belief that at certain definite times God was born, lived, and died as a man in India.

Hence, since every single Hindu incarnation is altogether mythical, the doctrine is dying, and will inevitably pass away. The changes it has undergone in the educated mind during the last half-century are symptoms of its dying condition.

Nor can the patriotic Hindu wish the doctrine to survive. He cannot desire that the poor of the people should be fed with mythology. A strong Indian nation can never be bred on such diet.

C. It is the spirit of the West that has wrought these changes in the incarnation doctrine. Two forms of Western influence have been specially active in this part of Hinduism. First, the sense of history has laid hold of the most cultured men, and has led them to study the growth of Hinduism frankly and openly. Hence, some have been found to confess that the incarnation tales are mythical. But most say nothing on the subject, or, like Baṅkim Chandra Chatterji, try to persuade themselves and others that the man-god Kṛishṇa is historical. Secondly, the presentation of the historical Jesus has produced very large results. His sure place in the world's history, His personal claims, His boundless personal interest, and the historical grip of the New Testament have proved very potent in rousing the Hindu mind.

D. On the other hand, the acceptance of these incarnation stories by such vast multitudes of the people of India and of Eastern Asia is all the more significant, when we realize how baseless they are. How deep and how powerful must the instinct be to which these mythical stories are a response! The instinct for the living God is undoubtedly the deepest and most insistent of all our natural religious faculties; but, clearly, amongst those that come next none is more vivid or more powerful than the longing for God manifest in the flesh.

E. But the question now rises, If the avatāras are all mythical, what are Hindus to do? Are they simply to drop the doctrine and do without it? The large place it has held in Hinduism for more than two thousand years shows how highly the Hindu religious spirit appreciates the idea of GOD WITH US. To give it up would be to confess, not only that the Hindu mind mistook myth for history, but that it has been seriously mistaken in one of its chief religious intuitions. If we cannot trust the Hindu spirit in a large matter such as this, in what can we afford to trust it?

F. The Christian standpoint is much less sceptical. The man who accepts Jesus as the incarnate Son of God certainly confesses that the Hindu mind has mistaken the Rāma and Kṛishṇa myths for history; but he holds that the Hindu spirit was right in looking for God manifest in the flesh. Must not this be the attitude of the true Indian patriot? In loyalty to truth he cannot but confess the incarnation stories to be mythical; but, if he feels any confidence in the spiritual capacities of his people, he will expect to find in human history a real divine descent into human life. Thus Jesus, whose teaching so wonderfully crowns the ideas of Hinduism, is needed to give stability and reality to the Hindu belief in incarnations. Without Him, it must pass away like the baseless fabric of a vision.

G. But have Christians any rational ground for asking the Hindu to accept Jesus as the incarnate Son of God? The following lines of thought may bring the foundations of Christian conviction before the reader.

1. Those who knew Jesus best declared that in Him they had seen God revealed. The whole of the New Testament is

evidence of what they thought and how strong their faith was. Here is what a modern historian says of the fact:

> Where in the history of mankind can we find anything resembling this, that men who had eaten and drunk with their Master should glorify him, not only as the revealer of God, but as the Prince of life, as the Redeemer and Judge of the world, as the living power of its existence, and that a choir of Jews and Gentiles, Greeks and Barbarians, wise and foolish, should along with them immediately confess that out of the fullness of this one man they have received grace for grace? [1]

2. The whole history of Christian influence in the world proves conclusively that Christian truth produces its characteristic results on a community only when Jesus is recognized as the Son of God. Unitarianism is a beautiful plant, but it is always sickly. Hindus have an object lesson before their eyes in the vigour of the Christian Church as compared with the weakness of the Brāhma Samāj.

3. When we turn to the teaching of Jesus, as handed down to us in the Gospels by His disciples, we find not only that Jesus calls Himself the Son of God, but that His teaching from beginning to end is steeped in such ideas as could have been held only by a mind that conceived itself as possessing divine authority.

(*a*) Jesus summons His hearers to personal surrender to Himself, to complete obedience, to public confession of their allegiance to Him, to readiness to suffer or even to die for His sake:

> He that loveth father or mother more than me is not worthy of me; and he that loveth son or daughter more than me is not worthy of me. And he that doth not take his cross and follow after me, is not worthy of me. He that findeth his life shall lose it; and he that loseth his life for my sake shall find it.[2]

> Why call ye me, Lord, Lord, and do not the things that I say? [3]

> Every one therefore who shall confess me before men, him will I also confess before my Father which is in heaven.[4]

[1] Harnack, *History of Dogma*, i. 76.
[2] Matt. 10, 37–39. [3] Luke 6, 46. [4] Matt. 10, 32.

> Blessed are ye when men shall reproach you, and persecute you, and say all manner of evil against you falsely, for my sake.[1]

He also set Himself forth as the example which we should copy:

> Come unto me, all ye that labour and are heavy laden, and I will give you rest. Take my yoke upon you, and learn of me; for I am meek and lowly in heart: and ye shall find rest unto your souls.[2]

Now the strange thing is that men have discovered that, in order to live such a life as Jesus calls us to live, it is necessary not only to attend to His teaching carefully, but to surrender ourselves to Him as Lord in the precise way which the above texts prescribe. The demand of Jesus that we should give Him absolute obedience is verified as a right thing religiously, in Christian experience. Here is what Harnack says:

> The Gospel can only be grasped and held firm by a believing self-surrender to the person of Christ.[3]

James Drummond, one of the leading Unitarian writers of recent years, says:

> Jesus is, to the heart that loves him, 'a quickening spirit,' one who forms the interior life, and fills it with an abounding energy.[4]

What is implied in this wonderful spiritual relation between Christ and the soul?

(*b*) That is precisely the question which Jesus Himself asks. He does not obtrude His person on us, but becomes our servant and helper, doing the more for us the more completely we yield to Him. Then He asks each one of us in the quiet of our own hearts the question which He asked of His disciples,

> Who say ye that I am?[5]

(*c*) When first we make the acquaintance of Jesus, one of

[1] Matt. 5, 11. [2] Matt. 11, 28–29.
[3] *Dogmengeschichte*, iii. 69. I owe this quotation to Mackintosh, *Person of Jesus Christ*, 347.
[4] *Studies in Christian Doctrine*, 291. See Mackintosh, 340.
[5] Matt. 16, 15.

the things that puzzle us most is the fact that He usually calls Himself the Son of Man. Careful study reveals that He thought of Himself as the head of the human race, and that He felt Himself directly related to every man, woman, and child.[1] He believed that every man needed Him:

> And blessed is he, whosoever shall find none occasion of stumbling in me.[2]

As the Son of Man, He believed that He had authority on earth to forgive sin.[3] Finally, He was convinced that, as the Son of Man, He must die for men:

> For verily the Son of man came not to be ministered unto, but to minister, and to give his life a ransom for many.[4]

(*d*) Feeling so keenly that all men needed His teaching and help, He said that His disciples, to whom He committed the carrying on of His work, occupied a position of the utmost responsibility with regard to all men; and He urged them in the most solemn way to fulfil it:

> Ye are the salt of the earth.[5]
>
> Ye are the light of the world.[6]
>
> Go ye, therefore, and make disciples of all the nations.[7]

(*e*) Since Jesus thought in this way about His life and work, we are not astonished to find that, in relation to the Jewish people, He called Himself the Messiah, and said that He had come to introduce the Kingdom of God. When He was tried by the Jewish Council, the President definitely asked Him the question. In reply He declared Himself the Messiah; and, finally, He allowed Himself to be crucified rather than give up the claim.

(*f*) In relation to God the Father, Jesus called Himself the Son, and He affirmed that He alone could reveal the Father:

> All things have been delivered unto me of my Father: and no one

[1] Matt. 25, 40–45. [2] Matt. 11, 6. [3] Mark 2, 10.
[4] Mark 10, 45. [5] Matt. 5, 13. [6] Matt. 5, 14.
[7] Matt. 28, 19.

knoweth who the Son is, save the Father; and who the Father is, save the Son, and he to whomsoever the Son willeth to reveal him.[1]

These, in briefest, simplest form, are the foundations of the Christian conviction that Jesus is the incarnate Son of God. We do not talk of proving that He is the Son. Like all the deepest things of religion, this is a matter of moral and spiritual apprehension, not of logical demonstration. Jesus comes to every educated Hindu to-day, and says, 'In the light of all the history of Hinduism, of the history of the world, of my teaching, of my Cross, of your own religious experience, who say you that I am?'

IV. The following paragraphs are intended to throw light on the relation in which the historic Christ stands to the mythical incarnations of India.

Poets sang of the avatāras, and saints of many schools meditated on them, until a common portrait took definite form and became a national ideal; so that the main features are found in the Kṛishṇa of the *Gītā*, the Buddha of the *Saddharma Puṇḍarīka*, the Rāma of Tulsī Dās, and even in Māṇikka Vāchakar's conception of the frequent theophanies of Śiva.

A. The central conception of the doctrine is this, that God became a man, was born, lived, and died a man. Here, as we have seen, lies the real power of the whole movement over the mind and heart of India and of the other lands that have accepted it. There are many passages in the books which give expression to the sense of wonder which the belief creates, and the lowly adoration stirred by it. Thus, according to the *Gītā*, when Kṛishṇa showed his transcendent form to Arjuna, the latter burst into a hymn of adoring praise, of which we quote a few stanzas:

> Hail, hail to Thee! a thousand times all hail!
> Hail unto Thee! again, again all hail!
>
> . . . . . .
>
> In power boundless, measureless in strength,
> Thou holdest all: then Thou Thyself art All.

[1] Luke 10, 22.

If, thinking Thee but friend, importunate,
O Kṛishna! or O Yādava! O friend!
I cried, unknowing of Thy majesty,
And careless in the fondness of my love;

If jesting, I irreverence showed to Thee,
At play, reposing, sitting or at meals,
Alone, O sinless One, or with my friends,
Forgive my error, O Thou boundless One.

Therefore I fall before Thee; with my body
I worship as is fitting; bless Thou me.
As father with the son, as friend with friend,
With the beloved as lover, bear with me.[1]

We see the influence of the same emotions in the passionate love of Hindus for the baby Kṛishṇa and the innumerable idols of the little crawling boy to be found in Indian homes all over the country. So Tulsī Dās is filled with wondering reverence for the humility and condescension of Rāma in being born a man; and Mānikka Vāchakar is never done pouring out his praises to Siva for the love and self-humiliation of his theophanies.

Yet, in the case of every Indian incarnation, the humanity assumed by the god is unreal. His human body is but a disguise; his human weakness and emotion are assumed; his limitations are but a pretence. The glory of the Supreme is scarcely dimmed by the muddy vesture of human flesh in which for the moment the great Actor robes himself. To the Hindu anything beyond this would seem to be unworthy of the Highest. There is never the idea that the incarnate God was confined to human conditions or limited to the powers of human nature. In the *Gītā* all the stress is laid on the divinity of Kṛishṇa: he has a man-like form, but he is never conceived as a true man. He is always the god concealed in the seemingly human form.

We meet the same conceptions of Gautama in the *Saddharma Puṇḍarīka*. Everything that he does is *līlā*, sport.

[1] xi. 39-44. Mrs. Besant's translation.

His coming to earth and his passing to Nirvāṇa are mere pretences: he remains all the time on Gṛidhrakūṭa. His death is but a device, an expedient, a piece of deceit, necessary for the good of men.

Similar phrases are used by Māṇikka Vāchakar of Śiva. All his operations, whether in the universe or in the soul, are only sport, *līlā*. They are typified in his dance. All his theophanies are illusion. He is constantly called the great Deceiver. He appears and works as a cooly, as a groom among horses, and in various other ways; but on each occasion he is the god disporting himself: there is no human toil, no true human experience.

The same terms reappear in Tulsī Dās. All that Rāma does is sport. He is an actor; he is the great master of the unreal; he constantly uses his deceptive, illusive power. He pretends to feel pain, sorrow, astonishment, or pleasure, but it is all mere acting:

> For the sake of his faithful people, the very God, our lord Rāma, has become incarnate as a king and for our supreme sanctification has lived as it were the life of any ordinary man. As an actor in the course of his performance assumes a variety of dresses and exhibits different characters, but himself remains the same; such, Garuḍa, is Rāma's divertissement, a bewilderment to the demons, but a delight to the faithful.[1]

In the case of Jesus, however, the very reverse is true. He was truly a man. He was no actor, no sportive illusionist. All was actual from beginning to end. He was born a helpless babe and grew in knowledge as He grew in body.[2] As a baby, He had no divine powers to display to a terrified mother, like Rāma in Tulsī Dās's poem.[3] By the age of twelve, He knew and loved His heavenly Father, but He was subject to His parents.[4] He was trained as a carpenter,[5] and toiled at the bench, earning bread for Himself, His mother, and the others by the sweat of His brow. There was no divine power used

[1] Growse, 533.
[2] Luke 2, 40.
[3] Growse, 96–97.
[4] Luke 2, 41–51.
[5] Mark 6, 3.

to lighten His labour. It was no few minutes of pretended toil, like Śiva's cooly labour. He made yokes and ploughs and such-like, until He was thirty years of age,[1] thus ennobling and hallowing all manual labour for man.

Throughout His public life He remained a real man, our brother, living our common human life under all the restrictions and limitations which narrow and shut us in. He was homeless,[2] suffered from thirst,[3] from hunger,[4] from fatigue.[5] His knowledge was limited: He frequently asked for information, never making any pretence of ignorance, and once at least He said He did not know.[6] Miraculous powers were given Him for His work, but they were always used to help others, never once for Himself, not even in the hunger that followed a forty days' fast,[7] not even in the agonies of crucifixion.[8] His favourite name for Himself was 'the Son of Man'. It is the glory of the Son of Man that He shared all the toil, sorrow and sufferings of His brothers and sisters of the human race.[9]

We here reach the point where the divergence between the Hindu incarnate ideal and Christ is at its greatest. 'How can Jesus be divine, since he was crucified? If he had been divine, he could have easily overcome his murderers. God cannot be defeated by man.' In such wise has many a Hindu argued. The Jews who stood round the Cross argued in the same way:

> And it was the third hour, and they crucified him. And the superscription of his accusation was written over, THE KING OF THE JEWS. And with him they crucify two robbers; one on his right hand, and one on his left. And they that passed by railed on him, wagging their heads, and saying, Ha! thou that destroyest the temple, and buildest it in three days, save thyself, and come down from the cross. In like manner also the chief priests mocking him among themselves with the scribes said, He saved others; himself he cannot save. Let the Christ, the King of Israel, now come down from the cross, that we may see and believe.[10]

[1] Luke 3, 23. [2] Matt. 8, 20. [3] John 4, 7. [4] Matt. 4, 2. [5] John 4, 6. [6] Matt. 24, 36. [7] Matt. 4, 4. [8] Matt. 27, 39–44. [9] Heb. 2, 14–18. [10] Mark 15, 25–32.

But is it not evident that, if Jesus came to earth to be the Saviour, it was His duty to save others, not Himself? The innermost secret of Christ's method is this, that He gives Himself up in self-sacrifice to win the sinner back to God. The Crucifixion is only the final exhibition before all the world of what had been going on in the life of Jesus from the beginning:

> For the Son of man came not to be served but to be a servant, and to give his life a ransom for many.[1]

The devout Hindu will probably be sore amazed at the idea of the incarnate One being truly a man; for it stands wide apart from Hindu conceptions. But here, in the central mystery of the Word become flesh and the only-begotten and well-beloved Son self-devoted on the Cross, lies the very heart of the Christian faith, the very fountain-head of the Christian life.

The Indian religious instinct divined that God would become man, but did not realize the depths of the divine humility and self-sacrifice. The main idea is right, but the detailed out-working is a failure. Even at its best Hindu incarnation is no true incarnation; God only seems to become man. Even if by some writers the human body be conceived as a reality, God has not become man, but only appears within a human shell. In Christ, on the other hand, the Son of God actually becomes man, shares our pains and sorrows, our temptations and moral difficulties, and lives under the same conditions as we do. Thus, Jesus fulfils the Indian thought. He is the realization of the Indian ideal; but in this case, as in every other, the reality sent by God is far better and more wonderful than the imagination of man.

B. The *character* of the incarnate One is described with a good deal of detail in some of the books, and is regarded by modern Hindus as a matter of considerable moment. It has two aspects.

[1] Matt. 20, 28.

(*a*) The idea that the incarnate One should be an example to men scarcely occurs in the literature. Yet for many centuries the *Rāmāyaṇa* of Vālmīki has been used as a mirror of character, Rāma being regarded as the ideal man and husband, and Sītā as the ideal wife. Fortunate is the Hindu people in having this piece of literature. Rāma and his faithful wife are indeed beautiful and healthy examples of Hindu life. Men of every race will heartily admire them. Yet it would be unwise to think of them as likely to exercise any serious ethical influence on the world. They are good Hindus; and there is much that is noble and helpful in their characters; but they do not lead the van of human life. It is also necessary to note that it is the original part of the poem, in which Rāma and Sītā are still purely human characters, that has proved fruitful in this regard.

From the time when Rāma and Kṛishṇa were thought of as the Deity incarnate, there is no longer any idea that their earthly life can afford moral examples to men. That is the reason why the *Gītā* says not a word about the earthly life of Kṛishṇa beyond what is implied in the situation. If we wanted to study the character and behaviour attributed to him in the literature, we should have to turn to the *Mahābhārata* and the *Purāṇas*; and there the material is the very opposite of promising. Fortunately, we are saved the trouble of dealing with it; for the *Bhāgavata Purāṇa*, one of the chief Kṛishṇaite authorities, warns us in the most serious way that men must on no account imitate the actions of gods. Tulsī Dās fully concurs in this judgement. Both passages have been already quoted.[1]

In spite of this solemn warning, a modern Hindu, roused to emulation by the Christian attitude to Christ, has written a work called *The Imitation of Śrīkṛishṇa.* It is a daily text-book, consisting of extracts from the *Gītā,* the *Mahābhārata*, and the very book which condemns such imitation, the *Bhāgavata Purāṇa.*

[1] Above, pp. 394–395.

In order to avoid misunderstanding, we may point out that in the *Bhagavadgītā* the actionless action of the transcendental Kṛishṇa-Brahman is put forward as an example of karma-yoga for men to follow. This is not the action of the incarnate One, however.

(*b*) But the character and life of the Incarnate are everywhere regarded as a revelation of the unknowable Brahman, whether he be construed as personal or impersonal. The outlines of this character are described in the various books with a good deal of unanimity.

His most prominent trait is sportiveness: he is full of play, tricks, and pretences. His illusive power enables him to do anything and to appear in any guise. One never knows what he will do next. In this way all the old mythology, which was current about Śiva, Vishṇu, Rāma, and Kṛishṇa before the doctrine of incarnations and of humanitarian theophanies arose, is retained, and is used to give variety to the character and incident to the life. Next in importance comes his indifference. He has the same feeling to every creature born. He is as kind to the evil as to the good. The *Gītā* says he neither loves nor hates. Although he is always active, his activity is not purposeful action, but mere sport. Hence he is always at peace. Thus far the character is precisely the same as that attributed to the Ātman in the Upanishads.

But, where God is conceived as personal, other traits appear in the character of the incarnate One. He is compassionate toward all, and is ready to give his grace to those who show devotion to him. He is their refuge, friend, and comforter; and he is ready to release them from sin. From the time of the Tamil poet-saints the Incarnate is always said to be a god of love. Hence the statement of the *Gītā* quoted above is not repeated. Māṇikka Vāchakar frequently insists on Śiva's humility, and Tulsī Dās thinks similarly of Rāma. Finally, Māṇikka speaks of Śiva as having suffered for men, and Tulsī Dās also emphasizes the sufferings of Rāma.

It is a most remarkable fact that the characteristic features of the most beautiful moral ideal ever created in India, namely, the ideal for ascetics, which we have already dealt with, was never ascribed to the incarnate One. World-renunciation, self-effacement, meekness, gentleness, forgiveness, and endurance were the marks of the monk, but were not thought of as characteristic of the avatāra, the reason being that he was always the divine in human disguise, never a real man.

We now turn from these wonderful creations of the Hindu religious imagination to the character of the historical Jesus.

(1) As He was truly a man, His character is genuinely human. We watch the growth of His moral nature; and we recognize in Him all the strain and struggle which we experience ourselves. His character grew gradually to ripeness. He had to fight His way upward against temptations, just as we have to do; only He never yielded, but kept free from all sin. He was dependent upon His Father as ordinary men are. This becomes completely apparent when we study His prayer-life. He struggled to learn and to do the will of His Father, putting down the human heart, which tended to rebel against the awful ordeal He had to pass through. He prayed whole nights, and cried to His Father with tears and mighty wrestlings of spirit. In fighting temptation and enduring persecution He learned obedience, and won His way to the perfection of the full moral stature.

(2) The most extraordinary fact about His character is this, that He, in whom the moral ideal was so lofty and so exacting, who knew sin so thoroughly as to hate it perfectly, who demanded repentance, and brought so many to it, never expresses any consciousness of sin, never shows the slightest trace of repentance or confession. Clearly He was that supremest miracle, a sinless soul. Through boyhood, youth, and manhood He lived so close to His Father that He was kept utterly pure. It is this above all things that sets Him apart from the greatest of men. He alone was utterly without stain. In Him the moral ideal was realized. He is the fairest of the sons of men, yea altogether lovely. Men of all

nations have recognized that the character of Jesus is perfect, that there is no difference between His teaching and His life.

(3) Since Jesus, then, lived up to the highest moral ideal ever conceived by man, He is the highest example for us. In Him we see what we ought to be. He is our religious as well as our moral example; for, being a true man, He lived by prayer, dependence on God and worship, as we do. Readers will realize how impossible it would be to form such a conception as this in the case of the incarnations of Hinduism.

(4) But, since Jesus exhibited in character and life the moral ideal at its very height, He was also the revelation of God. When we say that God is ethical, we mean that He Himself conforms to the standard which He bids us live by; but no religion, except Judaism and Christianity, has had the courage to say this frankly. It is the message of the Old Testament. It receives concrete expression in the character of Jesus, who, being the revelation of the Father, the express image of the righteous God, is also the example for men.

In Him the Indian incarnate ideal is more than fulfilled. The sketch of the divine character given by Hindu writers is here filled with a glory and a beauty they never dreamt of. And what the Hindu books declare to be impossible, namely, that the incarnate One should be a model to men, was actually accomplished by Jesus. In revealing the Father, He became our Exemplar. The chief points of character ascribed to the avatāra are raised to glory in Him. He lived in the peace of His Father's arms, and sought to lead men to the same. The indifference to men, which is the Indian ideal, is in Him raised to that love for the human race which was the mainspring of His life. His humility far surpasses anything told of Śiva. Compassion showed itself in daily toil for the sick and the suffering. Tulsī Dās and Māṇikka Vāchakar make their heroes endure suffering for the sake of men; but there is nothing in either poet to compare with the Cross of Christ.

(5) But strange to say, Jesus fulfils the Indian ascetic ideal

also. The main difference between Him and the Indian ascetic is that He did not seek suffering nor inflict pain upon Himself. Humiliation, contempt, slander, mockery, shame, desertion, treachery, hunger, thirst, pain, torture, death—all came to Him in the course of His daily endeavour to serve mankind. 'He was despised and rejected of men, a man of sorrows and acquainted with grief.' 'Behold and see if there is any sorrow like unto his sorrow.' Yet all the meekness, gentleness, and forgiveness laid down as an ideal for the monk appear in actual fact in His daily life, the product of the love which inspired Him.

C. The incarnate God of Hinduism and Buddhism is a great teacher.

This aspect of the ideal is very weak in all the literature referring to Rāma. In Vālmīki's *Rāmāyaṇa* he is no teacher at all; the same is true of the late Rāma Upanishads; and in Tulsī Dās, though here and there he gives religious advice, it scarcely amounts to teaching.

The original man-god Kṛishṇa of the second stage of the *Mahābhārata* is also no teacher: his work was the destruction of monsters. But in the *Gītā* the situation is very different. The god is no longer required to rid the earth of demons. A new need has arisen: the Vaishṇava layman needs a theistic theology. Hence Kṛishṇa is transformed into a guru of the school of the Vedānta, and teaches the ancient lore of the Upanishads, with the addition, that he himself is Brahman incarnate. Hence he is called 'World-teacher, worshipful and most reverend.'[1] In the *Saddharma Puṇḍarīka* Gautama, transformed into an incarnate god, teaches as he actually did during life, only his message is new. It was probably the example of Kṛishṇa that led to the idea that Śiva frequently appears on earth as a guru. Māṇikka Vāchakar attributes his own conversion to a theophany of this type.

The *Gītā* has had an extraordinary influence in India for

[1] xi. 43.

at least seventeen centuries, and the *Saddharma Puṇḍarīka* has played almost as great a rôle in China and Japan. But, while we venerate works which have touched men's hearts so deeply, we cannot read them to-day as the teaching of Kṛishṇa and Gautama. They are sisters, children of the same pregnant period, but the names of the great men who wrote them are altogether unknown.

In the Gospels, on the other hand, we have the undoubted teaching of Jesus of Nazareth. From Him came Christianity. So the ancient Romans tell us, and the Jews, as well as His own followers. Of the source of Christianity there is no more doubt than there is as to the source of Muḥammadanism, of Buddhism, or of the system of Rāmānuja.

Jesus conceives Himself as the World-teacher. He invites all to come and learn from Him. He makes His offers to everybody. His disciples are the salt of the earth, and the light of the world,[1] and His Gospel will be preached throughout the world.[2] There are no national limits in His teaching. He thinks of all men as children of God, and of God's love as blessing all men. When He sits as Judge, all the nations will be gathered before Him.[3]

In the preceding chapters of this book we have seen something of the character and power of the teaching of Jesus, its spirituality, its universality, and the wonderful way in which it fits into the needs of modern India and crowns the noblest ideals of the old religion. As we have already seen, His teaching is distinguished from the teaching of all other religious leaders in this, that He lays down no detailed laws for our guidance, but merely states the universal spiritual principles which lie at the basis of human life and conduct.[4] This is the secret of the fact that His moral and religious ideas are applicable in every country in the world and to men in all stages of civilization. Wherever a religion has undertaken to lay down a detailed religious law, it has thereby localized

[1] Matt. 5, 13–14.
[2] Matt. 26, 13.
[3] Matt. 25, 31–32.
[4] See above, pp. 58–59.

itself. No matter how excellent such laws may be, they cannot be applied to all the world. Conceive of Manu imposed on the Esquimaux, or the law of Moses given to a cannibal tribe in Central Africa. There is nothing in Christ's teaching that binds human freedom, nothing that offends against the laws of health, nothing that hinders simple human intercourse. He gives us the great principles, and each nation is left free to work out its own practice in harmony with the latest discoveries of science, and in such a way as to suit its own peculiar history and environment. Christ's teaching is universally applicable, and everywhere lays the foundations of freedom.

Every man may see the outcome of these facts in the world to-day. Christ's teaching is really preached in all the world. Indeed there is no race of men of any importance on earth that does not contain Christians. The message of Jesus has already proved itself universal in actual experience.

Although Jesus deals with universal principles, His words are supreme in their simplicity. His sentences are terse, epigrammatic, unforgettable. They are homely in the extreme, richly illustrated, parabolic. The consequence is that His teaching is utterly unlike any other piece of literature in the world. It is cast in such a form that it is universally comprehensible, even by men scarcely out of barbarism. This is the reason why the Gospels can be so readily translated into every language on earth. When translated, these books are not only intelligible to the simplest men: they retain the power of the original; they are as mighty to touch human hearts, as potent in producing repentance and faith and holiness, as the original itself. Where is there in all the world another book that shows this universal adaptability and simplicity? Imagine the *Gītā* and the *Chhāndogya Upanishad* translated and put into the hands of the cannibals of New Guinea, the savages of Terra del Fuego, or even the Outcastes of India! But the Gospels are actually known and treasured by men of these races, men who through Christ have escaped from savagery. You may go and hear them read the Gospels at family prayers. Thus does Christ daily prove Himself in fact the Teacher of the human race.

D. The Incarnate comes to save.

In the earliest period of the doctrine the saving work of Rāma and Kṛishṇa consists in killing monsters. Kṛishṇa kills Kaṁśa, the murderous king, Puṭana, the demon-nurse, and Kāliya, the snake-king. Rāma kills the demon-king Rāvaṇa. It was the gods who required help against Rāvaṇa: it was as their Saviour that Vishṇu became incarnate as the four sons of Daśaratha.

In the *Gītā* we have a much wider outlook. Kṛishṇa is represented as saying:

> To save the righteous, to destroy evil-doers, to establish the law, I come into birth age after age.[1]

He now saves the righteous and establishes *dharma*[2] as well as destroys demons.

In the *Saddharma Puṇḍarīka* another step forward is taken. Destruction is dropped out of the task of the Incarnate. Gautama is represented as saying:

> Repeatedly am I born in the world of the living.
> I am the Tathāgata, the Lord, who has no superior, who appears in this world to save.[3]

There is the same point of view in Aśvaghosha. To save all beings is said to be the aim of the Buddhas.[4]

Śiva, as we have seen, does not become incarnate, but manifests himself in human form. In these theophanies Śiva usually springs from a liṅga, or else takes the form of a Śaiva guru; but he may come in any guise. He appears either to teach or to help his devotees in need. Māṇikka Vāchakar says:

> Assuming diverse forms, and diverse habitudes, . . . Iśa, Lord of the bull, that the world might be saved,—He and the Lady, His partner,—came in grace.[5]

[1] iv. 8. [2] See p. 218. [3] *S. B. E.*, xxi. 308; 124.
[4] Suzuki, 98. [5] Pope, 9.

Tulsī Dās includes many things in the work of Rāma, but he never represents him as a guru. Here is his statement of the reasons for his incarnation:

> Whenever virtue decays, and evil spirits, waxing strong in pride, work iniquity that cannot be told, to the confusion of Brāhmans, cows, gods, and earth itself, the compassionate Lord assumes some new bodily form, relieves the distress of the faithful; destroys evil spirits; reinstates the gods; maintains the way of salvation; and diffuses the brightness of his glory throughout the world. Such are the motives of Rāma's incarnations.[1]

He confesses frankly that Rāma was no Saviour of men when he was on the earth; but he declares that 'his name' has saved millions:

> Rāma himself redeemed only one woman, the ascetic's wife;[2] but his name has corrected the errors of millions of sinners.[3]

These two last writers also introduce the touching thought of vicarious suffering. Māṇikka Vāchakar says:

> Thou mad'st me thine; didst fiery poison eat, pitying poor souls;
> That I might thine ambrosia taste, I meanest one![4]

Tulsī Dās:

> From the love that he bore to his followers, Rāma took the form of a man, and by himself enduring misery secured their happiness.[5]

It is very remarkable how the crude original idea of an incarnation, undertaken to rid the gods of an almost omnipotent demon, was gradually purified in the course of the centuries. The advance in the *Gītā* is very great, but the highest thought of all is the vicarious suffering taught by the Tamil and Hindu saints.

From these fascinating imaginations we turn to the actual life of Jesus. At this point the most significant thing for us to notice is that the whole of His public life was one continuous piece of saving activity.

He was the first religious teacher to take up a healthy

[1] Growse, 63. [2] Namely Ahalyā. See p. 298.
[3] Ib. 16. [4] Pope, 102. [5] Growse, 16.

attitude to the human body. He knew full well the value of the soul:

> What shall it profit a man, if he shall gain the whole world, and lose his soul?[1]

Yet he recognized the place of the body, as all modern thought does, and left us His example of loving care for it. He spent a great deal of time and energy in healing the body. All that modern science has got to say as to the importance of attending to our physical well-being is in accordance with the spirit of Jesus. All that we can do to bring medical aid to the sick, to introduce sanitation into Indian villages, to destroy the germs of disease, and to transform unhealthy conditions, and all our plans for healthy physical exercise, for outdoor games, for drill and gymnastics, are completely in accordance with His teaching and practice. India needs to learn to look after the body.

He sought to save human society, to make social intercourse happy, healthy, pure, and free. Having the heart of a brother to every son of Adam, He was the most sociable and the most hospitable of men. He would not have people go hungry nor a festive occasion fail. This is the reason why He spread His table on the rich green grass of Bethsaida for more than five thousand guests. He knew well the deep influence exerted on character by every aspect of social life; and, therefore, He wished to fill it with His own spirit of love. He wished to mould society as well as religion. He also used such occasions to win the hearts of those around Him, so as to draw them to His Father.

One of the chief aims Jesus had in view in His social life was the breaking down of social barriers, the actual establishment in practice of the new social idea, that a man may honourably eat and drink with men of every race and of every social grade. How completely new, how explosively revolutionary, this idea was then, every student of antiquity and of

[1] Matt. 16, 26.

India knows. Jesus was ready to sit down and eat with any one. He dined with wealthy men belonging to the strictest Jewish sect, the Pharisees; He dined with those who were considered hopelessly beyond the pale of respectable or religious society.

But Jesus goes still further. To Him human society is a mystic, a divine thing, of incalculable influence; our daily bread comes from our Father's hand; food eaten in common, whether at a family meal or in some larger gathering, ought to bind us to one another as well as to the great Provider: its significance is inexhaustible. Hence He chose the last meal He had with His disciples to be the Memorial of His own dying Love, and to become the central and most precious element in Christian worship.

But Jesus came into the world to save men from sin; and therefore the chief toil of His life was teaching, and the greatest of His acts was His redemptive death. Māṇikka Vāchakar and Tulsī Dās realized that the Incarnate One in His compassion and love would suffer for the sake of men: Jesus fulfilled their thought on the Cross of Calvary. Every student of the Gospels realizes that in His death Jesus laid down his life deliberately, voluntarily, in full obedience to His Father's will, realizing that the Cross was needed to secure our emancipation from the chains of sin. His blood was the only possible ransom. It was shed for us. He died on the tree, fast bound to the sacrificial post, the victim slain for our transgressions. Great High Priest of the human race, He offered up Himself, at once High Priest and Sacrifice, that we, redeemed through His death, might share His life here and hereafter. As He hung on the Cross, His enemies said in mockery, 'He saved others: Himself He cannot save,' not realizing that their sarcasm was the highest possible praise, that they had, without knowing it or intending it, marked Him out, once and for ever, as the True Saviour.

CHAPTER XI

THE RELIGIOUS ORGANISM

I. THE root of all religious life is the relation between God and the individual; yet religion is never found in actual life in that bare condition. As known to observation, religion is always found in a community, in an organized, historical form; and each individual receives it from the community in that shape. This is what distinguishes a religion from a mere theory, whether philosophical or religious. A religion is a religious theory controlling, in organized form, the life of a community. Bare theories may have very great interest for thought, and they may even influence the action of the individual to some extent; but their work in the world is not at all comparable to the action of a religion. One single fact by itself is sufficient to reveal at a glance the radical difference there is between a religious theory or a philosophy, on the one hand, and a real religion, on the other, namely this, that behind every theory, whether religious or philosophic, there will always be found an organized religion, from which the theory has sprung and under whose aegis it lives. If the theory succeed in becoming a religion, as happened in the case of Buddhism, the old religion will be repudiated and deserted; but, in order to exist apart from the old organized religion, it is absolutely essential that the theory should transform itself into a religious organism; and many religious and philosophic theories are quite incapable of such a transformation.

A real religion as opposed to a bare theory shows very distinctive powers. It forms society and the family in its own likeness. It produces a morality, and imposes it on the community. From its central belief there arises such deep feeling that it cannot but express itself in worship.

II. The Hindu system, which we studied in its simplest form in Chapter V, has proved itself throughout many centuries a really living religion. Men have believed in it and lived by it. It has controlled their thinking and their social and family life, and has produced a characteristic morality. Its religious energy has been above all displayed in its cult, which has not only swayed the Hindu people most powerfully, but has expressed itself in a very great and varied literature, and has created architecture, sculpture, painting, and music. The survival of the race is largely due to the nature of the social and family organization of Hinduism. A similar phenomenon faces us in China. Hence, we cannot wonder at the extraordinary hold which these things have on the people. The consciousness of their importance for the race lives within them, planted by the events of history and worked into their innermost mind by the cumulative action of heredity.

A. Yet our chapters have shown conclusively that most of the elements which go to form the Hindu system produce very unhealthy results; the whole is now breaking down under the pressure of Western influence. The characteristic features of the Hindu family, of which the Hindu Social Reform movement provides a most radical criticism, spring from religious beliefs which educated men no longer hold. Indian politicians unite with social reformers in condemning caste as the chief cause of the weakness of the Hindu people; and we have seen that behind each of its rules there is a religious doctrine which no cultured man believes. The position of the Brāhman priest and, in consequence, of the whole system of Hindu worship and teaching, is thus completely undermined. No educated man to-day believes that the souls which are born as Brāhmans are the most spiritual souls in all the world; yet that dogma is the sole basis of the exclusive sacerdotal powers of the Brāhman. Idolatry, the chief source of the vast incubus of superstition which prevents the Indian villager from rising out of his inefficiency and poverty, springs from the belief, no longer held by the educated class, that every idol is a living god. The whole course of the religious history of India exhibits a sustained effort on the part of thinking Hindus to get away from the impersonal God and to reach a God of love and grace. The sādhu, the living modern outcome of the philosophic-ascetic movement, is pronounced useless by the modern man. Finally, we have seen that the doctrine of karma and transmigration, the most pervasive and powerful of all Hindu ideas, has proved a most unhealthy influence in theology throughout the centuries, has been the real strength and justification of the beliefs on which the caste system rests, and has given the Hindu a deep religious reason for the most punctilious fulfilment of every detail of religious law and custom. The average educated man, not realizing clearly the foundations of Hindu belief and practice, thinks he still believes the theory, and expresses his conviction that it is one of the greatest principles ever thought out by the human mind; yet we have found abundant proof that Western thought and influence have destroyed belief in the deeper and more important aspects of the doctrine.

B. We must now realize that, though the multitudinous superstitions under which the Hindu people are labouring affect the Hindu mind and character most deleteriously, yet on every single one of them some glint of the spiritual world shines. These suggestions of the spiritual world do not alter the evil character and pernicious results of these practices, yet it is these gleams of light that have made the practices seem to the Hindu mind to be truly religious. We here mention a few of them.

1. Take the crude custom of bathing in the Ganges to wash away sin. The custom is not only absurd, but seriously immoral. Here is how a Hindu writes of it:

> If we can commit sins and wash them away by bathing in the waters of certain rivers, how easy have things become! Such ideas are most dangerous to man's moral evolution. They encourage the commission

of sin by holding out the hope of cleansing through the holy water of the Ganges.[1]

Yet there is behind it the true religious instinct, that there must be a way whereby man can get his sin forgiven, that, since God exists, there must be a fountain for sin and uncleanness.

2. At first sight it is difficult to understand how Hindus were able to practise the cruelties which were once regularly carried out in certain sects. The British Government has prohibited the worst of them, such as hook-swinging, tongue-extraction, thigh-piercing, and the impaling of animals. The self-torture of ascetics has been already dealt with. One may see any day the ordinary pilgrim measuring his length along the road to some famous shrine. Yet, however inhuman and irrational these things may be, two long lines of light stream from them, the hope (however vain it may be) of conquering the stubborn passions of the body by means of repression, and the thought that a man may rightly endure anything and give up anything if he can thereby win the favour of God.

3. We have seen above that satī, the very thought of which fills a modern mind with shame and horror, rests in its ultimate analysis on a very high ideal of wifely loyalty and purity, and a deep faith in the reality of heaven and the reunion of loved ones there.

4. Religious suicide has been not infrequent in India, both in Jainism and Hinduism. To the modern mind the man who takes his own life is both irreligious and cowardly: he will neither accept God's will nor face the battle of life. Yet behind religious suicide there is the noble desire to discard this sensuous frame, to give up this poor life so as to win the real life. It is a pitiful travesty of Christ's great principle:

Whosoever would save his life shall lose it; and whosoever shall lose his life for my sake and the gospel's shall save it.[2]

[1] See above, p. 41. [2] Mark 8, 35.

5. There is no more shallow superstition than the common Hindu belief in the spiritual value of the mere utterance of the name of the god one adores, or of the repetition of the sectarian *mantra*, or watchword. Two things have led to the rise of these unreasoning beliefs; first, the fact that the divine name and the sacred mantra, being the expression of the uttermost reverence of the soul, are uttered with the very deepest feeling; and secondly, the belief that the idea contained in the mantra is the sum of all spiritual truth, is, in fact, the spiritual food which has to be assimilated by the soul.

6. The beliefs of the ordinary Hindu villager about the Brāhman priest of his village are about as absurd and incredible as they can well be. He can not only sacrifice to the gods and declare their will, but can wield unlimited power over nature and man. He could blot the sun out of the heavens with a word; he could destroy the village and all its inhabitants with a nod. Yet the root from which all this most harmful superstition has grown is the belief that the Brāhman is a spiritual being of the highest rank, and that, on account of his spirituality, he has been chosen and appointed by the gods a priest to his people, to stand between them and their gods in sacrifice, in the revelation of the divine will, and in the use of supernatural power.

7. Here is how a Hindu writes about sacrifices to the village divinities:

> Again, it is a sorry spectacle to witness Hindus still worshipping the village gods and goddesses in the most hideous and superstitious manner. In my own place there is a 'kavu' (temple) where thousands of fowls and sheep are every year butchered for the propitiation of the supposed god and goddess. The sacred temple is literally transformed into a slaughter-house. Can any man conceive a more horrible and degrading way of worshipping the supreme Father of the universe?[1]

Yet sacrifice is perhaps the most constant and the most real element in the average Hindu's worship. How are we to account for its persistence for so many thousand years?—We must

[1] See above, p. 41.

recognize that it ministers to some of the deepest needs of the human heart, giving expression to man's gratitude to God, his desire to be on friendly terms with God, his desire to make atonement for wrong-doing. All that mass of noble belief and feeling is behind the gross practices which the modern man sees must not continue. But it is most necessary to realize that they cannot be removed, until something equally powerful, but spiritual, takes their place.

8. In most modern Hindu sects the disciple bows down before his guru and places some of the dust of his feet upon his own head. In some cases he drinks the water in which the guru has washed his feet. These are not mere manifestations of humility or expressions of respect: they are modes of receiving spiritual help. How can men believe such things? The grossly superstitious character of such practices stares us in the face; yet there is at their root the instinct that God will provide a teacher for us, and will pour into him such grace and wisdom that spiritual health and strength will flow to others from him.

9. To this day in certain castes, if a Hindu cross the ocean, he has to submit to *prāyaśchitta* (atonement) on return. It is a hideously unclean and sickening ceremony to which no self-respecting modern man can honestly subject himself. Yet, doubtless, the men who first gave form to the ceremony were very conscious of sin committed and of the necessity of a serious act to cover the wrong. Strangely enough, the revolting character of the ceremony arises largely from the Hindu belief in the peculiar sacredness of the cow.

10. The passion of the Hindu for purity is one of his most notable characteristics. Unfortunately, the various rules for securing purity are so exclusively external that they have benefited the Hindu only in so far as they have led to cleanliness of person, food, clothes, and house. But the strength of the Hindu desire for purity can be explained only by recognizing that it arises from the inner spiritual consciousness of the need of true purity.

11. Was ever anything more hateful done in the name of religion than that which is done by the Hindu mother when she dedicates her daughter to a life of religious shame? Yet even in that evil act there lies the idea that nothing is too good to be given as a gift to God, that devotion to Him should know no limits or restrictions. That this is the idea which has kept the practice alive is clear from the literature.

To the modern man it is scarcely conceivable that such true ideas and noble thoughts should express themselves in such debasing practices as we have here dealt with. When, however, we realize that to the Hindu mind God is not necessarily moral, we begin to see the possibility of such things.

Thus the Hindu system, despite the fact that it is filled with superstitions, is weakening the Hindu people, and must be laid aside, is yet a dark apocalypse. It is a realm of wrong and shame, of superstition and folly, yet everywhere there are gleams of light. One feels haunted by symbol and suggestion. The spirit is therefore twice burdened, and can but pray most earnestly that the day may soon come when the Hindu people will pass, in the words of Newman's epitaph, *ex umbris et imaginibus in veritatem.*

C. It is the dim consciousness of the presence of this basis of spirituality and truth in the worst parts of the religion that makes the educated Hindu burn with righteous indignation against Christian condemnation of Hinduism. He has felt the power of these things in his own life; and therefore, although he is as conscious as the Christian is of the folly and immorality of many of the practices, he feels it is most seriously unjust to condemn all without qualification. Nor can there be any doubt that the Hindu is right. The missionary who fails to acknowledge the presence of these right ideas amidst all the vice, cruelty, and superstition does not deserve to get the ear of the educated classes.

The average educated man also objects most seriously to articles such as those reproduced in our Introduction and quoted in this chapter, articles written by Hindus in condemnation of Hindu superstition. He looks upon them as acts of treachery, a playing into the hands of the enemy. So far as that objection is concerned, every thinking man will sympathize with the writers and not with their critics. But there is a deeper and much more serious source of their displeasure: they feel that such denunciation leads nowhere, that it does not solve the problem. The immorality and the superstition are there, quite true; yet they are the only religion the villager has. We do not require to be reminded that it is evil and degrading. What we want to know is, How is it to be changed?

D. A little reflection will show any one that each of the spiritual beliefs and motives which we have found underlying the grosser superstitions of Hinduism reappears in Christ, set in healthy institutions and spiritual practices. He provides a religious system at once effective and truly spiritual.

III. We must now realize the relation which the Hindu system has borne throughout the centuries to the philosophy, asceticism, and theistic theology of India.

A. The philosophies and theologies are, in their very essence, a series of attempts to transcend the organized religion. Their principles, both metaphysical and ethical, are far higher than the ideas of the old faith. Hence the sannyāsīs of the Upanishads renounced the whole Hindu system, flung all its literature and worship, its society, and its family life, behind them, and sought to live a new life in a higher region, above and beyond the gods and sacrifices which they despised, the petty distinctions of caste, the profits of the world, and the pleasures of domestic life. The same is true of Jains and Buddhists. The philosophic theology of the Vaishṇava and Śaiva sects seeks, not the petty gifts the gods give in return for sacrifices, but emancipation from the sense world and from transmigration. The whole movement is, essentially, a radical criticism of organized Hinduism.

B. But turn to Śaṅkara, in whom the thought of the Upanishads first finds perfectly articulated expression, and you find that he defends, explains, and accepts the whole system, the gods, their sacrifices, the priesthood, the literature, and the laws. He tacks on to his philosophy the whole of that Hindu system which the early monks had repudiated as valueless.

Buddhism and Jainism had no worship to begin with; but gradually they became conscious of the need of a cult; and the system they adopted was the idolatry which they saw around them, the gross external system which their founders had repudiated with loathing.

The Vaishṇava and the Śaiva talk in their theology of the spiritual, invisible, inconceivable Brahman, 'beyond thought and speech,' yet personal, possessing all good qualities, and full of love and grace. But their worship, both in the temple and in the home, consists in offering food and drink to an idol in the one case, to a phallus in the other, which (whether idol or phallus) is believed to be alive and to live on the offerings.

C. What is the explanation of these most strange historical facts? It is this, that the Vedānta, whether impersonal as taught by Śaṅkara, or personal as taught by the Vaishṇava and the Śaiva, and also the systems elaborated by Mahāvīra and Gautama, are philosophic theories lacking altogether that creative power which alone can produce a living religion. These theories attract the individual and influence him powerfully, but they do not succeed in creating that wonderful organism which seizes a community and forms it by producing for it a cult, a morality, a social and a family system. No single one of all this mighty group of philosophies has succeeded in creating a religion, or in organizing itself as a religious system. In each case the cult is simply the idolatry of the traditional Hindu system appended to the philosophic theology, and justified in a crude and clumsy way. The impersonal pantheism of Śaṅkara, the atheistic metaphysic of Gautama and of Mahāvīra, and the personal theism of the great sects, have each, as the expression of their innermost reverence, a polytheistic idolatry.

D. From the point of view of religion, the Hindu system has proved itself far more valuable than the philosophy. It has continuously done the work of a religion for the Hindu people. It supported them, comforted and guided them during the centuries when the philosophies were taking shape, providing not only the seeds of these systems but the fertile soil and the stimulating environment necessary for their growth. When their essential incompleteness became manifest, the Hindu system again came to the rescue, and became the ill-fitting, yet attractive and comfortable, garments of these naked theories. Without the ancient system, the poor of the people throughout the centuries would have had to be content with the ancient animisms of their ancestors. So that the work done by the Hindu system has been very great indeed.

E. But, though we recognize the religious power of the Hindu system as compared with the philosophy, we must acknowledge, on the other hand, that the system has proved a prison to the philosophies. The shell within which they lived cramped them. No spiritual worship was possible for them. They could not get away from caste. The *Gītā* offered emancipation to women and Śūdras, but they were not allowed to read the Upanishads. Rāmānuja, Nīlakaṇṭha, Rāmānanda, Tulsī Dās and many others recognized that the Outcaste was fit for spiritual religion, but he was not set free from his degrading position. Images of Outcaste saints are here and there worshipped, but no Outcaste is ever appointed a priest in any temple. The love of God never broke through the caste system. Now and then a leader would say, 'If an Outcaste is spiritual, eat with him,' but it remained a piece of sentiment. Finally, the philosopher and the theologian had to acquiesce in all the folly and filth of Hindu worship and its accompaniments. The only point where philosophy broke through ancient custom was in regard to animal sacrifice. The Hindu system thus proved stronger than philosophy, and stunted its natural growth in every direction.

IV. A. It is also most significant that those who defend

Hinduism to-day are being more and more driven, in similar fashion, to the acceptance of the whole of the ancient Hindu system. Twenty-five years ago no educated Hindu dreamt of defending idolatry and the grosser features of caste and Hindu family life: to-day almost every type of Hindu revivalist defends the whole of Hinduism. The Ārya Samāj still maintains its polemic against polytheism and idolatry (although many an Ārya still bows to idols); and here and there a Hindu may be found who condemns certain aspects of customary Hinduism; but all the rest defend the system as such. The reason is laid bare by the history: the Hindu system is a real religion, while Hindu philosophy, despite its spirituality and power, cannot develop by itself into a religious system.

B. It is abundantly evident that the Hindu people cannot enjoy light and freedom until they are liberated from the Hindu system. Yet the modern Hindu leader and the Theosophist put forward certain reasons for their policy of retaining the whole of the ancient faith. Vivekānanda writes:

> To the reformers I will point out, I am a greater reformer than any one of them. They want to reform only little bits. I want root and branch reform. Where we differ is exactly in the method. Theirs is the method of destruction, mine is that of construction. I do not believe in reform. I believe in growth. . . . I cannot join any one of these condemning societies. Why condemn? There are evils in every society; everybody knows it; every child of to-day knows it; he can stand upon a platform and give us a harangue on the evils in Hindu society. Every uneducated foreigner who comes in globe-trotting takes a vanishing railway view of India, and lectures most learnedly on the awful evils in India. We admit it. Everybody can show what evil is, but he is the friend of mankind who finds a way out of the difficulty.[1]

These apologists of Hinduism point to the gleams of spiritual light visible in customary Hinduism, some of which we have dealt with above. They explain that these truths are the

[1] Vivekānanda, 540, 542.

real source and origin of the religion, and that the immoralities and superstitions, the existence of which every one acknowledges, are later accretions and corruptions. The religion in itself is altogether holy and pure. Therefore, they argue, nothing must be lost. Every law and institution is of priceless worth. Reform along the lines advocated by social reformers is, first, destructive of that which is beyond price, and, secondly, it does not go deep enough. Make the spirit of the people right, and true reform will come of itself. We quote Vivekānanda once more:

> Therefore, this I have to tell to the social reformers of Madras, that I have the greatest respect and love for them. I love them for their great hearts and their love for their country, for the poor, for the oppressed. But what I would tell them with a brother's love is that their method is not right. . . . Most of the reforms that have been agitated for during the last century have been ornamental. Every one of these reforms only touches the first two castes, and no other. The question of widow marriage would not touch seventy per cent. of the Indian women, and all such questions only reach the higher classes of Indian people who are educated, mark you, at the expense of the masses. Every effort of these classes has been spent in cleaning their own houses, making themselves nice and looking pretty before foreigners. That is no reformation. You must go down to the basis of the thing, to the very roots. That is what I call radical reformation. Put the fire there and let it burn upwards and make an Indian nation.[1]

C. Our analysis of the family, karma, caste, and idolatry has conclusively shown that this reasoning is altogether mistaken. It is the character of the Hindu system itself that is at fault. It is the very laws of the Hindu family that require to be laid aside. It is karma itself that has weakened Hindu theology. The basal conceptions of the caste system must be repudiated, if Hindu society is to become healthy. The whole system of idolatry is essentially polytheistic and pagan. The gleams of light which stream from these things do not justify them. The paragraphs above which draw out the

[1] Vivekānanda, 546, 543.

lines of spirituality visible in the grossest parts of the religion further illustrate the principle.

D. Will any modern Hindu defend religious prostitution, because, throughout the centuries, the mother has had a noble thought in her mind in dedicating her daughter? Would the reader be ready to dedicate his own daughter on that basis? Shall we petition the British Government to rescind the laws against satī, cruel religious rites and obscenity, because in each case some gleam of the ideal is visible in the evil practice? If we are to act on that principle, the worst excesses of cannibalism and religious promiscuity are defensible; for in every such rite some true idea lurks behind. These noble accompaniments of ignoble practices do not hallow the vile things they accompany; and they are not lost when the immoral and superstitious rites and institutions are laid aside.

The folly of this policy is above all things apparent with regard to caste and idols, although, without any doubt, Vivekānanda's party and the Theosophists owe their popularity to their defence of these institutions. How can any patriotic Indian or intelligent Western follow them in their policy of maintaining the caste system? The conscience of Hinduism has already revolted against the treatment of the Outcastes: if caste is defensible, on what grounds are they to be set free? Hinduism is perfectly explicit about them. If we are to obey the laws of Manu, we must shut them up in hopeless degradation. It is easy to spin explanations and defences of idolatry; but the question for the modern man is this, Do we wish to condemn the Hindu race to eternal imprisonment in debasing superstition? Shall we seek to maintain institutions which destroy Indian vitality and intelligence, simply because they are parts of the traditional Hindu system? The time has come when the Indian patriot must choose between tradition and the health of his country.

V. We have already seen how Christ provides the fulfilment of each of the highest aspirations and aims of Hinduism.

A little reflection on the material contained in this chapter will show that every line of light which is visible in the grossest parts of the religion reappears in Him set in healthy institutions and spiritual worship. Every true motive which in Hinduism has found expression in unclean, debasing, or unworthy practices finds in Him fullest exercise in work for the downtrodden, the ignorant, the sick, and the sinful. In Him is focused every ray of light that shines in Hinduism. He is the Crown of the faith of India.

INDEX